PEACE MOVEMENTS WORLDWIDE

Volume 1: History and Vitality of Peace Movements

Marc Pilisuk and Michael N. Nagler, Editors

CONTEMPORARY PSYCHOLOGY
Chris E. Stout, Series Editor

 **PRAEGER**

AN IMPRINT OF ABC-CLIO, LLC
Santa Barbara, California • Denver, Colorado • Oxford, England

Library of Congress Cataloging-in-Publication Data

Peace movements worldwide / Marc Pilisuk and Michael N. Nagler, editors.
    p. cm. — (Contemporary psychology)
    Includes bibliographical references and index.
    ISBN 978-0-313-36478-5 (hard copy : alk. paper) — ISBN 978-0-313-36479-2 (e-book) — ISBN 978-0-313-36480-8 (vol. 1 hard copy : alk. paper) — ISBN 978-0-313-36481-5 (vol. 1 e-book) — ISBN 978-0-313-36482-2 (vol. 2 hard copy : alk. paper) — ISBN 978-0-313-36483-9 (vol. 2 e-book) — ISBN 978-0-313-36484-6 (vol. 3 hard copy : alk. paper) — ISBN 978-0-313-36485-3 (vol. 3 e-book)
    1. Peace movements 2. Peace movements—History. I. Pilisuk, Marc. II. Nagler, Michael N.
    JZ5574.P44 2011
    303.6′6—dc22   2010037446

ISBN: 978-0-313-36478-5
EISBN: 978-0-313-36479-2

15 14 13 12 11   1 2 3 4 5

This book is also available on the World Wide Web as an eBook.
Visit www.abc-clio.com for details.

Praeger
An Imprint of ABC-CLIO, LLC

ABC-CLIO, LLC
130 Cremona Drive, P.O. Box 1911
Santa Barbara, California 93116-1911

This book is printed on acid-free paper ∞

Manufactured in the United States of America

CONTENTS

ACKNOWLEDGMENTS

The three volumes of this book were invited by our publisher who saw, as we do, the value in an overview, as far as it was possible to take one, of the peace movement as a whole. First Debora Carvalko and then Lindsay Claire and Denise Stanley have been immensely supportive throughout. We soon found that the task of inviting, identifying, and editing selections from academics, officials, and activists from the varied aspects of the search for peace was a challenge to our time and organizational talents. To all of our contributors, some world renowned, all busy, we extend our thanks and appreciation for working with us, sometimes on short notice, to include their chapters. We remain amazed and grateful for the work for peace described in their contributions and the courage and persistence of the people they write about. The Metta Center for Nonviolence receives a special thanks for providing us with a welcoming place to meet.

This collection could never have seen the light of day without the dedicated involvement of a number of people. Gianina Pellegrini spent long hours beyond the few for which she was compensated to keep us on task, to communicate respectfully to hundreds of people through thousands of messages. She edited manuscripts, recruited other graduate students from Saybrook University to help, organized tasks and meetings, volunteered to write two articles on her own that we truly needed, fell behind in her own studies but never despaired or lost a chance to encourage others. Chris

Johnnidis of the Metta Center provided initial help in setting up an interactive filing system. The project got a boost when Gianina spread the word at Saybrook University. Saybrook deserves thanks for finding some of the most talented and dedicated students anywhere. Rebecca Joy Norlander provided endless hours of editing, evaluating, and reformatting articles and is a co-author of an article. Angel Ryono likewise helped write, edit, and find authors to fill gaps, and is a co-author of two articles. Other students whose generous help included becoming chapter authors are: Nikolas Larrow-Roberts, Rev. José M. Tirado, Ellen Gaddy, and Melissa Anderson-Hinn. Two other colleagues, Mitch Hall and Daniel J. Adamski, saw enough in the project to pitch in with major editing tasks and went on to be co-authors of chapters. Many others whom we were not able to include in the anthology helped us tremendously, sharing their specific expert knowledge and contacts to help us frame the task. These include Donna Nassor, Sandy Olleges, Kevin Bales, Curt Wands, Glen Martin, Byron Belitsos, Ethel Tobach, Douglas Fry, Ahmed Afzaal, Susan McKay, Joel Federman, Gail Ervin, Dan Christie, and Josanne Korkinen.

Marc wants to express appreciation for the inspiration of two mentors, Anatol Rapaport and Kenneth Boulding; of his parents, who always valued peace and justice; and to his wife Phyllis, who tolerated his sleep-deprived state for close to a year understanding what he was trying to do. He thanks Michael N. Nagler for being a partner whose knowledge and belief in the peace movement is just amazing.

Michael wants to thank the staff at the Metta Center for giving him the space and the encouragement to see this task through; his friends and colleagues in the peace movement for stepping up with translation (Matthias Zeumer), ideas, and other contributions; Marc Pilisuk for inviting him on board in the first place; and above all his mentor and guide, Sri Eknath Easwaran of the Blue Mountain Center of Meditation, for showing him his life's path and never losing faith that he would follow it to the end.

Set Introduction

The only thing we can, and therefore must control, is the imagery in our own mind.

—Epictetus

We humans have great abilities to create images, and with them, to build a significant part of our reality, and therefore to nurture or to destroy our species and its surroundings. We have used these abilities creatively but not always kindly, or wisely. As our science and technologies have made it possible to appreciate how our lives are part of one global world, they have also provided us with the means to destroy earth's capacity to support life. The peace movement that is growing throughout the world gives recognition and power to the first side of the balance, reacting against violence and war, raising aloft a higher vision of harmony and peace. It provides us with a living history of the strength of people, of communities and tribes, and sometimes of governments, to create social institutions and ideas that give peace its chance to grow. It is in the search for peace, for a way to live in harmony with each other and with the natural order that we seem to come most alive and closest to the meaning of our existence on this earth. The peace movement is likely the only undertaking that holds out a promise that the remarkable experiment of life can go on.

We consider peace to include both the absence of unnecessary violence and the pursuit of a world that offers deep contentment with the process of life. We feel some dismay as we look at paths taken by humans toward large-scale violence. But the destruction and suffering we find is not the whole story. There is another and far more hopeful story, partly old, partly new, and partly yet to be written.

Peace connotes a world with harmony among people and between people and their environment. It is surely not a world without anger or one without conflict. But it is a world in which the fulfillment of human needs can occur without inflicting preventable violence and human beings can grow closer to one another in spirit, which, as St. Augustine said, is the ultimate purpose and underlying desire of our very nature (see Volume 1, Chapter 2). Like science, which has a capacity for change as new evidence emerges, the pursuit of peace is an ongoing process in which its adherents can and do learn from the past and continually make new discoveries. Like democracy, the pursuit of peace does not always produce a better world right away, but that pursuit unquestionably has the capacity to bring correctives into the directions of our evolution as a species. The peace movement is an exciting and empowering wave of worldwide change that can harness the power of each of us, individually and collectively, for love and for life.

There are many books about peace. In the three volumes of this anthology we have chosen not to be an encyclopedia of the efforts for peace, peace,[1] or a history of worldwide efforts to realize it;[2] nor for that matter a celebration of a hopeful future. Rather we have tried to present a mosaic that gives due recognition to the obstacles to be overcome while sampling the amazing creativity of what has been and is being done to overcome them. The doers are scientists and poets, professors and peasant women, intergovernmental agencies and community art projects, soldiers and pacifists, environmentalists and defenders of human rights. Rather than force a rigid analysis on how all their efforts combine we have tried mainly to let the voices be heard.

Volume 1 focuses on different ways people have looked at peace—to construct a theory of its nature and possibilities. We present a framework for peace studies set forth by Johan Galtung, who more than anyone living deserves to be considered the founder of the field (peace entered academic discourse as a discrete subject only very recently), and we go on to writings that examine the deeper meanings of peace. The ubiquity of human aggression and violence leads some to the despairing conclusion that we are inherently warlike. We report on the new perspectives in biology, anthropology, and psychology that paint a different picture of what humans are or are not constrained to do by our nature, and take issue with the prevalent concept that we are "wired" to fight—or even to cooperate—which implies a determinism that is denied by science and common experience. Because world

peace will require some transformative changes in the way we view ourselves and our world, a section is devoted to the issue of human identity and
the culture of peace. We look at the contribution of organized religion to
the quest for peace. (Spirituality, as somewhat distinct from organized religion, and other broad topics are treated in Volume 3). Volume 1 ends with
chapters taking a hard look at the magnitude of change required for peace
and the institutional, particularly economic and monetary, forces, that need
to be transformed if peace is to reign.

Volume 2 looks at what is being done in response to war and other forms
of violent conflict. Moving along the chain of causality, we cite efforts to
prevent mass killing by monitoring and controlling weapons that in some
cases are capable not only of ending lives needlessly but of obliterating life
as we know it, as well as the ongoing efforts to expose corporate beneficiaries of war and to invest instead in enterprises that promote human and
environmental health. Then we examine the aftermath of violence—the
trauma, the scars, and the all-important processes of reconciliation and
healing. We end Volume 2 with accounts of select national and regional
movements, the world over, that have grown in opposition to war.

Volume 3 is the proactive and constructive complement to the anti-war
movements described in Volume 2. Here we illustrate efforts at building a peaceful world and its cultural infrastructure through peace education and reform of
the media that at present do little to counter those powerful forces that promote
a culture of violence and even instigate incidents of mass violence. We sample
some highly creative ways that peace is being built at levels from courageous
individuals to developing villages and on to international treaties and institutions. Then we examine, with examples, the process by which people can experience transformative change on a personal level that empowers participation in
building a peaceful world.

When "peace" is taken in its full meaning, when one backs out from the
simple cessation of one armed conflict or another to begin to sense the pre-
conditions, the "dispositions" (as Erasmus says) that produced the outcome
of conflict and its cessation, one begins to realize that the search for peace is
almost coterminous with the evolution of human consciousness, of our destiny. Such a discussion obviously cannot be covered even in an anthology of
this size. What one can do, and what we have tried to do, is sketch out a picture reasonably faithful to the variety, the intensity, and the unquenchable
audacity of the men and women who have taken up this struggle from above
(through law and policy), from below (from grassroots to civil society), and
most characteristic of the present, from within (through personal transformation). For this goal, many have laid down their very lives. We come away

from our survey of all this activity, dedication, and sacrifice with a combined sense of awe and inspiration.

At the end of the day, it is this inspiration that we wish to share with you. For as various writers in all three volumes have noted, all the ingredients for an evolutionary step forward toward this as-yet unrealized world are in place—some of them have been for some time. What is missing is the overview, the sense of the big picture, and the confidence in the heart of each one of us that we can make a difference. This we can do even in face of the apparently never-to-be-dislodged juggernaut of war: the mindset, the dehumanizing training, the institutions, the frightening technology. In face of that enormity, a countering awareness has arisen of the unquenchable drive for peace and what *it* has brought into being. The art, science, and practice of peace are having impacts on human understanding, institutions, and behaviors that are indispensable—if not for the courage to get engaged, at least for our sanity. But we hope for more; we hope you will come away from this set of books with re-fired determination to join this struggle, and a slightly sharper sense of where to make your best contribution. Nothing would please us more.

NOTES

1. Lazlo and Yoo, 1986; Kurtz and Turpin, 1999; Powers and Vogele, 1997.

2. Among many examples, see Chatfield and Kleidman, 1992; Chatfield, 1973; Beales, 1971; and http://www.peacehistorysociety.org/. For conscientious objection worldwide, see the works of historian Peter Brock.

INTRODUCTION TO VOLUME 1

The three volumes that constitute this collection move, as we have pointed out, from an investigation into what exactly peace *is*, along with some early efforts to achieve it (or restore it, if we consider the warless state of early societies as a state of peace), to resistance efforts in the modern period that have largely arisen as reaction to war and repression, and finally to more proactive attempts to build a peaceful world from positive resources—the equivalent of Gandhi's "constructive program."

In this first volume, accordingly, we look at the ways people have sought to understand peace through various lenses available to them—philosophical, psychological, sociological, religious, and gender-based. We add a section on "the challenge before us" to give some feeling for the situation in which we find ourselves at time of this writing (Fall 2009). We have not reached "the end of history," by any means. We will never reach it until war is laid to rest. That belief is shared by virtually all the authors in this collection. As one of the interviewees in Laura Bernstein's chapter on a typical grassroots peace effort put it, "I don't want my grandchildren to read about this conflict in the newspaper; I want them to read about it in history books" (see Volume 3, Chapter 14). The expectation that our grandchildren will see that state either with regard to the Israel-Palestine conflict or the planet at large may not seem likely; but the hope that our descendants will reach it *sometime* can never be abandoned.

In 1938, a number of English writers took up a similar task to ours: to motivate readers to work for peace by marshalling some ideas, language, and metaphors that might help them. Storm Jameson was one of them. In her essay she sheds light on the great paradox: why is peace, which is so "devoutly to be wished," as Augustine said, that no one does not wish for it, so rarely chosen and worked for in practice? She said, "Yes, we wish for peace; but we do not *will* it." Although it is quite incorrect to say that war is "instinctual" (see Part II in this volume), there is clearly something deeper than ordinary thinking that drives us into war—and that, when harnessed to another path, could loft us toward peace.

It is interesting to read the various chapters in this volume (and from others that could be added) with the question in mind, How does *wish* become *will*; when and how will peace be an idea whose time has come? With this question in mind we examine some of the cultural mechanisms in human societies past or present to keep warfighting at bay and/or create the institutions of a robust peace. It is encouraging to note that the way we understand peace has developed, albeit slowly, through cultural history; for surely if we want to build something we must have some idea of what it is. Arnold Toynbee once said that what rouses will is "an ideal that takes the imagination by storm, and a definite, intelligible plan for carrying that ideal into practice." Combining the insights into the possibility of peace that we have in this volume with the practical efforts to achieve it, negative and positive, that are offered in the next two might just fill that bill.

A young German friend of ours recently wrote a moving song about war with the refrain, *Sei es immer so heilig, ich mache nicht mit* ("sacred as it may be, I won't take part"). Surely as long as war is thought of as sacrosanct no will can be mobilized to renounce it. In this regard, the human capacity for contradiction is impressive. Although "the name of God is peace," as Jewish and Islamic scriptures declare, and the greatest gift of God is that eternal peace, which is his very being, as Augustine and many others report, most people seem to believe that the most reliable way to sanctity is to die in the act of killing others. On the wall of the Munich cathedral one can see a bas-relief of a soldier rising out of the grave, Wehrmacht helmet and all, to receive a crown at the hands of God: *Sie verdienten eine Krone am Hande Gottes,* "they earned a crown at the hand of God." It is hard to understand the persistence of this belief other than as a desperate attempt to whitewash with sanctity a behavior about which we in fact feel an intolerable kind of guilt (the abundant scientific evidence for this guilt is described in the discussion by Lt. Col. Dave Grossman and psychologist Rachel MacNair's concept of perpetration-induced traumatic stress outlined in Volume 2,

Chapter 21. Martydom, a Jewish invention of the second century BCE, is a dangerous idea, as we see in the minds of terrorists today.

In 1981, Michael Nagler wrote a brief article called "Peace as a Paradigm Shift" for the *Bulletin of the Atomic Scientists* that was widely read and translated. Thomas Kuhn's concept had given us a way to name and thus better understand the kind of transformation of consciousness that would be required to strip killing and death-in-killing of their aura of sanctity and rediscover the sanctity of life and the protection of life. How paradigm shifts happen is still a mystery, just as it is difficult to explain how crowds (or for that matter mobs) take up a dramatic idea and run with it, or large groups of people spontaneously self-organize and carry out complex tasks. But these are not quite as mysterious as they were, thanks to some studies that could not be included in this volume. That is important, because there is widespread agreement that these questions *must* be better understood because the scale and the urgency of the shift is such that we cannot wait for it to happen of itself. Perhaps the diverse insights offered by the chapters of this volume can help in that understanding.

PART I

The Meaning of Peace

Properly speaking, peace does not have a meaning. It *is* the meaning behind everything we do, even biologically, as St. Augustine eloquently points out in the *City of God*. Peace is the *summum bonum* that requires no elucidation from an outside concept but is the elucidation of all concepts.

That said, with rare exceptions our awareness of peace falls far short of that vision, and so we must try to understand it through the lenses we have ground ourselves. One of them is "philosophy," handled in this brief section. It begins with Michael Nagler's attempt to bring out some of the foundational insights in the peace section of Augustine's magisterial *City of God*. This passage has, in our view, been neglected and underappreciated. Though it is the first extended and articulate discussion of the peace concept in the Western tradition, as far as we know, it was far ahead of its time in recognizing that peace is positive, not merely the absence of war or violence, and contains other insights that should have put the discourse on peace far down the road. No doubt the fact that Augustine frames his discussion in religious terms, seeing peace as not *a* but *the* positive reality, allows many to label him as religious and dismiss him as impractical. There is a parallel in the objection that was raised in India to Gandhi's adopting the ancient term *swaraj*, used to denote spiritual freedom, for political freedom. He replied that he had adopted it deliberately, because he did not see a wall of separation between the spiritual or eternal freedom and the political and temporal freedom for which they were struggling. If there were such a wall, would not all religious thinking be irrelevant?

Barry Gan then brings us down to contemporary thinking on many of these questions. He stresses, albeit implicitly, the interconnectedness of life when he points out that in peace thinking today *all* life must be held in respect—one of the surest differentiating tenets from the views that accept force and violence. Similarly, he refutes the doctrine that ends justify means, which by a stroke knocks the justification out from under war reasoning. (Because of this truth, as Gan points out, "for all intents and purposes all modern war is immoral.")

Johan Galtung, considered the founder of peace studies, contributes the synoptic overview, a practical philosophy of where peace creation is and where it will have to go from here. Galtung is not technically a philosopher. His degrees were in mathematics and sociology and his work, through TRANSCEND, is to reduce conflicts and avert wars through peacemaking, peacekeeping, and where possible, peace building. These now standard terms Galtung invented are referenced at various points in this book, but for convenience, they are defined as follows:

- Peacemaking equals stopping an ongoing conflict and bringing about *rapprochement* between or among contending parties.
- Peacekeeping equals policy and monitoring a fragile peace and preventing relapse into violence.
- Peace building equals restoring the underlying conditions the distortion of which caused the conflict.

His descriptions of direct, cultural, and structural violence are critical to the conception of peace in this anthology. The peace movement we identify works as diligently to remove injustice and inequality as to prevent shooting wars. What Galtung brings to the table is his uncommon familiarity with peace activities and peace thinking worldwide, and his analytical ability to categorize them usefully.

Toward what goal is the peace movement (or the movement towards peace) going? Surely the movement toward peace requires an appreciation of this unfolding vision and beautiful phenomenon. To understand peace one must recognize that it is still slowly evolving and understand as well the relationships among its many facets. The concept of peace is at once amazingly simple and compelling, and yet still part of an unsolved mystery. The chapters in this section illustrate that the study of peace is indeed a discipline that has come of age and has begun to shed some important light on the path.

—Marc Pilisuk and Michael N. Nagler

CHAPTER 1

Eternal Peace

Michael N. Nagler

Even on the level of earthly and temporal values, nothing that we can talk about, long for, or finally get is so desirable, so welcome, so good as peace.

—St. Augustine, *The City of God*, XIX.11, p. 451

Before there were peace movements, there was the "movement toward peace." This was pioneer peace researcher Kenneth Boulding's term for the inexorable, slow mobilization of the human desire for creating and maintaining peace,[1] an ongoing, evolutionary process that is taking place unevenly in all societies, as opposed to the more visible work of civil society organizations and—occasionally—governments. While much of these three volumes will be concerned, quite appropriately, with that more formal and more easily documented side of peace creation, I focus here on a few highlights in the development of an underlying culture, a shared understanding of peace. This underlying vision is the infrastructure of formal organizations and eventual policy. The longing for peace that Augustine so poignantly describes is not going away; it is part of our nature. In fact, this movement toward peace, he and many others believe, is nothing less than the unfolding of human destiny. Note, in this connection, that while it is fitting to speak of peace *movements* in the plural, there is only one movement toward peace.

THE PREVAILING PARADIGM AND ITS CONTRADICTIONS

In February 2009 a Sri Lankan, Umar Jaleel, was abducted by nine gunmen from a house in Basilan, the Philippines. Nothing unusual, unfortunately, except that Jaleel, like Tom Fox, who met his death at the hands of kidnappers three years earlier in Iraq, was in Basilan as a peacekeeper. Specifically, he was a field team member for Nonviolent Peaceforce (NP), an organization that is building a worldwide service of nonviolent intervention along the lines Gandhi chalked out much earlier for his *shanti sena*, "armies of peace."

Armies of peace may sound a bit paradoxical, but paradoxes and double negatives characterize the universe of discourse on peace. The reason is that the prevailing, popular concept of peace takes war and violence to be real, while peace and nonviolence can be enjoyed only in their interstices: take away war and what's left is peace. It's not that easy. Nor is it easy, apparently, to grasp that peace and nonviolence (the mother of all double negatives in this field) are real and that war is the *absence* of them. The first news reports of Jaleel's abduction stated that he had an armed bodyguard who saved himself from the attackers by gunfire! This proved to be an outrageous falsehood, and NP spokespeople were quick to correct it (but as usual the damage was done). It is hard to realize that people are risking their lives, and in some cases forfeiting them, partly to help humanity correct its vision, to wean us from what was long ago declared a heresy but still holds sway over our minds: the idea that evil is real and good only its temporary suppression.

For the record, there was no bodyguard, much less an armed one. When a more amateur peace team prepared to enter Sarajevo in 1995 and members of the UN protection force, UNPROFOR, offered to escort their thrown-together convoy of buses down the dangerous "sniper alley," the team refused and pointed out that to accept such "protection" would negate the whole point of their mission. In they went, without a shot fired (though by that year the snipers had wounded 1,030 people and killed 225 [60 of whom were children]).[2] I invited the head of Air Force Military Science to speak to my nonviolence class some years ago, and raised examples like this one. My friend came back with, "Well, that's nice, but please, when you do something like that, have a rifle platoon behind you to back you up." One of my students, whose whole family was Air Force, calmly said, "No, sir. We believe nonviolence is its own protection."

What's at stake here is much more than an annoying misunderstanding. It is a paradigm. Starting from the "take away war" concept, from what is called today negative peace, humanity has never gotten past Vegetius: "if

you want peace you have to prepare for war," or if you want a modern reincarnation, President Reagan's doctrine of "peace through strength." Untold
damage has been done by that belief, which is as tenacious as it is mischie-
vous. In an attempt to correct it during Reagan's tenure (he wanted,
remember, to dub the MX missile "peacemaker"), I wrote an op-ed with the
provocative title "Strength through Peace." I was pleased when it was
accepted by a major newspaper—but my smile faded when the piece
appeared with the title "Peace through Strength." An editor had, no doubt
unconsciously, "corrected" my title to the conventional form. Yet, as the
Old Testament psalm says, "The horse is a vain thing for safety; neither
doth he deliver anyone by his great power" (33:17). There is no doubt that
war can accomplish a great deal, but it cannot accomplish peace. Gandhi's
vision provides a bracing contrast:

> The world rests upon the bedrock of *satya* or truth. Asatya meaning
> untruth also means non-existent, and satya or truth also means that
> which is. If untruth does not so much as exist, its victory is out of the
> question. And truth being that which is can never be destroyed. This is
> the doctrine of Satyagraha [soul-force, literally clinging to truth] in a
> nutshell.[3]

In the historical record of the understanding of peace in the West there
have been two major breakthroughs.

Peace Is Positive

In her 1981 study of the vocabulary of war and peace in the early Greek
poets, Dominique Arnould points out that the various words for peace are
fewer than those for war at all periods.[4] As she says, *Le déséquilibre entre les
deux domaines est très net*: the vocabulary of peace is far poorer. What's more,
she points out, each term for "war" in this universe of discourse brings up a
set of specific activities; it is both a concrete and articulate semantic field.
As she asks rhetorically, *Mais la paix a-t-elle des activités propres?* What,
indeed, are the activities proper to peace? Sitting under one's own fig tree,
for example, are activities that peace makes possible: but what makes *peace*
possible? What is peace itself? Understanding how our present concepts of
peace (for they are plural) developed, and where they still need to go, can
suggest some answers.

The asymmetry Arnould turned up in the early Greek poets only
increases as one moves down toward the Classical period, and in the end,
she discovers (p. 107) such metaphors that you get for "peace" are only the
negatives of war metaphors. And that dyslexic vision, as we've just seen, is

in part still with us. Some years ago the Department of the Navy defined peace as "perpetual pre-hostility." People misuse the hallowed name of peace to mislead themselves and anyone listening. Augustine points this up clearly: "anyone who is rational enough to prefer right to wrong and order to disorder can see that the kind of peace that is based on injustice . . . does not deserve the name of peace."[5] But it often does get that name.

Much public discourse today is an awkward mixture of these fundamentally incompatible definitions of peace, as positive and negative reality. In 1979, Mother Teresa was awarded the Nobel Prize for Peace (the history of the prize is itself an interesting study of confusions and ambiguities). One reason she richly deserved it is that when she heard that disabled children had been abandoned in an orphanage in Beirut during the intense bombardment of 1982 she went in and rescued 37 children—and both sides stopped fighting to let her do so. The only problem was that Prime Minister Menachem Begin, who had ordered the shelling, had *also* gotten the Nobel the year before.

Now, in practical terms, it is possible to arrive at peace within a given system by systematically eliminating war *and the possibility of war* from that system. Actors poised on the brink of "pre-hostility," or even somewhat further back, cannot meaningfully be said to be at peace; but it is conceivable that by systematically dismantling every threat of war in their environment they could in time find themselves left with peace. It is unlikely that that happy state could last very long, however, unless some positive concept of peace were there to reorient, guide, and sustain the parties who are trying to uphold it. This is why Gandhi, who was so far ahead of his time, created what was to be called the Constructive Programme (CP) alongside his Satyagraha (active resistance) from the earliest days of his public activities in South Africa (1894). One of his arguments for CP was that while an "effervescent" uprising can at times throw off a despised regime, a sustained campaign can never be held in place by "non-cooperation with evil" (here using King's well-known phrase); it requires "cooperation with good." Likewise, when the peace movement was confronting the very real (and still not dispelled) possibility of nuclear holocaust, it eventually found, or at least some of its representatives did, that survival was not a compelling idea that could keep the movement going forward because even cockroaches would survive such a holocaust. Something more positive was needed as a rallying cry—and unfortunately no agreed upon candidate was ever found.

As is pointed out elsewhere in this book (Volume 3, Chapter 17) the litany of environmental and other disasters with which well-intentioned activists seek to rouse the public is only paralyzing and disempowering people.[6] Even the rallying cry of sustainability, I would argue, does not sufficiently stir our imagination. To get from apathy to enthusiasm, Toynbee pointed out that first of all we need an idea that "takes the imagination by storm." This is why we need to claim and even enlarge on Augustine's legacy.

Immanuel Kant began his brilliant sketch *Towards Perpetual Peace (Zum ewigen Frieden, ein philosophischer Entwurf,* 1795) by contrasting what he was about to describe with the words *ewigen Frieden,* "perpetual peace," seen on a gravestone. The peace that he is arguing for is not "the peace of the grave," but what is it? For him it is a peace based on a set of arrangements that would head off—not eliminate or convert—whatever it is that causes humans to go to war. In this, Kant is a particularly brilliant example of the "perpetual peace" tradition that began as early as the 11th century in France and included such luminaries as Erasmus, Hugo Grotius, Abbé St. Pierre, Rousseau, and William Penn. The sketch is a brilliant example of an attempt to back into a positive idea of peace by eliminating war *permanently.* Yet fully 1,300 years earlier than Kant's treatise, Augustine had offered a far more positive definition of peace, grounded in a much deeper reality. *His* peace was closely identified with life itself, and he uses this telling parallel (p. 457):

> Notice that there can be life without pain, but no pain without some sort of life. In the same way, there can be peace without any kind of war, but no war that does not suppose some kind of peace.

That is, even those who wage war do so to achieve some kind of "peace," however limited by their faulty understanding (p. 451f):

> The whole point of victory is to bring opponents to their knees—this done, peace ensues. Peace, then, is the purpose of waging war; and this is true even of men who have a passion for the exercise of military prowess. . . .[7]

Augustine's point is that peace is such a compelling value—indeed *the* value to which all others refer—that even war is waged in its name. This can be a reprehensible and dangerous hypocrisy, as we know to our cost, but is at least a back handed acknowledgment of the priority of peace. The great value of this argument is in how clearly it demonstrates that peace—and all fundamental goods, for at their core they all seem to converge—is the ontological reality of which war is the absence, exactly as Gandhi stated in Indian and (paradoxically) more modern terms.

Augustine wrote the *City of God* (from ca. 410 to 426 CE) to restabilize a badly shaken world that was reeling from the unthinkable sack of Rome, the eternal city, by barbarian hordes, who of course did not think of themselves as such. The parallels to 9/11 readily recommend themselves. His goal was to overcome the all-but-inevitable feeling of many Romans, Pagan and Christian, that the disaster befell them because the empire had left its ancient traditions (the formal adoption of Christianity as a state religion was just 100 years old). The main thrust of his argument, built on his penetrating critique of human civilization in relation to its divine prototype and ultimate future—the city of God—is that sufferings of this kind are not only inevitable within but a means of leading us beyond our present flawed state and urge us to strive for the goal that the new religion has revealed. At intervals throughout the work (and his other writings) there occurs as a mantra, if you will, this explanation for our present mixed or flawed condition: *duo amores faciunt duas civitates.* Literally this would mean "two loves bring about two cities"; but in modern terms it really means that two drives within us that would create (if allowed to function fully) two contrasting world orders (because there was not yet the concept of a "nation" between the city-state and the empire—Rome was both). We live in a mixture of two orders that arise from these two contrasting, indeed opposing drives—the one toward self-gratification and the other toward the service of God. This brings us to the second breakthrough on which I wish to comment.

Peace Comes from within the Person

The concept of "inner peace" is very common today, at least in certain circles—and I dare say it is universally recognized, if nothing else than as a poignant absence. "If anyone wanted peace," Gandhi says of the tumultuous days of the South Africa Satyagraha, "he had to find it within." He is describing peace as a kind of refuge from the turmoil of the world; but there is much more: of late more and more people (though by no means a majority) are coming to recognize that inner peace is the *source* of all outward peace—in the family, society, or world.[8]

In another magisterial work of Christian inspiration, Dante's *Divine Comedy,* the poet says to souls who want him to convey a message to the upper world (*Purgatorio* V. 61):

voi dite, ed io faró par quella pace
che . . .
di mondo in mondo cercar mi si face.
(Do you but speak, and I shall do it in the name of that peace
which . . .
makes me seek after it in world after world.)

When Jewish monotheism swept through the West as what we now call Christianity, it was a major enabling condition for a deeply grounded peace that is still far off in the future. Monotheism actually involves two simultaneous breakthroughs: it symbolizes the unity of humankind—one's "God" concept is a code for the underlying reality of the world—and, perhaps even more importantly if less obviously, it implies the sanctity of the human individual. The idea that there is but one God brings with it the idea that each person is made in the image of that supreme reality; he or she is a microcosm of that wholeness (the meaning of the Hebrew *shalom*), that integrity. I am reminded of George Orwell's reflection on watching a man walk to his hanging in Burma: "One life less, one world less."[9]

There was also an important shift that created a model of history that we now take for granted that happened prior to Christianity in classical Greek thought, namely, the shift from a *devolutionary* concept of the world process—the idea that paradise existed in the past and we are doomed to fall progressively further from it as time goes inexorably by—to a modern *evolutionary* view, that paradise lies, at least potentially, ahead of us *and we therefore can and must strive to attain it.* This shift was fully capitalized on and given articulate imagination in Augustine's Christianity. His vision takes up a position in conflict with, for example, Manichaean Christianity, which denied that anything could be done about the world because it was inherently evil, and in opposition to most forms of paganism, which denied anything needed to be done about it because it was already good—as we would say, "this is as good as it gets." This was also a crucial shift, since if the only possible paradise lay in the past there was no point in striving for it (and not much point in living, when you stop to think about it).

It is therefore not only the ethic of Jesus, his profound gentleness, that placed in stark contrast the ethic of Judea's Roman conquerors, but his vision of the microcosm of the individual and his challenge of creating a world that would allow him or her to flourish. Modern historical research has emphasized that when the accretions of mythological status are stripped away, the "Jesus of history" stands forth as a supremely nonviolent figure who, even if he did say that he had come "not to bring peace but the sword" (Mt. 10:34), meant that he would bring to the surface vast violence that was ignored or taken for granted (what we call today structural violence) so that it could be resolved. This is exactly what Gandhi would do in our own time with the structural violence of foreign domination in India. That domination, as he correctly pointed out, was causing far more violence than the more open violence he had to risk unleashing to relieve it.[10] While the nonviolence of Jesus was lost soon enough in the construction of a "pragmatic" religion from the scarce remains of his known legacy, it never disappeared entirely from view. Indeed, its periodic rediscovery has been seen as the punctuating events of Christian history, for example, by Geoffrey Nuttall.[11]

Perhaps its reincarnation today in groups like Pax Christi, Witness for Peace, and many others, is writing another chapter of that punctuated equilibrium.

The discovery of the inner life slowly caught on among more receptive individuals and communities throughout antiquity,[12] and can be said to climax with Christianity—at least the "mystical" Christianity of one like Augustine. In my view, it was precisely the ability of thinkers within the Christian movement to describe inner experience and prescribe the care and management of inner life that lead to its astonishing success. In any case, no one was more at home in this interior landscape than Augustine, whose God was "more inward than my most intimate within" (*Conf.* III. vi) and this is evident throughout his teachings on violence and peace: "Imagine thinking that one's *enemy* could do him more damage than the *enmity* he harbors against him"[13] (*Conf.* I. xxix).

With his doctrine of the two loves Augustine states that the peace of the world must arise from the peace within the person (though he says little in this discussion about how that is to be done). The beauty of inner peace is that it can never be destroyed, but is there to renew the peace of the world that we seem to destroy periodically. This idea of causality is still controversial, particularly in the West. There are those like Orwell, who see the only hope for peace in the righting of social arrangements, while there are those like Dickens who see it coming from a change of heart, in line with the famous statement of Spinoza that "peace is not an absence of war, it is a virtue, a state of mind, a disposition for benevolence, confidence, justice."[14] It is not achieved by putting a different kind of people in power but by awakening a different kind of power in people.

Let me quote from a highly revered seer of modern India, Sri Ramana Maharshi. When a devotee asked him why the peace he felt in the great man's presence was not lasting, he explained:

That Peace is your real nature. Contrary ideas are only superimpositions. This is true bhakti, true yoga, true jñana. You may say that the peace is acquired by practice. [But] the wrong notions are given up by practice. That is all. Your true nature always persists. These flashes are only signs of the ensuing revelation of the Self.[15]

Compare Augustine, who says that a wrongdoer

. . . hates the peace of God which is just and prefers his own peace which is unjust. However, he is powerless not to love peace of some sort. *For no man's sin is so unnatural as to wipe out all traces whatever of human nature.* (emphasis added)[16]

It is this belief more than any other that constitutes the core of the non-violent worldview and inspires people the world over to a commitment to restorative justice as a replacement for retributive justice in the civic sphere and peace development as a replacement for the war system at large. There is no such thing as *perpetual* pre-hostility; when parties nourish resentment and hostility against others, it is only a matter of time before those hostilities express themselves in action. But more than this, would we want to live in such a state?

PRACTICAL OUTCOMES

For an increasing number of peace researchers and activists the question of peace has become how to awaken inner peace so that it can express itself through remaining "superimpositions" of our conditioning. Very few are naïve enough to believe that this is all we must accomplish: we can work on the development of peace from within or without, and indeed the wisest course is to do both. Inner and outer peace react on each other. What the Maharshi calls superimpositions can seem overwhelming, artificially, but powerfully maintained by culture. Let us go back to Augustine for a minute to see whether he has practical insights as vivid as his inspired vision.

Eternal peace *and its reflection within the mirror of the human soul* are the sources of human peace. The former acts as a "great attractor"; the latter acts as the guarantee that humans can in theory always be attracted. But there's a problem.

To what degree is Augustine's peace—and we see this in the epigram to this chapter—within the reach of human societies in any foreseeable future? What good is an ideal if we can't realize it except in Heaven (in which many cannot fully believe)? Actually, quite a lot. Progress requires a goal, an ideal to work *toward*, whether or not one expects fully to achieve it; the ideal of eternal peace is a paramount example. To cite Gandhi again,

> I may be taunted with the retort that this is all Utopian and, therefore, not worth a single thought. If Euclid's point, though incapable of being drawn by human agency, has an imperishable value, my picture has its own for mankind to live. Let India live for this true picture, though never realizable in its completeness. We must have a proper picture of what we want, before we can have something approaching it.[17]

Elise Boulding, Joanna Macy, and many other contemporary peace-workers have made use of precisely this potential to promote the *imagining* of peace as a vital step toward achieving it: "Without a vision, the people perish" (Proverbs 29:18). Augustine's time Christian communities were still

coping with the realization that the "second coming" of Christ had not happened as expected, that is, within a lifetime or so of the apostles. It was
therefore unclear whether the millennial expectations had a time frame and
should be anticipated as a realistic, if distant future. He does make it perfectly clear, however, that the tradition is not (only) individualistic or other-
worldly:

> For if the life of the saints had not been social, how could the City of God
> . . . have a beginning, make progress, and reach its appointed goal?[18]

As for us, nothing we now know about human nature today compels us
to believe that a stable regime of universal peace is beyond the realm of possibility. Under the right conditions, some very early societies may have
achieved it;[19] some technologically simple societies living quietly around
fringes of our own world today are holding onto it.[20] And even if one were
not to believe in such a possibility (which Gandhi said was to disbelieve in
the goodness of God), even small progress toward that happy state would
constitute an enormous improvement on a world order that in many ways
is scarcely better than Augustine's. Those who work for peace are motivated by a feeling of connection with others that extends even to those yet
unborn; therefore, the prospect of an *eventual* peace gives them intense
motivation to work for it. In this way Augustine's vision of absolute peace
was in some sense the goal of human life. Whether that vision is "true" or
not is vastly more useful than the negative peace which is as far as many
people can go in envisioning peace even today.

Although Augustine says little in the *City of God* about how the individual can undertake personal transformation to express his or her inner
endowment for peace in the social realm (that is the job of *Confessions*, and
in fact Augustine at one point or other in his many writings discusses every
method of meditation known in his time), he does at least offer us a model.
His model for the expression of eternal peace on earth is the well-ordered
home under the loving guidance of the *paterfamilias* who, suitably idealized,
"ought to look upon [his] duty to command as harder than the duty of
slaves to obey." This condition of benevolent authority is to last until there
is no need to wield authority of any kind over others who are already perfectly happy—such as in the state of immortal life.[21]

Not only anarchists but many people on the political left who make up the
bulk of those arguing and/or working for peace in today's secular world have
been profoundly uncomfortable with Augustine's acceptance of the markedly
vertical structures of dominance that are obtained in his world and are still
obtained in our own to various degrees. We want equality. The infamous
Milgram experiments have shown how dangerous "obedience to authority"

can be as an enabling condition of violence. Interestingly enough, however, this was not Gandhi's position. He was perfectly comfortable with authority, because when it was working correctly it was the only way to avoid the thing he *was* profoundly uncomfortable with—hatred and violence. Chaos, in his experience (and has anyone's been different?), did not resolve itself into an egalitarian order, but caused the greatest anguish and generally resulted in strict authoritarianism. He had no difficulty presenting himself, for example, during the heat of Satyagraha campaigns, as a "general"—as long as he was wanted in that capacity. Authority of some kind was unavoidable, he felt, and even unobjectionable.

To make it work, however, you needed another advance that goes beyond Augustine's thinking. In Augustine's world (and it would be unfair to hold him to moral standards that have since evolved), even a benevolent authority would, albeit reluctantly, apply corrective punishment to subordinates with *verba seu verbera* "words or whipstrokes."[22] Judicial torture was, as we've seen, a regrettable and transitory necessity given the fallen condition of humanity.

But Gandhi knew of another kind of family, if you will, the ashram, or intentional community gathered around a spiritual guide. In that role himself, he hit on a solution to the deplorable necessity of punishment, and by extension, of domination and torture which Augustine had to accept as provisional and "penal in character." When faced with some misbehavior by some young people under his care, Gandhi felt that some corrective had to be applied but that in an ashram punishment has no place. The solution? He fasted. There was some justice in this—had he been a more perfect model for them they would not have made the slip—but more to the point it was a highly effective remedy. This was pure Satyagraha. In Satyagraha, as distinct from all other forms of power, means must prefigure ends, which has led Johan Galtung to define nonviolence as "peace by peaceful means."[23] In this view, war, by virtue of its destructive means, cannot be "just"; it carries injustice in the instrumentality of violence itself, regardless of the end toward which it is aimed.

When Augustine takes the well-ordered home as "a beginning or fragmentary constituent of a civic community"[24] he is thinking of the homes of the wealthy, of course, which were indeed small societies consisting of an extended family and in some cases hundreds of slaves. That well-ordered home (when it was well ordered), was the "world order model" for peace: "the ordered harmony of authority and obedience among those who live together has a relation to the ordered harmony of authority and obedience between those who live in a city,"[25] which was, as mentioned, the largest unit in the world order itself. "After the city comes the world community."[26]

This model invites comparison with Gandhi's "Oceanic Circle" (this is the utopian model he was referring to in the earlier quote):

> In this structure composed of innumerable villages, there will be ever-widening, never-ascending circles. Life will not be a pyramid with the apex sustained by the bottom. But it will be an oceanic circle whose centre will be the individual always ready to perish for the village, the latter ready to perish for the circle of villages, till at last the whole becomes one life composed of individuals, never aggressive in their arrogance but ever humble, sharing the majesty of the oceanic circle of which they are integral units. Therefore the outermost circumference will not wield power to crush the inner circle but will give strength to all within and derive its own strength from it.[27]

These are both "bottom up" models of order, at least once one gets beyond Augustine's family unit, which itself is hierarchical because of our fallen condition Gandhi's village unit was a bit different, as the traditional village was governed by a *panchayat* or council of five elders. Anyone familiar with peace theories today will take this bottom-led direction for granted, but it was somewhat startling in Augustine's time. But to think that structures alone can change the character of a regime is what Galtung once called "the most naïve fallacy." We must also consider what kind of energy, or bond, holds the parts of the given structure together. Here Gandhi goes a step or two further than Augustine in his recognition that the system's whole energy comes from the bottom, the individual, and that the bond of self-sacrificing love that constituted that energy would show up, *in extremis*, as a willingness to perish for the next larger unit. He had, of course, mobilized this very power in his various Satyagrahas, and was not just speaking from speculation or wish-fulfillment. And in his case we can see also that this same love was very different from rote obedience. Once roused, "person power" not only should not but could not be held down by higher circles of authority.[28]

A just appreciation of Augustine's achievement would have to take into account that he had to overcome the disadvantage of his own vocabulary. As Zampaglione, Illich, and others have pointed out, the Latin word for "peace" *pax*, derives from *pac-tum*, "arrangement." In fact, *pax* meant the cessation of conflict that the vanquished beg for, as in our expression "sue for peace." Very Tacitean indeed; as such it invites comparison with the Greek word, *eirene*, from the root *ar*, "to articulate, fit together" which, while it at least implies an agreement between equals rather than a form of defeat for the vanquished, still frames peace as a contract—in other words, a pause between wars.

Both these Western terms appear shallow in comparison to either the Hebraic *shalom,* implying wholeness (among other things) or the Sanskrit *shanti* that includes in its semantic range the satisfaction of all longing. Ivan Illich brought this out in a brilliant article of 1981, where he compared (in a picture recalling Augustine's *paterfamilias*):

> . . . a Jewish patriarch when he raises his arms in blessing over his family and his flock. He invokes shalom, which we translate as peace. Shalom he sees as grace, dripping down from heaven, "like oil dripping through a beard, through the beard of Aaron the forefather." For the Semitic father, peace is the blessing of justice which the one true God pours over 12 tribes of recently settled shepherds.

This stands in sharp contrast to Roman peace (*pax romana*) that was declared by the victorious general when he planted the standards of his legion on a conquered land.[29]

We are the inheritors of both these traditions, and trying to function awkwardly with that contradiction. Take the term "nonviolence," for example (or worse, in the earlier spelling, non-violence). I am among those who believe that Gandhi was right that the emergence of his nonviolence "is the harbinger of the peace of mankind." But is it to be thought of as the German *Gewaltlosigkeit,* "absence of violence" or the Tagalog *alay dangal,* "to offer dignity"? Is security gained by force or the threat of force a deterrence (literally "frightening off"), or in the emerging framework of common security and human security, a condition free from, not dependent on, fear and including all dimensions of human well-being (economic sufficiency, health care, etc.) rather than the single, military dimension?[30] The realization that peace is positive, and the second realization that it is to be found within us feel—admittedly, I am going by intuition here—like sides of the same coin. Thus the evolution from *pax* to *shalom* (or *shanti*) is ultimately a shift in the conception of human nature, and thus is part of a very large paradigm shift that has been struggling to emerge now for several decades.[31]

As we have seen, however, these are not all-embracing historical steps; in fact, most people alive today have not made either of them. They are, nonetheless, "attractors" that are quietly, slowly, and with many undertows that take us back toward chaos, the destiny of the planet.

Recently there was a remake of a science-fiction classic, *The Day the Earth Stood Still.* In this wish-fulfillment fantasy, highly (technologically) advanced aliens send an emissary to earth to force humans to make peace— that is, stop making war. Even these enlightened aliens, we should note, have no particular love for us, but are actuated purely by self-interest (the unleashing of the atom threatens other planets). Moreover, they make no attempt to persuade dense mortals but operate entirely by threat (at least in the original version of the film). Whatever breakthroughs have been made in the understanding of peace, East or West, they have not penetrated very far into the popular discourse or, consequently, the halls of policy makers.

Augustine's exalted vision of the true meaning of peace, a sober critique of the relative peace that is the best that can be enjoyed here, in the city of man provides a lodestar toward which his contemporaries could orient themselves—and this is still true a millennium and a half down the road. He was ahead of his time. Unfortunately, he also seems to be ahead of ours. We have some catching up to do.

NOTES

1. Cf. Lazlo and Yoo, 1986.
2. Wikipedia, 2010.
3. Gandhi, 1926.
4. Arnould, 1981.
5. Walsh, 1950. All quotes, unless otherwise indicated, are from this translation here p. 454.
6. Nordhaus and Schellenberger, 2007.
7. Aristotle had said that war is never waged for its own sake; Augustine here goes a step further in saying that it is actually waged for the sake of peace.
8. See Kumar, 2009. According to the Indian concept of peace (the) individual is basic source of its creation and development. In other words, human being is the first centre of peace.
9. Orwell, 1968.
10. In the Bengal famine of 1943, for example, somewhere between 1 to 3 million Indians died of starvation when the rice crop was appropriated for the British army. See Greenough, 1980.
11. Nuttall, 1958.
12. Cf. Snell, 1953. Socrates was the first, it seems, to regularly use words like "within" to describe the psyche in any but a physical sense.
13. St. Augustine, translated 1950.
14. Spinoza, 1670.
15. Maharshi, 2000.
16. St. Augustine, 454.
17. Gandhi, 1926.
18. St. Augustine, translated 1950.
19. Cf. Anthony, 2007. One influential example is Marija Gimbutas's popular writing on "Old Europe," but recent scholars have found it naively optimistic.
20. Melko, 1973.
21. St. Augustine, translated 1950.
22. Ibid.

23. Galtung, 1996. Some have seen support for this view even in the breakdown of classical causality in quantum physics.

24. St. Augustine, translated 1950.

25. Ibid. For a pre-city parallel, cf. Odysseus's bed, which is built on a still living oak tree: the life and order of nature yields up the *oikos* or extended home unit, the largest recognized by name at that time.

26. Ibid, 7, 446.

27. Gandhi, 1946.

28. "Person power" is a term I have coined to supplement "people power," the well-known opposition to the power of the state in nonviolence circles. Even people power is a collective of the power of individuals.

29. Illich, 1981.

30. Likewise, to the concept of *peacekeeping* Galtung has added *peacemaking*—resolving the conflict—and *peace building*—restoring just conditions that preempt war. Also see Paul Kimmel's chapter in this volume.

31. "For our culture as a whole," Huston Smith recently pointed out, "nothing major is going to happen until we figure out who we are. The truth of the matter is, that today we haven't a clue as to who we are. There is no consistent view of human nature in the West today," Quoted in Glazer, 1999.

CHAPTER 2

A PHILOSOPHY OF PEACE

Barry L. Gan

Following reports that the United States had killed over 100 civilians one evening in a bombing raid in Afghanistan following the 9/11 attacks on the World Trade Center and the Pentagon, U.S. Secretary of Defense Donald Rumsfeld remarked, "There is no question but that when one is engaged militarily that there are [*sic*] going to be unintended loss of life."[1] Apologists for the atomic bombing of Japan also justify the deliberate killing of civilians by a calculus that subtracts the number of civilian dead from the alleged number of U.S. troops who might have been killed in a land invasion of Japan. Just war theory itself fashions a defense of war on the basis of a calculus of intended outcomes.

But such attitudes and reasoning extend beyond war. Modern popular culture has placed efficiency on a pedestal. In popular culture today, our ethic is: "Git 'er done," and we have ceased to regard patience as a virtue. Instead, we raise people who break the rules to the level of heroes, slash the Gordian knot, and justify their actions on the basis of the goals they seek. In the end we don't care if the goal was achieved unjustly or illegally. It's all about outcome, not about process. We justify our actions by the ends at which they are aimed, and we justify our characters by the outcomes we intend or achieve, not by the means by which we pursue them.

Portions of this chapter were previously presented as part of the Presidential Address at the 2006 annual meeting of Concerned Philosophers for Peace at St. Bonaventure University and also at a 2009 symposium in honor of Robert L. Holmes at the University of Rochester.

The infamous 1970 Ford Pinto case, in which Ford justified its decision to continue to manufacture cars that were firetraps on a calculation that it was cheaper to settle lawsuits over people incinerated in accidents than to redesign the cars, is matched more recently, in 2009, by the Peanut Corporation of America, which knowingly distributed contaminated peanut products to groceries, restaurants, and other food services rather than swallow a short-term loss in profits. Again, following September 11, 2001, under the George W. Bush administration, civil liberties were regularly set aside on the grounds that such measures were necessary for national security, even though most people understand that civil liberties in the first place are a central feature of what is meant by security in one's nation. Even in games, in sporting events, rule-breaking has become part of the larger strategy.

A philosophy of peace pursues a different path. It recognizes that every action either builds community or destroys it. Every action either uses something solely as a means to an end, or shows respect for what is used as an end in itself as well. One who pursues a philosophy of peace seeks to plant oneself as fully as possible in the realm of building community, in the realm of respecting everything in the world as an end in itself. To do less is to destroy community and to disrespect others.

Yet few, if any, of our actions occupy one realm or the other exclusively. Often we destroy community as we attempt to build it. Often, despite our respect for others, we use them for some ends other than their own. This is practically unavoidable because, as Albert Schweitzer put it: "I am life which wills to live, and I exist in the midst of life which wills to live."[2] Indeed, it may be impossible to live a philosophy of peace to the fullest.

Nonetheless, a philosophy of peace may inform our lives and infuse our values far more often and far more deeply than is our current practice. People pursue peace in many ways, from "the war to end all wars" to mindful meditation. Peace scholars of the late 20th century distinguished between negative peace—an absence of war—and positive peace—the presence of justice and well-being in a society. But ultimately, peace is not merely a condition; it is the specific means by which any condition is sought. Nor is it the single end of positive peace alone but a way of pursuing any and all ends. A philosophy of peace exercises itself in both means and ends, seeking to avoid the destruction of community, seeking to preserve and promote all ends by the manner in which it pursues them. A rich philosophical history informs such a philosophy of peace.

THE PHILOSOPHICAL AND ETHICAL BASIS FOR A PHILOSOPHY OF PEACE

Perhaps Plato provides the oldest secular support for such an orientation. In his dialogue *Crito*, Plato portrays Socrates arguing with Crito:

[We must not] when injured injure in return, as the many imagine; for we must injure no one at all. . . . [W]e ought not to retaliate or render evil for evil to anyone, whatever evil we may have suffered from him. But I would have you consider, Crito, whether you really mean what you are saying. For this opinion has never been held, and never will be held, by any considerable number of persons.[3]

Some people understand Jesus' dictum of turning the other cheek in exactly this way. Others, including Jesus himself, in one passage, anyway, see it as "heaping coals upon the heads of one's enemies." But a philosophy of peace sees such behavior not as retaliation but rather as both a tactic for breaking the cycle of violence and also as the extension of a hand of friendship in spite of past differences, a willingness to endure injury rather than perpetrate and thereby perpetuate it.

In his second formulation of the categorical imperative, the principle of humanity, Immanuel Kant offers an arguably less extreme position but one, which, regardless, requires a deeper respect for all persons than is commonly practiced. He says, "Always act so that you treat humanity, whether in your own person or that of another, always as an end and never as a means only."[4]

Kant's point is not that we may never use people as means to our ends, but that if we do so, we must ensure that our use of them does not frustrate their pursuit of their own ends but rather, respects it or, ideally, enables it. For instance, a professor may offer instruction to students to fulfill her own ends, namely, to earn a living or to take satisfaction in the progress of those we help. But such a pursuit, when done well, enables students to fulfill their own ends as well. It is only when one pursues one's ends at the expense of another's ends that Kant takes exception.

Martin Buber, the great Jewish thinker of the 20th century, makes a similar distinction but draws the line even more sharply. In the opening pages of his masterpiece, *I and Thou*, he says:

To man the world is twofold, in accordance with his twofold attitude . . .
The *I* of man is also twofold.
For the *I* of the primary word *I–Thou* is a different *I* from that of the primary word *I-It* . . .
As experience, the world belongs to the primary word *I-It*.
The primary word *I-Thou* establishes the world of relation. . . .
First . . . with nature . . . Second, with men . . . [and t]hird, with spiritual beings.[5]

According to Buber, human existence depends on experience, on using the world for sustenance, but it fails to be fully human if it never enters into a relation that is all-consuming, a relation that regards the other not as an other but as the being in whose light all else lives.[6]

In this respect Buber's concepts resemble strongly Gandhi's call for people to shed fear, to shed attachment to the material world, and to pursue
truth wholeheartedly. And again, although it may not be possible to do so
permanently, fully, without jeopardizing one's very life, the striving for such
an ideal is what makes more likely a heaven on earth, or, in Kant's terms, a
kingdom of ends, where everyone's individual pursuits are so regardful of
others that everyone's ends are entwined and mutually reinforcing.

Some of the greatest peacemakers have attempted to capture these
insights in various ways. Gandhi said, "The means may be likened to a seed,
the end to a tree: and there is just the same inviolable connection between
the means and the end as there is between the seed and the tree."[7] A. J.
Muste, a major figure in American nonviolence during the 20th century
said, "There is no way to peace. Peace is the way."[8] And Martin Luther
King, Jr., said, "Darkness cannot put out darkness: only light can do that.
Hate cannot drive out hate: only love can do that."[9] The insight might also
be characterized by the Zen Buddhist maxim, "Attention!" a maxim that
urges one to focus on the task at hand, to focus more on the present means
than the future ends.

Each of these thinkers or approaches offers a point of view that stands
apart from that of the multitude. Although many people regard means as
justifiable by reference to the ends, others—like the thinkers above, far
fewer in number but present throughout all ages—see the necessity of linking the justifiability of the ends necessarily to the justifiability of the means.

Robert L. Holmes, in a lengthy footnote in his book *On War and Morality*,
establishes this necessary moral connection between means and ends. He says:

> One is justified in performing an act only if he is justified both in
> employing the means necessary to its performance and in performing
> any subsidiary acts constitutive of it. I cannot be justified in watering
> my garden unless I am justified in attaching the hose and turning on
> the water . . .
>
> Some, of course, would argue that if the end is justified, then so must be
> the means. And this is true, if properly understood. But it does not follow
> from it that the end justifies the means. For there is an asymmetry here.
> One must justify the necessary means before one can justify pursuing the
> end, whereas the reverse is not the case. I do not need to justify watering
> my garden before I justify hooking up the hose and turning on the water; I
> may do these things as a means to a different end, such as washing the car.
> If the end is justified, the means will in fact *be* justified. But that is because
> one must justify them in the course of justifying the end, not because the
> justification of the end in isolation somehow justifies them.[10]

Most people are either ignorant of this moral relation between means and
ends—or are dismissive of it. But its implications are manifold and far-reaching.

THE IMPLICATIONS OF A PHILOSOPHY OF PEACE

One of the major implications of such a philosophy of peace, as Holmes argues in his book, is that for all intents and purposes all modern war is immoral. Since the means used to wage war regularly entail the killing of innocent lives—more innocent lives in the 20th century than lives of combatants themselves—it is only possible to justify war if one can justify the taking of innocent lives, and in modern war, extraordinary numbers of innocent lives. While some may argue that modern war is often, also, a question of *saving* large numbers of innocent lives, one cannot know in advance whether one's actions in a modern war will, in fact, result in saving more innocent lives than would otherwise be lost. This is so, at least in part, because the decision to end a war, once begun, is never up to one side alone. Do what I may, just or unjust, I cannot be certain how others will respond to what I do. And thus, to use unjust means—in hopes that others will respond as I wish and thereby bring about a worthy end—is, in the final analysis, simply to do injustice.

Another major implication of a philosophy of peace is that the pursuit of profit for the sake of profit is immoral. The pursuit of profit requires that people buy products and services, and if the people who buy these products and services become incidental to the profits sought, then the philosophy of peace is violated. So when one sells a piece of furniture, a cell phone, or an inkjet printer that is known to break within the first two years of normal use, or an automobile that gets recalled regularly, or a balloon mortgage that far outstrips a person's long-term ability to pay, or an academic program to students who have a poor record of success as students, one violates a philosophy of peace.

Whether or not an invisible hand guarantees a long-term outcome beneficial to all, the philosophy is violated because the means are sacrificed for an intended outcome—profit—that becomes everything. The process by which the outcome is achieved becomes irrelevant. A philosophy of peace rejects such an approach.

Even within the field of nonviolence itself one can find violations of a philosophy of peace. Strategic nonviolent action—recently widely touted as a new way of changing policy, overthrowing dictators, doing battle—distinguishes between means, which it calls tactics and strategies, and ends, which it calls goals or objectives.[11] Insofar as the tactics and strategies always offer one's opponents a choice—do as I wish or make me suffer, then nonviolent strategic action fits well within a philosophy of peace. But when the strategies and tactics take on a different tone—do as we wish or you will suffer, then the dynamic begins very much to resemble the dynamic of war itself.

The notion of doing as I wish or making me suffer is allied very closely with Jesus's dictum of turning the other cheek. The willingness to suffer demonstrates to the opponent and to others that one is willing to suffer for what one believes in. Its dynamic is antithetical to the dynamic of war, for it invites one's own suffering and shows one's opponents that one will not visit harm on them. It says, "I will stand for what I believe in, but I will not harm you because of it."

Perhaps the best example of this attitude, of the practice of a philosophy of peace, can be found in parenting. Not all parents, of course, do a perfect job of raising their children, but almost all parents aspire to an ideal that is difficult if not impossible to realize. That ideal entails a goal—a child who will become a productive, likeable, fair-minded, and fulfilled adult, or something along those lines. But no good parent would dream of treating the child in harmful ways to achieve that result. Many good parents sacrifice much for the sake of their children, preferring to sacrifice themselves in little ways like missing meetings or larger ways like giving up job opportunities so that their children might flourish, might learn, might grow into the adults we hope they will become. But only a foolish parent—and many such parents exist—would employ unjust or harmful means to accomplish such a purpose. Most of us would view such means as inimical to the very goal we seek. Why, then, would we not extend such reasoning to other means and ends in our lives?[12]

The world is violent, not only because natural phenomena like earthquakes, tsunamis, and tornados violently destroy much of what people value, but also because we ourselves choose to destroy much of what we value. Often we do violence in relatively inadvertent ways; more often we regard violent choices that we make as having undesired side effects, what the Pentagon euphemistically calls collateral damage. Undesired side effects vary: they may be a dozen insects smashed on a car's windshield during a summer drive to the beach, a dozen children killed in a school by a misguided missile, or the bulk of the civilian population of a Japanese city obliterated or radiated by an atomic bomb. But these side effects are foreseeable consequences of our actions, and all too often the desired effects of our actions are more wishes than likelihoods.

Few people disagree on what ends we desire. Almost all of us seek a peaceful home, a peaceful community, a peaceful nation, a peaceful world. No, what we differ on, what distinguishes peacemaking from other work, whether one is an electrician, a retail clerk, or a philosopher, is the *means* by which one does one's work.

The insight was driven home to me even more when I made one of my infrequent visits to a synagogue, in this case the synagogue in which I had grown up as a teenager in Rochester, New York. I noticed that since I had last been there, the prayer books had been replaced. And I also noticed that in the new prayer books the translation of a very famous line from Isaiah had also been changed. Each week, one of the Sabbath prayers that I had uttered and heard as a teen had been:

Lo yiseh goy el goy herev, v'lo yl-medu od ml-hamah.
"Nation shall not lift up sword against nation. Neither shall men learn war anymore."

But though the Hebrew remained unchanged in the prayer book, the English translation had changed. It now read: "Nation shall not lift up sword against nation. Neither shall men *experience* war anymore."

That's curious, I thought. In the original Hebrew the idea was that paradise would be a place where people would not *learn* war anymore. But now the idea had shifted from a world in which nations would not *learn* war to a world in which nations would not *suffer* war.

After the service I approached the rabbi and asked him about this change. I asked him whether the Hebrew word *yl-medu* meant "learn" or "experience." I knew what it meant, and so did he. It means "learn." It does not mean "experience." But he made excuses for the translation.

And it was clear to me, at least, why such a translation in an American prayer book had been altered. Israel and the United States both spend a great deal of money, time, and effort in *learning* war. Both nations have turned away from the paradise envisioned by Isaiah.

The wishes of both nations are that neither of them experience war in their own territories. Neither wishes to suffer war, but both are willing to learn it. Both are willing to learn war in the mistaken view that by doing so they will not suffer it. But the Bible strongly suggests that paradise is the circumstance that obtains, not when nations suffer war no more, but when they *learn* it no more.

One cannot reach the end one desires by pursuing means inimical to those ends.

AN OBJECTION

And so we return to the question: what is a philosophy of peace? This much, is clear: a philosophy of peace does not countenance making war. It does not entail harming others intentionally or out of negligence. To put it in Platonic terms, it requires that we not make others worse off. If one is making *any* others worse off, one is not engaged in peacemaking.

But some think otherwise. Some think, along with the Pentagon, that it is often necessary to use violence to prevent harm to innocent people. In 2006,

I heard Archbishop Celestino Migliore speak at the annual conference of the Peace and Justice Studies Association. Migliore at that time was the Pope's representative to the UN, and, though I shouldn't have been, I was surprised to hear some of his remarks. When asked whether the Church would condone the use of violence in some circumstances, he said that it would be wrong sometimes to turn the other cheek. I was curious to see how he would explain this since it contradicts what Jesus says in the Beatitudes, and he obliged me by trotting out the following worn example: "Imagine a person carrying a baby, assaulted by a third person. Should the person charged with the care of the baby turn the other cheek? No, said the archbishop, not if it means that the baby would be assaulted—because one has an obligation to protect innocent third parties." If there were a Frequently Asked Questions book for pacifists and nonviolentists, it would begin with this example. The responses are also standard, but they point the way toward a deeper understanding of genuine peacemaking.

One response is put forward by Leo Tolstoy,[13] who speaks not of a baby allegedly about to be assaulted but of a child allegedly about to be killed. He says first, that the person wishing to protect the child could not know whether or not the child would be harmed before it is. Nor, he continues, could one know that the world would be a better place if the child instead of the third person were saved. Both assumptions presume that we can know another's intentions. To know that the child would be harmed is to know not only the capabilities of the other person but also his or her intentions. To know that the world would be a better place if the child were spared at the expense of the alleged attacker is to know what each being will make of himself or herself in the future. And both assumptions presume that we can know that the outcomes of our actions will be as we desire them. Both assumptions are unprovable.

Another response is to acknowledge that many actions short of doing violence might stop an attack. One of my friends was once accosted in Kansas City at gunpoint in an attempted street-corner robbery. He looked the potential robber in the eye, spoke quietly to him, and talked him out of the robbery. There is, of course, no guarantee that such efforts will always yield such outcomes, but what must be realized is that there is no guarantee that *violent* efforts will always yield desirable outcomes, either.

In the end, the most important question one can ask oneself is: what sort of person do I want to be? Do I want to be the sort of person who injures others, who occasionally kills others? Or do I want to be a person who shows faith in the goodness of others, and who is willing to absorb a blow or two rather than deliver one?

Most people, like the archbishop, would hedge on that question. They would say that, well, yes, it would be nice to be the sort of person who never injures or kills others, but sometimes duty requires me to injure another. After all, I don't want to be the sort of person who allows innocent third parties—such as babies—to be injured.

Built into such a response, in certain circumstances, is a major moral misunderstanding. I am not obliged to do whatever I must to prevent innocents from suffering wrongdoing. I am certainly obliged not to contribute to their suffering. But I am not obliged to do *whatever* is necessary to prevent wrongdoing to innocents.

We may have an obligation to inform others that what they are about to do is morally questionable, or wrong, especially if those others are people under our care. I would call this bearing witness, in much the same way that Socrates and Thoreau bore witness to what they believed to be wrongdoing. But bearing witness to alleged wrongdoing should not involve harming others or, as Socrates argued in the *Crito*, harming the concept of law by which people govern themselves. Gandhi notes that we are finite beings who cannot know with any certainty that wrongdoing is about to occur. Thus we should not knowingly or negligently harm others in an attempt to prevent what may not happen. This is one major insight at the basis of Gandhi's philosophy of *ahimsa*, though he did allow that when wrongdoing was virtually *certain* to occur (the well-known "madman with the sword" scenario), one must use harmful, even lethal force in such emergencies. If one tried as far as possible to do so without anger or fear or conviction that this is an ideal way to solve such emergencies in the future, it could be considered a nonviolent act.

Again Robert Holmes captures this insight rather neatly in his book *Basic Moral Philosophy*.[14] There he distinguishes between what he calls mediated and unmediated consequences of actions. An unmediated consequence of an action, he says, is a consequence that results directly from my action, without the intervention of another human being's actions. The example he offers is that of breaking a window. The broken glass is an unmediated consequence of my throwing a stone through it. A mediated consequence, on the other hand, is a consequence that results indirectly from one of my actions by the response my action generates in another. If I admonish a student in front of other students and he runs to the dean and complains that I've humiliated him, his complaint to the dean is a mediated consequence of my action.

Gandhi would have said that as finite beings, we cannot know the mediated consequences of our actions, only the unmediated consequences. Thus we cannot justify unmediated consequences of our actions on the basis of expected mediated consequences.

For this reason it is quite possible that the readiness to do violence in the defense of innocent people is one of the major sources of all violence in the world. This is true because those who do violence allegedly for this purpose are often fooling themselves and/or trying to fool others, and they are often not even trying to learn from their experiences. Of course, such a reaction could only be considered nonviolent—and fully justified, in an emergency. Gandhi said this argument could not be used to justify *preparing* to use harmful force against a future threat because if one had the time to do that he or she would also have the time to prepare *non* violence.

But there is yet another response to the archbishop's example, and trite though this response may at first appear, nothing about it is trite at all. One can ask: what are you doing with a child in a dark alley, anyway? How did you get there? And what did you expect to find? Somehow, for some reason, while walking with this child, or carrying this baby, you decided it would be perfectly all right to walk down this dark alley, to place yourself in a circumstance where a crisis was, if not likely, at least reasonably possible. Why?

If I have someone in my care, then I have obligations with respect to that person, obligations that include planning intelligently what I will be doing while that person is in my care. For example, last year I offered to drive some friends to the nearest major airport, a good 70 miles away. I knew I had a couple of tires on my car that would soon be in need of replacement. I decided to replace them a bit early rather than run into a problem while these friends were in my care. In this way I avoided a potential crisis.

Here's another example: we knew that the dikes in New Orleans needed repair long before Hurricane Katrina hit, but we did little or nothing to address that problem until it became a crisis. Yet another example is the continuing spread of nuclear weapons. Almost half a century ago the nuclear nations of the world had an opportunity to begin disarmament of their weapons and thereby reduce incentives for other nations to acquire nuclear stockpiles. Today the United States and Russia each still have well over 6,000 nuclear weapons each in their arsenals, and the United States is complaining about North Korea's detonation of a nuclear device so small that at first people weren't even certain the explosion was an atomic explosion. The United States and Russia both had the opportunity, beginning in 1970 or even earlier, to reduce desire among the nations of the world to acquire nuclear weapons. But unwillingness to make significant reductions, even to levels of hundreds rather than thousands of nuclear weapons, ensured that other nations would seek to acquire the same power. Unwillingness to address an acknowledged problem before it became a crisis guaranteed that the problem would become a crisis.

Some may still object that what I am doing is blaming the victim. Doesn't one have the right to walk with a child down any dark alley one chooses without having to worry about being assaulted? Isn't the person who assaults me the person who should be blamed?

Actually, there is a legal principle, well established, that addresses a similar question. It is the principle of "last clear chance." The principle asserts that a person who had a last clear chance to avoid injury or damage but chose not to do so may not recover damages. This principle is not a principle of criminal law; it's a principle of civil law, and in recent years it has been replaced in most states with the notion of comparative negligence. But it captures, nonetheless, the intuition at the heart of this particular argument, namely, that people have some responsibility to avoid placing themselves in circumstances where injury is likely, especially if they seek to recover damages from the party that injured them.

CONCLUSION

So we can draw some conclusions about a philosophy of peace.

As we said at the outset, a philosophy of peace distinguishes means from ends but finds them practically and morally inseparable. One cannot justify means that harm others or might harm others by appealing to the ends that we seek. In short, a philosophy of peace, of necessity, is nonviolent in all of its means, all the time.

Second, a philosophy of peace demands long-term work. If one is in crisis mode, odds are good that one is not doing genuine peacemaking, especially if crisis mode means that one is acting in ways that may harm others. Labeling something as a crisis is often though not always another way of justifying the doing of violence to those we perceive as "enemies." Newton Garver, a philosopher, Quaker, and pacifist, once remarked: "I think that crisis management is itself a disease." A philosophy of peace requires patience. Nice!

I am reminded of this each time I recite the prayer that is called St. Francis's Prayer (even though it is not). The prayer begins, "Lord, make me an instrument of thy peace. Where there is hatred, let me sow love. Where there is injury, pardon." The prayer does not talk about *supplanting* hatred with love, *supplanting* injury with pardon. It talks about planting love, planting pardon. It implies that these orientations are like seeds, or seedlings, to be nurtured, watered, protected, and, above all, not to be hurried along because they *can't* be hurried along.

Third, a philosophy of peace recognizes, as Plato said, that it is better to be harmed than to harm.[15] A philosophy of peace, in other words, recognizes Gandhi's insight that people, as finite beings, cannot know the mediated consequences of their actions and thus cannot justify unmediated consequences of actions on the basis of expected mediated consequences. We know the effects of many of our actions on the environment. We know the effects of over-consumption. We know when we have more than we need. We harm others, negligently if not deliberately, in allowing such a great divide between rich and poor, and also in allowing over-consumption. As Nietzsche said, "The superfluous is the enemy of the necessary."[16]

Finally, a philosophy of peace requires a creative tension. It is the tension between working on oneself to become a better person while working to make the world a better place. The world is never made a better place if we become so certain of ourselves that we think we are entitled to harm others to achieve our vision of a better world. Should we work to make peace by working on ourselves or by working on others? We must do both.

Socrates asserted that a wise person knows that he doesn't know. And such wisdom precludes one from ever undertaking to do violence to others. To do so is to be smug, to be certain, to regard oneself as more than finite. This is why one must develop one's own character while working to develop the character of the world.

The earth and all its creatures should be regarded as our family. Schweitzer's observation that we are life that wills to live in the midst of other life that wills to live reveals (1) that we are not privileged in creation in our will to live and that, (2) because of that, there is a presumption against destroying any of what many would call God's creations. A philosophy of peace requires that we must show them patience, forbearance and love, and care for the earth and all its creatures; and we must have faith that, whether we live to see the fruits of our actions, whatever those mediated and unmediated fruits may be, at least, in not deliberately or negligently harming others, we have done the right thing.

NOTES

1. CNN.com Transcripts, 2001.
2. Schweitzer, 1987.
3. Holmes and Gan, 2005.
4. Plato, 360 BCE.
5. Buber, 1958.
6. Ibid., 8.
7. Gandhi, 1926.
8. Muste, 2009.
9. King, reprinted 1986.
10. Holmes, 2007.
11. Sharp, 1973; Ackerman and DuVall, 2000.
12. Ruddick, 1989.

13. Tolstoy, reprinted 1987.
14. Holmes, 2007.
15. Ibid.
16. Nietzsche, reprinted 1997.

CHAPTER 3

PEACE AND DEVELOPMENT TODAY: AN OVERVIEW

Johan Galtung

To work for peace is to work against violence: by analyzing its forms and causes, predicting in order to prevent, and then acting preventively and curatively. Peace relates to violence much as health relates to illness. Of particular concern is *genocide*, or *massive category killing*, across the fault-lines in human society: nature (between humans and their environment), gender, generation, race, class, exclusion, nation, and state. Whether as direct violence or as the indirect slow, grinding violence of social structures that do not deliver sufficient nutrition and health at the bottom of world society, enormous suffering, the Buddhists' *dukkha*, is the effect of violence.

To work for peace is to build *sukha*, liberation, wellness in a world at peace with nature, between genders, generations, and among races—where the excluded are included but not by force and where classes, nations, and states serve neither direct nor structural violence. In such a world they would all pull together for better livelihood for all. That would be true globalization, unlike the present abusive reduction of that term to represent only state and corporate elites in a handful of countries. The best instrument of true globalization would be an improved UN, with a UN People's Assembly for global democracy, and without any veto power for privileged states, probably located where most people live, somewhere in the Third World, like in Jerusalem or Hong Kong.

An improved UN would build on civil society actors—nongovernmental organizations (NGOs) and local authorities (LAs)—and Transnational Corporations (TNCs), underutilized as peace actors. The modern state system, from the "peace" of Westphalia 1648 on, has clearly been over-utilized. It is a war system, giving states the right of war (except for Japan: Constitution, Article 9 still denies Japan that right). An improved UN would also have to learn to build on *nations*, striving for autonomy, not privileging *states*.

States were not created to bring peace into the world but to satisfy "national interests" defined by elites of elite nations. Peace has lower priority as seen comparing the size of the state institutions for war and for peace. Very problematic are predatory states who see national interests located outside their territory—euphemistically called their "sphere of interest"—and inside the smaller states. When states pretend to work for peace it is very often as a way of solidifying their sphere of interest. Should the effort be honest it is usually painfully clear how little they know and how amateurish their endeavors. Nothing of this, however, prevents them from claiming a monopoly on peace, even as they do on war.

From this it does not follow that non-states, in the world civil society as NGOs and as LAs, or TNCs, or individuals, are necessarily competent. Nor does it follow that states cannot be improved, nor that states cannot often be excellent peacemakers across the other divides defined by nature, gender, generation, race, class, and exclusion. Such efforts are codified in a major instrument for peace, human rights (universal, indivisible), and partly protected by the institutions of democracy. But these two institutions are far from culturally neutral. And their practice in inter-nation and inter-state relations, at the macro and mega levels of the human construction where state and regional egotisms prevail, supported by democratic majorities of dominant nations and civilizations, leaves much to be desired. To put it mildly.

Hence, this explains the rise early last century (but with forerunners in the high Middle Ages) of non-state actors working for peace. There are at least three generations of such approaches, so far.

To understand them better, the definition *peace equals ability to handle conflict, with empathy, nonviolence, and creativity* may be useful, since so much violence is due to mishandling of conflict.

Conflict equals attitudes plus behavior plus contradiction: an ABC triangle. At the root of the conflict is a *contradiction*, the incompatible goals. Hateful/apathetic *attitudes* and *behavior* often come later, all three stimulating each other. After some time the situation crystallizes, polarizes around friend/self and foe/other, the former surrounded by increasingly positive and the latter by increasingly negative attitudes and behavior. Friend-and-foe images become megalomaniac and paranoid, unable to include anything negative in the former and positive in the latter. We can talk about social pathologies bordering on collective psychoses the way we classify individuals with similar traits. Rationality evaporates. Deep culture with grotesque ready-made polarization takes over. Violence, even with mass destruction, is not far away. The Cold War was a case of this ABC dynamic that was only dissipated when forces in civil society had a sobering, depolarizing effect. So are conflicts in and around Yugoslavia, the Middle East in general, and over terrorism by state or non-state actors.

We can use the ABC triangle to identify deep attitudes, deep behavior, and deep contradictions, assuming that they steer or at least influence the surface level of the incompatible goals, of what people say they feel or think and how they act and behave. "Deep" would mean subconscious, hidden, under the surface. We can identify those three with deep culture, basic human needs, and deep structure, the latter referring to the eight fault-lines in the human social construction mentioned above.

We then get peace approaches by trying to change all six, the attitudes, the behavior, the contradictions; at the surface level and deeper down. And we get three generations of peace approaches:

1. *First Generation of Peace Approaches: Up to World War II*
   A—oriented: peace movements, advocating, demonstrating;
   B—oriented: war abolition, eliminating war as social institution;
   C—oriented: global governance, globalizing conflict transformation.
   The three were related, with people expressing themselves through the movements, with governments searching for regional and global harmonization, and for war abolition through mechanisms of democracy, human rights, and regimes. Motto for this generation: Peace is too important to leave to the generals.

2. *Second Generation of Peace Approaches: After World War II*
   A—oriented: peace education/journalism, for knowledge/information;
   B—oriented: nonviolence, to be able to struggle, but nonviolently;
   C—oriented: conflict transformation, solving conflicts creatively.
   The three are related, evolving from the first generation. People start doubting that peace ranks high among the interests pursued by governments, and doubt their capability, watching them stumble at the brink of nuclear abyss, through the Cold War. People start demanding education and research for peace, and turn to the streets to fight, inspired by Gandhi and Martin Luther King, Jr., Mandela, and Tutu. Patterns of people's NGO diplomacy start emerging to solve conflicts rather than waiting for governments. Motto for this generation: Peace is too important to leave to the states.

3. *Third Generation of Peace Approaches: After the Cold War*
   A—oriented: peace cultures, going into deep cultures if needed;
   B—oriented: basic human needs, as non-negotiable pillars;
   C—oriented: peace structures, repairing fault-lines like gender.

This period is characterized by a search for foundations for peace below the surface, generalizing Freudian-Jungian needs and culture approaches and Marxian ones of needs and structure. Motto for this generation: Peace is too important for shallow approaches.

The first generation was a reaction against war. People demanded peace through governmental cooperation, above nations and states. The second generation is a reaction against governments. People become increasingly skeptical and want to work for peace themselves. In the third generation there is a reaction against simplistic peace approaches, realizing how deep-rooted—and linked to development, to the satisfaction of basic needs—these problems are.

CONFLICTS HAVE LIFE CYCLES, OR PHASES, WITHIN THEM

- Phase I: Before violence:
  1. Peacemaking (conflict transformation),
  2. Peace building
- Phase II: During violence:
  3. Peacekeeping,
  4. Peace Zones
- Phase III: After violence:
  5. Reconciliation (with reconstruction),

This overall scheme opens possibilities for cooperation with states. Non-states are not contesting state monopoly on violence, but its practice, along with any state monopoly on peace action. Cooperation among various actors is needed for all five approaches above. Non-state actors may be able to transform conflicts; states may follow and formalize an outcome in a treaty. Peace building is essentially the antidote to polarization and the individual and social pathologies mentioned, used preventively in Phase I and curatively in Phases II and III. Peacekeeping (violence control) and Peace Zones (models of normality) are best practiced by military, police, and civilians together. And reconciliation to heal traumas of violence and bring about closure of a conflict has to include state actors if the latter used violence. Reconciliation between Serbs, Croats, and Bosniaks in Bosnia-Herzegovina and Serbs and Albanians in Kosovo/a is needed, but so is reconciliation with French and Dutch UN peacekeeping forces, with NATO, with U.S./UK bombers, and Austrian and German protectorate administrators.

How do we obtain peace? It has to cover all approaches, and more, and draw on theory from micro (intra/inter-personal), meso (intra-social), and macro (inter-nation and inter-state) levels of human organization. The old model of one semester or summer courses will have to yield to treating peace studies like health studies with its own university faculty, and a four- to five-year study with practice, preparing for professional activity.

We thus have a number of approaches that together can model a more peaceful world:

- *Peace Movements*: NGO advocacy of commitment to peace by all states and all corporations, making them accountable to peace programs.
- *War Abolition*: more states without armies; outlawing research-production-distribution-use of major arms, as for hard drugs.
- *Global Governance*: democratizing the United Nations through direct elections to a People's Assembly and abolition of the veto power.
- *Peace Education*: to be introduced at all schools all levels all over like civics, hygiene/sex education, and knowledge of one's own culture.
- *Peace Journalism*: that all decent media inform the public about ways out of conflicts, building a solution culture, not a violence culture.
- *Nonviolence*: that nonviolent ways of fighting for a cause and to defend one's integrity, for example, one's basic needs, become common skills.
- *Conflict Transformation/Peacemaking*: conflict-handling knowledge and skills as part of training citizens anywhere, again like hygiene.
- *Peace Culture*: that people start discussing their own culture, what can be done to make it more peace-productive—and then do it.
- *Basic Needs:* that basic needs, particularly of the most needy, is the guideline for politics and economics; peace and development.
- *Peace Structure:* from exploitative and repressive structures with nature, genders, races, classes, nations, states to equity, parity.
- *Peace Building:* build good *and* bad rather than good *or* bad images of the world's actors, and build positive ties in all directions.
- *Peacekeeping:* with minimum violence as a protection for the defense-less and as a protective in-between for the violent.
- *Peace Zones:* starting with oneself as one-person peace zone based on the principles above, constructing archipelagoes of peace.
- *Reconciliation:* learning to apologize and accept apologies, how to ask for forgiveness and forgive, how to heal and close conflicts.

More can doubtless be added, as human experiences of peace and the construction of peace accumulate. Does the model have a chance or is it only a *fata morgana*, some mirage over a desert overheated by the excessive violence, not to mention the threats, of the 20th and 21st centuries (the little we have seen so far?). Well, it can be argued that humanity has been through much worse; and that there is no reason that military and civilians, politicians and people could not do all of this together, given more knowledge, skill, and will. And much reason, of course, why they must.

PART II

THE PEACE INHERITANCE: SCIENCE AND THE PROMISE OF HUMAN NATURE

When church leaders and scientists rose in opposition to Darwin's theory of natural selection in the famous Oxford debate of 1860, their fear was that Darwin would make nature self-regulating, thus making God superfluous. The theory did have some such effect, but its real damage to human well-being and understanding has been the legitimization of competition and violence that popularists made of it—something Darwin never intended at the time and from which he distanced himself more and more as his understanding grew.

The two chapters of this brief part attempt to suggest a much greater topic: that the hand of cooperation and peace can be seen at work at every level of evolution, indeed perhaps in the structure of reality itself as understood in the post-Newtonian age and certainly in the psychology of human consciousness. Nature was "red in tooth and claw" only when we looked on her with sanguinary eyes; the true story is more complex, more hopeful, and more challenging.

Michael N. Nagler and Angel Ryono attempt to outline the changing outlook of science with regard to the peace potential, starting with the quantum revolution, then touching on the new ethology that is balancing out the distortions of the Lorenzian and popularizing era of "innate aggression," and climaxing with eye-opening discoveries made possible only since the late 1980s by precise, noninvasive studies of the living brain and central nervous system. Their point is that while we think that science is giving us a picture of reality, we are really, as Carolyn Merchant (1980) pointed out in her groundbreaking book *The Death of Nature*, telling science what to tell us, based on already formed preconceptions—getting the science we deserve, so to speak. This makes the current expansion of science into more positive areas most encouraging, and as Nagler and Ryono imply, peace work should take full advantage of it.

Marc Pilisuk and Mitch Hall provide a remarkably condensed overview of some of the important ways that the "softer" psychological disciplines shed, similarly, much light on the often disregarded human capacity for empathy and peace. They focus on the special circumstances in the lives of children that make some more, and others less, prone to violence and the intensive sanctions required to turn ordinary people into soldiers. They stress the human capacity to construct the worlds of symbols in ways that can make cruelty seem either like second nature or outrageously inhuman.

Huston Smith remarked some years ago that there would be no significant progress for this civilization until we came up with an agreed-on, reasonably accurate image of the human being. These two chapters, brief as they are, seem to offer a beginning template for the elaboration of that new image.

There is one important topic that neither of these studies touches on: the existence, historically and in the present, of "peaceful societies" that live without war and often without much conflict of any kind (they are briefly referenced by David Adams in Chapter 8). These human experiments are of two kinds: most are pre-industrial societies like the Semai of Malaysia and many others (an early paper on this subject bore the title "Fifty Peaceful Societies"). Anthropologist Douglas Fry[1] reports his finding of 70 well-documented nonwarring societies. These societies are not utopias. They face many of the problems of living with environmental conditions and with other humans. But they demonstrate well that nothing we have learned about the evolving human animal can cast doubt on the living proof that humans can live in peace for very long periods of time. Clearly we should be learning from them with diligent attention, particularly as many of them, like the Mbuti of central Africa, are disappearing.

The other type is quite different: "enclaved" communities like the Mennonites, Amish, Hutterites, and Quakers who live in the midst of, but have maintained a measure of cultural separation from modern industrial societies. Both are beginning to receive due recognition in the form of a Web site, http://www.peacefulsocieties.org, that includes the beginnings of an encyclopedia.

Of these peaceful societies, two observations should be made: (1) they vary in the degree to which they actually practice active forms of nonviolence as opposed to conflict avoidance, and more significantly perhaps, (2) their institutions and cultural memes are not always applicable in the industrialized world. In particular, many of them have perfected peaceable customs that give them a quite stable regime *within* their relatively isolated environment. Among the Semai and the Mbuti, for example, there is no love lost between themselves and respectively the lowland Malays or the surrounding African peoples. More than this, they have worked out mechanisms that do not survive the inevitable contact with industrial "civilizations"; and when that contact occurs they often react with violence, sometimes *more* violence than other groups. For example, the Semai, so peaceable within their own territory, broke out in bloodthirsty behaviors when they were swept up in the Cold War struggles for power in Southeast Asia. There is a lesson to be learned here, too. As so often in peace development we must avoid romanticism (or any kind of naiveté); however, we must never fail to learn from an experiment that has even partly succeeded. Too much is at stake and there is too little time to reinvent those slowly evolved cultural patterns that provided ways to live without inflicting serious harm on one another.

—Marc Pilisuk and Michael N. Nagler

NOTE

1. Fry, 2007.

CHAPTER 4

The Evolution of Peace

Michael N. Nagler and Angel Ryono

King started from the essentially religious persuasion that in each human being, black or white, whether deputy sheriff or manual laborer or governor, there exists, however tenuously, a certain natural identification with every other human being; that, in the overarching design of the universe which ultimately connects us all together, we tend to feel that what happens to our fellow human beings in some way also happens to us, so that no man can continue to debase or abuse another human being without eventually feeling in himself at least some dull answering hurt and stir of shame. Therefore, in the catharsis of a live confrontation with wrong, when an oppressor's violence is met with a forgiving love, he can be vitally touched, and even, at least momentarily, reborn as a human being, while the society witnessing such a confrontation will be quickened in conscience toward compassion and justice.

—*Marshall Frady*

STEPPING OUT OF THE SHADOWS

Kenneth Boulding, the distinguished economist who was one of the giants in peace studies, used to say that the field of nonviolence is like that of science in that it seeks to discover truth. In any field of science, falsehood or misinformation, once disclosed, is always rejected while truth, once discovered, is kept. It should be noted that in all sciences, the pursuit of knowledge is an evolving process—old views are subject to review and to alterations through better understanding. However optimistic Boulding's assessment may appear, it does seem that science as a whole is broadening its perspective, particularly on the nature of human beings. The science of human and animal behavior is moving from a preoccupation with the dysfunctions that can lead to aggression and war to exploring the inherent potential of the human being for nonviolence and peace. A landmark development in the exploration of our capacity for peace was the ringing publication *The Seville Statement on Violence* that was disseminated under UN auspices in 1986.[1] Eighteen distinguished ethologists, psychologists, and bioscientists systematically refuted the assumptions that we are by nature defined by competitive behaviors and biologically inclined to war-making. The driving concern of the authors of *The Seville Statement* was that the myth "war is intrinsic to human nature" is widespread and presents a real challenge to the progress toward peace.[2] Although there is violence in nature and in human societies, there is also nonviolence in the form of cooperation, sharing, mediation, reconciliation, and even self-sacrifice. Moreover, biology, as understood in its most common definition, does *not* exclusively determine human behaviors. Humans have the ability to accept or override biological influences. As Nagler has said in oral presentations: "We are not wired for violence, and we are not wired for nonviolence. We are wired for *choice*."[3] Therefore, it is either overreaching or naïve to say that war-making—a phenomenon and an institution that involves a highly complex system requiring intricate and extensive planning and the dedication of vast resources—is "inevitable."

Like the sciences, a parallel widening of the lens is discernible today in the field of history. Gandhi once argued, "Hundreds of nations live in peace. History does not and cannot take note of this fact. History is really a record of the interruption of the even workings of the force of love or the soul. History, then, is a record of the interruptions of the course of nature. Soul-force [satyagraha], being natural, is not noted in history."[4]

Conversely, psychology and psychiatry, like other sciences, have been increasingly confronted with the "dual-use dilemma" of their work.[5] Although scientists usually do not consider "ominous applications" for their research, the dawn of contemporary studies of human brain processes and behavior rose inseparably with the increasing sophistication of war-making institutions.[6] Although only a small number of clinicians in psychology and psychiatry worked for the military in World War I, the employment of psychologists and psychiatrists in various aspects of military and central intelligence institutions saw a dramatic increase about a year after World War II began. "By the end of the war, 1,710 psychologists were serving in the U.S. military, an astounding figure because in 1945, APA [the American Psychological Association] had only 1,012 full members."[7] Although similar increases have occurred in other parts of the western world, the U.S. government and military is, by far, the biggest employer of psychologists and psychiatrists.

In the United States an inexhaustible military budget has brought significant patronage to studies of the brain and human behavior. War-making institutions have expanded the research and duties of psychologists and psychiatrists beyond strategies to resist enemy interrogation or to improve the morale of troops during battle; they have been asked to exploit the human potential for and consent to acts of violence, among other disturbing "applications" of their expertise[8] (see Latonick-Flores and Adamski, Chapter 9, Volume 2 of this set). In fact, some of today's most established subfields in psychology and social sciences were born out of U.S. naval research projects.[9] Psychologists were thus deeply involved in one of the most disturbing uses of science in the modern world: we have improved on the crude methods used in the past to overcome the natural human aversion to injuring or killing another person. Science, at the service of the military, has succeeded in dehumanizing military personnel so that the actual gun-firing rate of men in combat could be raised from an estimated 15 percent in the Korean War to over 90 percent in the Vietnam War.[10] Further, in 1947, the establishment of a U.S. Central Intelligence Agency (CIA) commenced a long and "disturbing" relationship with APA officials.[11] It has been documented that APA officials were involved in the development of ethical standards "governing psychologists' participation in interrogations and those involved in overseeing and facilitating the Bush administration's . . . programs of torture."[12] Other psychology experiments or research like those conducted in the 1960s by Stanley Milgram and in the 1970s by Philip Zimbardo focused on investigating the negative tendencies of human behavior in the context of group pressure or in response to authority. Milgram's research on obedience and Zimbardo's discovery of the Lucifer Effect, although helpful in understanding such social phenomena, nevertheless influenced our worldview that humans under certain not uncommon circumstances are constitutionally violent and destructive.

Today, as global-scale problems threaten all human beings, if not all life on earth, studies of the mind and brain science are turning the corner to explore the other edge of human potential: ". . . while ordinary people have the potential to do evil, they also have the power to do good."[13]

THE SUBATOMIC WORLD

The development of quantum theory paints a picture of the universe at the subatomic level that is far more unitary and resonant with the consciousness-pervaded reality understood by the mystics and sages than the

Newtonian model or classical mechanics. For instance, the dual characteristics of light, being both a particle and a wave, and Einstein's Theory of Relativity challenge Newtonian laws of physics and the paradigm that the universe can be fully explained through cause and effect. Physicists must now take seriously the idea that consciousness is affecting experimental outcomes: non-determinism. These ideas are friendlier, at least as analogy, to the interconnected world of peace research, and much else. As quantum theorist Henry Stapp states,

> The assimilation of this quantum conception of man into the cultural environment of the twenty-first century must inevitably produce a shift in values conducive to human survival. The quantum conception gives an enlarged sense of self . . . from which must flow lofty values that extend far beyond the confines of narrow personal self-interest.[14]

Indeed it must, though the flow has yet to become a river to sweep away the mechanical and deterministic world view that has influenced the imagination of the general public or many scientists. Much is still to be explored in the notional importance of a paradigm shift in the physical science and how it impacts our general worldview, and specifically its implications for peace.

THE SUBHUMAN WORLD

In 1975, primatologist Frans de Waal observed a flare-up among the chimpanzees in the colony at the Arnhem Zoo. He also witnessed the animals bring themselves back to their calmer state, and got curious about what he had just seen, clearly a form of conflict resolution and reconciliation. When he went to check the literature on this second phenomenon he made an interesting discovery: there wasn't any. De Waal observes:

> Fires start, but fires also go out. Obvious as this is, scientists concerned with aggression, a sort of social fire, have totally ignored the means by which the flames of aggression are extinguished. We know a great deal about the causes of hostile behavior in both animals and humans, ranging from hormones and brain activity to cultural influences. Yet we know little of the way conflicts are avoided—or how, when they do occur, relationships are afterward repaired and normalized. As a result, people tend to believe that violence is more integral to human nature than peace.[15]

In biology, particularly in relation to evolution, biological psychology, and neuroscience, we are beginning to appreciate how grievously Darwin's ideas have been misinterpreted to protect the misleading notion that nature and the general life process are a ruthless competition for physical survival.

New findings in research are beginning to vindicate Peter Kropotkin's argument that cooperation plays a key role in evolution.[16] Ironically, the simplistic notion of "survival of the fittest" or the purely material universe composed of random events—in which, as Alvin Toffler has said, we are made to feel like an anomaly, like "gypsies of the universe"—is held aloft to support a belief in a world in which no one really wants to live.[17] To think of ourselves as part of a competitive, mechanical, and statistically based reality has obscured our true relationship with one another and the environment, and has discouraged us from discovering who we truly are.

It is worth citing an example of how the biological sciences are evolving away from a limited view based on scarcity and competition. Much of the evidence about aggression in our animal ancestors relied on one of the genetically closest primates, the common chimpanzee (*Pan troglodytes*), which exhibits seriously aggressive behavior, particularly in the captive environments in which they are constrained (and almost all observation of them took place until recently). Then, in 1928, a German zoologist, Ernst Schwarz, discovered evidence of a related species, now known as bonobos (*Pan paniscus*), that was flourishing in a small area of the Democratic Republic of the Congo. Bonobos are genetically quite similar to the chimpanzee (and consequently to us), but their social structures and behaviors are remarkably different. They practice sex differently and conflict very differently, such that if they had been discovered first we might have derived a more tempered understanding of our biological inheritance for violence and aggression and their opposites.

New research evidence shows that pre-human animals possess the entire repertoire of behaviors and emotions that we do, violent and nonviolent. In a brilliant experiment, de Waal placed a group of stump-tailed macaque monkeys—a relatively egalitarian and pacific species—among the hierarchically organized and fight-oriented rhesus monkeys. At first, the Rhesus monkeys were puzzled that the placid stump-tailed macaques did not respond in an expected way when attacked, *neither running away nor fighting back*. In fact, stump-tailed macaques interacted with the dominant rhesus monkeys by *offering an extremity for a ritual bite that never causes harm, but serves to end the confrontation*. Interestingly, the pacific behaviors of the stump-tailed macaques were, over time, adopted by the aggressive rhesus and remained even when the stump-tailed monkeys were removed. As de Waal writes, *"we had infused a group of monkeys of one species with the social culture of another."*[18] What we have put in italics are three well-known principles of active nonviolence, uncannily represented in the subhuman world. A final note from de Waal: "My main purpose is to correct biology's bleak orientation on the human condition. In a decade in which peace has become the single most important public issue, it is essential to introduce the accumulated evidence that, for humans, making peace is as natural as making war."[19]

Primate research is admittedly complex: behaviors differ in the wild and in captivity, between species and even within the same species when they are found in harsh versus plentiful and secure environments. Scientists have interpreted studies in ways that emphasize either the war-like or the peaceful activities of the great apes. But a fair view would suggest that our closest primate relatives show capacities for avoiding violence and transforming or redirecting the impulses that lead to it. Monkeys show capacities for peace. They are already affected by the apparent universal dynamics of nonviolence.

WHAT ARE WE "WIRED" FOR?

We arrive now at some of the important discoveries in neuroscience and biological psychology that have helped balance the story about the human capacity to build a more peaceful society. Much of this progress has been made possible by new, noninvasive studies of brain activities in living, waking subjects. On another level, they also arise from a felt need to balance the picture by looking at both sides of the human potential.

Recent studies have shown that empathy is involved in mediating aggression, developing emotional literacy, and increasing competency in interpersonal communications. The limbic system is considered the neuroanatomical center of human emotions. It is composed of subcortical structures that mediate interactions or information flow between the primitive brain stem and the cerebral cortex, control the release of major bodily hormones, and modulate the storage and recall of memory.[20] By identifying structures that are involved in emotional responses and understanding how they are central to a multitude of brain processes scientists have gained a tremendous amount of information about how, for example, emotions are involved in daily, conscious behaviors.

A summary of key facts about the neuroscience of emotions can be gleaned from Kandel, Embry, Adkins, and the larger body of research on emotions:[21]

- Human emotions are now "visible," thanks to modern scanning devices that measure electrical activity in the brain and biochemical levels in the body.
- Emotional states directly affect attention and therefore play a crucial role in memory.

- Emotional responses are both a product of inherent tendencies and environmental influences.
- Neural pathways for emotions demonstrate *neuroplasticity*, meaning that experiences and environmental factors can physically alter the way brain cells interact over time.[22]
- Although activity in the primitive structures of our central nervous system can override more complex emotional (and consequently cognitive) processes, studies have shown that the reverse occurs as well.

Recent studies on neurochemicals and hormones reveal important information about the mechanics of positive social behaviors such as attachment, the forming of relationships, and compassion for others. Breakthrough investigation of the hormone oxytocin has generated compelling data about positive behaviors of individuals and even information about interpersonal relations.[23] For one example, studies of the combined effects of the hormone oxytocin and activation of the vagus nerve show that they produce behaviors that are clearly opposite of aggression leading to a theory of "tend and befriend."[24] The vagus nerve is perhaps the most significant communication line between the brain and the rest of the body, particularly in regulating the heartbeat. It is the longest running nerve, extending from the brain stem to the abdominal area. It is in exploring oxytocin's impact on the vagus that researchers begin to understand the physiological foundations of the human ability to focus on "the other." Individuals who feel secure are likely to engage in "prosocial behaviors" such as protecting another person, acting compassionately, and so forth. Feelings of security and affiliative behavior have been measured in children to be correlated with the "resting tone" of the vagus nerve.[25] The resting tone of the vagus nerve has been discussed in many studies to help individuals attend to social cues and process information like facial expressions and body language about others during interpersonal communication.

In 1988, Iaccomo Rizzolati and Vittorio Gallasse made a revolutionary discovery in the field of brain science. Their research with the frontal lobe of macaque monkey brains showed that the same group of neurons in the ventral premotor area appears active whether the subject is performing a set of complex tasks or whether the subject watches others perform the same tasks. These neurons have been appropriately termed *mirror neurons* and have significantly advanced our ability to explain how the brain functions during social activities or while engaged with more complex interactions with the external world.

Mirror neurons, fundamentally motor and association neurons that are located throughout the brain, have been discovered to "imitate" the actions that we observe and are involved in basic encoding of the intentions of the observed actor. Further research with human subjects at the University of

California, Los Angeles (UCLA) showed that mirror neurons reinforce and maintain learned skills through "simple observation" and that the mere observation of similar behaviors or movements, or simply hearing the sounds of such behaviors (like kicking a soccer ball or putting a cup down on the table), or even imagining the behavior in question also trigger the same brain processes.[26] The resonance between one person's brain and the perceived actions and behaviors of another person can be so intense that a set of "super mirror neurons" must intervene to remind the observer that his or her own responses are independent of the observed expressions or behavior.[27]

In studies of autistic children, brain wave recordings reveal that a dysfunctional mirror neuron system is linked to difficulties in showing empathy.[28] Mirror neuron findings suggest that we have the capacity to fully identify with another person's behavior to the point that we require other neuromechanisms to inform us that we *are not* that other person. As he puts it, "mirror neurons . . . show that we are not alone, but are biologically wired and evolutionarily designed to be deeply interconnected with one another."[29] A striking neurophysiological parallel that a few scientists have begun to document speaks to the disastrous psychological and neurochemical effects of inflicting pain on another.[30] (See Rachel Chapter 21, Volume 2 on the effects of killing.) Iacoboni summarizes from his mirror neuron research: "although we commonly think of pain as a fundamentally private experience, our brain actually treats it as an experience shared with others."[31] Briefly, but cogently, Iacoboni asserts that we are "wired for empathy," and "we have evolved to connect deeply with other human beings. Our awareness of this fact can and should bring us even closer to one another."[32] Indeed it should.

What light does King's belief that "no man can continue to debase or abuse another human being without eventually feeling in himself at least some dull answering hurt and stir of shame" shed on the enormous amount of violence played out constantly on television and movie screens? Iacoboni argues, "if all this violence could somehow disappear for one week (we are so wired for empathy that) *it would never come back.*"[33]

All this having been said, it is important to note that the existence of a neural network *or any physical or physiological mechanism* has never been proved to directly *cause* human beings to have certain emotions or carry out specific behaviors. Rather we understand that biochemical events and psychological events, heavily invested with meanings we have created, are reflections of a single reality and one that humans have helped to construct. We humans have evolved higher control systems, consistent with a complex cerebral cortex that make people quite able to override impulses generated from hormones and other neural pathways. We are in this sense our own pilots. To believe otherwise is to set aside human will, freedom, and responsibility—as

Shakespeare puts it, it is an "admirable evasion of whoremaster man." The innate aggression theory encouraged the all-too-common exclusion of will, choice, and responsibility in human behavior. When scientists set aside the will, which the 14th-century classic on contemplation called the *Cloud of Unknowing* calls the highest part of the soul, they are unwittingly contributing to the dehumanization that precedes all violence.

In spite of the new research in brain science, "[o]ther findings show that mirror neuron activity is instrumental for interpreting the facial expressions and actions of others but may not be sufficient for decoding their thoughts and intentions."[34] The discovery of mirror neurons is without doubt a major breakthrough in neuroscience, but there are legitimate doubts among researchers that we currently have the ability to explain fully how humans understand, respond to, or are changed by observed social behaviors. Jacob and Jeannerod caution science against explaining social interactions as simply the brain imitating the observed movements and behaviors of others, and Goldman believes that mirror neurons are at best the brain's preliminary system for recognizing, coding, and understanding actions.[35] As the Buddha said, "Our life is shaped by our mind," which resonates with findings in neuroscience—our hormones or our genes do not exclusively shape us. The recent discovery of neuroplasticity, mentioned above, gives a physical reality to this ancient insight. Hormones and genes, and neural networks are only a part of a constellation of factors that affect our behavior.

More recently, neuroscientists and others, including the general public, are taking a renewed interest in the effects of constructive social behaviors, peaceful and nonviolent practices, and even attitudes, on the brain. This enthusiastic and long overdue turning away from war-based research has brought modern, "'hard" scientists in touch with the ancient practice of meditation: ". . . [B]rain research suggest[s] that compassion can be learned and increased with practice, similar to any skill or talent. Some researchers believe that compassion meditation may benefit depressed people or young people who struggle with aggression and violence."[36] Meditation is above all a continuing act of will, and as such it is no surprise that measurable brain activity associated with the practice typically begins in the frontal or prefrontal area of the cerebral cortex. Fascinating connections have been found in monitoring and imaging the brain during meditation that reveal voluntary control of or at least influence over the limbic system, especially in regulating the activity of the amygdala, a limbic system structure that has been associated with producing aggression and anxiety.

In this connection, one important study must be added to what we have discussed so far. We are aware that altruistic acts are accompanied by surprisingly intense pleasure responses in the brain equal to feelings that accompany addictive drug experiences.[37] Neuroscience has suggested that we are "wired for empathy," in other words, our central nervous system contains important mechanisms that resonate with the mental states of others—giving a scientific basis, for those who require it, to the nonviolent effect Frady mentions. Another supportive finding for nonviolence is that the biological inheritance that predisposes us to fear and aggression, built deeply as it is into our very brain stem and in higher brain structures, can be overridden.[38] A clever study by two Princeton scientists, Mary Wheeler and Susan Fiske, showed that the simple act of asking a research subject questions like "does the person you're about to see like crunchy or smooth peanut butter" successfully suppressed the amygdala's "fight or flight" reaction that normally accompanies seeing the face of an unknown person from a different race.[39] One can reflect on how this study helps to support the idea that by seeing a person as an *individual* rather than a stereotype, that is, by *rehumanizing* that person, the negative conditioning embedded in millions of years of evolution can be neutralized.

Meditation involves not only the slowing down and concentrating of our normally rapid and scattered thought processes but also, and by some yet to be understood corollary, the conversion of destructive to constructive *content* of our thoughts.[40] Perhaps the most popular form of meditation in the West today is Vipasanna, or "insight." As seen by brain scientists, this practice "is associated with enhanced prefrontal cortical regulation of affect through labeling of negative affective stimuli."[41] Thus, isolating the act of mindfulness is contributing to the understanding that humans have the ability to control and change their aggressive behaviors, especially if the ability is practiced over a long period of time.

In 1901, Wilhelm Roentgen received the first Nobel Prize in Physics for his serendipitous discovery, six years earlier, of what we now call X-rays. By that time the British army of the Sudan already had a portable X-ray unit traveling with every company. It would take *50 years* more, however, before X-ray technology was widely available for peacetime medicine. To study the human potential for peace is obviously not as easy to do *or* as well supported as research designed (or subsequently used) to manipulate people and otherwise cause violence and fear. It will be a great day for science, and humanity, when that priority is reversed.

NOTES

1. Frady, 1992, 70.
2. Adams, "The Seville Statement on Violence," 1989.
3. Ibid.
4. Gandhi, 1944.
5. Mauk, 2007.

6. Ibid.

7. Summers, 2008.

8. Ibid.

9. Ibid.

10. Grossman, 1995.

11. Raymond, 2009.

12. A recent *New Yorker* article revealed that G.W. Bush's administration consulted with professionals who helped to build an interrogation program that "appl[ied] theories of 'learned helplessness' on [human] detainees based on findings from experiments with abused dogs." See Jane Mayer, "The Secret History: Can Panetta Move the CIA Forward without Confronting Its Past?" *New Yorker,* 2009.

13. Landau, 2008.

14. Stapp, 1989.

15. de Waal, 1989. This realization has lead to a long series of superb books by de Waal.

16. "Mutual Aid: A Factor in Evolution." In *Encyclopædia Britannica,* 2000.

17. Prigogine and Stengers, 1984.

18. de Waal, 1996. For further discussion of these issues see Clark, 2002.

19. de Waal, 1989.

20. *"Emotion." In Encyclopædia Britannica,* 2000.

21. Kandel, 2000; Adkins, 2009.

22. Doidge, 2007.

23. Kok, 2008.

24. Ibid., 5.

25. Ibid., 7.

26. Tyson, 2009.

27. Iacoboni et al., 2005.

28. "Autism," 2005.

29. Iacoboni et al., 2005.

30. See Rachel MacNair, vol. 2: ch 21.

31. Iacoboni et al., 2005.

32. Iacoboni, 2008.

33. Iacoboni to Michael Nagler during a recent interview.

34. Goldman, 2009.

35. Jacob and Jeannerod, 2005.

36. Ingles, 2008.

37. Angier, 2002; Rilling et al., 2002. (We do not believe, of course, that the neuronal activity is the "basis" of cooperation).

38. As would be suggested by de Waal's study of the Rhesus and Stump-tailed monkeys cited earlier in the chapter.

39. Wheeler and Fiske, 2005. Getting subjects to see faces as individuals rather than (racial or gender) categories overrides Amygdala reactions to stereotypes.

40. An effective form of meditation built on this very synergism is "passage meditation" developed by Sri Eknath Easwaran (cf. www.easwaran.org).

41. Creswell, et al., 2007.

CHAPTER 5

Psychology and Peace

Marc Pilisuk and Mitch Hall

There are two peace psychologies, one expressed in studies, the other in stories. The first involves the work of psychology scholars who apply their tools to understanding why humans engage in violence and war or in peaceful and cooperative relations.[1] The second gives witness, through stories, to what is happening in the hearts and minds of people confronting a world awash in violence. In such stories, we hear the voices of those who have suffered violence, fought in wars, and initiated nonviolent reconciliation of conflicts. From those who have found ways to repair the wounds of violence, we learn of capacities for forgiveness, healing, reconciliation, and love. Both studies and stories provide insights into why people kill and go to war, how to reconcile differences without violence, how the trauma of violence and fear affects us, and how we recover and sometimes become advocates for peace. We begin with two characteristics of the human species: our ability to create psychological constructions of social reality and our potential to kill large numbers of our own species. The two are likely related.

PSYCHOLOGICAL ABILITIES TO CONSTRUCT OUR WORLD

Our earliest human ancestors survived against more powerful predators by collaborating with others, using tools, and storing information in large, complex brains. They created intricate languages for communication and taught successive generations what was learned through experience.

We now live in a world we have largely created—a physical world we have changed more in the last 300 years than nature has done in 3 million—and in a symbolic world of mental images that define what we assume to be true. The most comprehensive symbols are the prevailing myths about who we are as humans and as members of larger groups. The myths identify our place and purpose in the world, provide a framework for our beliefs, and lead to ritual practices observed with dedication.[2]

Our images of larger social entities, such as nations and religions, exist only because we believe they are real. We invest them with sovereign powers and sacred attachments. Many willingly kill or die for them. We live by role expectations prescribed by our cultural worldviews and social-group identifications. This, according to terror management theory, enhances our self-esteem, gives meaning to our lives, and buffers us from the anxiety and terror that our uniquely human awareness that we are going to die can induce in us.[3]

Soldiers are assigned a special role in the world of attachment to national symbols. They are depicted as heroic defenders against alien forces who would hurt us. No matter how endangered the soldiers, leaders manipulate the national myths and tell us that we cannot pull out of an armed conflict because it would dishonor the troops.

How people behave in roles within these larger symbolic realms is often confused with inherent "human nature." Violent conflicts among larger groups are commonly attributed to human aggression. That view fails to recognize the myths of nationhood and, of relevance here, the dominant Western worldview.

All cultures give special value to insiders, who in some languages are identified by the same term that means "humans." For cultures with hegemonic aspirations, the myths surrounding prejudicial favoring of one's own group may determine whether outsiders are to be converted, conquered, enslaved, or annihilated. Cultural attitudes toward outsiders are therefore essential for understanding aggressive societal policies. Our stored constructions of people from other parts of the world depend largely on whether they are brought to us by media. When Iran held 51 American hostages their well-being was a global concern. When thousands of people are abducted and killed extra-judicially by state terrorism in Guatemala, Colombia, Haiti, Indonesia, or Egypt, governments favored by the United States, their plight is not part of our reality. Human compassion may well extend to individuals, even to species never personally known to us, but this cannot be tapped to stop violence when the facts are concealed.

WESTERN WORLDVIEW

The dominant Western worldview is among the most potent, though often latent, psychological constructions of the contemporary developed world. Its propositions encompass ownership of resources, inequality, legitimacy of power, amorality, force, and inevitability.[4] This worldview is a constellation of beliefs and values that include:

- All people are free to compete for success, typically defined as expanded wealth.
- The world's resources exist for exploitation by those best able to take advantage of its gifts.
- Private property is favored by law over either unowned nature or public property.
- Freedom to speak includes the unlimited right to use wealth to influence opinion and public policy.
- Problems can be fixed with technical solutions.[5]
- Corporations shall have the protection by law afforded to citizens.
- Corporate investors are the creators of wealth and jobs.
- Efficacy is more important than ethics in the attainment and protection of wealth.
- Disparities in wealth of any magnitude are natural and acceptable.
- Poverty is due to deficiencies in the poor.
- Military force is justified to protect corporate interests (often defined as national interests).
- Limited parliamentary democracy (mandating elections while allowing wealth to be used for persuasion) is the much-preferred form of government.
- Psycho-cultural values of power, masculine domination, acquisition, and development are aspects of the natural world order.
- Those not accepting these views or the policies that flow from them pose a danger and must be either trivialized or eliminated.

The above beliefs and values define what is thought to be the inevitable and universal path to progress.[6] These beliefs define a system with little tolerance for alternatives. Against the background of such belief systems we can evaluate the contribution of human aggression to the occurrence of war.

WAR AND HUMAN AGGRESSION

In developed societies, unless we live in high-violence urban zones, our images of how violent humans are derive less from what we witness directly and more from media depictions. Media always select and frequently distort.

Media create an unrealistically violent view of our communities and world. By reporting the tragedy of victims without serious analysis of what social and economic conditions foment violence, they increase our fearfulness of people. Despite the highlighting of violence in media, people mostly cooperate, share, care, compete peacefully, act altruistically, and forgive. Despite the frequency of conflict, most humans go through a typical day without being either a perpetrator, victim, or witness of any type of physical violence. Across continents and cultures, conflicts are mostly handled by talking over differences. Ridiculing, persuading, coaxing, arguing, shouting, grumbling, or walking away are all common. One finds people agreeing to compensate for damages, compromising, reconciling differences, and negotiating settlements, often using third parties to help.[7] Most individuals cope with bullying, insults, competitive conflicts, and disappointments without resorting to violence or inflicting serious harm on adversaries. Even in cultural settings considered violent, most daily behavior is entirely nonviolent. Comparative studies show that major violence in societies, while common, is not universal and that human nature does not make war inevitable.

AGGRESSION

Human capacities for anger and aggression are deeply rooted in our bodies. Cruel, selfish, and violent activities appear to be as fundamental a part of human nature as creative, caring, and cooperative actions. So we examine one aspect of what makes war possible: the capacity and the motivation of humans to be aggressive and to kill other humans.

Erich Fromm's *The Anatomy of Human Destructiveness*[8] describes diverse forms of aggression—some benign, accidental, or playful. Many forms are seen by the aggressor to be purely defensive or instrumental to achieving a noble purpose. Such actions often reflect a need to conform to the prejudices of one's group. And some aggression is malignant and intended mainly to destroy. Frustration frequently increases the arousal of aggressive tendencies. But from the time of our foraging ancestors, those bands whose symbolic worlds included means to resolve conflicts without killing off their members were those that remained. Angry temptations are universally present, but it is more than fear of consequences that keeps us from physically harming one another. Internalized cultural symbols, particularly moral standards, also help. The world in which such moral standards abound is one that humans have created. In simple foraging societies, violence, if it does occur, is personal and not the basis for long-term feuds. Tribal hierarchies sometimes permit organized group violence that is typically short-lived. It is at the level of nation states that organized military force to inflict war becomes possible.

Even within larger hierarchical societies, people are typically living peacefully even as powerful leaders prepare for war. The world in which organized violence or war can be considered a choice is a world predicated on the way fear-arousing symbols are mobilized.

FACING AND AVOIDING DANGER

The psycho-physiological ability to mobilize thoughts and behavior rapidly in the face of threats is essential to survival. If we were continuously frightened by an immediate threat of nuclear annihilation or of floods to come with global warming, we likely would be overwhelmed with emotion and unable to act. Avoiding recognition of real-world dangers is a manifestation of psychological *denial*. Pushing danger from awareness has implications for the prevention of mass violence. Not fearing the enormity of such dangers, we may increase their risks by delaying action to prevent them. Fortunately, we humans have the capacity to deal with long-term issues with creative dedication and with opportunities to engage with others in building solutions. Movements for peace and justice lie within human psychological abilities.

US AND THEM: DEHUMANIZATION AND ENEMIES

We retain long-term conceptions of others; some are known personally, others known only by images offered to us by secondary sources. An intriguing experiment by Bandura[9] shows how easy it is to set up negative images of an unknown group. In this case it was just overhearing some derogatory comments. People acted on this information by applying more intense shocks, (or so they believed) to the negatively represented group than to others. To engage in killing other humans, or to sanction such killing, we make use of a capacity to withdraw a human connection to the target person or group. Dehumanization is a composite psychological mechanism that permits people to regard others as unworthy of being considered human. On a conscious level it can be fostered by blinding appeals to hate a particular evil adversary. Beneath the level of awareness, dehumanization permits us to resolve self-doubts by finding a scapegoat as the target for blame. Terror management researchers argue that many cultural beliefs and identities are symbolic attempts to buffer us from the terror of inevitable death. We may hide such existential terror by projecting bad intentions onto members of out-groups who are deemed evil.[10] War depends on a designation of out-groups as enemies. It is a special "game" in which governments grant license to kill.

CREATING SOLDIERS

For most people at most times, personal violence against others is not part of what we condone.[11] How then do we turn people into professional warriors? Lt. Col. Dave Grossman who has studied soldiers' willingness to kill approximates that only 2 percent can kill with no feelings of remorse. They are dangerous, psychopathic people who often choose work in missions with special forces involving the chance to kill. The task of turning most civilians into soldiers who kill is more difficult. The U.S. Army had to change training methods from one war to the next over the past century to increase the percentage of soldiers capable of killing. In World War II, Grossman reported, only 15 to 20 percent of soldiers in combat fired their weapons. By the Korean War, the percentage increased to 50 to 55 percent, and by the Vietnam War, it had risen to 90 to 95 percent.[12]

Recruitment to the military is presented as a patriotic endeavor to defend one's homeland, prove masculinity, and learn skills. The recruit is brought into an institution with an absolute hierarchy of command based on rank. Boot camp is harsh and aims to create a soldier who will follow orders, act courageously, and be able to kill. While training mentions the obligation of soldiers to follow the accepted rules of warfare, the military tolerance for insubordination or questioning an order is small. Retired marine Sergeant Martin Smith reflected on the poor and poorly educated recruits he trained:

> a recovering meth(amphetamine) addict, a young male who had prostituted himself to pay his rent, an El Salvadorian immigrant serving in order to receive a green card, a single mother who could not afford her child's healthcare needs as a civilian, and a gay teenager who entertained his platoon by singing Madonna karaoke in the barracks. They were a cross-section of working-class America hoping for a change in their lives from a world that seemed utterly hopeless.[13]

U.S. soldiers in recent wars were typically from poor or middle-class backgrounds, distinguishing them from the privileged government officials who had decided to engage in war. Recruiters promised them education and job training they could not otherwise afford. No part of their recruitment or training described the likelihood of their own death, the consequences to their families, or the effects that the experience would have on them for the remainder of their lives. In contrast, the upper classes that benefit most economically from war have been practically absent from military service.[14] The transformation of people into warriors has less to do with human motives to fight than with the absence of other opportunities for education, job training, socially respected employment, and participation in the larger society.

The professional soldier does not describe his or her work as killing but rather to engage in a designated mission, to protect fellow soldiers, to eliminate a ruthless enemy, or to secure a territory held by dehumanized enemies. In the increasingly common circumstance of war against insurgents opposed to military or police occupation of their countries, and supported by local kin and sympathizers, the façade of professionalism often wears thin. Anger rages against suicide bombers and unreliable collaborators who are able to kill one's buddies. In such cases, angry abuse of insurgents and of civilians defies the professional rules of law.

Recognition for self-sacrificing contributions to a larger cause has long been understood as a benefit of war. In 1906, William James, perhaps the first peace psychologist, called for a moral equivalent to war, a cause that would command the dedication and focus of young people for building communities rather than for destruction of enemies.[15] More recently, Chris Hedges provided a compelling look at the group psychology of war.[16] The peace-movement community would benefit from studying his book and finding ways to offer people the same sense of identity and belonging in the work of peace building that they otherwise find in supporting or participating in war.

COPING WITH THE AFTERMATH OF WAR: TRAUMATIC EXPERIENCE

Soldiers return from war harmed physically or psychologically. Brain damage from head trauma, spinal cord injuries, amputated limbs, loss of sight or hearing, and shattered dreams are all common for thousands of wounded veterans. "Somebody's got to pay the price," said Col. Joseph Brennan, a head and neck surgeon, "And these kids are paying the price."[17] The colonel did not challenge the premise that such wars have to occur. His reference to soldiers as "kids" evokes an unconscious, collective myth organized around the ancient archetypal theme of child sacrifice, a dominant cultural symbol, in the biblical stories of Abraham's willingness to sacrifice his son, Isaac, and the crucifixion of Jesus as "God's only begotten son."

Not counted in the casualty figures are soldiers who suffer delayed psychological trauma of combat. During the Vietnam War these psychological effects became so common that the mental health category of *post-traumatic stress disorder* (PTSD) was created. In coping with trauma, what is first buried from awareness continues to live on. Symptoms include persistent reliving of the traumatic event, hyper-vigilance, sleep disturbance, nightmares, a numbing of emotions, feelings of estrangement, inability to experience intimacy, withdrawal from feelings of connection to the outside world, and avoidance of frightening reminders. People with PTSD sometimes experience heightened fearfulness, amnesia, irritability, and uncontrollable outbursts of anger. Among combat veterans, high rates of alcoholism and drug abuse reflect efforts to dull the torment, while high rates of domestic violence, child abuse, and suicide reflect the difficulty of doing so. Some researchers have documented that soldiers who have killed develop perpetration-induced traumatic stress symptoms that are even more severe than the PTSD in soldiers who have been traumatized in combat but have not killed.[18]

Young children are often traumatized by the sights, sounds, and losses of war. But similar fears may be brought on by punitive parenting, by inconsistent or unpredictable discipline, and to a great degree, by neglect. Such parenting occurs in all social classes and among many cultures, but it is exacerbated by poverty and by forced displacement of people from their familiar origins. Like war veterans, many of these children still maintain a remarkable resilience and ability to recover their sense of caring, especially if they benefit from at least one caring, empathic relationship with, for example, a grandparent, teacher, or other mentor.[19] Also like traumatized veterans, some children who remain traumatized from early abuse and/or neglect, will remain prone to act out violently against others and themselves and will be easily recruited into gangs or armies in which their impulse to strike out can be rewarded. Involvement in violence, and particularly in killing, has long-term consequences.[20]

FINDING ENEMIES

Designating some people as evildoers who must be found, imprisoned, or killed is common in the lead-up to executions and to war. Certain behavior, real or fabricated, is interpreted as a reason for killing. But this interpretation reflects what psychologists have long studied as *attribution error*, the tendency to ascribe behavior to the enduring characteristics of individuals while ignoring circumstances that are often more important factors. Often, attempts by one country or group to defend against assault are interpreted by adversaries as aggressive.[21] During the Cold War, the common perception among leaders and public alike was that the opposing country, the United States or the Union of Soviet Socialist Republics (USSR), could not be trusted and that none of its policies could be considered other than aggressive in intent. Bronfenbrenner described this as the mirror image in U.S.-Soviet relations.[22]

The Nazis who committed genocidal killings of unprecedented magnitude are viewed as pathological killers. Yet, in her study of Nazi storm troopers, Hannah Arendt noted that the most remarkable thing about the Nazis was how like the rest of us they were.[23] Social psychologists have put forth compelling evidence to support the view that the capacity to engage in evil or harmful behavior lies within all of us and that surrounding circumstances play the major role in releasing violent behavior.[24] This is the *situationist* perspective, in contrast to the view that ascribes behavior to individual *dispositions*. In a famous series of experiments that inform the situationist position, Milgram[25] showed that ordinary American citizens could be induced into administering what they believed to be harmful electric shocks to strangers under circumstances in which the experimenter explained to them that this was what they should do. Remarkably, administering even a potentially lethal shock could be induced among most subjects, males and females, across all ages and educational levels. Sixty-five percent of the subjects would do this if the experimenter said it was okay, if they saw their peers doing it, and if the victims were presented as being in some way inferior. According to Zimbardo,[26] a contractual agreement, verbal or written, contributes to the willingness to justify immoral violence. One critical factor is the cover story that what is being done is for a good cause. The depiction of Panama's Manuel Noriega as a brutal drug lord or of Iraq's Saddam Hussein as a political leader stacked with concealed weapons of mass destruction are examples of cover stories that were false but never the less helped to legitimize violence. Another major factor is the promise that the cruel activity can be done anonymously and without individual identification. The cloak of the hangman and the uniforms of soldiers contribute to such anonymity. Societies that mutilate their victims in warfare typically provide masks to their warriors.[27]

The people behind the cloak appeared on Christmas Eve, 1914, on a World War I battlefield in Flanders. As the troops were settling in for the night, a young German soldier sang *Stille Nacht* ("Silent Night"). The British and French responded by singing other Christmas carols. Eventually, soldiers from both sides left their trenches and met in the no-man's-land between them. They shook hands, exchanged gifts, and shared pictures of their families. Informal soccer games began, and an informal service was held to bury the dead of both sides, to the displeasure of the generals. Men who have come to know one another's names and seen family pictures are less likely to want to kill. War often seems to require a nameless, faceless enemy.[28]

DEVILS AND BAD APPLES

We distinguish in language heroic warriors from undisciplined killers. The evidence that most of us can be drawn by circumstances into committing violence does not preclude the alternative perspective that there are vast differences among people in the willingness to inflict pain or to kill.

A psychological developmental perspective helps to account for such differences. Formative early relationships predispose us toward certain behaviors, which current situations may also influence.

Because we have learned that killing is wrong, those who readily engage in such behavior often reflect a traumatic history that has blunted their capacities for empathy. Young children are helped by the predictable assurance of a parent figure to fix within their neural pathways an ability to return from perceived danger to a psychologically safe zone. Abuse and/or neglect early in their lives can interfere with early bonding and affect the long time ability to form later attachments. Such adult assurance is again important in adolescence so the developing person can cope with fear and anger as controllable parts of the self. Punitive child-rearing, particularly inconsistent punitive discipline, leaves children vulnerable to feelings of worthlessness, easily catapulted into violence by their own emotions and prone to find assurance from gangs of others like themselves. Early violent experience often limits our ability to re-examine dangerous events, rather than striking out in anger.[29]

Trauma has been associated with neuronal and brain-chemistry dysfunction affecting areas of the brain responsible for emotion regulation and empathy. Individual trauma history and the presence of subsequent healing relationships account for the fact that not all of those who were severely abused are prone to react with impulsive acts of aggression. Others who were egregiously neglected are more likely to perpetrate calculated, predatory violence.[30] Arendt's cogent observations on the "banality of evil" among the Nazis did not take into account the developmental perspective later presented. Historical data include accounts of widespread abusive child-rearing practices in Germany at the turn of the 20th century that probably contributed to the childhood traumatization of many who later became Nazis.[31] Hitler's own background is one example affirming Stephenson's studies of 14 modern tyrants. All had suffered multiple childhood humiliations, were shame-based, and had grown up in violent, authoritarian families.[32] While their rise to power may well reflect the current situations faced by their populations, the contribution of childhood trauma affecting the predisposition to violence should not be ignored. The research on impacts of early trauma is complicated because some individuals with a history of unhealed, violent trauma have a socialized, normal-appearing personality housed in one part of the brain, along with dissociated alter personality in which feelings of terror, helplessness, rage, humiliation, and identification with the perpetrator of early traumatic experience are stored and, under certain circumstances, activated.[33]

Observations of killing at the level of the individual homicide contribute to understanding a complex relation between personal and situational factors. Many are related to family or group pressure (for example, honor killings or street gang activity). Convicted killers do not all share the same personality type. Some fit the image of mean, aggressive, impulse-driven males with little sign of sensitivity or compassion for others. But another group of first homicides are committed by people who are more androgynous or feminine, gentle, shy, and with no prior record of violence.[34] One study of blood chemistry of violent inmates found two distinctive, abnormal blood profiles; one was associated with episodic, explosive violence followed by remorse, and the other with frequent, assaultive behavior followed by no remorse.[35] The forensic psychiatrist Gilligan, who worked for 20 years with violent inmates, found a primary cause of their violent acts was overwhelming shame that they unsuccessfully tried, through killing, to replace with pride. They did not perceive themselves as having alternative nonviolent ways of relieving themselves from feelings of shame, humiliation, and low self-esteem. Also, they lacked the capacity to experience the feelings that normally inhibit violence, such as love and guilt in relation to others and fear of consequences for themselves.[36]

Social psychologists Milburn and Conrad and linguist George Lakoff have presented evidence that punitive political attitudes, including the favoring of war as an instrument of national policy and capital punishment, are consequences of punitive upbringings and venues through which people, particularly males, beaten, terrified, and shamed by parental authorities as children, displace their childhood anger onto political issues and outgroups.[37] In light of these findings, it is significant that James Dobson, the influential, conservative, evangelical leader, child psychologist, best-selling author, radio and television journalist, and founder of Focus on the Family, explicitly advocates the physical punishment of children, along with not allowing them to cry in pain for more than two to five minutes before they are hit again.[38] Dobson is an example of the misappropriation of both psychology and religion in the service of an authoritarian personal and political agenda that, to the extent it is implemented, increases levels of violence in the home, society, and the wider world. Individuals who are more prone to violence find inducements to act violently in a culture that accentuates individual achievement through competition and glorifies retribution against evildoers. Such retribution begins in the homes of some fundamentalists who teach their children that they are born sinful and who use physical punishment in child-rearing more than do other groups.[39]

THE PSYCHOLOGY OF STRUCTURAL VIOLENCE

Ordinary soldiers fight in wars begun by others who rarely engage in direct combat themselves and who decide on national interests and the costs to be tolerated in their pursuit. Moreover, Johan Galtung has drawn attention to structural violence, which requires no fighting but takes a far greater number of casualties than wars and other forms of direct violence.[40] Consider the statistics. The World Health Organization has reported that 1.5 million people are killed worldwide each year due to direct violence of all kinds, including war.[41] This tragic reality is compounded by structural violence, which causes from 14 to 18 million deaths per year as a result of starvation, lack of sanitary water, inadequate access to medical care, and other consequences of poverty.[42] Direct violence, Galtung noted, is episodic, and typically harms or kills people quickly and dramatically. Episodes of overt violence are often intentional, personal, instrumental, and sometimes politically motivated. Structural violence, by contrast, represents a chronic affront to human well-being, harming or killing people slowly through relatively permanent social arrangements that are normalized and deprive some people of basic need satisfaction. Structural violence results from how institutions are organized, privileging some people with material goods and political influence while depriving others. Acting without hostile intent, some people make routine decisions in the global marketplace that necessitate the destitution of others—depriving them of their land, their resources, their jobs, and their hopes. These decisions are not accidents or mistakes but rather understandable consequences of a distorted process. The horrors of this indirect violence, as well as the benefits attributed to these market decisions, are products of the system, not of an omnipotent conspiracy. Most of the harm that privileged political, corporate, financial, and military elites cause has been sanctified by custom and law, which protect their privileges.

Beneath the eyes of the citizenry, a high level of planning in a high-stakes game of attaining competitive advantage takes place, at times in secret meetings or in normal operating procedures.[43] The perpetrators of structural violence who order wars and economic exploitation are rarely studied. They often make use of game theory to calculate strategies for winning and levels of acceptable costs. It is permissible within game theory to consider which country might be coerced into ensuring a greater amount of oil for the United States, but impermissible to ask whether more oil is desirable.

LEGITIMIZING GLOBAL VIOLENCE

The mindset in which the world and its inhabitants are all instruments in an elite game to gain competitive advantage is very much a part of the belief system that legitimizes global violence. Human beings, on either side of a conflict or competition, are not considered for their feelings, needs, and rights, but are abstractly viewed as expendable pawns. In a military occupation where torture is used to find, punish, and intimidate resistance, the game has been redefined as one in which the rules permit such abuse. Toxic chemicals, radioactive pollution that will harm lives for millions of years, unhealthy fast foods, or brain-injured war veterans all enter into cost-benefit analyses. The acceptability of risks may look different for executives of a corporation producing toxic chemical pesticides used to dust crops than to the migrant-laborer parents of a child with leukemia. The dehumanized mode of thought of game theorists requires that we consider everything, including material products, human lives, natural resources, and the sound of songbirds, to have a monetary value.

To justify apparently immoral and illegal intervention activities, former Secretary of State Henry Kissinger once explained we have no principles, only interests. Even within the game-theory framework, its practitioners are prone to offer technical advice on playing the wrong game. So many situations that might turn out better if the parties are allowed to engage in trust and to seek mutually rewarding solutions are recast by the strategists (with media help) into zero-sum contests, obliging someone to get hurt. Completely absent from this formulation is appreciation of human motivations for empathy with other humans, for altruistic behavior that defies the balance sheets of self-interest and greed and for the gratifications that come from sharing, cooperation, and nurturing those in need. Leaders know their followers may be mobilized to follow their game plan, for short periods, with fear-arousing threats. But they also know that most people do not like the violence of war. A government that has chosen to act with military violence since the end of World War II is continually in need of justifying its compassion. For example, in a famous exchange on TV in 1996 between Madeleine Albright and reporter Lesley Stahl, the latter, while speaking of U.S. sanctions against Iraq, asked the U.S. ambassador to the UN and future secretary of state: "We have heard that a half-million children have died. I mean, that's more children than died in Hiroshima. And—and you know, is the price worth it?" Albright replied, "I think this is a very hard choice, but the price—we think the price is worth it."[44] Internationally agreed-on rules for the game of war preclude unprovoked, preemptive military attack, the kidnapping, extradition, and torture of captives, and starving of civilians. Under existing international laws for the conduct of war, those responsible for the war in Iraq have engaged in criminal behavior. However, like Madeleine Albright, they find justifications and see themselves as serving good ends that justify any means.

We all compartmentalize the symbolic maps that guide us. People in power may not be devoid of compassion, although they may be in psychological denial of the human suffering their decisions cause and of their own consequent culpability. In the roles afforded them by governments or corporate structures, their realities are shaped only by what can be measured as winning. Perhaps paradoxically, organizational psychology finds that ignoring one's nonmeasurable and unselfish potentials is detrimental to achieving even competitive military and corporate objectives. The army knows this and uses it to build teams of soldiers.

ALTERNATIVE WAYS TO RESOLVE CONFLICTS

Whereas conflicts are often inevitable, creative, nonviolent ways to resolve them exist. A conflict can be a sign that democratic participation in decision making is alive and well. A premise of coming together on conflicts over divisive beliefs or ideologies is that the parties should be able to hear and acknowledge each other's actual position, which is more difficult than it would appear to be. One model requires each party to restate the other's position in a manner satisfactory to the other party. Once this is mutually achieved, the next step would be to validate points of agreement and to note symmetries. While neither adversary is converted to the other's views, both sides can see their similarities with and differences from each other. The common ground humanizes the adversary and opens a space for compromise.[45]

Mediation is the most studied form of third-party intervention. For apparently intransigent conflicts, Fisher and Ury[46] pioneered a model that encourages empathy, separates personal characteristics from underlying issues, avoids criticism, and invents creative options that provide mutually advantageous outcomes. Here psychology helps by teaching not to use "war words" and by distinguishing expressed positions from the actual needs they serve. When alternative ways to meet the needs are found, conflicts can often be resolved. Many creative options for coming together use the principle that antagonists who need each other to attain a shared goal will lessen their hostilities through common action. Even when parties have been locked into a pattern of hostility and distrust, methods are available to reverse the escalation of hostilities. Charles Osgood's proposal of graduated reciprocation in tension reduction[47] enables one of the parties to take the courageous first small step by announcing a specific minor conciliatory initiative and following through regardless. The practice is repeated. Eventually the opposition is tempted to reciprocate, if for no other reason than to establish its credibility as the nonbelligerent party. This process has been shown to work in controlled psychological experiments.[48] Historically, the process occurred in the Kennedy and Khrushchev era of the "thaw" in the Cold War.

Methods of alternative conflict resolution are wonderful if they avert violence. They can also be misused in situations of unequal power. A large corporation charged with destroying a community's habitat or chemically poisoning their groundwater may avoid full costs of restitution by mediating with some of the victims. Families impoverished by injury or illness, by loss of a wage earner, or by property made worthless, lack the resources to contest corporate lawyers in a drawn-out process. They are pressed during mediation to settle for a compensatory financial agreement along with a promise not to discuss the case. Similar dynamics exist in negotiations between small countries and international funding organizations. Such examples show the difference between conflict resolution and peace. When conflict resolution maintains injustice, it perpetuates structural violence.[49] To address this problem, *transformative* mediation aims to establish a relationship between parties, improve mutual understanding, and open a channel for continued dialogue.[50] Overall, nonviolent conflict resolution strategies are a remarkably effective substitute for violence. The problem is not their efficacy but the unwillingness to try them.

Fairly viewed, psychology teaches us that humans can restrain their hostilities and find creative ways to live together with respect. We can be caring, fair, and peaceful. But to do this, we will need to remake the constructions we have made of militaries, mega-corporations, and nations, and to amplify our reverence for life.

NOTES

1. For a comprehensive review of what peace psychologists in this group have done, see Christie et al., 2008; Blumberg et al., 2007; Kool, 2009.
2. Langer, 1942.
3. For a comprehensive presentation of terror management theory, see Pyszczynski et al., 2003.
4. Pilisuk and Zazzi, 2006.
5. Postman, 1992.
6. Pilisuk and Zazzi, 2006.
7. Seager, 1993; Bredemeier and Toby, 1972.
8. Fromm, 1973.
9. Bandura, 1988; Bandura, et al., 1975.
10. Pyszczynski, et al., 2003.
11. Fry, 2007.
12. Grossman, 1995.
13. Smith, 2007.
14. Roth-Douquet and Schaefer, 2006.

15. James, 1995.
16. Hedges, 2003.
17. Robichaud, 2007.
18. See Rachel MacNair, vol. 2: ch. 21.
19. Perry, 2008.
20. Schore, 2003.
21. Holsti, 1982.
22. Bronfenbrenner, 1986.
23. Arendt, 1968.
24. Zimbardo, 2007.
25. Milgram, 1974.
26. Zimbardo, 2007.
27. Watson, 1973.
28. Wallis, 1994.
29. Perry, 2008.
30. Schore, 2003.
31. Miller, 1983; DeMause, 2006.
32. Stephenson, 1998.
33. Schiffer, 2002.
34. Zimbardo, 2007.
35. Bitsas, 2004.
36. Gilligan, 1996.
37. Lakoff, 1996; Milburn and Conrad, 1996.
38. Blumenthal, 2009.
39. Grille, 2009.
40. Galtung, 1969.
41. World Health Organization, 2009.
42. Gilligan, 1996.
43. Pilisuk, 2008.
44. Stahl, 1996.
45. Rapoport, 1960.
46. Fisher and Ury, 1983.
47. Osgood, 1962; Rubin, 1994.
48. Pilisuk, 1984.
49. Pilisuk, 2008.
50. Bush et al., 1994.

PART III

A Societal Perspective

Why can't we just get along and live in peace? Much of the answer depends on what is meant by "peace" and much depends on what is meant by "we." Peace is not just a state that may descend on us but rather a pattern of actions and ideas that can and should be incorporated into the basic beliefs and daily activities—the culture—of the human family. Peace, in this view, must be reflected in the institutions we create to encourage caring and to hold ourselves accountable for violence and injustice. Earlier selections (Nagler and Ryono, and Pilisuk and Hall) have established the case that we humans are defined in large measure by our ties with others, by the symbols and images we share, and by the images of our own identities. We wear lenses that bias our stored realities and limit our appreciation of the realities of others. Such differences, if not understood with empathy, can lead to dangerous assumptions of the intentions of others. This is especially true when shorthand stereotypes abound in the media and help to reinforce our blinders. Human contact at every level can help to increase awareness of our prejudices and opportunities to engage in dialogue as the way to deal with differences. But this is only true if we are aware of what we each bring to the table and if we come with an open mind and a caring heart. In this part Paul Kimmel suggests the depth of enculturation into beliefs about the groups that provide our identities and our images of those who are considered others. He highlights the ways in which cross-cultural misunderstandings can be turned into cross-cultural understandings and the importance of training in cultural awareness for reconciliation efforts to succeed.

On the deepest personal level the definition of "we" is challenged by the awareness of how intimately interdependent humans have always been in their connections with others and with their immediate environment. At this time that awareness clearly includes ties with others whom we will never meet from places we will never visit and with a global environment that affects the air, water, resources, and climate on which all of us rely. The question of what basic identification we need with the web of living things for a planet to be capable of survival is raised by Norlander and Marsella. It adds something of beauty to a self-image that already borrows much of this identity from teachings of the world's great religions (see Chapter 9, "The Spirit of Change," by Rothberg, and Chapter 1, "Eternal Peace," by Nagler).

Finally, David Adams describes an international movement to create an identifiable culture of peace that transcends national borders. In response to a dominant, media-driven culture of war, Adams describes a UN General Assembly-initiated effort to describe a universal standard for a culture of peace. Its eight principles stand as a beacon for the global society that must evolve if there is to be a future worthy of the values we profess for humanity.

—Marc Pilisuk and Michael N. Nagler

CHAPTER 6

CULTURAL UNDERSTANDING IN PEACEKEEPING, PEACEMAKING, AND PEACE BUILDING

Paul R. Kimmel

We have come to realize that it is not enough to send peacekeeping forces to separate warring parties, or to engage in peace-building efforts after conflict has taken place. It is not even enough to conduct preventive diplomacy. We need to act at a deeper level for the prevention of violent conflicts before they arise. We need, in short, a Culture of Peace.

—Kofi Annan, UNESCO Guidelines, 2000

CURRENT DESTRUCTIVE CONFLICTS

Since 1989, there has been a shift in the genesis of organized violence from national states toward groupings of peoples that I will call "cultural states." Whereas the analysis of national wars is the domain of political scientists and specialists in international relations, the analysis of cultural wars is more suited to the theories and perspectives of psychologists and sociologists. The emergence of cultural states is related to a decline in the power of many

This chapter is a revision and update of "Cultural and Ethnic Issues of Conflict and Peacekeeping," which appeared in H. Langholtz, ed., *The Psychology of Peacekeeping* (Westport, CT: Greenwood Publishing Group, 1998), 57–74.

national states both internally (the loss of patriotism) and externally (the breakdown of international relations).[1] National states with growing cultural movements of peoples whose identities are anchored in existential feelings, called "primordial sentiments"[2] can develop a diminution of the individual's sense of being a state citizen.[3] Subgroups of peoples dedicated to cultural identities surface with cultural imageries that often idealize their group and demonize others. The conflicts in Bosnia, Sri Lanka, Afghanistan, Lebanon, Rwanda, Cambodia, Somalia, and Sudan exemplify the resurgence of political structures and identities based on the primordial sentiments of ethnicity, language, race, tradition, religion, and region, and the primal violence that follows.

National wars are becoming less frequent while cultural and ethnic wars are multiplying.[4] In battles among cultural states, the organized, technologically managed warfare of nations has been replaced by primal violence.[5] Violent conflicts involving peoples who believe they are fighting for the survival of their way of life are more personal and inhumane than wars for economic or political advantage fought by nation states. Because the cultural enemy is often seen as totally inhuman and maximally threatening, there are fewer rules and standards regarding the wounded, captured, and civilians in cultural conflicts than there are in international wars. There is less likelihood of a cease-fire, truce, or armistice in a cultural conflict. There are many more attacks on noncombatants, including massacre, torture, rape, starvation, and incarceration.[6] Cultural conflicts lead to struggles that demand genocide, fights to the finish, ethnic cleansing, and unconditional surrenders. They are especially cruel and vicious and have long-term repercussions.

Recently, the phenomenon of nation states initiating and/or prolonging cultural and ethnic wars has also added to the shift from international to primal violence. The recent U.S. interventions in Iraq and Afghanistan are illustrations of this phenomenon.

CULTURAL IDENTIFICATION AND ETHNOCENTRISM

The social actualities of language, ethnicity, customs and traditions, religion, race, and region evoke existential feelings or emotions called primordial sentiments[7] during each individual's enculturation. They are the basis for social connections called "primordial bonds." Associations based on primordial bonds create a consciousness of kind that separates us from those who are different. Sumner[8] coined the term *ethnocentrism* to describe the acceptance of those who are culturally like oneself and the rejection of those who are different. As individuals are socialized, their thoughts and emotions reflect the primordial sentiments of their people. In addition to learning that there are differences between one's own cultural group and other cultural groups, children also learn that the standards of their people are better than other peoples' standards; that they have superior ways of handling the tasks of human existence. This growing sense of in-group superiority and out-group inferiority is the result of enculturation.

All humans go through the same processes of enculturation, albeit with very different emphases and content. Thus, the roots of identity in everyone are chronologically and historically primordial.[9] The movement from the chauvinism of the infant to the ethnocentrism of the child is the first step in this enculturation process.[10] As Volkan[11] pointed out:

> For centuries, neighboring tribes had only each other to interact with, due to their natural boundaries. Neighboring groups had to compete for territory, food, and physical goods, for their very survival. Eventually this primitive level of competition assumed more psychological implications. Physical essentials . . . evolved from being tokens of survival to becoming large group symbols that embodied an ethnic group's self-esteem and glory.[12]

Peoples organized around primordial sentiments—that is, groups emphasizing their ethnicity, language, race, tradition, religion, and/or region—have the personal sense that their values, norms, and systems of thought are right and sensible and those of others are wrong and illogical. If they have not moved beyond this stage of cultural development, they are more prone to engage in cultural wars when they conflict with others, especially those who are also primarily ethnocentric. Such conflicts can occur within or between nation states.

The identification process is the bridge between the culture and the individual personality that binds people together as cohesive groups. This process creates strong roots that provide security, familiarity, and order. There are other, less ethnocentric possibilities for individual identity formation beyond one's primordial roots, of course, but the primordial groupings of family and local community come first and are strongest in the individual's enculturation. Primordial sentiments' pervasive influence on the individual is difficult to overcome, since they generate an internal sense of normality (as, for example, in the use of one's native language).

The salience and characteristics of cultural identification vary with the social and psychological situations of cultural groups. Primordial bonds and sentiments are the source of constructive (patriotic, humanitarian) and destructive (nativistic, xenophobic) behaviors. When a people feel secure and content, they are unlikely to demonize and attack other cultural groups. Their civic activities may include programs designed to improve and enhance the life conditions of the entire populace according to the dominant social norms (for example, the American dream). Rather than being preoccupied with the dangers and uncertainties of the present and the ills and injustices of the past, peoples with a positive future based on a satisfactory present can work together toward political and economic goals and visions. Their social and psychological security allows them to tolerate and even appreciate a wide range of cultural differences in their society and the world. Cultural identification serves a positive social function in such evolving civic states. They have gone beyond ethnocentrism and reached the stage of tolerance in their cultural identity.[13]

However, when a people's social or psychological security is severely threatened, their primordial sentiments are more easily aroused by cultural differences so that cultural identification serves a negative function: the promotion of their group values, norms, and patterns of thought at the expense of those of other groups. When peoples perceive themselves to be threatened, there is a tendency to become more ethnocentric and to seek an enemy as the focus of their fears and anger. Peoples whose identities depend on less-flexible primordial sentiments rather than on more-adaptable civic actualities are less able to deal with rapidly changing economic and political conditions. In difficult times, political and ethnic leaders can incite these peoples to become frightened, angry, defensive, and intent on getting even.[14] There are many well-known social and psychological processes that lead to violence in such situations. These include dehumanization, scapegoating, negative stereotyping, fundamental and ultimate attribution errors, propaganda, groupthink, censorship, black and white images, and moral superiority.

CONFLICT MANAGEMENT AND CONCEPTIONS OF PEACE

Conflict is inevitable in human groups and societies and is often constructive. Western social scientists have developed peace processes and training programs to make conflicts more productive.[15] There are three conceptually distinct approaches to stopping violence and managing conflicts: peacekeeping, peacemaking, and peace building.[16]

According to Galtung[17] the traditional peacekeeping approach views peace as a somewhat negative concept, the controlled absence of violent conflict between the inevitable wars of history. Conflict management is peace enforcement: the application of military force to separate combatants and stop violence when there have been breaches of peace.[18] Although peace enforcement may be required when violent conflict is occurring, peace psychologists are wary of the use of force. Violence is malignant. It corrupts those using it and those that it is used against. It fosters revenge, vengeance, and other negative emotional states in the victimized and aggression and dehumanization in the victimizers.[19] It can arouse and reinforce negative cultural identities and promote ethnocentrism.

Peacemakers aspire to a more positive conception of peace. Peacemaking programs are designed to bring potential and former combatants together to manage their differences through negotiation, mediation, and conciliation. Lawyers, diplomats, and social scientists believe that with their assistance as mediators people can work through their problems, reach compromises, and manage their conflicts more constructively.[20] They can become tolerant of each other. The most proactive view of peace is that of the peace builders. They have as their goal the creative resolution of conflicts without any use of force or coercion.[21] Conflict management depends on building and maintaining personal relationships and organizations that promote understanding and collaboration among a variety of individuals and groups. Old enmities are addressed and reconciled through active programs in forgiveness and reconciliation.[22] The peace-building approach has the most promise for managing current and future cultural conflicts productively.[23] Peace building reinforces positive cultural identities and promotes cultural understanding. Through peace building, cultures can move beyond tolerance to cultural understanding in their identities.

TRADITIONAL PEACEKEEPING

Traditional peacekeeping has been epitomized by the separation of combatants.[24] In today's world, traditional international peacekeeping often involves UN peacekeeping forces (see the UN home page on the World Wide Web for a listing of past and current UN peacekeeping operations, http://www.un.org). However, UN peacekeeping forces have expanded their missions. Examples of recent peacekeeping activities and locations include patrolling cease-fire lines (Cyprus), protecting humanitarian relief shipments (Rwanda), demobilizing troops (Bosnia), disarming militias (Somalia), organizing and supervising elections (Cambodia), instilling respect for human rights in police, soldiers, and government officials (Central Africa), and even functioning as surrogate governments (El Salvador). Intervention in the form of peace enforcement often precedes these peacekeeping activities. The timing and procedures used in these expanded peacekeeping missions involve cultural considerations. These considerations are particularly important in violent conflicts among cultural states.[25] As Paris[26] has pointed out, nearly half of the peace processes managed by the international community have failed within five years. These failures are especially pronounced in complicated cultural conflicts.

Today's peacekeeping missions provide intercultural challenges for peacekeepers. Because UN forces come from different countries and are usually working in unfamiliar cultures, culture shock and cultural misunderstandings are inevitable. Communication is a constant challenge in any intercultural endeavor, more so under the stress of violent conflict or its aftermath among cultural states. Peacekeepers are not always welcome in the wake of peace-enforcement programs, as the situation in Bosnia vividly illustrated. Bureaucratic confusion adds to the difficulties. Peacekeepers experience tedium, boredom, and a lack of privacy in the field. They suffer from loneliness, isolation, and intimidation. Differences and inconsistencies in organization and training among multicultural peacekeeping forces create pay and privilege differences and bias among some contingents toward host populations.[27] Any past political and economic alliances among the nations of the peacekeepers and those of the combatants can further complicate matters, as expectations about friends and enemies come into play. Though the majority of peacekeeping activities have been free of conspicuous difficulties, newspaper reporters have documented charges of sexual harassment, graft, torture, and murder involving some peacekeeping troops in Cambodia and Somalia, allegations of waste from officials in some countries hosting peacekeepers in Africa, and assertions of conflicting loyalties among some UN troops and national authorities in Bosnia.[28]

The level of cultural identification among the peacekeepers is a critical factor that affects all of these problems. The risk of violent confrontations between peacekeepers and combatants and among combatants is increased when trust and communication break down and cultural differences are emphasized. Peacekeepers need training in cultural awareness to help them, not only with the combatants, but also with the local customs, meaningful contacts with citizens and other peacekeepers, and being good role models. Without such training, the peacekeepers' own primordial sentiments often are aroused, making them part of the problem rather than part of the solution.

The primal violence associated with destructive cultural conflicts decimates human relationships.[29] The reestablishment of a civic culture after such conflicts requires new and innovative programs. Traditional international peacekeeping and peacemaking efforts, as seen in recent UN activities, have not been effective during or after primal violence. It is difficult to undertake even the most limited missions using military forces without becoming snared in the dynamics of primal violence (witness Somalia and Cambodia). The continued salience of the primordial sentiments aroused during the violence makes elections, the relocation of refugees, and communal activities prone to renewed violence.

It has been found to be more productive for combatants to work jointly on the more technical and economic problems of rebuilding, letting the development of community and the refocusing of their cultural identities from primordial to civic follow from these more impersonal problem-solving efforts. Such rebuilding activities can contribute to the construction of civic institutions and identities.[30] To facilitate rebuilding and the construction of new identities, peacekeepers need training in cultural awareness.

TRAINING IN CULTURAL AWARENESS

Cultural awareness training could be conducted (1) in the countries from which the peacekeeping contingents are coming (screening stage), (2) in a common location near the place of their mission (assignment stage), and (3) in the field as they carry out their duties as peacekeepers (performance stage). Effective military training and a sense that the peacekeeping mission reflect national policy is related to more effective functioning in the field.[31] Successful completion of the first phase of training along with military training in the home countries would be a prerequisite for selection to certain peacekeeping forces and missions. Some trainees would be screened out of the peacekeeping force based on poor performance in this phase. Successful completion of the second, more intensive phase of cultural awareness training at a common location would be a prerequisite for assignment to certain positions or duties. More advanced trainees could be assigned to more challenging duties. Culture-specific information on critical aspects of the mission would be provided in the field for each individual peacekeeper during the third phase of the training, as needed for their successful performance.

During this training, peacekeepers would learn how their experiences with and feelings about conflict and other cultures impact their work. Current problems faced by the peacekeepers on their assigned missions would be specifically addressed. All of the different parties' beliefs regarding conflict and peace are crucial to such training. Especially important is information on the primordial sentiments that have been aroused in each party by the conflict.

Cultural awareness training must be adapted to the existing levels of awareness of the trainees.[32] For those trainees whose identity is at the ethnocentric level of awareness, the main goal of the initial training is to provide a better understanding of cultural differences and their implications for their own behavior. For these trainees, the training would emphasize the relativity of some of their own values and assumptions. As Stewart, Danielian, and Foster[33] put it, "The primary intention of such an approach would be to increase his [sic] awareness of the possible limitations of his own cultural frame of reference and of the possibility of alternative ways of perceiving a situation." In other words, to help them reach the level of tolerance in their awareness.

For trainees with more cultural experience and knowledge of cultural differences, it is possible to illuminate some of their values and assumptions and to improve their skills in intercultural communication. They can be helped to go from tolerance to cultural understanding. I have found a model of intercultural perception and reasoning that Edmund Glenn[34] and I developed to be very helpful in working with such trainees.[35] Using this model, the trainer can summarize and integrate discussions of individual and social growth as well as illustrating intercultural communication in face-to-face situations.

These training programs would increase the level of cultural awareness of peacekeepers so they can go beyond their ethnocentric roots and primordial sentiments. The graduates of these programs would be better managers of the conflicts to which they are assigned and would help others in the field become more culturally aware. Cultural awareness training would give the peacekeepers a common orientation toward their mission, motivating them to become more involved with each other, nongovernmental organizations on the same mission, and local populations. Understanding that they are role models would encourage them to get better acquainted with other troops and the local populations. These new relationships and challenges would reduce the problems currently associated with UN peacekeeping missions as peacekeepers become partners with each other, other organizations, and the local populations rather than outsiders pushing an agenda or enforcing separation.[36]

PEACEMAKING, PEACE BUILDING, AND LEARNING HOW TO LEARN

Bringing the former belligerents together moves the peacekeeping operations to peacemaking groups. Successful problem-solving groups in conflict intentionally avoid interpersonal issues in their initial meetings.[37] These meetings focus on technical concerns, while personal concerns are held in abeyance, so that conflicting cultural identifications are muted. Over time, successful interactions establish trust and greater understanding occurs as members become involved with common problems. The more group members come to understand and explain their interests, positions, and relationships to each other, the greater their shared vision of a desirable future.[38] At this point, these problem-solving groups become cultural retraining groups. Unfortunately, most of them never reach this point during and after cultural conflicts.

To become cultural retraining groups, the participants in peacemaking groups need special training to gain more conscious control over their own cultural identities. Face-to-face communications call for new skills, such as high tolerance for uncertainty, constructive use of evidence, positive feedback, meaningful nonverbals, suspension of judgment, considering cultural as well as personal attributions, and listening responsively. Basic to the development of these new skills and concepts is training in intercultural exploration. Representatives must learn how to learn in these complex situations if their peacemaking efforts are to be successful. Training in learning how to learn is needed to develop the required skills and concepts through direct experience with and feedback from intercultural communication specialists.

The major challenge for any program designed to help individuals manage conflicts among cultural groups more effectively is that their reference culture and identities are sociologically and psychologically different from those with whom they are in conflict. Thus, the program must help them to become aware of and able to modify their own cultural assumptions and accommodate other assumptions in their interactions with their antagonists. This is the process of learning how to learn. Programs that provide the needed training in learning how to learn are different from most current conflict-management programs.

Training in learning how to learn begins with cultural self-awareness and results in the ability to participate effectively in intercultural dialogues or intercultural explorations.[39] Those with these skills have the capacity to be cultural integrators.[40] Cultural self-awareness enables the individual to make conscious the deep culture internalized in an unconscious manner over a lifetime. Trainees must become more aware of their enculturation from the basic level of perceptions to the abstract level of values if they are to cope with their primordial sentiments and cultural sentiments. Such awareness must precede training that develops the individual's abilities to examine, understand, and control their judgments, feelings, and conceptions in intercultural situations (see below). There is little possibility for better intercultural communication and effective peace building without cultural self-awareness.

Many of the skills for successfully interacting with individuals from different cultural backgrounds are similar to skills developed during enculturation. However, the problem-solving, decision-making, and negotiating skills learned in one's own culture will interfere with successful communication in an intercultural situation. More generic skills taught by someone who understands the other culture(s) in question are required. After increasing trainees' cultural self-awareness, a successful learning how-to-learn program will focus on the management of their communications with others, especially others whose primordial sentiments differ greatly from their own. Because all perceptions involve stereotypes that enable individuals to organize and categorize the characteristics of less-familiar groups, a program in learning how to learn must assess the positive and negative stereotypes in each participant's culture. In developing such programs, the trainers must also know which social actualities (race, ethnicity, religion, language, tradition, and region) are important and relevant in the history and political culture of the groups being trained.

Programs in conflict management presented through seminars, discussions, and lectures are unlikely to get at the emotional aspects of the cultural differences embedded in the cultures of the trainees. Mere information about one's own and others' cultures will not affect cultural awareness nor provide a solid basis for intercultural exploration. More emotional involvement and practical skills are needed. Training that stimulates real interaction and communication among the trainees will satisfy these requirements. Cultural topics provide context for such interaction and communication and the social actualities associated with relevant primordial sentiments generate the emotions that make them meaningful. As Stewart et al. noted, "It is only through the commitment demanded by a 'realistic task-oriented problem' situation that many trainees will confront and re-evaluate long-held assumptions and values about the nature of people and of the world" [41]

Cultural training in learning how to learn is specific, not general. Each training program must be tailored to specific trainees, jobs, and situations. Successful communication is learned within and in relation to specific cultures. Role plays that use scenarios containing such contextual information will help trainees understand and grow beyond cultural identities associated with primordial sentiments and bonding. Using such role plays, it is possible to increase the level of cultural awareness of individuals and help them communicate beyond their ethnic roots and primordial sentiments. Finding and empowering successful trainees among the local populace and the peacekeepers will be crucial to the long-term success of peace-building efforts. Funding them and providing follow-up evaluations of their efforts will require more resources from international agencies.

THE TRAINING DESIGN

The technique that I have found most useful for improving cultural understanding is the culture contrast training exercise,[42] in which trainees interact with role players who portray contrasting psychological views of culture. The role players' identities are constructed to contrast dramatically with relevant cultural values and assumptions of the trainees. Realistic scenarios are used to involve the trainees. Through lively discussions before and after the role plays, trainers can help trainees understand their normal reactions in intercultural situations. By directly experiencing misperceptions and miscommunications, they become more aware of their own cultural backgrounds and their impact on others. Through repeated participation in these lifelike simulations, trainees also improve their skills in intercultural communication and conflict management. Rather than trying to correct or change the perceptions and behavior of their counterparts, they learn how to communicate their ideas and values in ways that are better understood and acted on.

The culture contrast training program for increasing cultural awareness has seven phases: (1) a reconstruction of each trainee's relevant cultural experiences by professional facilitators to elicit meaningful behaviors, perceptions, and emotions in context; (2) an analysis of these reconstructions by intercultural communication specialists familiar with the trainee's culture to isolate crucial primordial sentiments and to relate these to cultural values, assumptions, and thought patterns; (3) the construction of cultural values, assumptions, and thought patterns that contrast with those of the trainee, and of riveting scenarios designed to bring out these contrasts; (4) the training of a professional role player to portray the behaviors and perceptions of a representative of the contrast culture; (5) the facilitation of a simulation using the scenarios (step 3) and role player (step 4) with each trainee; (6) a discussion of the simulation using an edited videotape to illustrate and examine misperceptions and misunderstandings between the trainee and the role player; and (7) the facilitation of additional scenarios with videotape (repeating steps 5 and 6) to refine cultural self-awareness and improve intercultural communication skills.

A key consideration, of course, is persuading the UN and contributing nations to develop and use cultural awareness training programs. Special military courses in peacekeeping in Canada, Denmark, Finland, Norway, and Sweden have been effective in the field.[43] However, policy makers and trainees in some countries may belittle unfamiliar training programs for peacekeepers. Opponents of such training must be convinced that it is possible to manage violent conflict nonviolently. Illustrations of peacekeeping successes produced by effective cultural awareness training programs can generate the credibility for these programs that victory in battle has for the military or catching criminals has for the police.

At its best, peacekeeping, like community-oriented policing, can serve a preventative function. For example, greater involvement in the communities of belligerents can inhibit terrorists or make them more obvious. Being on the street and interested in people leads to trust. Culturally aware peacekeepers will become concerned neighbors who want their adopted communities to prosper. They will create social conditions that encourage and enable the belligerents to undertake peacemaking and peace-building activities that avoid violence. UNESCO's Culture of Peace Program[44] is promoting the further development of peacekeeping activities within a more proactive model of peace and reconciliation. This program could be enlarged within the UN to support the kind of training proposed for peacekeepers.

CONCLUSION

Learning to detect the cultural biases in one's own assumptions, conceptions, perceptions, and behaviors and substituting for these interests, concerns, and messages that connect with the assumptions, feelings, and concepts of the other parties is basic to facilitating understanding and communication in intercultural interactions. Individuals who understand their own identities and are willing to learn about the identities of those from other cultures with whom they are communicating can reduce misunderstandings and facilitate the search for mutually acceptable solutions in conflicts. The relationships they form while working together can ameliorate or avert destructive cultural conflicts and promote agreements that lead to cultural understanding.

Training in cultural awareness begun today with peacekeepers in places like Ireland, Cyprus, Bosnia, and many Middle Eastern, African, and Asian countries will have repercussions for many others. This training will help peacekeepers overcome the stresses and frustrations that are inevitable in their missions. The interpersonal relationships and integrative programs created by trainees will develop a momentum of their own. Local meetings, organizations, and programs involving these individuals will facilitate peace building. Their relationships will avert conflicts based on misunderstandings and promote a positive sense of peace among the peoples with whom they are working.

Through increased cultural awareness and intercultural exploration, these peoples can overcome the negative ethnocentrism often associated with their primordial sentiments and cultural identifications and work toward positive peace. Our old concepts of peace as stability, quiescence, balance of powers, and avoidance are dysfunctional in today's world. Understanding and controlling our ethnocentric primordial sentiments through intensive and extensive training in learning how to learn can enable us to come together as a world community in the context of a global ecology, rather than identifying as diverse groupings in the context of our local social actualities. Developing cultures that promote intercultural exploration through teaching potential peace builders high tolerance for uncertainty, cultural awareness, constructive use of evidence, positive feedback, meaningful nonverbals, suspension of judgment, and empirical perception will help us create such a future.[45] Such peace building requires empathy, imagination, innovation, commitment, flexibility, and persistence from individuals devoted to the development of relationships and the creation of consensual meanings and outcomes.

We are now approaching the end of the UN's International Decade for a Culture of Peace and Nonviolence for the Children of the World. Many nations have signed the Manifesto 2000 for the Culture of Peace and

Nonviolence.[46] The networks for facilitating the kind of training that I have suggested are in place. What is needed is for the UN to convene groups of trainers, practitioners, and participants in peacekeeping to learn how to learn and begin spreading this ability to those in these networks that can benefit from it. The time for such meetings is now.

Of course, there is a great deal more to peace building than reducing intercultural misperceptions and misunderstandings. There are structural as well as relational considerations. Improvements in infrastructure, health care, and sanitation are critical. Civic institutions dedicated to cultural and political rights and freedoms are also necessary. Pluralistic assumptions and values achieved at the local level by problem-solving groups must be elaborated at the economic and political levels of the culture.[47] Cultural understanding is also vital for these structural changes to occur. Given enough citizens with cultural understanding and a growing number of healthy societies with pluralistic institutions, we can learn to work collaboratively in open groups on the issues that threaten us (like environmental sustainability) rather than threatening each other. Peace can become an active state of cooperation that maximizes the welfare of all.

NOTES

1. Fukuyama, 1995.
2. Geertz, 1973.
3. Kaplan, 1994.
4. Gottleib, 1993.
5. Emminghaus, 1997.
6. Suedfeld, 1989.
7. Shils, 1957.
8. Sumner, 1906.
9. Stewart, 1987.
10. Kimmel, 2006.
11. Volkan, 1991.
12. Ibid.
13. Kimmel, 2006.
14. Welch, 2008.
15. Black and Avruch, 1989.
16. These concepts were first described by Galtung, 1976; and elaborated by Pease, 1987.
17. Galtung, 1976.
18. Wurmser and Dyke, 1993.
19. Staub, 1996.
20. Burton, 1987; Cantril, 1961; Etheridge, 1987.
21. Wagner and Christie, 1994.
22. Feldman, 1991; Njeri, 1993; Volkan, 1991.

23. See Kimmel, 1984, 1985, 1989, 1994.

24. Galtung, 1976.

25. Montville, 1990.

26. Paris, 1997.

27. Segal and Gravino, 1985.

28. Bates, 1997; Fisher and Smith, 1997; Meisler, "Baby-sitters in Blue Berets," 1992.

29. Staub, 1996.

30. Galtung, 1976; Kimmel, 2006.

31. Segal and Gravino, 1985.

32. Bennett, 1986; Kimmel, 1994.

33. Stewart, el al., 1969.

34. Glenn, 1981.

35. Kohls, 1987; Kohls, 1977; Kimmel, "Facilitating the Contrast-Culture Method," 1995.

36. Donais, 2009.

37. Kelman, 1992.

38. Lumsden and Wolfe, 1996.

39. Kimmel, 1989.

40. Kimmel, 2006.

41. Stewart et al. 1969.

42. Stewart et al., 1969; Kimmel, "Facilitating the Contrast-Culture Method," 1995; Stewart, 1995; DeMello, 1995.

43. Segal and Gravino, 1985.

44. Adams, *UNESCO and a Culture of Peace*, 1995.

45. Kimmel, "Sustainability and Cultural Understanding," 1995, 2006.

46. UNESCO, 2000.

47. Donais, 2009.

CHAPTER 7

RETHINKING "IDENTITY" FOR A GLOBAL AGE: EMERGING RESPONSIBILITIES AND DUTIES

Rebecca Joy Norlander and Anthony J. Marsella

THE WORLD TODAY PRESENTS NEW CHALLENGES FOR IDENTITY CONSTRUCTION

In the search for a peaceful and just world, it is more common to suggest what must be done than to consider who should be responsible for actually doing it. When we try to identify the players, whether ruling elites, displaced people, groups advocating change, guardians of tradition—or even ourselves—we confront the fundamental reality that each person has an identity that gives meaning to one's life and the life of others. Every victim of violent conflict, every contributor to the destruction of people and planet has a life story in which his or her identities help to explain what guides his or her values, thoughts, and behavior. Some of the current identities to which we adhere are no longer consistent with survival of our species or of life on our planet. Identities are changing because we live in a time when traditional bases for identity formation are changing.

This chapter explores the nature and meaning of identity—its personal, cultural, and national nuances, and its relevance for a sustainable and just peace in a global era. Indeed, many of our traditional political, economic, social, and religious institutions—long a major source for shaping individual and collective identities—have become part of the problems we face in the formation and negotiation of identities now needed for the continuity of life. Amid the current changes we humans find ourselves assaulting life in all its forms; species are becoming extinct, bio-diversity is declining, global warming is occurring, and there is a depletion of our water, energy, and agricultural resources. Destructive conflict and war are endemic. This chapter proposes that a solution to many of the challenges we face may be to move beyond our conventional identifications to an identification with life.

We must now answer the age-old questions regarding identity—"Who am I?" What do I believe?" "What is my purpose?" "What are my responsibilities?" "How did I become who I am?"—amid a context of unavoidable competing and conflicting global forces that are giving rise to increasing levels of unpredictability, confusion, and fear. The critical question to be asked is whether such change can lead to universal identity that nurtures the splendor and mystery of life and the need for it to be sustained in a world committed to peace.

Changes in telecommunications, transportation, and economic ties are linking our welfare and well-being to events and forces in distant lands. Emerging social, cultural, political, and environmental problems around the globe are imposing intense and complex demands on individual and collective psyches; these are testing our sense of identity, control, and well-being.

Previous generations have been faced with major global challenges and opportunities. For example, the industrial revolution tore apart the identities of individuals shaped by their life-long participation in familiar tribes and kinship groups. Writing in 1936, anthropologist Ralph Linton referred to the fundamental social unit as the band. He expressed hope that growing industrialization would not push society further toward a collection of rootless individuals searching in vain for the bands they had lost. We have lived though an era of war and massive social change and upheaval in which rifts in our web of caring ties have produced high levels of alienation and anomie.

But the current situation is different. Never before, for example, have our destinies been so linked to one another in such an intricate maze of changing social forces, technologies, and institutions that are global in proportion and scope. Telecommunications, mass transportation, and interdependent economies have created a new global context for daily human life. In addition to the sheer depth and complexity of current global changes, there is also the problem posed by their time-compressed speed and unpredictability. There are specific syndromes of distress and disorder associated with this problem that have been labeled future shock, culture shock, acculturation stress, rootlessness, and identity confusion. There are societal and group disorders, such as cultural disintegration, cultural dislocation, social disillusionment, sick societies, failed states, urban blight and decay, social fragmentation, cults based on myths of superiority and hatred of scapegoats, and cultural abuse and collapse.[1]

Whether it has been done intentionally or willingly, our world has become the fabled "global village."[2] The scale, complexity, and impact of recent events and forces constitute a formidable challenge. In a global era, identity has become even more complex because we are exposed to the demands of a myriad of choices and pressures that go far beyond those previously limited to more confined cultural and physical settings. We are faced with new responsibilities that are part of the negotiation and management of global interactions and an implicit "world" citizenship. Comforting assumptions of the past that were both simple and unquestioned (if such certainties ever were true) have now yielded to the demands of confusing and conflicting needs, choices, and values that have a global context. And yet, the roots of identity—the locus in which we pursue and define it—remain at personal, cultural, and national levels.

PREVIOUS WAYS OF UNDERSTANDING IDENTITY ARE NO LONGER SUFFICIENT

To be adapted to the current context of globalization, we see a need for some revered bases of identity, namely, personal, cultural, and national to be transcended or transformed. One place to begin this difficult challenge is with an appreciation for and exploration of the function served by identity.

We all live in a world of symbols, an encyclopedia of constructed images held in our memory. They are organized into meaningful sequences and ordered according to degree of relevance to our respective self-concepts, all of which vary greatly across cultures. Some are indicative of close ties to others and to nature, other selves more bounded by individual bodies and motives. But every self comes with a set of markers by which we determine who we are. A sense of identity is at the core of human existence and meaning. It is the self-reflective and dialogical anchor—both conscious and unconscious—that grounds us amid the constant changes in our settings. It offers a sense of who we are and what we are. The varied forces that shape our identities are found in both unique and shared experiences. The accumulation of these experiences—their dynamic interactions and their constant appraisal, evaluation, and modification—form the crucible in which we as individuals and as members of groups claim place, position, and agency.

Erich Fromm (1900–1980), a social psychoanalyst, has argued that identity is a basic human need along with rootedness, belonging, frame-of-reference, and transcendence.[3] The positing of identity as an essential human need creates a timeless context for our human search for understanding our nature. Identity, for Fromm, is at the core of human existence and dominates the endless pursuit for human meaning and purpose. With Fromm's thinking, our understanding of identity soars beyond a simple description of the characteristics by which we assert identity (such as name, age, gender, religion, ethnicity, citizenship, physical features, memberships, traits, and dispositions) to a powerful statement of our very nature. We are driven to seek an identity and to pursue it constantly through relationships, beliefs, and belonging. And ultimately, we aspire to transcend, to rise above what we are and to move toward ever new levels of awareness, being, and experience. Such efforts are often seen in the pursuit of religion and spirituality.

One of Fromm's central theses is that human beings often feel isolated, lonely, and estranged from others and from life itself. The search for freedom and individuality comes with the burdens of increasing responsibility and separation from other people. Such demands are often overwhelming and people find themselves surrendering their unique identity in favor of group, organizational, and national identities that diminish their individuality and their possibilities for connection with anything that challenges the group's goals and ethos. We become the identity prescribed by one group, one nation, or one religious sect. Thus, we neither connect with humanity nor with life. Fromm stated:

> The problem of the sense of identity is not, as it is usually understood, merely a philosophical one, nor a problem concerning only our mind and thought. The need to feel a sense of identity stems from the very condition of human existence, and is the source of the most intense strivings. Since I cannot remain sane without the sense of "I," I am driven to do almost anything to acquire this sense. Behind the intense passion for status and conformity is this very need. It is sometimes even stronger than the need for physical survival. What could be more obvious than the fact that people are willing to risk their lives, to give up their love, to surrender their freedom, to sacrifice their own thoughts, for the sake of being one of the herd, of conforming, and thus of acquiring a sense of identity, even though it is an illusory one.[4]

For Fromm and others concerned with identity formation, understanding personal identity requires an understanding of cultural and national identities. These, too, are determined by the broad social and institutional contexts in which personal identity is negotiated, defined, and maintained. A more contemporary case for the embeddedness of identity in its social and cultural context is seen in the work of Kwame Appiah, a professor of philosophy at Princeton University. This context may be viewed both as an anchoring of a deep identity and as a submerging of aspects of identity.

Cultural identities are a critical determinant of individual identity. They express the affiliate groups by which individuals choose to communicate their personal sense of who they are and what they stand for—their ties and allegiances to family, gender, ethnicity, race, religion, and other local socialization contexts. Indeed, in some contexts, a cultural group identity can become so powerful that there is no longer a sense of pride in individual distinctness, but rather a near-blind loyalty to the cultural identity.

Cultural identities also bring with them a history of affiliation with specific social labels, roles, and contexts and their implicit and explicit values, attitudes, and behaviors. Inherent within each of these micro-cultural contexts are the forces for the socialization of "shared meanings and behaviors" that serve to affirm and anchor identities. Amartya Sen, the Nobel Prize winner in economics, writes:

> I can be at the same time, an Asian, an Indian citizen, a Bengali with Bangladeshi ancestry, an American or British resident, an economist, a dabbler in philosophy, an author, a Sanskrit, a strong believer in secularism and democracy, a man, a feminist, a heterosexual, a defender of gay and lesbian rights, with a non-religious lifestyle, from a Hindu background, a non-Brahmin, and a non-believer in an afterlife . . . This is just a small sample of the diverse categories to each of which I may simultaneously belong—there are of course a great many other membership categories too which, depending on circumstances, can move and engage me.[5]

Cultural identities emerge from our construction of reality learned within the daily socialization contexts in which we live. Such identities position us in society and help anchor our personal sense of who we are. One can only imagine, then, the difficulty—even trauma—that can accompany identity development and change among immigrant populations, especially those living under conditions of complete powerlessness and marginalization such as refugees, asylum seekers, and undocumented workers.

Appiah explains that our identities become subject to those labels used to describe members of our group. We internalize these labels and then behave according to labels—often pejorative—even when they are imposed by others. We become embedded in a complex of labels and markers that shape our thoughts and actions and the responses to them by others.

> Once labels are applied to people, ideas about people who fit the label come to have social and psychological effects. In particular, these ideas shape the ways people conceive of themselves and their projects. So the labels operate to mold what we may call identification, the process through which individuals shape their projects—including their plans

for their own lives and their conceptions of the good life—by reference to available labels, available identities. In identification, I shape my life by the thought that something is an appropriate aim or an appropriate way of acting for an American, a black man, a philosopher. It seems right to call this "identification" because the label plays a role in shaping the way the agent makes decisions about how to conduct a life, in the process of the construction of one's identity.[6]

In a global era that is challenging traditional constructions of reality and the roles that support them, personal, cultural, and national identities are under serious challenge. Pressures to conform, integrate, acculturate, accommodate, and assimilate are challenging our sense of who we are, what we are, where we are going, what we can do, and why we can do it. Certain identities are valued, privileged, or empowered over others. Labels and markers must now be negotiated in a global arena in which differences are more profound and more obvious. At stake is our sense of meaning and purpose. We are finding ourselves unable to anchor or position ourselves because of constantly changing demands for competency and mastery. We shift and change. We are more hesitant to define ourselves in fixed and concrete ways, at the risk of making ourselves vulnerable, protean, and obsolete.[7]

The dynamics of interaction are changing in the world. Technological advances and improvement in transportation are examples of how people who would have previously existed in relatively exclusive spaces now co-exist. Encountering "otherness" is by no means a new phenomenon. There are examples throughout history of different cultural and ethnic groups interacting. Yet the speed and extent to which this is now occurring demands particular attention. Identity is the pursuit of meaning and purpose.

Edward Said's groundbreaking theories in the field of identity construction focused on major distinctions in the claim for identity between regions he referred to as the Occident and the Orient. Since colonial times, social science had been responsible for "homogenizing vastly different peoples, places, cultures, and historics."[8] In his seminal book *Orientalism*,[9] Said first introduced the notion of co-constructed identities. He saw Western "experts" as depicting a homogeneous image of the East, solidifying a system of representation that served the interests of the West. The "us versus them" mentality reinforced power relationships. Said's work has been prescient, given the "clash-of-civilizations" rhetoric that has proliferated in the post-9/11 world. It is a rhetoric that has been perpetuating a stereotypic and intolerant stance toward non-Western peoples, ideas, and cultures.

According to Said, globalization was set in motion by imperialism. Said expands his ideas about identity by advocating what he termed "contrapuntal reading," a way of juxtaposing the ideas and attitudes of the colonizers and colonized.[10] The technique of contrapuntal reading is helpful for understanding the co-created relationship between the imperialists and those they exploited; the existence of each was constituted by and dependent on the presence and actions of the other. The traditional "us versus them" mentality, with its strong ties to the nation state, potentially engenders xenophobia.

Indeed, of all the identities that can characterize individuals or groups, a strong national identity (that is, identification with a nation) potentially constitutes one of the most dangerous, as evidenced by the long history of war associated with nationalistic fervor. There is an increased risk of violence that often accompanies unbridled patriotic fervor with its appeal to self-righteousness, conformity, and blind obedience.

We see this with the very term *homeland* that is now popular in the United States. Homeland has been used throughout history by many nations to evoke a strong need to defend one's home against invasion from outsiders. National governments gain increased control and conformity by appealing to high levels of fear and distrust and labeling certain groups as enemies (that is, enemification) and demonizing them, often invoking religious justification.

For Said, what we call "culture" becomes a combative source of identity. *Culture* is how we refer to the conglomerate of behaviors, practices, customs, and beliefs that determine who we are. Rallying behind an exclusive claim for the universal rightness of one's own perspective is unhelpful, even dangerous. It is dangerous because our ability to create a meaningful existence depends on our understanding of cultural identity. Said went on to argue that one of the paradoxical legacies of imperialism was that, in addition to bringing previously exclusive people together, it also allowed them

> to believe that they were only, mainly, exclusively, white, or Black, or Western, or Oriental. Yet just as human beings make their own history, they also make their cultures and ethnic identities. No one can deny the persisting continuities of long traditions, sustained habitations, national languages, and cultural geographies, but there seems no reason except fear and prejudice to keep insisting on their separation and distinctiveness . . . Survival in fact is about the connections between things.[11]

The social scientific tradition of the Western world—the objectivist tradition—has contributed to a political system based on separate and distinct unitary identities. The tradition in Western science is to isolate entities for study and to emphasize their distinguishing characteristics that may then be measured and subjected to empirical test. Critical theory has emerged to question whether such an approach can actually capture the essence of complex phenomena such as identity. A fundamental reality of the world is that it is pluralistic and that it became and remains this way due to the ongoing presence of the "other." The "other" ceases to be a separate entity and is brought in and made part of the center. This shift points the way to curb the perpetuation of inequality.

We create our own social fabric, and in turn are created by it. The "I" cannot be separated from the "other." Joan Halifax, in her book on creating cultures of peace, stated:

> We cannot turn our backs on the tendency to turn the world and its beings into objects which we call "other." We are called more than ever to realize the obvious, that we are not, nor were we ever, living in a world of isolation. We are completely and inescapably interconnected and interdependent.[12]

Culture (and therefore identity) is not homogeneous; any attempt at making it so will be detrimental: "All cultures are involved in one another; none is single and pure, all are hybrid, heterogeneous, extraordinarily differentiated, and unmonolithic."[13] For Said, it was imperialism that ushered in the process we now call globalization, because it "consolidated the mixture of cultures and identities on a global scale."[14] This has made it impossible to label people as "purely" one thing, because cultural purity is a myth in the era of globalization. "Labels . . . are not more than starting-points, which if followed into actual experience for only a moment are quickly left behind."[15]

National identities are a part of the growing challenge we face in our global era. Issues of diversity, opportunity, and the distribution of power become subjects of debate as appeals are made to protect certain identities and to devalue or deny others. This introduces an even more dangerous mix when power and the threats to it become part of intergroup and international conflicts and we begin to hear the clarion calls for patriotism and defense of the homeland—"Your nation needs you!" Under these circumstances, we seek new levels of protection and security that may isolate us from others in our nation, region, and across the world in a protective and xenophobic cocoon of imagined security. Our personal identity becomes extended to a larger national identity reinforced by appeals to fear and vulnerability.

Yet today, even as unbridled nationalism seems to be growing in some places, the need for nations is being contested as globalization pressures encourage the growth and empowerment of multi-national corporations—entities that hold no national allegiance beyond profit for shareholders. Via the Internet, people find others more like themselves in distant lands than in their own locales. With national governments being exposed as military and economic protectors of international investors, rather than of the well-being of their own citizens, regard for nations is weakened. The assault on our pursuit of identity is endless—from above and below.

As nation states collapse, many of the intense ethnic and religious rivalries, previously suppressed by a strong national government, become renewed and emerge again. Further, as the economic, political, and social pressures of hegemonic global political economy spreads, new groups, movements, and coalitions form to resist the pressures from above by asserting their local rights, needs, and impulses for recognition. They unite to assert or protect their identity. Local opportunities for mutual caring have challenged reliance on governments. Yet, for many, efforts to actively shape and control their personal and collective lives seem futile in the face of overwhelming globalization pressures.[16]

IDENTITY AS INTERCONNECTION

Each time we as human beings assert our identity, we are challenged to understand the essential principle of separation and connection. Existence is affirmed, meaning created, and connections and positions established with every utterance "*I am.*" But unless we learn that "I" is not a separate entity—but rather an interconnected and interdependent necessity—we run the risk of the "I" in our identity becoming a travesty with regard to what is possible and what is required. When we separate the "I" from all else, we engage in an affront to the most important cosmic principle revealed across time—we are part of something more than ourselves and if we reject or ignore this essential truth, we face the risks of isolation, disharmony, and destructive conflict. Identity, then, in all its forms, personal and collective, is ultimately, in our opinion, the pursuit of meaning and purpose, and is best found in those moments of conscious awareness that recognize that separation and unity can never be thought of apart from one another. The very principle of separation and unity—fission and fusion—constitutes an awe-inspiring and reverential statement about the nature of life and the cosmos itself. Fission and fusion are, after all, the principles by which the cosmos appears to have originated and to continue to exist. The idea is so profound that it taxes our comprehension because of the limitations in our language, logic, and learning. This principle of fission and fusion as represented in the dynamics of separation and connection is the fundamental challenge of identity formation and negotiation.

A critical consideration of identity necessitates a new understanding of ethical obligations, resulting in the notion of a global cultural citizenship. Successful participation in the global community suggests increased interaction with, and dependence on, former "others." Globalization is not a trend that will reverse. However, the effects of globalization can either be beneficial or detrimental to society. An ethical system, and corresponding sense of responsibility, emerges from a changed understanding of identity, allowing a model of globalization to advance that aims at reducing marginalizing tendencies and combats inequalities.

Identity and ethics are overlapping concepts. The identity of a person who engages in shooting another human determines whether the act is seen as one of heroism or of murder. New ideas about identity construction bring about new ethical considerations; at the same time, a changing ethical system introduces forces that shape identity. At the core of meaningful human existence is our ability to express and embody a meaningful social identity. The "success" of this identity is based on the choices that we make. In an increasingly globalized world, there are many forces competing for the ability to determine our decision-making capabilities. Traditional social, political, or religious institutions that used to be sources of determining identity are no longer adequate.

Appiah discusses the ineffectiveness, and even danger, of labeling people.[17] Labels have a dramatic social and psychological effect because of their ability to mold processes of identification. The construction of an identity takes place according to what is deemed "appropriate" within the confines of a particular label, which then has consequences for conduct and decision making. In their respective works, Appiah and Said both argue the same point: the necessity of recognizing society as increasingly pluralistic and constituted by otherness. Furthermore, both scholars push their ideas into the realm of ethics. The job facing the cultural intellectual is therefore not to accept the politics of identity as given, but expose the forces behind representations and show how they provide a rationale for inclusion or exclusion.[18] Although he rejects the term *globalization*, Appiah defines new global identity—his and ours—as being cosmopolitan. This understanding of identity is a shift away from national exclusivity and traditional boundaries and is not based on previous gendered and racial thinking. Cosmopolitan identity pushes humanity into the moral realm. A cosmopolitan world is culturally pluralistic and characterized by an increased vested interest in the "other," resulting in the need for global responsibility. Moving away from the falsely dichotomous "us and them" model, it becomes possible to develop an ethical system that is fair to and representative of all. In the spheres of communication, mobility, and environmental regulation there is ample evidence of the extent to which decision making by some impacts all. Decisions made about regulating carbon emissions or subsidizing agricultural production, for example, have global ramifications. We are undeniably constituted by and dependent on our interaction with others, implying a correlating ethical responsibility to them.

Said and Appiah, both implicitly and explicitly, work within the framework of moral philosophy. A discussion of culture, or cultures, necessarily has ethical implications. The more that society is understood as an enormous diverse web, the more urgently we need to locate specific ways to give meaning to our lives. Appiah's recommended ethical guidelines are rather loose, likely because he recognizes that positing a stringent moral system would undercut his point about cosmopolitanism. He suggests, therefore, that some universal values hold firm for everyone, but that there are also many local and specific values that are adapted accordingly, and that our understanding of ethics must allow for this. When it comes to morality there is no one single truth. His analogy of a conversation is helpful, referring not only to "literal talk but also as a metaphor for engagement with the experience and the ideas of others . . . Conversation doesn't have to lead to consensus about anything, especially not values; it's enough that it helps people get used to one another."[19] The point echoes with the emergence of transformative conflict resolution in which long-term appreciation of the adversary's position outweighs the benefit of a sometimes uneasy resolution.

A correct understanding of contemporary identity and ethics should ideally result in global-cultural citizenship. Many hesitate to use the term *global governance* because of the negative associations it conjures–anything from ambitious totalitarian regimes to American economic and military exploitation around the globe. World citizenship (not governance) is already implicit, due to the co-constitution of identity and interconnectedness of our decision making. Since it is already a reality, the need to determine what it should look like is urgent. Any notion of global citizenship must link concern for social justice and human rights with cultural respect and equal opportunity of expression and participation.

In our global era, replete with all of its contestations of individuals, groups, and nations, a widespread spirit of "versus-ism" emerges in which compassion, cooperation, and collaboration are urgently needed yet denied amid the felt need for protection. The old way of thinking about identity and ethics must be transcended, giving way to a re-imagined global mandate. The old paradigm is nationalistic, imperialist, patriarchal, conformist, militaristic, homogeneous, exploitative, and ideologically hegemonic. The new paradigm must transcend these former characterizations by being universally empowering, emancipatory, diverse, creative, peaceful, and based on principles of equitable resource distribution and concern for quality of life. To bring about this paradigm shift, education is essential.

There are two fundamental concerns that have emerged from the discussion about globalization that must be cultivated through education—responsibility and participation. Said and Appiah have convincingly portrayed globalization as a phenomenon occurring in the space of overlap between contemporary identity issues and ethical concerns. The necessary outcome, then, is to combine their theory with praxis—developing a sense of responsibility toward others and then making a commitment to increased participation. Post-colonial, cosmopolitan identity, as heterogeneous and co-constituted, should result in a participatory cultural citizenship. Likewise, any identity born out of recognition of the influence of otherness necessitates an ethical system that transcends the old paradigm. Moving beyond traditional concepts of citizenship into an understanding that encompasses cultural considerations of inclusion is the only way to achieve these goals. Educating global citizens is the first step toward changing the global reality.

IDENTITY—TRANSFORMED AND TRANSFORMATIVE

Arthur Koestler (1905–1983), the famous writer, theorist, and social commentator, noted in his book *The Ghost in the Machine*,[20] that within all living things from cells to human beings to universes, there are two basic impulses: a self-assertive impulse designed to support independent survival and an integrative impulse, designed to connect independent units with others, and in doing so, to produce and reveal a new and emergent dimension of being. And so it is with human beings. We can exist separately and unconnected to others, unconcerned about an expanded sense of our nature. But when we join with others, when we choose to serve the common cause, when we advance the collective, there is a new dimension to our being—we are part of something larger. From the point of identity, this impulse to be part of something larger may be an inherent characteristic of life itself. The quest for identity is not only a basic human need at a personal level, but also one that is sought at cultural and national levels of organization. Amid the destruction of life about us, it should now be clear that we need to identify with something more if we are to survive.

We can move beyond the struggles for identity at individual, cultural, and national levels, in favor of a more encompassing identity—life and the ecologies that nurture and sustain it. Identification with life could be recognized as our most essential and most authentic identity. This identity with life should, in our view, be placed above personal, cultural, and national identities. It is the most important because it implicates all other identities in a far more meaningful way. If we accept the truth that we are part of life, a new sense emerges of connection and harmony with the world about us. We experience the life-affirming impulses of evolving, developing, and becoming. There emerges a sense of humility and wisdom that offers insights into unforgivable carelessness and disdain we have demonstrated for life in all its forms—how much we have done to destroy life and, in the process, perhaps to destroy ourselves. With this affirmation and acceptance, we can build a foundation for connection to all forms of life, and we can move beyond the struggles for identity that are now present at individual, cultural, national, and regional, and global levels, in favor of the ultimate identity—we are life.

NOTES

1. For example, Marsella, 2009.
2. McLuhan, 1989; Fiore and McLuhan, 1968.
3. Fromm, 1941, 1955.
4. Fromm, 1995.
5. Sen, 2006.
6. Appiah, 2005.
7. Lifton, 1993.
8. Roman, 2006.
9. Said, 1978.
10. Ibid.
11. Ibid.
12. Halifax, 1999.
13. Said, 1993.
14. Ibid.
15. Ibid.
16. Sandel, 1996.
17. Appiah, 2005.
18. Said, 1993.
19. Appiah, 2006.
20. Koestler, 1968.

CHAPTER 8

CULTURES OF PEACE OR CULTURE OF PEACE?

David Adams

As far as I know, the first time that the UN General Assembly ever called for a global movement was in the 1999 Declaration and Programme of Action on a Culture of Peace.[1] This standard-setting instrument for peace, still relatively unknown in the United States although much better known elsewhere in the world, is the equivalent of the Universal Declaration of Human Rights for human rights. In one of the key paragraphs of the Programme of Action, it calls for a "global movement for a culture of peace" through partnerships between the UN, UNESCO, the Member States, and the civil society.

In fact, when we prepared the World Civil Society Report[2] for the midpoint of the UN Decade for a Culture of Peace and Non-Violence for the Children of the World in 2005, we found that while the UN, UNESCO, and the Member States had done little, the civil society had made a great deal of progress in the promotion of a culture of peace.[3]

Hence, it is appropriate to speak of a "global movement for a culture of peace." Unfortunately, this movement is not well known because it is not considered newsworthy by the mass media because, I would argue, the mass media are very much in the employ of the culture of war.

In this chapter, I wish to explain why the phrase is "culture of peace" and not "cultures of peace."

First, let us consider the nature of culture. For this, I rely on the work of the great anthropologist Leslie A. White and his seminal book, *The Evolution of Culture*[4]:

> We may think of the culture of mankind as a whole, or of any distinguishable portion thereof, as a stream flowing down through time. Tools, implements, utensils, customs, codes, beliefs, rituals, art forms, etc., comprise this temporal flow, or process. It is an interactive process: each culture trait, or constellation of traits, acts and reacts upon others, forming from time to time new combinations and permutations. Novel syntheses of cultural elements we call inventions . . .
> . . . The interrelationship of these elements and classes of elements and their integration into a single, coherent whole comprise the functions, or processes, of the cultural system . . .
> For certain purposes and within certain limits, the culture of a particular tribe, or group of tribes, or the culture of a region may be considered as a system. Thus one might think of the culture of the Seneca tribe, or of the Iroquoian tribes, or of the Great Plains, or of western Europe as constituting a system. . . . But the cultures of tribes or regions are not self-contained, closed systems in actuality, at all. They are constantly exposed to cultural influences, flowing in both directions with other cultures.

Although White never lived to consider an analysis of the culture of war (he died in 1975), I think he would agree with me that it is a culture that has dominated the world for thousands of years. It can be described, using his words above with my additions in brackets, as a culture that involves

> mankind as a whole . . . as a stream flowing down through time [involving] Tools, implements, utensils [i.e., weapons, weapon systems and other military supplies], customs, codes, beliefs, rituals, art forms, etc. [as] an interactive process: each culture trait, or constellation of traits, acts and reacts upon others, forming from time to time new combinations and permutations.

It is this universal culture of war that we set out to address when the UN General Assembly, in 1998, requested UNESCO to prepare a draft Declaration and Programme of Action on a Culture of Peace.[5] It is in the singular, because, as I like to say, if Dwight Eisenhower, David Petraeus, Napoleon, Alexander the Great, and Genghis Khan could be put into a room with translators, they would understand each other perfectly. And, in fact, it is said that Mao Tse Tung followed closely the advice of Sun Tzu's *Art of War*[6] which dates from the time of Confucius.

The culture of peace (not "cultures of peace") was formulated as an alternative to the eight principal aspects of the culture of war in the draft document that we sent in 1998 from UNESCO Paris to the General Assembly in New York. Here are some key excerpts:[7]

1. Education is the principal means of promoting a culture of peace . . . The very concept of power needs to be transformed—from the logic of force and fear to the force of reason and love. [Although education for the culture of war and violence is not specifically mentioned here, it is inferred that it is based on force and fear, i.e., the basic qualities of terrorism.]
2. Sustainable human development for all . . . This represents a major change in the concept of economic growth which, in the past, could be considered as benefiting from military supremacy and structural violence and achieved at the expense of the vanquished and the weak.
3. The elaboration and international acceptance of universal human rights, especially the Universal Declaration of Human Rights, has been one of the most important steps towards the transition from a culture of war and violence to a culture of peace and nonviolence. It calls for a transformation of values, attitudes, and behaviors from those which benefit exclusively the clan, the tribe or the nation towards those which benefit the entire human family.
4. Equality between women and men . . . can replace the historical inequality between men and women that has always characterized the culture of war and violence.
5. Democratic participation and governance . . . the only way to replace the authoritarian structures of power which were created by and which have, in the past, sustained the culture of war and violence.
6. There has never been a war without an "enemy," and to abolish war, we must transcend and supersede enemy images with understanding, tolerance, and solidarity among all peoples and cultures.
7. Participatory communication and the free flow and sharing of information and knowledge . . . is needed to replace the secrecy and manipulation of information which characterize the culture of war.
8. International peace and security, including disarmament. [It seemed so obvious that we did not bother to state that this is an alternative to the soldiers and weapons that are central to the culture of war.]

Following my years of work at UNESCO designing the culture of peace program with its national programs in El Salvador, Mozambique, and so forth and managing the International Year for the Culture of Peace (2000), I have lectured around the world on the culture of war and culture of peace. In Africa and Latin America, there is no difficulty eliciting the characteristics of the culture of war from the audience; they have lived through it. They quickly relate to the prospect of replacing the culture of war with a culture of peace (in the singular).

But in the United States, one encounters "American exceptionalism" that includes a preference to speak of "cultures of peace" instead of "culture of peace." Why is this? One reason may be that Americans are so isolated from the rest of the world that they are not aware of (or, in many cases, not interested in) the UN initiatives for a culture of peace and their standard-setting instruments.

To understand the need for a culture of peace in the singular, it is necessary to understand and accept the fact that the world is dominated by a culture of war in the singular. But for many in the Global North this has been difficult to accept. It was the representative of the European Union who, in 1999, insisted that all references to the culture of war must be stricken from the culture of peace resolution before they could sign on to it. As a result the final resolution refers only to the culture of peace and not to the culture of war. The American delegate agreed with this, but went further by insisting that the phrase the "human right to peace" must also be stricken from the resolution because "if this is adopted it will be more difficult to start a war."

American exceptionalism was evident in the lack of response to the Manifesto 2000 by which we mobilized people during the International Year for the Culture of Peace. Over 75 million people around the world signed the Manifesto, pledging to cultivate a culture of peace in their family and community. Here's where most of the signatures came from:

- India—35 million
- Brazil—15 million
- Colombia—11 million
- Korea—1.6 million
- Japan—1.2 million
- Nepal—1.2 million
- Western Europe—1.1 million
- Algeria—789,000 (with probably another half million not reported)
- Morocco and Tunisia—550,000

Where was the United States? Despite formal commitments to circulate the Manifesto and collect signatures by the National Council of Churches (50 million members) and the American Association of Retired Persons (another 50 million members), as well as a number of other major U.S. civil society organizations, there was a news blackout on the Manifesto and in the end there were only 45,000 signatures. As a result, most Americans have never heard of the Manifesto 2000.

Nor are most Americans aware of UN initiatives for the culture of peace, not only the Manifesto 2000, but also the International Year for the Culture of Peace (2000), the International Decade (2001–2010), or the standard-set-ting Declaration and Programme of Action on a Culture of Peace (1999). These have never been considered newsworthy by the mass media.

One rationale that I have heard for "cultures of peace" is from those who have sought to identify non-state societies that do not have a culture of war. Perhaps the best example is the Peaceful Societies Web site.[8] Indeed, it is possible that some societies, such as those described on this Web site, did not experience war, but if so they were exceptional. At least half of the particular societies listed on the Web site were observed in conditions where warfare was impractical because of extreme environmental conditions and/or populations that were widely scattered or pacified by outside forces. In fact, several societies listed on the Web site, including the Kung San and Mbuti pygmies, had historical accounts of warfare at earlier times when their peoples were more numerous and less scattered or were not "pacified" by other peoples.[9] In fact, there are so few reported cases of people without a history of war that when the cross-cultural anthropologists Mel and Carol Ember set out to examine the ethnographic record for predictors of warfare, "we could not compare societies with and without war to see how else they might differ, because there were too few unpacified societies without war."[10]

Some people point to ancient Crete as an example of a culture of peace, and indeed the traditional archaeological data tend to support this. However, in recent years there are new findings of extensive military fortifications on the island dating from the period that is considered to be its culture of peace. Hence, the question needs to be re-examined.

A related rationale for "cultures of peace" is from those who say that unlike the culture of war, a culture of peace needs to respect the autonomy and integrity of all cultures rather than forcing them to conform to a dominant global culture. Indeed, the basis of this argument is quite sound. One of the eight program areas of the culture of peace is international under-standing, tolerance, and solidarity that should be interpreted as respect for all cultures, including indigenous cultures. With this in mind, perhaps the most complete formulation should not be "culture of peace or cultures of peace" but rather "local and regional cultures and societies of peace in the framework of a global culture of peace." Such a formulation would reflect the need to replace the global culture of war by a global culture of peace, as well as the need for local and regional societies and cultures to flourish without being dominated by other cultures. In saying this, however, one should not overlook the understanding, as expressed above by White, that "the cultures of tribes or regions are not self-contained, closed systems in actuality, at all. They are constantly exposed to cultural influences, flowing in both directions with other cultures."

Is a global culture of peace possible, or is it a utopian idea with no chance of ever coming into existence?

The first question to consider is whether the culture of war reflects biological factors in human evolution that cannot be overcome through cultural change. Consider the Seville Statement on Violence[11] that has adequately answered this question by disposing of biological explanations. This opinion is supported by the American Psychological, Anthropological, and Sociological associations, all of which endorsed the Seville Statement with its conclusion, paraphrased from Margaret Mead, that "the same species that invented war is capable of inventing peace."[12]

But if a culture of peace is possible, who are the actors that will bring it to pass? Let us consider four sets of actors: the state, the UN, the civil society, and local authorities.

THE ROLE OF THE STATE

Traditionally, it has been assumed that peace (and by extension, a culture of peace) must be obtained through reform of the state. Hence, for example, peace movements direct their message to the state. The state is demanded not to make war, or, once a war has started, to stop the war and "make peace." Revolutionary movements also address their message to the state, calling for its replacement by a new revolutionary government with the assumption that the new state will bring peace.

I have come to believe that the state cannot make a culture of peace, and that a new strategy is therefore needed. This conclusion is based on my experience as the initiator of the culture of peace program of UNESCO (1992–1997) and director of the International Year for the Culture of Peace (1998–2001). And it is based on the study and writing of the first ever "history of the culture of war," which is now being published.[13]

To put it briefly, the last 5,000 years of the culture of war may be summarized as the progressive monopolization of the culture of war by the state. A graphic allegory is presented by the American Western film genre. Prior to the arrival of the sheriff, there is lawless violence in the frontier town, whether by Indians, outlaws, or feuds. The sheriff arrives and announces that he represents the state and that only the state has license to kill. The sheriff can deputize others to kill, but only in the name of the state. As Max Weber put it a century ago, the definition of the state has become the organization that has a "monopoly on the legitimate use of physical force within a given territory." And as it is seen at the UN, the definition of a "failed state" is one that has lost its monopoly of violence.

When the U.S. delegate objected to a "human right to peace" by saying that if this were adopted it would be more difficult to start a war, he was implicitly stating that the fundamental right of the state is the right to make war.

In this regard, the dream of a UN that could enforce international peace through universal disarmament had a fatal flaw. The flaw was article 2.7 of the Charter:

> Article 2.7: Nothing contained in the present Charter shall authorize the United Nations to intervene in matters which are essentially within the domestic jurisdiction of any state. . . .

This is a fatal flaw because one of the essential and indispensable functions of the culture of war for the state is the ability to use military force as a last resort to suppress *internal* opposition. And this is precisely what the UN is forbidden to address.

In 1995, I published "Internal Military Interventions in the United States," in the *Journal of Peace Research*.[14] Compiling the data from the U.S. Army and National Guard for the years 1892 to 1992, I showed that in the United States there were 18 interventions and 12,000 troops per year, on average, during the period 1886 to 1990 against striking workers, urban riots, etc. The rate has been more or less constant over time, when one includes the interventions to stem urban riots throughout the United States in the 1960s and again in 1992 in Los Angeles when 4,000 National Guardsmen and 4,000 U.S. Army soldiers and marines were deployed.[15]

The question of the internal function of military force in so-called "democracies" is a taboo topic, not only at the UN, but also in academia:

> The unchanging rate of internal military intervention in the USA and the lack of attention to such intervention in the literature on war and peace are in striking contrast to the rapid changes in other aspects of war and peace. It is argued here that this reflects an oversight which peace researchers and activists should address in the coming years.[16]

During the intervening years since this article was published, there have been only four academic references to it according to the Social Science Citation Index, even though the *Journal of Peace Research* is a prestigious journal that one would expect relevant researchers to read. I have searched throughout the academic literature and as far as I can see, no other researchers have taken up the challenge independently.

From all of the above, I conclude that the state is incapable of promoting a culture of peace.

THE ROLE OF THE UNITED NATIONS

As long as the UN remains an inter-governmental organization run by the Member States, one should not expect it to play a role other than that dictated by the states themselves. However, as will be suggested below, we can look forward to the day when the UN is no longer run by states but by another system that brings to pass the initial lines of the UN charter, which begins "We the peoples. . . ." The UN organization and its specialized agencies have the capacity to work for a culture of peace. When they are able to act without the direct control or interference of the states they are quite capable of representing the interests of peace and justice. A good example is the national culture of peace programs that I was privileged to participate in during the 1990s at UNESCO. As representatives of the UN, we were able to make great progress with civil society and local authority representatives in the El Salvador and Mozambique National Culture of Peace Programmes until it came time to involve the Member States. It was only later when these programs failed to get the necessary support from the powerful states in Europe and the United States that they had to be shut down.

THE ROLE OF THE CIVIL SOCIETY

In 1998, realizing that the powerful states would oppose and weaken the culture of peace resolution, we proposed in the draft Programme of Action for a Culture of Peace that it should be promoted by a global movement for a culture of peace including not only the UN and its Member States, but also the civil society. This provision was kept intact in the final version of the UN resolution, and as mentioned above, it was the first time that the UN General Assembly ever called for a *global movement*. The resolution calls for the promotion of this movement through sharing of information among its actors, including the civil society.

In this spirit, from 1999 to 2000, for the International Year for the Culture of Peace, we launched the global campaign, as mentioned above, for individuals to sign the Manifesto 2000 committing them to work for a culture of peace in their daily lives. Most of the 75 million signatures were obtained through the efforts by a great number of civil society organizations around the world.

In 2005, at the midpoint of the UN Decade for a Culture of Peace and Non-Violence for the Children of the World, we carried out a survey of actions for a culture of peace by 700 civil society organizations around the world. Most of them reported that they were making progress toward a culture of peace in their own area of work, but that few people knew about it because it was not treated as newsworthy by the mass media or the academic community.[17]

We found, in conducting the survey that the civil society promoting a culture of peace extends far beyond what is usually considered the "peace movement." When one considers all the civil society initiatives around the world working on the various aspects of a culture of peace, including human rights, sustainable development, women's equality, democratic participation, etc., then the civil society initiatives for a culture of peace touch the lives of most of the world's inhabitants. For example, all trade unions may be seen as working for the economic and social rights of workers. For another example, the initiatives for sustainable development include not only obvious ecology organizations, but also those working for local sustainable agriculture and farmers markets.

Because of the strengths of the civil society, its enormous scope and complexity and energy, it is tempting to think that the civil society itself, working independently of the state, and gradually coalescing into a global movement, could eventually bring about a transition from the culture of war to a culture of peace. No doubt, civil society is a powerful force for the culture of peace, and must play a very important role, but for the following reasons, I believe that the civil society, working alone, cannot accomplish the task.

First, civil society organizations are not truly representative of the peoples of the world. Civil society organizations are not elected by the people. Instead, they are self-appointed, and their leadership develops independently within each organization. Of course, they wish to be recognized by the people they serve. They try as much as possible to involve these people as a force to strengthen and expand their capacities, but, at the same time, they are not required to obtain a mandate from the people. In some cases, they give the people they serve a voice in the decisions about how and what actions to undertake, but the leadership of the organization itself is not usually decided by the people at large. This is both a source of strength and a source of weakness. On the one hand, it gives civil society organizations the freedom to be "ahead of their time" and be an educational force for the future. On the other hand, they do not have the democratic legitimacy to become a political counterforce to the culture of war of the nation state, and in the final analysis, the transition from a culture of war to a culture of peace is a question of political power, not just a struggle of ideas and good works.

Second, civil society organizations are often locked in a fierce competition, one against another, for limited resources. For example, many organizations must devote a high proportion of their efforts to finding enough money to pay their staff on an ongoing basis. In doing so, they are competing with other organizations doing the same thing, and the overall effect of the various organizations is often greatly reduced.

Third, there is often a lack of synergy among organizations working for different components of the culture of peace. Organizations working in one area, for example, freedom of the press, do not necessarily join forces with organizations working for other areas, for example, disarmament or women's equality. This "fragmentation" of the culture of peace is unlike the unity of the various components of the culture of war. For example, those working in the arms industry know full well that they are in synergy with those working for economic exploitation, male domination, propaganda for enemy images, and vice versa; those working in these other areas recognize their alliance with the arms industry, etc. The various forces of the culture of war pool their energies in the traditional political process, ensuring that most national presidential campaigns support the various aspects of the culture of war, explicitly or implicitly, and once the politicians are in office, the lobbies of the culture of war are synergetic.

Fourth, much of the energy of civil society is directed toward trying to change policies of the state. No doubt this is important and many important victories have been won, including the prevention of some wars. But in the long run, for the reasons I have provided earlier, it is not likely that the transition to a culture of peace can be accomplished at the level of the state. It will be more productive in the future, as I will argue further below, to put more of the energy of the civil society into making changes at the local level while continuing to think globally and acting in liaison with local authorities.

For all the above reasons, it makes sense to redirect the primary emphasis of the civil society toward working together with elected officials at the local level instead of the national level. That does not mean abandoning completely their work at national and international levels, which will continue to achieve important victories. But it does mean a radical shift of emphasis and priorities.

THE ROLE OF LOCAL GOVERNMENTS (CITIES, TOWNS, AND REGIONS)

Over the centuries, as the state has increasingly monopolized the culture of war, the city, town, and local region has lost its culture of war, ceding it to the national authorities. If we visit European cities, we can still see fragments of the old city walls with their turrets spaced at intervals so that archers or musketeers can shoot an invading enemy on all fronts. In many cases we will see the old gates that could be closed to keep out an invading enemy or to control who could come in and out of the city, much as today's states control the traffic through their customs at each port of entry into the state.

No longer do cities and towns maintain armies to protect against invasion or to put down internal rebellions. Police forces are armed to encounter one or a few potential "enemies," and one does not imagine them to have tanks, missiles, nuclear weapons, and the weapons of the modern battlefield. The same is true for the various other areas of the culture of peace in the context of local government. One finds that policies in most of these areas are much less aligned with the culture of war than their equivalents at the national level, and instead one finds considerable evidence of the culture of peace.

The strategy proposed here is to link civil society to local governments to developa culture of peace at the local level, and eventually to develop a new global democratic order based on regional networks of local authorities as a replacement for the role of the Member States in the UN.

This strategy is already being developed in city culture of peace commissions, beginning in Brazil and now spreading to other parts of the world. These commissions are official bodies of local government with a certain number of elected officials or city representatives and an even larger number of representatives from local civil society organizations. This strategy has a number of key advantages.

First, by working together with local elected officials, the civil society achieves a legitimacy of working for the people as a whole, and it increases the possibility of broadening the base of involvement to include everyone in the community.

Second, by working together with local elected officials, the civil society can find common ground, beyond the level of their competition for limited resources. For the projects with city or town officials, resources may be provided by the city or town budget or by foundations and other financial sources that will give their money to a city or town project while they might not give it to a particular nongovernmental organization.

Third, by working together on the culture of peace, the civil society organizations that would normally concentrate on their own particular area, can now take part in a more holistic and mutually reinforcing approach involving all of the program areas of a culture of peace.

Fourth, by putting energy into local government, they can help build the base for a new world order that is democratic, global, and free from the culture of war.

At the same time, the involvement of civil society makes possible contributions of the city to a culture of peace that would not otherwise be done by local government working alone:

1. Passion, energy, and local experience provided by civil society organizations in each of the various areas of a culture of peace.
2. Linkage to global civil society movements concerned with each of the various areas of a culture of peace.
3. Continuity when local government changes hands in election reversals.

TOWARD A NEW WORLD ORDER BASED ON LOCAL GOVERNANCE

Already there are global organizations of cities working on sustainable development, such as the International Council of Local Environmental Initiatives, and democratic participation (the International Observatory of Participative Democracy); one can imagine similar global initiatives of local initiatives for the other eight program areas of the culture of peace. These global initiatives of local authorities show that it is not necessary to pass through the nation state to achieve global governance based on a culture of peace.

In this regard, I can imagine an eventual shift of the UN from its present dependence on the Member States to a dependence on regional representatives of local governments (perhaps organized by continent) that are aligned locally with civil society for a culture of peace.[17] To cite an example of such regional organization, ICLEI (International Council for Local Environmental Initiatives [now officially called Local Governments for Sustainability]) has regional offices in South Africa (for Africa), Japan, Korea, Germany (for Europe), Argentina (for Latin America and the Caribbean), Canada, United States, Australia (for Oceania), India (for South Asia), Philippines (for Southeast Asia), and Mexico.

Just imagine how the agenda of the Security Council would change if it were dependent on representatives of local government. For example, nuclear disarmament would be one of the first items on the agenda.

Of course, such a shift would not take place under normal conditions, but it seems likely that the world is headed in the next few decades for one of its periodic breakdowns of state power. In the past these breakdowns have been associated with World Wars I and II and with the Great Depression as well as the breakdown of the Soviet Empire at the end of the 1980s. When the state system breaks down, there is a void and a period of opportunity for radically different approaches.

What concerns me is not so much that there will be such a crash, historical void, and period of opportunity, but rather that it will come too soon for us to prepare for it. In the past, the crashes of empires and states often have been followed by fascism and/or revolutionary governments that reflect the culture of war of the revolutionary movements that brought them about. The institution of a culture of peace instead would be a radically different response, without historical precedent, and perhaps the greatest challenge our species has ever faced. The time to begin developing this alternative is now.

NOTES

1. United Nations, 1999.
2. World Civil Society Report, 2005.
3. Ibid.
4. White, 1959.
5. United Nations, 1998.
6. Tzu, 1910.
7. Adams, 2008.
8. Peaceful Societies.
9. Adams, "Why There Are So Few Women Warriors," 1989.
10. Ember and Ember, 2001.
11. Adams, "The Seville Statement on Violence," 1989.
12. Adams, 2008.
13. Ibid.
14. Adams, "Internal Military Interventions," 1995.
15. Adams, 2008.
16. Adams, "Internal Military Interventions," 1995.
17. Adams, 2009.

PART IV

Religious Dimensions of Peace

It is said that at a dinner party in Cairo, Jaan Christian Smuts, Gandhi's chief political opponent in South Africa, said to Winston Churchill that Gandhi succeeded because he could appeal to the religious feeling of his followers, while they (Churchill and Smuts) could not. Churchill failed to get the point; but it is true nonetheless. Religion has had a major role in the creation of ethical standards and the sense of individual and group identity. Some have argued that it has greatly hindered peace by framing differences in absolute terms. Such rigid, exclusionary identities provide obstacles to dialogue and produce artificial incentives to fight against those not accepting one's own faith. Others say that without religion, our merely secular beliefs would lack the moral strength that enable us to resist temptations for violence. Both are correct. Because religion, for better and for worse, touches deeper commitments and feelings than almost any other area of our lives, it has been the greatest stimulus to both peace and war. Despite the secularization of peace concepts at the beginning of the last century, no attempt to understand the dynamics of peace even in today's nominally secular world can avoid it.

We introduce this part with an overview by Buddhist practitioner and teacher Donald Rothberg of the theologies of most of the major religions as they treat the all-important issue of war and peace, down the ages and today. Some the world's best known advocates for nonviolence, Christ, Gandhi, and Martin Luther King, Jr., drew their inspiration from their faith. This is followed by special attention to two of the traditions, Christianity and Islam. Specifically, Catholic Christianity is examined as the basis of life-long activism by the revered nonviolence trainer Hildegard Goss-Mayr who, with her husband Jean, helped bring nonviolent and anti-war movements to fruition in the Philippines, Central America, and elsewhere (see Chapter 10, Volume 2, for the work of Maryknoll Missionary Father Roy Bourgeois who was inspired by his faith to resist the violence traced to School of the Americas, a military training school).

The next contribution in this part is directed more to a scholarly analysis of Catholic doctrine, though its young author has also been quite the activist. Eli Sasaran McCarthy deals with a specific question within the Catholic social teaching on peace, namely, its recent shift from a rule-based or morality-derived set of norms to a more pragmatic position. Sasaran's chapter is pertinent to the entire field of peace thinking (and consequently peace creation), which has long been at a disadvantage when peace and nonviolence have been thought of, sometimes even by practitioners, as based on abstract norms rather than practical realities, in an age when such norms are often disregarded as, in fact, only abstractions.

At times of heightened conflict, extremists within a religious group sometimes find an excuse for violent activities in the words of their sacred texts. These same words are sometimes used to justify hatred by outsiders toward an entire religious faith. The word *jihad*, is a current example. Typical in such use of religion to fan violence is a distorted view of what the actual teachings of the world's great religions do in fact promote. It is at such moments that examining the actual beliefs within a religion becomes important. In doing so we find the world's great religions reflect serious dedication to the goals of living in peace, rejecting injustice, and respecting other humans.

Mohammed Abu-Nimer is one of the most widely regarded scholars of Islam and its teachings on nonviolence and peace. Here, he and Jamal Badawi go in depth into the Islamic tradition's teachings on these subjects, showing as they do how many facets of ethics and many aspects of life are integral to a peace perspective and culture. No one should pretend that the scriptural bases of peace, sampled in this section, are all that one needs to bring peace about, for they are often honored more in the breach than the observance; but no one should pretend either that they are not, at least potentially, an invaluable support to the seekers after peace in their respective traditions.

—Marc Pilisuk and Michael N. Nagler

CHAPTER 9

The Spirit of Change: Spiritual and Religious Resources for Peace and Justice Movements

Donald Rothberg

Spiritual and religious traditions at their best have provided powerful resources for peace and justice movements. Out of such traditions have come the principles of justice, nonviolence, interdependence, and equality; visions of peace, reconciliation, and the "beloved community"; analyses of the roots of suffering and injustice; an emphasis on cultivating core virtues, such as love, compassion, courage, patience, equanimity, and wisdom; and the life stories of numerous exemplary figures.

Such resources, sometimes appearing in modern, secular forms are, I believe, invaluable to help us respond to the challenges, local and global, that we now face. In what follows, these resources will be identified, both ancient and contemporary.

DEFINING SPIRITUALITY AND RELIGION

But first it's helpful to clarify the often confusing terms, *spirituality* and *religion*. For the purposes of this chapter, *spirituality* involves the *lived transformation of self and community toward fuller congruence with or expression of what is understood, within a given cultural context, to be sacred.* This transformation may or may not be supported by doctrines, practices, and social organization.

The term *religion* is used as a broader term signifying *the organized forms of doctrine, ritual, myth, experience, practice, spirituality, ethics, and social structure, which together constitute a world in relation to what is known as sacred.* In this sense, religion has a wider scope than spirituality.

It is important to note that, following these definitions, there can be both nonreligious (that is, nonorganized) spirituality and nonspiritual religiosity. Furthermore, neither spirituality nor religion as such is inherently good or bad. Those acting in the name of spirituality and religion at times have manifested great love and wisdom, on the one hand, and great brutality, on the other.

THE MODERN SPLIT BETWEEN RELIGIOUS TRADITIONS AND SECULAR SOCIAL MOVEMENTS

Those wanting to use the resources of spiritual and religious traditions for contemporary peace and justice movements, however, have to contend with the modern world's fundamental split between religion (and implicitly spirituality) and secular social movements. Modernity, emerging in the 17th century, takes as one of its basic starting points a series of fundamental critiques of religion—as irrational, dogmatic, superstitious, and unsupported by evidence, as linked with oppression, and as based on psychological immaturity. Such critiques have led typically to the outright rejection of religion (or at best its marginalization). At times, particularly recently, spirituality has been distinguished from religion and seen as valuable, but only as an inner, private phenomenon.

Therefore, the idea of using spiritual and religious resources in *public* social movements goes against the grain of modernity. Furthermore, many modern social and political movements have been explicitly *anti-religious*; we might think of the 19th-century anarchist slogan *"Ni dieu ni maitre"* (neither God nor master) or Marx's analysis of religion as the "opium of the people." In this context, many secular social activists consider spirituality and religion as oppressive and delusive, as at best an irrelevant escape, and a misguided attempt to emphasize transformation—the transformation of economic, social, judicial, and political institutions and policies.

THE VISION OF A CONTEMPORARY SPIRITUAL ACTIVISM

Yet a case can be made that *progressive* forms of *socially engaged spirituality* may play a crucial role in helping contemporary peace and justice movements. By socially engaged spirituality, I refer to both traditional and contemporary forms in which spiritual qualities are developed not by leaving the everyday social world (whether as a monk or nun, hermit, wanderer, or a member of a separated intentional community), but rather in the context of involvement in family, work, community, society, and/or politics. By "progressive," I generally refer to those who attempt to integrate the "achievements" of modernity—especially science and democracy—with spirituality, and explicitly distinguish progressive from "regressive" forms of socially engaged religion and spirituality, notably from various forms of fundamentalism.

I have argued elsewhere[1] that progressive forms of socially engaged spirituality represent a potential transformative force that might help us preserve what is most valuable about modernity and elicit the emergence of "postmodern" forms better able to help us respond to the needs of our times.[2]

In what follows, I focus on four broad traditions: (1) the prophetic traditions of social action in Judaism, Christianity, and Islam; (2) Hindu and Buddhist traditions of nonviolent social action, grounded in meditation; (3) indigenous (particularly Native American) traditions, with their emphases on community- and earth-based spirituality; and (4) contemporary efforts to connect spiritually based action to depth psychology, concerns related to gender and ecology, and interfaith cooperation.[3]

THE PROPHETIC TRADITIONS OF JUDAISM, CHRISTIANITY, AND ISLAM

The prophetic traditions originating in Judaism have arguably been, directly or indirectly, the most significant source for many generations of peace and social justice movements in Europe and the Americas. Many of the most prominent spiritually minded social activists and writers of the 20th and 21st centuries trace their lineage directly back to the prophets of Israel. Furthermore, many interpreters of Western radical and revolutionary movements understand the penetrating moral and analytical critiques of capitalism, and the related attempts at radical social transformation as based in secularized versions of the prophetic tradition.

The Jewish, Christian, and Islamic prophetic traditions continue to offer many important resources. I will focus on three: (1) the archetype of the prophetic figure who speaks out on behalf of the oppressed—seeking righteousness, compassion, and justice—as a model for activists and public intellectuals; (2) the centrality of the principles of justice and peace, linked with trenchant moral critiques of injustice and violence; and (3) powerful visions of the just and peaceful society.

THE PROPHETS FROM ISAIAH TO JESUS

The prophets of ancient Israel, such as Isaiah, Jeremiah, Amos, Hosea, and Ezekiel, lived mostly during a two-century span, from the mid-8th century BCE up to the time of the Exile. Later, Jesus framed his ministry in prophetic terms, understanding his own life as a completion of the work of the prophets, saying, "Do not imagine that I have come to abolish the Law or the Prophets. I have come not to abolish but to complete them" (Matthew 5:17–18).

The original prophets called on their contemporaries to realize God's will in their societies, to manifest a just and peaceful society. Toward that end, they pointed out the problems of their times—moral transgression, religious hypocrisy, and self-centeredness—that led to a lack of compassion for those not well off. According to Heschel, the prophets both shook people's complacency and inspired them. They were, he wrote, "some of the most disturbing people who have ever lived."[4]

Isaiah spoke of how many of his contemporaries had abandoned Yahweh (Isaiah 1:4), pursuing self-interest: "All are greedy for profit and chase after bribes" (1:23). The people wear all sorts of ornaments (3:18–24) and lack piety: "Once integrity lived there, but now assassins" (1:21). There is no compassion—for the oppressed, the orphan, the widow, the poor—or justice (5:23). Yet, as Isaiah communicated, "I, Yahweh [God], love justice, I hate robbery and all that is wrong" (61:8). He proclaimed the "good news" to the poor, those whose hearts are broken, captives, those in prison, and those who mourn (61:1–3).

Similarly, Jesus criticized the religious hypocrisy of the scribes and Pharisees, and the lure of money—throwing the money changers out of the temple. He spoke for the oppressed, the downtrodden, the suffering, "those who mourn . . . those who hunger and thirst for what is right . . . the merciful . . . the pure in heart . . . the peacemakers . . . those who are persecuted" (Matthew 5:1–10).

The prophets complemented their strong criticisms with enduring visions of living according to God's will. Isaiah invoked the image of a world beyond war, an image that would be carried through speech and song to many social movements: "These will hammer their swords into plowshares, their spears into sickles. Nation will not lift sword against nations, there will be no more training for war" (2:4). Jesus announced the coming of the kingdom of God, based in the love of enemies, reconciliation, and the ending of an "eye for an eye" (Matthew 5:38).

CONTEMPORARY JEWISH PROPHETS

In our own times, there are many who have continued to offer prophetic resources. Abraham Joshua Heschel (1907–1972), one of the most important interpreters of the Jewish prophetic tradition (1962), was a rabbi and refugee from the Nazis. In the latter part of his life, he became a friend and colleague of Martin Luther King, Jr., participating actively in the civil rights movement, and linking Hasidic mysticism and prophetic social action.

Other major contemporary Jewish prophetic voices include Heschel's daughter, Susannah, who has been prominent in helping to develop Jewish feminist analyses,[5] along with Judith Plaskow and others. Michael Lerner,[6] a student of Heschel's, is perhaps the most prolific and visible Jewish prophetic exponent of our times.

CONTEMPORARY CHRISTIAN PROPHETIC FIGURES AND MOVEMENTS

Twentieth- and twenty-first-century Christian prophetic figures and movements have understood themselves to be following the example of Jesus. The following are some of the most prominent.

Martin Luther King, Jr.: Spiritual Responses to Racism, Poverty, and Militarism

Martin Luther King, Jr., arguably the most powerful moral and spiritual actor and speaker in the history of the United States, combined prophetic action with fiery moral critiques of racism, militarism, and poverty, as well as inspiring visions of his "dream" of the "beloved community."[7] His work was particularly focused on healing what may be the core wound of the United States—the unresolved legacy of centuries of slavery and racism—although later in his life he also addressed more fully the related systemic issues of poverty and militarism.

King's initial approach was predominantly ethical and spiritual, modeled especially on Gandhi's nonviolence and expressed through active resistance to and noncooperation with the "evil" of racist laws. In such action, often entailing civil disobedience, the actor voluntarily takes on suffering, whether through going to prison or making oneself vulnerable to the violence of police or vigilantes. The strategy of nonviolent action is to break the cycle of violence, by not reacting to violence with further violence. It is also to appeal to the capacity for good of the oppressors and those who passively support the oppressors, as their hearts are opened by witnessing the suffering of nonviolent actors. The distinction between the sin (in this case, racism) and the redeemable sinner suggests the possibility of reconciliation.

Liberation Theology: Spiritual Responses to Poverty and Injustice

Liberation theology is a contemporary Catholic movement, centered especially in Latin America, but also very influential in Asia, Africa, and North America. Born from the worldwide social ferment of the 1960s, it can especially be seen as a response to the suffering connected with *poverty, inequality, and injustice.* Phillip Berryman writes that liberation theology is "an interpretation of Christian faith out of the suffering, struggle, and hope of the poor."[8] Such an interpretation leads liberation theologians to develop critiques of social, political, and economic systems, as well as cultural and political ideologies, which keep poverty in place, critiques that are often aimed at the past and present Catholic Church itself.

Being and working with the poor and oppressed, the "salt of the earth" (Matthew 5:13), has since the time of Jesus been a fundamental moral response of many Christians, and for some it is at the heart of Christian faith. And so liberation theologians have worked closely with grassroots groups and particularly encouraged the development of "base communities." Typically led not by priests but by laypersons, a base community of 10 to 20 persons might meet once a week to reflect on life issues in the light of the Gospel. Liberation theologians have thus redefined the role of theologians and priests; Leonardo Boff, a Brazilian theologian silenced for a year by the Vatican, has written that all prayer must be linked with "a lived commitment to the liberation of the oppressed."[9]

Contemporary Christian Peace and Justice Activists

Many other Christian prophetic activists have also been prominent in the last century. Dorothy Day, the co-founder in 1933 with Peter Maurin of Catholic Worker houses in the United States, was also primarily focused on serving the poor and destitute. For her, the heart of the gospel was to "comfort the afflicted and afflict the comfortable."[10]

A number of Christian activists, particularly Jesuit priests Daniel and Phillip Berrigan and John Dear, have focused on countering militarism and war. They have engaged in a number of highly public symbolic acts to draw attention to the institutions of war—destroying draft records, symbolically damaging weapons at military bases, and committing civil disobedience—participating in what they have called, echoing Isaiah, the Plowshares movement. The Trappist monk, Thomas Merton, also wrote extensively about the roots of war and peace.

Other prophetic figures have focused on concerns of justice. Jim Wallis,[11] the editor of *Sojourners*, has helped to develop an evangelical prophetic voice, with particular attention to economic, political, and moral issues. Cornel West[12] has developed a contemporary prophetic stance, at once philosophically nuanced, historically grounded, socially active, and attuned particularly to concerns of race and democracy.

Rosemary Ruether has, along with other Christian feminists, developed critiques of sexism in the Christian tradition, and developed innovative spiritual practices and theological perspectives that might support more egalitarian gender relationships. Ruether rests such efforts on the claim that the essential Christian message is not sexist, that it is rather the (nonsexist) "prophetic-liberatory" approach of both Judaism and Christianity that is normative.[13]

In Europe, a number of Christian theologians and activists were prominent in opposition to fascism, both during World War II and in the post-war period; their examples remain very significant. We might think especially of Simone Weil (1909–1943), Dietrich Bonhoeffer (1906–1945), and Dorothee Sölle (1929–2003).

SOCIALLY ENGAGED SPIRITUALITY IN THE ISLAMIC TRADITION[14]

For Muslims, the Prophet Muhammad is the archetypal example of a human being of highly developed character concerned with issues of morality, social justice, oppression, and humanitarianism. As such, he set the example to be followed by all Muslims. In a *hadith*, Abu Sa'id al-Khudri said, "I heard the Messenger of Allah, may Allah bless him and grant him peace, say, 'Whoever of you sees something wrong should change it with his hand; if he cannot, then with his tongue; if he cannot, then with his heart.'"[15]

Zakat, the giving of charity, is one of the "five pillars" of Islam. Muslims are required to give at least 2 percent of their yearly income to the poor. Both historically and in the contemporary Muslim world, there have been many organizations working to re-distribute wealth to help the poor. The belief is that allowing some to remain in poverty while others have excessive wealth is an injustice that should not be tolerated.

Such mainstream Islamic forms of socially engaged spirituality have been overshadowed in recent times by other forms often linked with fundamentalism and violence, such as the Iranian revolution, the Muslim Brotherhood in North Africa, Salafism, Wahabism in Arabia, the Tablighi Jamaat, and Deobandism in South Asia. Although many of their roots can be found in some (arguably dogmatic) aspects of Islam, they can also be understood as a significant part in reaction to what we might call the shadow side of modernity: Western dominance of Muslim regions, and in many cases, national and cultural humiliation.

Nonfundamentalist spiritually motivated action in the manner of the Prophet is much more representative of modern Muslims. For example, Abdul Sattar Edhi in Pakistan has established a social welfare system that includes caring for orphans, providing medical care, saving abandoned babies, recovering and burying dead bodies, and training Muslim women as nurses. There is also Muhammad Yunus, who established the Grameen bank, helping people to establish small businesses without incurring major debt. A number of contemporary Muslim women, such as the scholar-activist Amina Wadud[16] and Meena of Afghanistan, have been motivated by their spiritual beliefs to increase women's roles in the mosque and in world affairs, and to ensure that the rights of women according to Islamic law are upheld.

HINDU AND BUDDHIST RESOURCES FOR CONTEMPORARY PEACE AND JUSTICE MOVEMENTS

From among the multitude of offerings from many centuries of Hindu and Buddhist traditions, I want to select four crucial resources: (1) the Hindu idea of karma ("action") yoga as a spiritual path; (2) the principle of *ahimsa*—nonharming or nonviolence—particularly as interpreted and enacted by Gandhi; (3) the parallel Buddhist grounding of social transformation in meditative practice; and (4) the Buddhist archetype of the bodhisattva, dedicated to the liberation of all beings.

Karma Yoga

The idea of *karma yoga*, of spiritually guided action, dates back at least to the time of the *Bhagavad Gita* (ca. 2nd century BCE). In the *Gita*, *karma yoga*—the cultivation of union with the divine through action—is presented as one of the four main spiritual paths, along with *jñana yoga*, coming to the divine through intuitive insight; *bhakti yoga*, loving devotion to the divine; and *raja yoga*, a primarily meditative path.

In the *Gita*, Krishna, in dialogue with the warrior Arjuna, reminds Arjuna that action is inescapable, that one is always acting, and that therefore the question is *how to act*. Krishna recommends a formula that Gandhi later exemplified: choose the right action, use the right means to attain it (that is, nonviolence), and cultivate an attitude of *nonattachment to the fruits* (that is, the personal benefits) of one's action (*Gita* 2:48). The message of the *Gita*, again embodied by Gandhi, is that working through our attachments to outcomes while simultaneously (and paradoxically) acting fully and responsibly, in a kind of increasingly "selfless service," is a basic path of spiritual realization.

Nonviolence and the Legacy of Gandhi

Mohandas Gandhi (1869–1948) linked the idea of *karma yoga* with the equally ancient Hindu idea of *ahimsa*, or "nonharming." Gandhi's great innovation was to apply the ideas of *karma yoga* and *ahimsa* to large-scale social transformation, in his case, to the movement for the independence of India in the first half of the 20th century. For Gandhi, only nonviolent action could produce a new and free society. Indeed, a nonviolent movement is itself a "transformation of relationships"[17] that results eventually in a transfer of power. Echoing the ancient Hindu, Jain, and Buddhist texts, Gandhi declared that "hatred can be overcome only by love. Counter-hatred only increases the surface as well as the depth of hatred."[18] Such nonviolence, whatever its origins, provides one of the great resources for peace and justice movement drawn from spiritual traditions.

Nonviolence for Gandhi was an ongoing spiritual practice that one must apply not just in social action, but in all activities and all relationships. As in the model of *karma yoga*, the task is to purify one's mind and heart of desire and hatred, coming closer to one's true nature, while at the same time confronting violence and oppression. *Ahimsa*, nonviolence, and love, Gandhi tells us, are the very essence of our being; this is why nonviolent action is an expression of spiritual truths and why it eventually works, why the oppressor or violent one eventually responds.

The basic principle of nonviolence is that of noncooperation with what is oppressive and unjust. The activist or *satyagrahi* (one who "holds to truth") works to purify him- or herself from any hatred against the oppressor, even though one's noncooperation may well lead to suffering and even death. Gandhi in fact hoped that through nonviolence the British might move from the position of oppressor to that of reconciled friend—as they did.

Meditation in Action: Socially Engaged Buddhism

Socially engaged Buddhists have also articulated the importance of spiritual practices for social action, particularly focusing on the practices of mindfulness, loving kindness, and compassion. They have taken as central the teachings of the Buddha about the transformation of greed, hatred, and ignorance into generosity, compassion, and wisdom, and understood such transformation as occurring on both individual and collective levels.[19]

In Asia,[20] socially engaged Buddhists have responded to violence with peace walks; nonviolent demonstrations; massive meditative rallies (in Sri Lanka, one rally in 2002 gathered some 650,000 persons); dialogue; and nonviolence trainings. They have formed resistance and reconciliation movements in the midst of war and/or oppression in Vietnam,[21] Tibet, Burma, and the Chittagong Hill Tracts of Bangladesh. In Sri Lanka, the Sarvodaya Shramadana Movement, a massive network of village-based community development activists led by Dr. A. T. Ariyaratne, has for over 50 years linked personal and social liberation.

In the West,[22] socially engaged Buddhists have worked on human rights issues, especially having to do with Asian countries such as Tibet, Burma, and Cambodia. They have also participated in various other movements, protests, and activities—anti-war, anti-violence, anti-racist, and environmental, among others. There have been numerous meetings and conferences of Buddhist women, concerned especially with the patriarchal strands of Buddhist teachings and organizations, the revisioning of Buddhist practices, and sensitivity to gender issues in Buddhist communities.[23] Socially engaged Buddhists have also brought Buddhist teachings to prisons, developed hospices and centers for people with AIDS, and worked with the homeless.

In these activities, there has often been an explicit connection of action and meditative practice, a connection particularly relevant for contemporary peace and justice activists. Traditional formal daily practice, weekly or monthly days of practice, and periodic retreats provide an essential support for action in the world, helping to provide balance and renewal, as well as powerful tools both to cultivate states of clarity, compassion, love, and equanimity, and to work skillfully with difficult states, such as anger, despair, grief, or confusion. Some socially engaged Buddhists have also developed new ways to bring meditative resources (and wisdom teachings) to engagement in the fields of interpersonal relations, group dynamics, conflict, work, service, relationships with the nonhuman world, and social change strategies.[24]

The Bodhisattva

Like the figures of the prophet or karma yogi, the Buddhist figure of the bodhisattva[25] has captured the imagination of many contemporary spiritual activists. The bodhisattva, literally a "being" (*sattva*) oriented to "awakening" or "enlightenment" (*bodhi*), suggests a life of spiritually grounded service to others, a life centered in the aspiration to liberation—for self and others.

INDIGENOUS RESOURCES FOR A SOCIALLY ENGAGED SPIRITUALITY[26]

Indigenous spirituality, both traditional and contemporary, is in many ways less accessible than the traditions of the world religions, yet nonetheless offers important resources for peace and social justice movements. We might selectively summarize those resources, particularly as drawn from Native American traditions, as (1) the grounding of spirituality in community, and in relationship with the earth and all beings; (2) the understanding of spirituality, everyday life, and social action as of one piece; and (3) the use of particular practices relevant to peace and justice work.

The Centrality of Community, Relationship, and Interdependence

We can characterize indigenous traditions as consciously based on locally, ecologically, and seasonally contextualized truths that are narratively anchored in natural communities. Stories and ceremonies help individuals to find internal and external balance within a relational conversation that *participates* in the life of ancestors, animals, plants, stars, humans, rocks, mountains, and other beings.[27] Because of the tendency to idealize or romanticize Native American peoples, it seems important to understand this general characterization as *paradigmatic* in indigenous cultures, but not necessarily fully achieved.

Indigenous spiritual practice can thus be seen as an engagement that arises locally yet goes beyond one's own community. The traditional Hopi, like other tribes, see their responsibility for keeping their villages in balance not just as an obligation to their own tribe, but to the entire world.

Many indigenous authors speak of the ongoing conversation with all beings. In the Sámi language, this has been expressed as *humalan eatnama*, "I converse with the earth." In Aymara, it becomes *nayasa kollo achachilampi uywaysastssta*, "I am letting myself be nurtured by the *apu*—the spirit of the mountain—as I am nurturing the spirit of the mountain. Peruvians use the

Spanish *criar y dejarse criar*, "to nurture and let oneself be nurtured," as equivalent to the Aymara wording.

The Integration of Spirituality, Community, and Social Action

Native people do not typically separate "sacred" and "secular," frequently stating that *everything* is sacred. According to Beck and Walters,[28] Native Americans understand life as sacred and as pervaded by a mystery—of all things moving in circles, dependent on each other. They also describe the personal commitment made to the sources of life through purification, blessings, sacrifices, offerings, and prayerful conversation. Given indigenous participation in this ongoing sacred engagement, it seems that such participation is by its nature spiritual and socially engaged, as well as communally and ecologically based.

Indigenous Practices Relevant for Activists in the Context of the Recovery of Indigenous Mind

On the deepest level, individuals seeking a socially engaged spiritual practice that is informed by native traditions might see themselves as involved in what has been called "recovery of indigenous mind." This term has been suggested directly and indirectly by Native American thinkers, among them Apela Colorado, who point to the importance of European Americans returning to the earth-based knowledge of their ancestors.

Working with the issues of racism and genocide seems to be a crucial ingredient in relating to indigenous traditions. Kremer[29] points to the need for working through cultural shadow material:

> With me walks a shadow. Before me I project the shadow of forgetting where I came from. Behind me trails the shadow of the tears of native peoples. Below me I march on the shadow of the lands my peoples have raped. Above me looms the shadow of the spirits which I am blind to . . . I hope to heal by remembering and seeing the shadows that walk with me so that I can become complete.

Hopefully within such a context of recovery of indigenous mind and decolonization, versions of some practices based in indigenous cultures have begun to enter into the repertoire of spiritual activists. Many organizations use a variant of "Council," originally from the Iroquois,[30] as a way to speak publicly in groups so as to deepen community, work with conflicts, and open up communication. Others may periodically enter into wilderness to come more in touch with deeper motivations and directions, or be inspired by other native ways of working with conflicts.[31] A deepened appreciation of the place of ritual and ceremony may also help frame action in a sacred way.

FOUR FURTHER CONTEMPORARY SPIRITUAL RESOURCES FOR PEACE AND JUSTICE WORK

Four further general resources for a socially engaged spirituality have roots in these contemporary areas of inquiry and action: (1) depth psychology, (2) gender, (3) ecology, and (4) interfaith collaboration.

Depth Psychology

Depth psychology, originating in the pioneering work of Freud and Jung, and continuing through later psychoanalytic, Jungian, existential, phenomenological, humanistic, and transpersonal approaches, offers some powerful theoretical models and therapeutic methods, many of them spiritually oriented, relevant for peace and justice movements. Although some depth psychologists have made significant connections with social movements, many possible connections remain relatively undeveloped. This lack of development has been particularly influenced by the well-known Freudian critiques of religion as psychologically immature, and the pervasive asocial and individualistic interpretations of depth psychologies in the last 70 years, particularly in the United States.[32]

Generally speaking, what seems most valuable about depth psychology for spiritually grounded peace and justice work are: (1) the identification of unconscious dimensions of human experience connected with injustice and conflict, including both individual, familial, social, cultural, and universal aspects, that need to be understood to work for justice and peace; and (2) the development of a variety of therapeutic methods that help to bring awareness, healing, and transformation where there has been unconsciousness and suffering.

Contemporary Approaches to Gender and Socially Engaged Spirituality

As we have seen, a dynamic revisioning of gender is widespread in the contexts of the world religions, involving: (1) identification of nonpatriarchal texts and approaches within a given tradition; (2) arguments for the tradition's "essence" as pointing beyond patriarchy; (3) understanding historically how and why the patriarchal strands have gained ascendancy; (4) imagining and enacting interpretations of their traditions in which men and women are seen as increasingly equal in terms of political and spiritual power and potential; (5) emphasizing the "immanent" aspects of spirituality, particularly community, relationships, the body, emotions, and the earth; and (6) linking analysis of gender to issues of race, class, sexual orientation, and ecology.

Others have in parallel ways found nourishment and inspiration in reconstructing, through scholarship and contemporary practice, various "goddess" traditions and pre-patriarchal ways of life in which the "feminine" seems central, with much less polarization of male and female roles.[33] Still others have revived "pagan" traditions of Wicca, healing "witchcraft," and magic, sometimes[34] with social and political engagement.

Ecology and Spirituality

Similarly, awareness of the urgent need for corrective and restorative action around a host of ecological issues has influenced both the world's religions and emerging spiritual forms and practices. Paralleling the critical self-examinations made in terms of gender issues, many have examined their traditions both for problematic aspects, as well as resources for responding to ecological issues.[35] Three contemporary resources are particularly valuable for contemporary peace and justice activists: (1) deep ecology, (2) ecofeminism, and (3) earth-based practices and rituals.

Deep ecology[36] is an attempt to identify a spiritually grounded framework for recasting human relationships to other beings and to the earth. Its core principles put in question many characteristically *modern* views (many of them held by mainstream environmentalists), namely, (1) a view of humans as "above" the natural world, rather than immersed in it; (2) the centrality of the individual, separate self, as opposed to a sense of self-in-community; (3) an emphasis on central government, rather than local autonomy and decentralization; and (4) a denial of the ethical import of non-humans, including land and place, rather than what deep ecologists call an "ecocentric" ethic.

Ecofeminists (some more secular, some more spiritual) have identified the connection between the domination of women and the domination of the earth. Originating from a number of sources, ecofeminism has strongly influenced many in the world religions.[37]

Partly influenced by these contemporary perspectives, many have also developed new earth-based spiritual practices.[38] Particularly influential has been the work of Joanna Macy, who has developed a large body of group practices, such as the "Council of All Beings" (with John Seed) and "Deep Time" practices, in which one relates to past and future generations.[39]

Interfaith Approaches

Interfaith dialogue and cooperation has occurred in many settings and through organizations such as the Fellowship of Reconciliation and Religions for Peace. Increasingly, those of different traditions (and those outside of traditions) are recognizing that the great challenges of our times—increasing conflict, violence, and fear; the mounting gap between rich and poor; ecological crisis; and challenges to democracy and civil liberties in an age of globalization, militarism, and imperial ambition—are sufficiently demanding as to require a *spiritual* response to summon the *depth* required to face them skillfully, a response *dialogically across many traditions and approaches* to offer the *power* required to meet them adequately, and *access to many traditions* to have the *resources* needed to meet our challenges.

NOTES

1. Rothberg, 1993.
2. I will *assume* rather than attempt to establish the plausibility of that important and complex argument.
3. I have been selective, and not mentioned a number of traditions and authors that might be covered in an expanded treatment.
4. Heschel, 1962.
5. Heschel, 1983.
6. Lerner, 2006.
7. Washington, 1986.
8. Berryman, 1987.
9. Boff, 1992.
10. Day, 1952.
11. Wallis, 1994.
12. West, 1999.
13. Ruether, 1983.
14. This section has been helped by the work of my student, Anisah Bagasra, the main author of a much longer treatment of this theme to which I also contributed: Rothberg et al., 2007.
15. Imam Muslim, 2009.
16. Wadud, 1999.
17. Merton, 1965.
18. Ibid.
19. Loy, 2008.
20. Queen and King, 1996.
21. Hanh, 1993.
22. Queen, 2000.
23. Gross, 1993.

24. Macy and Brown, 1998; Rothberg, 2006.

25. Leighton, 2003.

26. This section depends in large part on the work of my colleague, Dr. Jürgen Kremer, in Rothberg et al., 2007.

27. Kremer, 2004.

28. Beck and Walters, 1977.

29. Kremer, 2000.

30. Zimmerman and Coyle, 1996.

31. For example, as fictionalized by Storm, 1994.

32. Ferrer, 2002; Jacoby, 1986.

33. Eisler, 1987.

34. For example see Starhawk, 1987.

35. Gottlieb, 2003.

36. Devall and Sessions, 1985.

37. Diamond and Orenstein, 1990.

38. Gottlieb, 2003.

39. Macy and Brown, 1998.

CHAPTER 10

When Prayer and Revolution Became People Power

Hildegard Goss-Mayr

We know that not one step, not one seed, not one action that is carried out in the spirit of nonviolence is ever lost. It bears fruit, in the history of nations and of the world. But even though we know this, it is encouraging and helpful to be able to see the practical results of nonviolent action from time to time. That is why I would like to share with you some of the things that happened in the Philippines during the recent liberation struggle, although—I should like to add immediately—it is only a first step in the struggle for a life of dignity for all Filipinos.

The international press has covered it quite well, but there are aspects of what the people of the Philippines lived through that very few journalists have been able to grasp. The press could not relate the events that occurred to the traditions and the attitudes of the people that made them possible.

Nonviolence—this power of truth and love—always develops out of a given historical and cultural background. The Filipino people were under Spanish domination for three centuries, and were a U.S. colony for half a century. Later on, during World War II, they were occupied by the Japanese and liberated by the Americans. Although the United States did not set up another

This chapter appeared in Richard Deats, *Marked for Life, The Story of Hildegard Goss-Mayr* (New City Press, 2009) and was originally printed in *Fellowship* (March 1987): 8–11.

colonial regime, it established a strong military presence in the Philippines and made that country economically dependent on the multinational firms.

Three centuries of Spanish rule brought Christianity to the Philippines, leaving behind, as in Latin America, a mostly Catholic country in the Spanish tradition. It is important to understand that the majority of the Filipino people are a believing people, with a faith like that of children, but not in a negative sense, at all. Our children often have a very close relationship to God. There is no theology in between. Many Filipino people are like those in Latin America who have said to me, "God has spoken into my ear, He said this and this." Sometimes the Gospel comes directly into the hearts and minds of the people, in a way that is not rationalized, as it is in other countries.

More recently, there were almost 20 years of the Marcos regime with the suffering of the people increasing, seen in unemployment, hunger, and misery. Whenever groups in some of the dioceses began to form in the struggle for justice, repression set in immediately. Very great atrocities were committed. This repression came down on the peasants, students, labor unions, and committed Christians. Only a small part of the Church opted to stand on the side of the people and work for social justice. There were perhaps some 30 dioceses where Christian Base Communities were formed.

Bishop Claver in Mindanao was one of the first to develop nonviolent liberating actions in his diocese. Some of the sisters and priests were persecuted, but the majority of the Church leadership and most of the middle class were linked to the regime. As in Latin America, the Church as an official institution was linked to those in power much too long. It is easy to understand why idealistic young people—seminarians and lay people alike—saw no other way out but to join the guerillas. Known as the New People's Army (or the NPA), they were established as the armed branch of the Communist Party, more or less on a Maoist basis. These young people saw no other way to struggle for justice against an unjust regime. I think the Church must bear a large part of the responsibility for the development, due to the cowardice of large sections of the official Church.

People cannot remain passive under certain circumstances. Unless there is the offer of a nonviolent alternative, they will have to take to counterviolence. Gandhi has said that the lowest possible attitude is to remain passive; if you don't know another way, you choose counterviolence. This is not to defend counterviolence, but I think it is a reality of which we must be aware. Wherever the moral authorities—whether it be Christian churches or other moral authorities—do not take the lead in nonviolent resistance there will be counterviolence and, sooner or later, civil war. I think we should understand this, and never condemn those who join the guerillas because they see no other way. But we must try to live that alternative.

Another important event in the Philippine story was the assassination of Ninoy Aquino. This opposition leader had been imprisoned for seven years when he became very ill and had to be operated on in the United States. It may not be well known that while he was in prison Ninoy Aquino underwent a radical change, a kind of conversion. He was certainly an honest person, but like all politicians he had been trying to get power. While in prison, he read the Gospel and Gandhi and began to understand that a politician must serve the people. He decided then that if he ever had the chance to assume responsibility for his country, he would try to be a politician who worked with nonviolence and served the people rather than himself. It is important to understand that this man, who sought leadership in a country where corruption among the political and economic leaders was a way of life, underwent a deep conversion.

When Ninoy Aquino returned to the Philippines in 1983 he knew he had been condemned to death. When he stepped off the plane and was shot to death, his act of courage in returning held great meaning for the Filipinos. They saw him, as we say in the Old Testament, as a "just one," who gives his life for the people, rather than take the life of the enemy. And we also know from the early Church that the blood of the martyr is fruitful; it has the strength to renew people, to bring a challenge and change those who are passive, or those who are collaborative with the dictatorship. Ninoy's giving the gift of his life was really the beginning of a strong popular effort in the Philippines to try to overcome the dictatorship through nonviolence. Following the assassination, demonstrations began to take place all over the Philippines. The fact that one person had the courage to give his life encouraged thousands and thousands of others to overcome the fear that had kept them passive. They poured into the streets to witness to truth and justice, and to demand that martial law be discontinued and human rights respected.

The demonstrations lasted for months, but there was no ongoing nonviolent action; people were not yet prepared for that. Polarization increased; repression became fierce; and the economic situation continued to deteriorate. NPA actions were on the increase in two-thirds of the provinces of the Philippines.

It was then that a few religious communities wrote to Jean and me, asking if we would come just to study the situation and see whether there might be the possibility of developing a well-organized, coherent nonviolent resistance to the existing injustice. We thought perhaps our Latin American experience might help us understand the Philippine situation, so we accepted. We went to the Philippines for the first time in February 1984. With the help of religious sisters and priests, we traveled throughout the islands and met many people: people close to the regime, people in opposition, peasants, laypeople, union leaders, priests, bishops, and politicians.

Jean and I felt that we were coming into the situation with nonviolence at a very late hour. I think we must say to our shame that we all closed our eyes for a long time in the face of injustice. Very often those who see no other way than counterviolence are the first ones to take action against injustice. It is very difficult to come in later and say no, we should take another path. We, as Christians, should be the first ones to open our eyes to injustices, and to speak out and bring the power of nonviolence into the revolution. We felt it was late, but we felt that there were people really searching for the nonviolent alternative.

One thing that made us decide to accept the challenge was when, on the last day of our first visit, the brother of Ninoy Aquino—he's called Agapito ("Butz") Aquino—came to see us. He said to Jean and me: "A few days ago, we were approached by arms merchants, who said, 'Do you think you will be able to overthrow this regime with demonstrations? Don't you think you need better weapons than that? We're offering them to you. Make up your mind.'" And then he said to us: "It is providential that you have come at this time, because ever since their visit I have been unable to sleep. Do I have the right to throw my country unto a major civil war? What is my responsibility as a Christian politician in this situation? Is there really such a thing as nonviolent combat against a system as unjust as this one?" Jean and I told him that at least he could try. "You don't lose anything if you try with nonviolence," we said. "But you must make up your own mind, and if you decide to try it, you must prepare yourself inwardly, because nonviolent methods are the fruit of the vision of man that we have. If you want to have seminars in preparation, let us know, and we will come back."

A few weeks later, we were invited back to carry out a series of seminars on nonviolent liberation. One of these seminars was with the group of bishops that had already committed itself to working for social justice. Bishop Claver had organized a seminar for them. The others were mainly for leaders from the political opposition, for labor unions, peasants, students, and church people—priests, sisters, and laypeople.

In each of these seminars, we would first analyze the situation of violence together, and how we were a part of it. The seed of the violence was in structures, of course, and in the dictator. But wasn't it also in ourselves? It's very easy to say that Marcos is evil. But unless we each tear the dictator out of our own heart, nothing will change. Another group will come into power and will act similarly to those whom they replaced. So we discovered the Marcos within ourselves.

In some of these seminars, there were political leaders of the opposition, and there were peasant leaders. In one seminar, the peasants would not speak to the politicians. "We have no faith in the politicians," they said.

"Even if they are from the opposition, they have betrayed us too often." So one evening when we celebrated the Eucharist together, Father Jose Blanco, a Jesuit priest, distributed the host immediately after consecration. "Let us now break the bread," he said, "and bring one part of the host to someone with whom you have not yet talked during our seminar." There was a deep silence. Finally one person from the labor unions got up, walked to up to one of the political leaders present, and shared his host with him. Deeply moved, the politician promised that if he got the chance of political leadership, he would firmly stand on the side of the poor. This was the breakthrough: unity was achieved. This unity is the pre-condition for nonviolent liberation work Those seminars were more than just training people in methodology. The goal was for each one of us to undergo a deep change, a conversion.

The nonviolent movement of the Philippines, called AKKAPKA, developed out of these seminars, under the leadership of Father Blanco. AKKAPKA is Tagalog for "I embrace you," as well as an acronym for Movement for Peace and Justice. Everybody who took part in a seminar was asked to pass on what they had learned, what they had experienced. And during the first year AKKAPKA was in existence, those few people held 40 seminars in 30 provinces of the Philippines. They saw an urgent need to share what they had learned, so that the people might be prepared, at least to some extent, for nonviolent change in the country.

When the so-called "snap" elections were announced at the end of 1985, AKKAPKA discontinued the training to work at preparing for the electoral process. They encouraged people to have the courage to vote for the person who they really believed should be the leader in the country, and to refuse to accept the money that was offered by the government for Marcos votes. They prepared people to defend the ballot boxes. Young and old, men and women, priests and laypeople, stood unarmed around the urns that held the ballots in the face of armed agents who came to steal them.

AKKAPKA also decided that from the middle of January to the end of the struggle, they would have "prayer tents." One tent was set up right in the banking center in Manila, where the financial power of the regime was concentrated. This big prayer tent was set up there in a little park. And around it, people who promised to fast and pray had a presence day and night. We cannot emphasize enough the deep spirituality that gave the people the strength to stand against the tanks later on. People prayed every day, for all those who suffered in the process of changing regimes, even for the military, and for Marcos: that he would find the strength not to use his huge arsenal against the people—that what little love for his people that was perhaps left in his heart might prevent him from giving the order to shoot into the millions of people who were demonstrating.

It makes a great difference, in a revolutionary process where people are highly emotional, whether you promote hatred and revenge or help the people stand firmly for justice without becoming like the oppressor. You want to love your enemy, to liberate rather than destroy him.

Radio Veritas, the Catholic station, helped tremendously in this task. It coordinated the whole resistance, around the clock, with news of the events as they happened. Day and night, they read passages from Martin Luther King, the Sermon on the Mount, Gandhi, and so forth—asking the people to follow those examples. Radio Veritas also encouraged the soldiers to remember their vow of loyalty to the nation, and not to one person. They kept urging the troops, "Refuse to shoot at the people, on whose side you should stand. Refuse unjust orders."

To do all this in a situation where the dictatorship was still powerful took more than human courage. It was marvelous to see the atmosphere in which it all took place, where prayer and revolution had become one. The revolutionary effort was really a revolution of the strength of truth and love. This is why, in the midst of it all, people were able to sing and dance. They knew they had a strength within them that was stronger than their own little human strength, that the power of love and truth was carrying them along. Therefore, although they were afraid, they knew at the same time that victory was possible. Because truth is stronger than lying, and love is stronger than the hatred and the repression of the regime, it will win in the end.

Now I should like to say a word about Cory Aquino[1], because it seems like a miracle that this nation was able to unite in so short a time. One factor was certainly the deep suffering the people shared. Their suffering and their faith united them. But I think the pole around whom everything revolved was Cory Aquino. In the eyes of the people, she represented the opposite of all the corruption, oppression, and violence of Marcos. When the Filipino people united around Cory Aquino, I think it was because they felt the authenticity of this woman.

In the end, there were only two pillars of the regime left. One was the United States, which gave its support to the Marcos government until the very last moment. And one was the army. While we were there last year, with Cory Aquino, Cardinal Sin, and the others, a number of scenarios of possible conflicts that might evolve in the struggle were developed. The scenario everybody feared the most was that the army would split. We knew that if the army split, a great deal of blood would be shed. We had to ask ourselves what could be done if this should happen. That was, in fact, the scenario that evolved. When the reform movement of the army separated from Marcos, he gave the order to his armed forces to crush the dissidents. As planned, Radio Veritas immediately called on the people to fill up the streets, to stand in front of the tanks, to speak to the soldiers. Eventually there were several hundred thousand people who spent a whole weekend in the road, blocking the tanks so that they could not move against the dissident groups. They spoke to the soldiers, gave them flowers, hugged them, and said, "You belong to the people; come back to those to whom you really belong."

While it was very important for the people to experience the strength of the poor and the power of love and truth to overcome evil, we all know it is only the first step. What is before the Filipino people now is at least as difficult, if not more difficult, than what has gone before. It will require perseverance. And it will need the continued conversion of those who still adhere to the old regime, who have important places in the provinces; to dismantle the private armies of the landlords; to carry out land reform so that the mass of the people can live in dignity; to negotiate with the Muslim minority; to negotiate with the NPA, so that perhaps they will be willing to put down their arms and become one of the democratic parties in the country; to rebuild the economy.

It is important that we do not forget Cory Aquino and those who support her, and our prayers accompany her. We must also encourage our own governments to give economic and moral support to this new government. Not the kind of economic support that makes the Philippines dependent on others, but economic support that will enable the Philippines to realize its own model of economy and its own model of social reforms.

The nonviolent revolution in the Philippines comes to us as a great gift. It has given hope to countries like Chile, South Korea, and others where there are still dictatorships. Perhaps the peace movement, where we have experienced a little bit of what the strength of God in the poor can mean, can also receive this gift, if we really believe in it and if we act accordingly.

NOTE

1. President Corazon Aquino died on August 1, 2009 after the writing of this article.

CHAPTER 11

CATHOLIC SOCIAL TEACHING: INTEGRATING THE VIRTUE OF NONVIOLENT PEACEMAKING

Eli Sasaran McCarthy

Much of the resistance to the possibility of a robust, lasting peace today comes from people who think that claims of nonviolence and peace are "moral," by which they mean rule-based rather than pragmatic.[1] In contrast, those who work diligently for peace are coming by and large from an entirely different philosophical framework, namely, that peace is a worthwhile endeavor and a potentially achievable political arrangement like any other, and the claims of nonviolence are entirely scientific, that is, practical (as Gandhi always insisted, apparently without much success in some quarters). In this chapter I will examine a particular and potentially influential arena in which this argument is shifting toward integrating the "moral" and pragmatic through virtue ethics, namely, Catholic social teaching.

Catholic social teaching (CST) is both a tradition of religious discourse and of translating such discourse into arguments for policy. Contemporary CST stands in a tradition of ethical discourse that has been moving toward integrating human rights and virtue. However, CST still maintains the tendency toward rule-based assessments of nonviolent peacemaking.[2] This tendency gets expressed in a rights-based approach to confronting conflicts, especially acute conflicts, and this approach offers some contributions but also some significant limits in correctly assessing nonviolent peace making.

I maintain that CST ought to employ a virtue-based assessment of non-violent peacemaking supplemented by aspects of human rights theory.[3] This move would yield a more adequate way of understanding and describing nonviolence in CST documents and more readily bring to light as well as sustain us in a set of core practices.

CATHOLIC SOCIAL TEACHING ON NONVIOLENCE

CST's rule-based assessment of nonviolent peacemaking often truncates the imagination of nonviolent practices, both for daily life and public policy, and gives inadequate attention to forming the persons and groups interpreting and applying the rules.[4] Further, CST primarily measures the success of nonviolent peacemaking practices by their protection of human rights, that is, a set of rules. CST tends to argue that nonviolence is often unable to protect and promote certain human rights, such as the right to self-defense or the duty to defend the innocent. In turn, CST has held that nonviolent peacemaking was only or primarily for individuals. Thus, this rights-based ethic also reinforced an emphasis on just war theory and more recently on humanitarian intervention, more than nonviolent peacemaking practices, especially those that concern government or state actors. It is at least partly for this reason, I believe, that U.S. Catholic leadership often failed to adequately challenge U.S. political and military leadership on the use of war and preparation for war, for example, the atomic bomb in World War II. Scholars have pointed out other significant limits of a human rights-based approach.[5]

However, a gradual recognition of the importance of virtue has been increasing in CST, especially since Vatican II, but also more clearly since the U.S. bishops' 1993 document *The Harvest of Justice Is Sown in Peace.*[6] The combination of drawing more readily on the Bible, especially the Christian Scriptures, with its clearer resonance to virtue ethics, and the extending of the call to holiness to all persons has contributed to positions in CST that have increasingly questioned the possibility of a just war and increasingly valued the potential of nonviolent peacemaking practices for public policy. The particular practices of nonviolent peacemaking illustrated by Gandhi, Martin Luther King, Jr., and the many successful nonviolent movements of the 1980s, especially the Solidarity movement in Poland, have also contributed to these positions arising in CST.

Pope John Paul II, who was a key contributor to the Solidarity labor movement in Poland and the largely nonviolent movements that toppled communism in Eastern Europe, taught that peace is the fruit of solidarity, which he also described as a key virtue.[7] He increasingly taught the priority of nonviolence and the need to end war, which Christianson argues was summarized in his statement about "violence, which under the illusion of fighting evil, only makes it worse."[8] The Pope had even argued that "violence is evil."[9] He exhorted persons not to follow leaders who

> train you in the way of inflicting death . . . Give yourself to the service of life, not the work of death. Do not think that courage and strength are proved by killing and destruction. True courage lies in working for peace . . . Violence is the enemy of justice. Only peace can lead the way to true justice.[10]

In the 1983 *Challenge of Peace*, the U.S. bishops offer some reflections on the value of nonviolent means of conflict resolution. Although a virtue-based ethic is not predominant in their document, the bishops acknowledge that some Christians since the earliest days have "committed themselves to a nonviolent lifestyle."[11] They note that:

> the objective is not only to avoid causing harm or injury to another creature, but, more positively, to seek the good of the other. Blunting the aggression of an adversary or oppressor would not be enough. The goal is winning the other over, *making the adversary a friend* [emphasis added].[12]

It is an emphasis consistent with viewing nonviolent peacemaking as a virtue.

In *Harvest of Justice* the U.S. bishops orient the document by discussing the theology, spirituality, and ethics of peacemaking.[13] The bishops argue that for Jesus's gift of peace to transform our world, it also requires "peaceable virtues, a practical vision for a peaceful world and an ethics to guide peacemakers in times of conflict."[14] The list of virtues includes:

> *faith and hope* to strengthen our spirits by placing our trust in God, rather than in ourselves; *courage and compassion* that move us to action; *humility and kindness* so that we can put the needs and interests of others ahead of our own; *patience and perseverance* to endure the long struggle for justice; and *civility and charity* so that we can treat others with respect and love.[15]

The ethics to guide peacemakers in terms of conflict consists of the increasing importance of nonviolent peacemaking and the increasing questions about just war theory.[16] On nonviolent peacemaking and public policy, they argue,

> Although nonviolence has often been regarded as simply a personal option or vocation, recent history suggests that in some circumstances

it can be an effective public undertaking as well . . . One must ask . . . whether it also should have a place in the public order with the tradition of justified and limited war . . . Nonviolent strategies need greater attention in international affairs.[17]

In the midst of the bishops' increasing questioning of just war theory, they consider the importance of character and a properly formed conscience:

> Moral reflection on the use of force calls for a spirit of moderation rare in contemporary political culture. The increasing violence of our society, its growing insensitivity to the sacredness of life and the glorification of the technology of destruction in popular culture could inevitably impair our society's ability to apply just-war criteria honestly and effectively in time of crisis. In the absence of a commitment of respect for life and a culture of restraint, it will not be easy to apply the just-war tradition . . . given the neglect of peaceable virtues . . . serious questions remain about whether modern war . . . can meet the hard tests set by the just war tradition.[18]

This increasing emphasis on virtue, character, conscience, and vision in CST strengthens CST's position that all persons, not just political leaders, are responsible for the common good. After describing an agenda for peacemaking,[19] the bishops conclude with discourse congenial to virtue, such as conversion and imagination:

> . . . today's call to peacemaking is a call to conversion, to change our hearts, to reject violence, to love our enemies . . . To believe we are condemned . . . only to what has been in the past . . . is to underestimate both our human potential for creative diplomacy and God's action in our midst which can open the way to changes we could barely imagine . . . For peacemakers, hope is the indispensable virtue.[20]

Pope Benedict XVI has also indicated a way of thinking that supports the trajectory of further integrating virtue ethics into CST. He argues that the centrality of love can be commanded because God has first given love.[21] In other words, the central theme of Christian ethics is about a response to a gift, an attraction to a good and more than assent to a command, duty, rule, or right. He attends to the interrelation of key virtues, such as charity.[22] In 2007, Pope Benedict spoke about the Gospel text "love your enemies." He described nonviolence for Christians as

> *not mere tactical behavior* but a person's *way of being*, the attitude of one who is convinced of God's love and power, who is not afraid to confront

evil with the weapons of love and truth alone. Loving the enemy is the nucleus of the "Christian revolution," a revolution *not based on strategies of economic, political or media power* [emphasis added].[23]

When we combine his reflections on love, which prioritizes attraction to the good over command and rule, with his reflection on the centrality of love of enemies and particularly nonviolence as a way of being rather than mere tactic or strategy, he further opens the conceptual space to understand non-violent peacemaking as a virtue, which realizes the good of conciliatory love.

However, the movement toward integrating virtue ethics still has signifi-cant growing edges. I have noted how CST has historically relied primarily on a rules-based and more recently rights-based assessment of nonviolence. Even within the [1983] document, rights language has a significant, if not primary role. The term "virtue" is only used 13 times, while the term "rights" is used over 50 times. In the vision of a peaceful world, the three components are each defined in terms of human rights. The just war tradi-tion is understood in terms of a state's right and duty to defend against aggression as a last resort, and as aiming at the kind of peace that ensures human rights. Humanitarian intervention, such as using lethal force, is per-mitted in exceptional cases as a right and duty. Securing human rights is one of the five components of their agenda for peacemaking. Seriously con-sidering nonviolent alternatives by national leaders is described as a moral obligation, or what Christianson calls a "prima facie public obligation."[24] Yet, in the ethics section, nonviolence is promoted as being an "effective public undertaking" under some circumstances, and thus, "nonviolent strategies" deserve more attention. In this instance, nonviolence gets portrayed primar-ily as a strategy or tactic, precisely in the context of arguing for its increased role in public discourse and policy. Further, in the 2004 compendium, the pri-ority of rights is even more pronounced and there is no mention of "peaceable virtues" or "nonviolence."[25] The relationship between peaceable virtues, non-violence, and human rights needs further clarification and development in CST, particularly for public discourse and policy.

VIRTUE OF NONVIOLENT PEACEMAKING

The scriptural evidence, particularly the witness of Jesus, makes it diffi-cult to argue that the pattern of nonviolent peacemaking or love of friends and enemies would not be *at least* one of the paradigmatic actions that corre-sponds to one of the key Christian virtues, and thus, not merely a utilitarian strategy.[26] However, a Christian virtue entails key features that are also sat-isfied by the portrayal of nonviolent peacemaking in the scriptural witness.

First, a virtue is a habit, disposition, or practice that realizes a specific good or instance of human flourishing. Drawing on Bernard Haring's work, we may say that the Christian virtue of nonviolent peacemaking realizes the good of conciliatory love.[27] This virtue would differ from the Thomistic virtue of charity in that it aims particularly at transforming enemies into friends, and deals with conflict or acute conflict, which calls forth a unique set of paradigmatic practices. Second, Joseph Kotva explains that virtues are a means to and constituent elements of human flourishing, that is, our human end or *telos*.[28] For Christians, Jesus is the way (the means) and the one who ushers in the present and coming-to-completion Reign of God (the *telos*). Thus, Jesus's pervasive and consistent practices of nonviolent peacemaking support the characterization of nonviolent peacemaking as a virtue, which constitutes our *telos*.

Third, William Spohn argues that "each virtue of the Christian moral life is shaped by the story of Jesus and preeminently by its conclusion, the cross and resurrection."[29] The instances of nonviolent peacemaking arise centrally in the narratives about Jesus, and the power of nonviolent peacemaking to realize conciliatory love is ultimately conveyed in the reconciling cross and resurrection. Fourth, a virtue entails the formation and transformation of character, rather than being primarily an external law or rule for us to obey by rote. Jesus's practice of nonviolent peacemaking aimed to disclose the conciliatory character of God and to transform the character of his disciples toward a conciliatory love, especially regarding the outcasts, poor, and enemies.[30]

Fifth, a virtue consists in being a practice rather than being a mere technique or instrument that produces goods tangential to the activity. Spohn explains that practices are primarily "worthwhile and meaningful in themselves; the enhancement and satisfaction they bring comes from doing them well." The primary intent of Christian nonviolent peacemaking entails a *satisfaction* found in expressing our love and gratitude for God's love, rather than primarily as an instrument to gain political power or receive the reward of heaven. As far as nonviolent peacemaking cultivates the transformation of our character, nonviolent peacemaking entails an *enhancement* from the activity itself, which is a constitutive element of a practice. Further, Spohn argues that practices are activities that make up a way of life. Jesus, again often called the "way," offered us a way of life, which entailed central practices such as those of nonviolent peacemaking.

Because the portrayal of nonviolent peacemaking in the scriptural witness satisfies these five key features of a Christian virtue, we ought to consider nonviolent peacemaking a distinct virtue rather than merely subsuming it in the paradigmatic practices of other virtues.

INTEGRATING THE VIRTUE OF NONVIOLENT PEACEMAKING IN CST

A virtue-based assessment of nonviolent peacemaking supplemented by some aspects of human rights offers particular contributions toward developing CST. These contributions consist of both a more adequate way of understanding nonviolence, and a set of practices that arise more clearly and will more likely be sustained.

The shift in understanding consists in assessing nonviolent peacemaking as a virtue, which realizes the specific goods of a conciliatory love that turns enemies into friends, and truth, particularly the truths of our ultimate unity and equal dignity.[31] Recognizing this virtue qualifies key virtues, such as justice, courage, solidarity, and humility, and uplifts a certain set of related virtues to more prominence, such as hospitality, mercy, and empathy. For instance, the virtue of solidarity with its focus on the poor and oppressed would affect our analysis of preparing and directly engaging in war, our analysis of those who exercise lethal force by emphasizing the question "what kind of persons are they becoming," and our care for the environment.[32] The virtue of justice would orient us to restorative more than retributive justice.[33] The virtue of courage that prioritizes endurance over attack would now include the practice of suffering out of reverence for the dignity of others (and self) by risking, perhaps even giving, one's life without the protection of violent force.

Further, particular aspects of human rights can supplement this virtue-based assessment, which presently has less moral traction in public discourse. The contributions of human rights theory in CST already include a strong presumption against war and a fuller range of human rights that includes socio-economic and political-civil rights.[34] These aspects enhance the priority of nonviolence, the challenge to the exorbitant and disproportionate U.S. military spending and selling, and even Gandhi's insight about the constructive program in nonviolence.

To take the approach outlined would set the stage for naming and elaborating a set of paradigmatic practices that correspond to the virtue of nonviolent peacemaking and its related set of virtues. I now turn to this set of practices as the second core contribution of a virtue-based assessment of nonviolent peacemaking for CST.

Seven paradigmatic practices would include: (1) celebrating the nonviolent Eucharist, with secondary components of prayer, meditation, and fasting; (2) training and education in nonviolent peacemaking, with the secondary component of forming nonviolent peacemaking communities; (3) attention to religious or spiritual factors, especially in public discourse, and learning about religion, particularly in the form of intra-religious or inter-religious dialogue; (4) a constructive program with its particular focus on the poor and marginalized; (5) conflict transformation and restorative justice, particularly in the form of Truth and Reconciliation Commissions; (6) third-party nonviolent intervention both in the form of international implementation and local peace teams; and (7) civilian-based defense.

The following examples are a further elaboration. Pope Benedict recognized the central role of the Eucharistic practice in drawing us into the "revolution" of nonviolent love.[35] Fr. Cantalamessa, the Preacher to the Papal Household in 2005, affirmed the growing attention to the Eucharist as the sacrament of nonviolence and God's absolute no to violence.[36] Rev. Emmanuel McCarthy argues that the words "suffered and died" in the Eucharistic prayer are theologically correct, but pastorally insufficient. He suggests the Eucharistic prayer include something like the following:

> On the night before He went forth to His eternally memorable and life-giving death, rejecting violence, loving His enemies, praying for His persecutors, He bestowed upon His disciples the gift of a New Commandment: "Love one another. As I have loved you so you also should love one another."
>
> . . . But, we remember also that he endured this humiliation with a love free of retaliation, revenge, and retribution . . . we recall also that He died loving enemies, praying for persecutors, forgiving, and being superabundantly merciful to those for whom [retributive] justice would have demanded [retributive] justice.[37]

This practice of connecting the Eucharistic prayer with nonviolent peacemaking can be extended to the practice of prayer in general, but also to the practice of meditation. The virtue of nonviolent peacemaking not only foregrounds the significance of these practices, but also informs how and to what end(s) they should be practiced. For instance, prayer and meditation can function to re-connect us with the source of our lives and with the interconnectedness of all being. These practices often generate solidarity and patience, as well as a capacity to locate and focus on the deeper issues, desires, wounds, and needs. When situations of conflict become particularly trying and long-lasting, these practices nourish our energy and sustain us for the long haul.

Fasting has often accompanied prayer or meditation. Fasting can function as a way of discernment, along with cultivating a sense of solidarity with the poor, hungry, and vulnerable. Further, Gandhi illustrated how fasting can function to stir the hearts, especially of loved ones to transform their ways from violence toward nonviolent peacemaking. Policy makers who engaged in prayer, meditation, or fasting informed by the recognition and appreciation of the virtue of nonviolent peacemaking would likely become the kinds of people who can better see, imagine, and commit to policies oriented to nonviolent peacemaking.

The attention to formation that a virtue-based assessment offers raises a second core practice: training and education in nonviolent peacemaking. The U.S. bishops have spoken generally about how our nation needs more research, education, and training in nonviolent means of resisting injustice. But the specifics can be clarified and the implementation can be enhanced by a virtue-based assessment.

Scott Appleby makes the argument that we need stronger religious education in nonviolent peace building, and that spiritual-moral formation is the key internal condition for moving beyond violence.[38] John Paul Lederach suggests an emphasis on the moral imagination as a way to transcend violence, which resonates well with a virtue-based assessment of nonviolent peacemaking.[39] Connecting the moral imagination to peace building, he argues that such education should provide early and continual space for exploring questions of meaning and the journey such as: Who are we? What are we doing? Where are we going? What is our purpose?—all questions that get further emphasis with a virtue-based assessment.[40]

Other examples of training and educating for nonviolent peacemaking include the development of peace studies programs and service-learning opportunities. A virtue-based assessment would uplift this need for more emphasis in our education on nonviolent peacemaking, and suggest relevant courses toward developing "deep nonviolence," such as meditation or contemplation, and nonviolent communication.[41] Other educational projects could include the movement to establish a Peace Academy,[42] analogous to the academies for the armed forces, a substantial increase in resources for the U.S. Institute of Peace, and perhaps the realization of a U.S. Department of Peace.

Closely related to the practice of training and education is the formation of communities committed to the virtue of nonviolent peacemaking. These communities provide a fertile and sustaining space to encounter nonviolent peacemaking, to grow in the virtue of nonviolent peacemaking and its related virtues, and to experiment with or imagine practices of nonviolent peacemaking. The Community of the Ark, the Bruderhof, and the Catholic Worker communities are good examples.[43] Catholic dioceses and even public policy makers at various levels could also set up pilot programs or experiment with the formation of nonviolent communities in the hope of drawing wisdom and practices eventually for the larger societies.

A third core practice arising more clearly in a virtue-based assessment of nonviolent peacemaking is attention to (1) religious or spiritual factors, especially for public discourse, and to (2) learning about religion(s), particularly in the form of intra-religious or inter-religious dialogue. A virtue-based approach emphasizes conceptions of the good life, which persons in the major religious traditions have been reflecting on and enacting for hundreds of years.

Appleby and Douglas Johnston have both elaborated on numerous examples of how the religious factor and religious actors can become a richer resource for peacemaking and U.S. statecraft.[44] The U.S. government has recently developed a Civilian Response Corps to provide civilian experts for deployment to regions at the risk of, in, or transitioning from conflict.[45] However, although they draw on various fields of expertise for this Corps, they do not but should include expertise in religion and religious peacemaking.

A fourth core practice is what Gandhi called constructive program or social uplift of one's own community. Martha Nussbaum's central capabilities theory, corrected by Lisa Cahill, represents a policy framework for actualizing the focus on the poor and marginalized found in the constructive program. The constructive program would also enhance our commitment to the Millennium Development Goals,[46] particularly since most of the goals are still not on target.[47] The Human Development Index, grounded in capabilities theory, would also receive more prominence in a virtue-based assessment, particularly compared to a Gross Domestic Product or economic development.[48] Further, since a constructive program would also aim to construct and sustain peaceful societies, we would take more seriously the policy implications of the Global Peace Index, which ranks the United States 83 out of 140 countries.[49] Finally, the fair trade movement would find stronger support with its emphasis on the poor and easily exploited.

A constructive program helps our understanding that nonviolence is in fact primarily a constructive endeavor. Stassen's cohort that developed the 10 practices of just peacemaking theory (JPT) is an example focusing attention on the practices that make for peace, rather than simply on avoiding violence—or indeed justifying war.[50] JPT resonates well with a virtue-based approach.

A fifth core practice is conflict transformation, particularly in the form of Truth and Reconciliation Commissions. By conflict transformation I follow Lederach, who describes it as envisioning and responding to "the ebb and flow of social conflict as life-giving opportunities for creating constructive change processes that reduce violence, increase justice in direct interaction and social structures, and respond to real-life problems in human relationships."[51] Conflict is not held to be problematic, something merely to manage or resolve, but rather as a creative opportunity for personal, relational, structural, and cultural growth or transformation.[52] Thus, conflict transformation arises more clearly in a virtue-based approach, which is personal, relational, and growth-oriented.

The accent on reconciliation in conflict transformation resonates well with Pope John Paul's addition of forgiveness to what Christianson calls the convoy concept of peace in CST,[53] and with the John Paul's message of "no justice without forgiveness."[54] Christianson argues, "Catholic Social Theory needs a theory of conflict and principles of conflict transformation and reconciliation."[55] Kenneth Himes acknowledges the underdevelopment in CST of alternative ways to achieve peace and particularly strategies for conflict resolution,[56] calling for CST to give more attention to the themes of reconciliation, truth-telling, restorative justice, and forgiveness, as well as to develop an ethic for resolving conflict that goes beyond the strategy of dialogue. Yet, when Himes alludes to developing an ethic for resolving conflict, he primarily points to more rules in the form of *just post bellum* norms, rather than a virtue-based ethic with the virtue of nonviolent peacemaking. A virtue-based ethic would more adequately address the need to cultivate the character, which can imagine ways to achieve peace and respond to conflict, particularly enhancing the conflict transformation themes he mentions and sustaining the persons in their practice. O'Neill and Philpott have contributed to a deeper integration of virtue regarding the notion of reconciliation.[57]

Conflict transformation and particularly Truth and Reconciliation commissions (TRCs) could greatly enhance contemporary policy decisions. For instance, policy leaders even in the peace-building field sent a proposal to the new U.S. administration in late December 2008 but left out conflict transformation and reconciliation because they are not "on the radar for many policy thinkers."[58] A virtue-based assessment of nonviolent peacemaking would contribute to this disconnect by clarifying the meaning and value of conflict transformation in general, and TRCs in particular. These commissions could enhance U.S. policies regarding Iraq and Afghanistan, among other issues,[59] as well as UN policy for example as at least a complement to the International Criminal Court, if not an eventual substitute.

A sixth core practice is third-party nonviolent intervention (TPNI), or as it is now called "unarmed civilian peacekeeping (UCPS)." This practice entails an outside party intervening in a conflict as a nonpartisan, with compassion for all parties, without violence, with the aim of reducing violence and creating a space for reconciliation and peace building. The virtue-based assessment of nonviolent peacemaking cultivates the kinds of persons who can imagine, prepare for, and enact UCP, as well as highlight the themes of compassion for all, aiming toward reconciliation and empowering all persons, including civilians. The Nonviolent Peace Force, which arose from reflecting on Gandhi's idea of *shanti sena* (peace army), is an attempt to professionalize UCP and take it to global scale.[60] Other examples include Christian Peacemaker teams, the Michigan Peace Team, and the recently formed Muslim Peacemaker teams in Iraq.[61]

The further development of UCP could contribute to CST and present public discourse and policies in the following ways. First, the UN peacekeeping force is still based on military operations, although it has been expanding its repertoire.[62] UCP povides an alternative form of peacekeeping, which would change the debate on UN peacekeeping, such as the use of private military contractors.[63] It could potentially shift the ground of UN peacekeeping from military operations to civilian operations; shift the training from military virtues to the virtue of nonviolent peacemaking and its related set of virtues; offer the specific practices of nonviolent modeling and interposition; and more adequately integrate the aim of reconciliation rather than primarily keeping parties apart.

Second, although the U.S. government has recently developed a Civilian Response Corps (CRC), the implementation of the originating directive has faced bureaucratic roadblocks and taken a backseat to the wars in Iraq and Afghanistan.[64] Further, the emphasis of the CRC is on mere stabilization with concern for U.S. national security interests.[65] A virtue-based approach to nonviolent peacemaking could enhance the policy of developing and implementing a CRC because it (1) raises the value of civilian participation and intervention, (2) clarifies UCP as well as the practice of conflict transformation and the particular form of TRCs, and (3) indicates that the CRC should also include experts in UCP.

Third, UCP could offer some insights to the just policing model or to policing in general. One of these insights is the creation of local peace teams as a supplement to and perhaps eventually a substitute for armed police. Both the Michigan Peace Team and the success of street outreach workers, such as the Street Outreach Team in Oakland, California, which entails training and deploying unarmed, nonpolice, street-smart persons to patrol high-violence areas, are movements in this direction.[66]

A seventh core practice that becomes clearer in a virtue-based and human rights approach is civilian-based defense (CBD). This practice entails using nonviolent resistance or force to defend against military invasion, occupation, or coups d'état. The resistors do not physically prevent invading troops from entering their territory. Everyone participates in the resistance, taking responsibility for their defense rather than delegating it to an elite group.[67] The power of this practice is in part grounded in the notions that (1) one who refuses to submit cannot be ruled, and (2) the distinction between resolutely acknowledging the humanity of persons, while resisting their unjust agenda.[68]

A virtue-based assessment is particularly congenial to everyone's personal growth, such as the participation and taking fuller responsibility, which CBD emphasizes. Further, a virtue-based assessment would be especially helpful in drawing our attention to developing the courage and solidarity to engage this practice, the sustenance to maintain it in the face of ongoing repression, the imagination to find ways to noncooperate, and the capacity to discriminate between the shared dignity of persons and their agenda. The recognition of shared dignity or humanity in CBD also entails relating to the other as potential friends, that is, with the conciliatory love that the virtue of nonviolent peacemaking enacts and aims toward.

Taking different forms, CBD has been tried a number of times in the past century and has recently been incorporated into the defense planning of some governments.[69] Drawing on Adam Roberts's four stages toward CBD policy,[70] the UN, the United States, and the Catholic Church, particularly Catholic schools, could all develop and emphasize policy on funding research and investigation into CBD (stage 1), as well as general public education in CBD with concentrated training and organizational preparations (stage 2).[71] If the United States would move toward a CBD policy, then this could help correct our excessive funding for military research and free up research funds for addressing root causes of violence, other social injustices, pollution, and human development.[72] Further, if Catholic schools of higher education were to give priority to the virtue of nonviolent peacemaking and similarly to prioritize research into corresponding practices like CBD, Reserve Officers' Training Corps (ROTC) programs on campus would require serious reconstruction of their curriculum, or indeed should be given a diminished authority on campus, if not completely discontinued.

In sum, I have argued that a virtue-based assessment of nonviolent peacemaking supplemented by aspects of human rights contributes to CST by (1) offering a more adequate understanding than a rules-based approach, and (2) offering seven core practices that arise more clearly and more frequently in our imagination, and that will more likely be sustained. These practices further the integration of virtue and rights, especially in CST, but also contribute to public discourse and policy.

NOTES

1. Peace primarily as a rule against war.
2. Cahill, 1994.

3. I use "peacemaking" broadly to include peacekeeping, peacemaking, and peace building.

4. Further limits articulated in McCarthy, 2009.

5. See Nussbaum, 2001.

6. U.S. Catholic Bishops, 1993.

7. Pope John Paul II, 1992.

8. Pope John Paul II, 1991.

9. Pope John Paul II, 2002.

10. Ibid.

11. U.S. Catholic Bishops, 1992.

12. Ibid.

13. U.S. Catholic Bishops, 1993.

14. Ibid.

15. Ibid.

16. Ibid.

17. Ibid.

18. Ibid.

19. Ibid.

20. Ibid.

21. Pope Benedict, 2005.

22. Ibid.

23. Pope Benedict, Vatican City, 2007.

24. Christianson, 2008.

25. Pontifical Council for Justice and Peace, 2004. It does refer to peace as the fruit of justice and love, which are often described as virtues in the broader document. Rather than "nonviolence," the compendium acknowledges the value of the "witness of unarmed prophets" but gives it little explication except to condition it on the defense of human rights (C.11, par. 494, 496).

26. Stassen and Gushee, 2003.

27. Haring, 1997.

28. Kotva, 1996.

29. Spohn, 2003.

30. Consider the Good Samaritan and the transforming initiatives noted by Stassen and Gushee, 2003.

31. Gandhi contributes the object of truth and its particular aspects.

32. Attention to who soldiers are becoming is particularly significant in light of the levels of PTSD, suicide, murder, abuse of women and children, and homelessness. See "Mental Illness Common among Returning U.S. Soldiers," 2007.

33. For more on the difference between the virtue of justice and the virtue of nonviolent peacemaking, see McCarthy, 2009.

34. For more on the integral relationship between virtue and human rights see King, 1986 and O'Neill, 2008.

35. Pope Benedict, 2005.

36. Fr. Cantalamessa.

37. McCarthy, 1992.

38. Appleby, 2000.

39. Lederach, 2005.

40. Ibid.

41. Rosenberg, 2003.

42. National Peace Academy supports, advances, and nurtures cultures of peace by conducting research and facilitating learning toward the development of peace systems–local to global–and the development of the whole spectrum, of the peace builder–inner and outer, personal and professional. In all its operations, internal and external, the National Peace Academy strives to embody and reflect the principles and processes of peace.

43. Founder: Lanza Del Vasto. See Shephard, 1990.

44. See Appleby, 2000. He argues this would inculcate forgiveness and compassion as political virtues and provide a stronger concept of reconciliation beyond the political realm. See Johnson and Sampson, 1994.

45. Office of the Coordinator for Reconstruction and Stabilization.

46. UN Millennium Development Goals, 2008.

47. Ibid.

48. United Nations (UNDP) 2010.

49. Vision of Humanity, 2010.

50. Stassen, 2008.

51. Lederach, 2003.

52. Lederach, 2007.

53. Christianson, 2008.

54. Pope John Paul II, 2002.

55. Christianson, 2008.

56. Himes, 2008.

57. O'neill, 2008.

58. Schirch, 2008.

59. TRCs have also been proposed in the United States. for issues like torture, racism and structural injustice, sexism and patriarchy, poverty and U.S. foreign policy in Central America.

60. Nonviolent Peace Force, 2002.

61. Muslim Peace Teams, 2005.

62. UN Department of Peacekeeping Operations.

63. Isenberg, 2008.

64. Bensahel et al., 2009.

65. Office of the Coordinator for Reconstruction and Stabilization.

66. Grant, 2004.

67. Nagler, 2004: 252–253.

68. Ibid.

69. Sharp, 2005; Lakey, 2010.

70. Roberts, 1967.

71. U.S. Catholic Bishops, 1983.

72. Zahn, 1996.

CHAPTER 12

ALTERNATIVES TO WAR AND VIOLENCE: AN ISLAMIC PERSPECTIVE

Mohammed Abu-Nimer and Jamal A. Badawi

Many Muslim and non-Muslim scholars and writers have emphasized the peaceful nature and message of Islam. They have identified values and principles such as unity, supreme love of the creator, mercy, subjection of passion, accountability for all actions, relying on the innumerable verses in the Qur'an commanding believers to be righteous and above passion in their dealings with their fellow beings. Love, kindness, affection, forgiveness, and mercy are recommended as virtues of the true faithful.[1] Other Islamic values are cited as directly connected to peace building and development, such as *Adl* (justice); *Ihsan* (benevolence); *Rahmah*[2] (compassion); and *Hikmah* (wisdom). *Amal, yakeen* and *muhabat* (service, faith, and love) are another set of Islamic values identified by Abdul Ghaffar Khan,[3] making the connection between Islam and peace building more prominent than the stereotypical violent characterization of the religion. In this chapter we categorize values and principles that have a direct relationship and applicability to peace building (here an umbrella term used to capture the various processes of conflict resolution, peacemaking, peacekeeping, and nonviolence resistance). In many cases the categories and their applicability to peace building will be self-evident, but in others the connections will be briefly clarified.

PURSUIT OF SOCIAL JUSTICE

A main call of Islamic religion is to establish a just social reality. Thus, the evaluation of any act or statement should be measured according to whether, how, and when it will accomplish that desired reality. In Islam acting for the cause of God is synonymous with pursuing *Adl*—justice. Islam calls for action whether you are strong or weak. The following Qur'anic verses have strong messages concerning social justice and responsibility. They show that it is the Muslim's duty to work for justice and reject oppression and injustice on interpersonal and structural levels.

> Allah commands justice, the doing of good, and liberality to kith and kin, and he forbids all shameful deeds, and injustice and rebellion (16:90). Allah doth command you to render back your trusts to those to whom they are due; And when ye judge between man and man, that ye judge with justice: verily how excellent is the teaching which he giveth you! (4:58) Ye who believe! Stand out firmly for justice, as witnesses to Allah, even as against yourselves, or your parents, or your kin, whether it be (against) rich or poor: for Allah can best protect both. . . . Follow not the lusts (of your hearts), lest ye swerve, and if ye distort (justice) or decline to do justice, verily Allah is well-acquainted with all that ye do. (4:135) O ye who believe, stand out firmly for God, as witnesses to justice and let not the enmity of others make you swerve from the path of justice. Be just: that is next to righteousness, and fear God. Indeed, God is well acquainted with all that you do. (5:8)

Continuously, the Qur'an reminds Muslims of the value of justice, thus it not only encourages, but divinely orders believers to pursue justice (5:8; 57:25; 16:90; 4:58; 42:15). Justice is an absolute and not relative value. It is a duty to be pursued among the believers and with the enemies.[4] The early Caliphates were known for their strong pursuit of justice, particularly Umar Ibn Khatab who had a distinctive tradition in pursuing it:

> Worship God and associate naught with Him and behave benevolently towards parents, kinsmen, orphans, the needy, the neighbor that is a kinsman, the neighbor that is a stranger, the companion, by the roadside, the wayfarer and those who are under your authority. Surely God loves not the proud and boastful who are niggardly and enjoin other people to be niggardly and conceal that what God has given them of His bounty. (4:36, 37)

The connection of peace building with justice is thus never far from the surface in Islam. Peace is the product of order and justice. One must strive for peace through the pursuit of justice. This is the obligation of the believer as well as the ruler, more than that it is a natural obligation of all humanity.[5]

"God does command you to render back your trust to those whom they are due. And when you judge between people, that you judge with justice. Indeed, how excellent is the teaching that He gives you. For verily God hears and sees all things" (4:58). "God loves those who are Just" (60:8).

Rulers are expected to follow the same message. In his message to Al Ashtar, the governor of Egypt, Ali instructed him:

> O Malik, let it be known to you that you have been appointed to the governorship of Egypt. All of your actions as the Governor will be open to the criticism of the people. You should do good deeds. Keep your passions under control. Your dealings with your subjects should be just and fair. Treat them affectionately and love them. There are two kinds of subjects to be governed, firstly your brethren in Islam, and secondly the minorities whose protection has been guaranteed. Intentionally or unintentionally the people are apt to make mistakes. It will behoove you to excuse them, as you expect that God will forgive your sins. Do not be ashamed if you pardon them. Never find pleasure in punishing them. Do not be short tempered. Never say that you are Governor above them, for it breeds a feeling of inferiority in them. Should you ever take pride in your exalted office then think of the power and grandeur of God, for that is the only means to check your arrogance. Remember that God hates the cruel and the arrogant. Be fair and just, for if you fail in it, you are a tyrant and tyrant is the enemy of God. God hearkens to the weak and the afflicted. Follow the path of moderation in your doings, and try to please your subjects.[6]

Within the pursuit of justice there is a consistent message to resist and correct conditions of injustice through activism and third-party intervention, and through divine intervention. Justice and peace are interconnected and interdependent.[7] In addition, the Prophet has called Muslims to mobilize and be steadfast against injustice, even if the injustice is originated by a Muslim: "O, Ye who believe, be steadfast in service of God's truth and bear witness for justice and let not hatred of a people seduce you so that you deal with them unjustly. Act justly for that is what piety demands." Again, "He who supports a tyrant or oppressor knowing he is a tyrant casts himself outside the pale of Islam."[8]

Peacemakers as well as disputants are expected to pursue justice in the means and ends of their conflict resolution processes.

SOCIAL EMPOWERMENT THROUGH DOING GOOD (*KHAYR* AND *IHSAN*)

As a religion, Islam was spread on the basis of helping and empowering the weak and the underdog, and it continues to be characterized as such a religion. Struggling against oppression (*Zulm*), assisting the poor, and pursuing equality among all persons are core religious values emphasized throughout the Qur'an and Hadith.

One should do good (*Ihsan*—grace, beneficence, kindness) not only to one's parents and relations but also to the orphans, the needy, the helpless, and the neighbor whether he is related to one in any way or not at all (17:24–26). The Prophet himself reinforces this by the saying: "A true Muslim is one who does no mischief to any other Muslims," but the true Mu'min (man of genuine faith who is superior to a formal Muslim in merit) is one who does no mischief to his neighbors and of 'whom they have no fear.'"[9]

The emphasis in Islam is on doing good (*Khayr*) not on power and force (*Quwwat*). Good deeds are associated with *Sirat El Mustaqim* (straight way) and with all the virtue of the Prophet.

> Those who believe (in the Prophet of Islam) and those who are Jews and Christians and the Sabians (that is who belongs to any religious group) who believe in God and the Last Day of Judgment) and whose deeds are good, shall have their reward with their Lord. On them there shall be no fear nor shall they grieve. (2:62)

To ensure social justice (distributive, administrative, or retributive) and empowerment, Islam has many teachings, rules, and institutes. Social and economic justice is so important in Islam that they are even equated with worshiping God.[10] The value of *Zakah* (almsgiving) and *Sadaqah* (voluntary charity) relate to individual and collective responsibility. These obligatory and voluntary duties are intended for the poor; there are also stipulations of fixed shares of inheritance for women, children, and a host of regulations regarding the just treatment of debtors, widows, orphans (90:13–16), and slaves (24:33).[11] *Zakah* and *Sadaqah* (charity) are central virtues for doing good in life and helping others particularly the needy people. *Zakah* is one of the five main pillars of Islam and it is aimed at ensuring distributive social justice and empowerment of the weak. Charity is a good deed that every Muslim has to carry out within his or her limits. Charity is prescribed in at least 25 Qur'anic verses, and all encourage Muslims to take more responsibility for the unjust systems that exist in their communities.

> It is not righteousness that ye turn your faces towards east or west; but it is righteousness to believe in Allah and the last day, and the book, and the messengers; to spend your substance, out of love for him, for your kin, for orphans, for the needy, for wayfarer, for those who ask, for the ransom of slaves; to be steadfast in prayer, and practice charity, to fulfill

the contract that ye have made, and to be firm and patient in pain (or suffering) and adversity. (2:177)

People are responsible and have obligations to those who are underprivileged in their community. Islam repeatedly stresses such principles: "Did He not find thee an orphan and provided for thee shelter (and care). And He found thee wondering and gave thee guidance and He found thee in need and made thee independent [in the financial sense]" (93:7–9).

The Prophet's compassion that he brought in his treatment of the underprivileged who suffered from personal misfortune or from social and economic injustices, was not the result of the Qur'anic teaching only, but was born from his own experience.[12] The Qur'an supported such compassion: "Therefore treat not the orphan with harshness, nor repulse the petitioner (unheard)" (93:9–10). Caring and helping those underprivileged constitute a central mechanism for social empowerment and for maintaining a sense of community. Abolishing slavery was a clear example of the ethical standpoints and principles that guided Muslims in dealing with oppression, poverty, and human suffering.

On the interpersonal level, preserving good relationships with others is an expectation that a Muslim must fulfill: "No Muslim can become a *Mu'min* (genuine believer) unless he likes for all others (not only Muslims) what he likes for him and he makes friends with them for God's sake."[13] "God Commands you to treat (everyone) justly, generously and with kindness." (16:90). "Be good and kind to others even as God is to you" (28:77).

Doing good extends beyond the interpersonal to a group or community level. A nation cannot survive according to Islam without making fair and adequate arrangements for the sustenance and welfare of all the poor, underprivileged, and destitute members of the community. The ultimate goal would be to create a situation under which they can eliminate their suffering and poverty.

In short, for Muslims, a conflict resolution process is expected to result in justice and good deeds that lead to empowerment in any interaction or behavior with other Muslims and non-Muslims.

PROMOTE AND PRESERVE THE UNIVERSALITY OF ALL HUMAN DIGNITY

Islam brings a firm and clear message through the Qur'an and Hadith of the universal man. This is conveyed through the belief in equal origin, calls for equal rights, treatment, and solidarity among all people. Man (and woman) is an integral part of an ocean of humanity. Man is the most dignified and exalted of all creatures. He has the potential to learn and know, the ability to decide which actions to take, and to bear the consequences of his actions. Man is God's vice-regent on earth. The Qur'an states: "when your Lord said to the angels verily I am going to appoint a vice-regent (*Khalifa*) in Earth" (17:70). Thus protecting human life and respecting human dignity is sacred in Islam. The honor that God bestowed on humans is also stressed: "We have honored the sons of Adam; provided them with transport on land and sea; given them for sustenance things good and pure; and conferred on them special favors, above a great part of Our Creation" (17:70).

Therefore, the work, worship, and life of a person should be aimed preserving, protecting, and achieving human pride and dignity as a main principle and value in Islam. Islamic scholars have cited several Qur'anic verses to establish the importance of human dignity and pride:

> We have indeed created man in the best of moulds (95:4). It is We Who created you and gave you shape; then We bade the angels bow down to Adam, and they bowed down; not so ibl'is; he refused to be of those who bow down (7:11). Behold, thy Lord said to the angels: "I will create a vice-regent on earth." They said: "wilt thou place therein one who will make mischief therein and shed blood Whilst we do celebrate Thy praises and glorify Thy holy (name)." He said: "I know What ye know not" (2:30).

It is considered a good deed to intervene or act to protect the basic dignity and pride of the person, because the creation of man by God makes him a creature who deserves respect and protection: "In Islam every person has the human sacredness and is under a protection and sacrosanct until he himself violates his sanctuary. He removes with his own hands such protection blanket by committing a crime that removes part of his immunity. With this dignity, Islam protect its enemies, as well as its children and elders. This dignity which God blessed humanity with each member is the base for all human relationship."[14]

Elder Muslim mediators and arbitrators have often utilized social and cultural techniques to preserve the human dignity of the victim as well as the offender (such mechanisms are used in conducting *Sulha*—a traditional ritual based on public ceremony to restore honor and dignity of the victims). In fact, in many cases successful resolution of a conflict depends on the capacity of these traditional mediators to restore the victims' social and cultural dignity in public (though sometimes by bringing public shame on the offender's family).

Thus participating and supporting international organizations that act globally to protect universal human rights and advocate for the basic rights and dignity of all humankind is an integral part of Islamic values and faith.

PROMOTING EQUALITY AND RESISTING DISCRIMINATION AND PREJUDICE

Islamic teaching goes beyond reaching a settlement in a specific dispute; it aspires to achieve one human family. Equality among the members of this family is promoted and acknowledged as a basic value, based on the common human origin of all people:

> O mankind! We created you from a single (pair) of a male and female, and made you into nations and tribes, that ye may know each other (not that ye may despise each other). Verily the most honored of you in the sight of Allah is (he who is) the most righteous of you. And Allah has full knowledge and is well-acquainted (with all things). (49:13)

In Islam, there is no privilege granted based on race, ethnicity, or tribal association. The only two criteria to be deployed are the faith (*Iman*) and good deed (*aml-I-salih*). There is no difference whatever between people except in their devotion to Allah, since God is the common creator of all.

A saying of the Prophet acknowledges the origin and universal equality among humans: "You are all from Adam and Adam is made of dust." Ibn Taymiya (a well-known Muslim scholar, 1263–1328) argued in these terms: "The desire to be above other people is injustice because all people are of the same species. A man's desire to put himself higher and reduce the others lower is unjust."[15] Islam underscores that all people are the children of Adam and Eve, and such sayings are often cited by traditional mediators and arbitrators as a recommendation or a call for brotherhood and harmony.

In a conflict resolution or other nonviolent processes, this principle of equality requires the third party to treat its disputants with equal measures throughout the entire process of intervention. Mediators or arbitrators, regardless of their affiliation, are obliged to promote equal rights and treatment of all persons.

PRESERVE THE SACREDNESS OF HUMAN LIFE

Peace building and development approaches assume that human life must be saved and protected, and that resources should always be utilized to preserve life and prevent violence. The Qur'an clearly suggests the sacredness of human life, "And if any one saved a life, It would be as if he saved the life of the whole people" (5:32). "And do not take a life which Allah has forbidden save in the course of justice. This he enjoins on you so that you may understand" (6:15). Each person's life is an integral part of the great cosmic purpose. Consequently, what the individual does matters profoundly. "Lord, Thou hast not created all this in vain!"[16]

Thus, destroying and wasting resources that serve human life is prohibited. Even when Muslims in the early period launched an armed conflict, their rulers instructed them to avoid destruction and restrict their wars. Abu Bakr, the first Caliph, made this well-known speech when he dispatched his army on an expedition to the Syrian borders:

> Stop, O people, that I may give you ten rules for your guidance in the battlefield. Do not commit treachery or deviate from the right path. You must not mutilate dead bodies. Neither kill a child, nor a woman or an aged man. Bring no harm to the trees, nor burn them with fire, especially those which are fruitful. Slay not any of the enemy's flock, save for your food. You are likely to pass by people who have devoted their lives to monastic services, leave them alone.[17]

Based on the above principle, nonviolence intervention in resolving conflicts becomes a primary guide for Muslims to resolve their conflicts. It also limits the type and nature of force that can be used in fighting the other. The strict conditions on how to treat innocent people are beyond any doubt prohibiting excessive force and violence as a means to resolve any conflict. According to these Islamic values, suicide bombing, beheadings, promotion of nuclear weapons and mass destruction is prohibited and illegitimate. Muslims are instructed to oppose these measures and avoid them when dealing with their enemies or other Muslims.

THE QUEST FOR PEACE

Peace in Islam is a state of physical, mental, spiritual, and social harmony. Living at peace with God through submission, and living at peace with fellow beings by avoiding mischief on earth is real Islam. Islam obligates its believers to seek peace in all life domains. The ultimate purpose is to live in a peaceful as well as a just social reality. However, it should be noted that there are certain conditions in which, for defensive purposes, Muslims are allowed to use limited force: "There are circumstances in which Islam contemplates the possibility of war—for instance, to avert worse disasters like the denial of freedom to human conscience—but the essential thing in life is peace. It is towards the achievement of peace that all human efforts must be sincerely diverted."[18] Peace is viewed as an outcome that can be achieved only after the full submission to the will of God. Thus, peace has internal, personal, as well as social applications, and God is the source and sustainer of such peace. Accordingly, the best way to ensure peace is by total submission to God's will and to Islam.[19]

Shunning violence and aggression in all its forms has been another primary focus of Islamic values and tradition. Many Qur'anic verses stress this principle, among them is: "Whenever they kindle the fire of war, God extinguishes it. They strive to create disorder on earth and God loves not those who create disorder" (5:64). Tolerance, kindness to other people, and dealing with all people in such manner with no exception is also emphasized in these verses: "God commands you to treat (everyone) justly, generously and with kindness" (16:90); "Repel evil (not with evil) but something that is better (*Ahsan*)—that is, with forgiveness and amnesty."

In supporting this value in Islam, Jawdat Said (1997) provided a famous Hadith, widely quoted in Islamic literature and often seen hung as a calligraphic adornment in the homes of people: "whenever violence enters into something it disgraces it, and whenever 'gentle-civility' enters into something it graces it. Truly, God bestows on account of gentle conduct what he does not bestow on account of violent conduct."[20]

The quest for peace is also clear in the Prophet's life. The use of violence as a mean to address conflict played a minor role in the Prophet's life, and the Qur'an, the Hadith, and Islamic tradition are rich in examples of nonviolence and peace-building strategies.[21]

During the Meccan period of the Prophet's life (610–622 CE), the Prophet showed no inclination toward the use of force in any form, even for self-defense. He conducted nonviolent resistance, through all his instructions and teaching during that period in which Muslims were a minority. The Prophet's teachings were focused on the value of patience and steadfastness in facing the oppression. For 13 years, the Prophet fully adopted nonviolent methods, relying on his spiritual preaching in dealing with aggression and confrontation.

In Islam, the quest for peace extends to both interpersonal and community cases of quarrel or disagreement. Muslims should not use violence to settle their differences, but rely on arbitration or other forms of intervention such as: "You should always refer it (disputes) to God and to His Prophet." "And Obey Allah and His Messenger; And fall into no disputes, lest ye lose heart And your power depart; and be patient and persevering: for Allah is with those who patiently persevere" (8:46).

Peace in Islam is reflected in the word itself and its meaning in Arabic. It indicates the "making of peace," thus the idea of "peace" is the dominant one in Islam. A Muslim, according to the Qur'an, is one who has made peace with God and man. Peace with God implies complete submission to His will who is the source of all purity and goodness, and peace with man implies the doing of good to his fellow man: "Nay, whoever submits himself entirely to God, and is the doer of good to others, he has his reward from His Lord . . ." (2:112). The centrality of peace is reflected in the daily greetings of Muslims of each other "Al Salam Alikum," "A peace be on you." The Qur'an states: "And the servants of Allah most gracious are those who walk the earth in humility and when others address them, they say 'peace!'" (25:63) "And their greeting therein shall be, Peace" (10:10). Peace is also a reward which the believers will enjoy in paradise: "They shall hear therein no vain or sinful talk, but only the saying, Peace, Peace (56:26). Peace is the ideal that Muslims strive to achieve and they are constantly reminded of this value through the names of God: "Abode of peace" (10:25).

In Islam, the goal and the nature of humans is to live in peace, and it is mirrored in the few basic principles about nature of man: (1) Man's fundamental nature is one of moral innocence, that is, freedom from sin; and (2) Man's nature is to live on earth in a state of harmony and peace with other lives. This is the ultimate import for the responsibility assigned by God to man his Khalifah (vice-regent) on this planet (2:30).[22]

The various Islamic principles and values of peace cannot be fully identified without addressing the value of jihad. In the Qur'an and Muslim practice, jihad refers to the obligation of all Muslims to strive (*jihad*, self-exertion) or struggle to follow God's will. This includes the virtuous life and the universal mission of the Muslim community to spread God's rule and law through teaching, preaching, and where necessary, armed conflict."[23] The debate over jihad is well described by Esposito as a common issue associated with the spread of Islam in which Westerners are quick to characterize it as a religion spread by the sword or through holy war, while modern Muslim apologists sometimes explain jihad as simply defensive in nature.[24]

Scholars agree that there are conditions that permit the use of force, and there has been a massive amount of research and lively debates by Muslims and non-Muslims to provide interpretations of the context and meaning of jihad. Many such studies conclude that jihad does not mean the constant use of the sword to resolve problems with non-Muslim enemies, or among Muslims. On the contrary, jihad has been interpreted as by "means of the Holy book itself" (25:52). In clear words the Qur'an states: "there is no compulsion in religion" (2:256). In addition to the previous verses that indicate the possibility of peaceful and nonviolent jihad, different sects in Islam have emphasized the principle that there are several levels of jihad and that the self-jihad is the most difficult to achieve.[25]

Regardless of the different definitions and interpretations of jihad that can be provided in this discussion, scholars agree that the current religious meaning and interpretation of jihad as a holy war has been broadened from the interpretation of Qur'anic jihad, and influenced by the role of Muslim jurists throughout the history, particularly true of the early periods, in which they justified the offensive jihad wars.[26]

STRIVE TO BE A PEACEMAKER

Open communication and face-to-face confrontation are considered in peace building as more conducive to building good relationships than avoidance or violence. They reduce the cost of an ongoing conflict and address grievances of all parties. The role of the third party, as an integral part of a peace-building intervention, is mainly to facilitate the communication, reduce tension, and assist in rebuilding relationships. Such interaction is functional and necessary to engage the parties in a true peace-building process. Islamic values encourage such process through an active intervention, particularly among Muslims themselves.

> If two parties among the believers fall into a quarrel, make you peace between them. But, if one of them transgresses beyond bounds against the other, then fight against the one that transgresses until it complies with the command of Allah. But, when it so complies, then make peace between them with justice and be fair. For, God loves those who are fair. The believers are but a single brotherhood; so make peace between your brothers and fear Allah that you may receive mercy. (49:9–10)

These verses have been pointed out by scholars who search for a legitimate base for the use of violence in Islam and to disqualify the pacifist hypotheses. Nevertheless, they clearly support the concept of mediation and third-party intervention to resolve disputes using fairness and justice as the primary values of intervention. In addition, they reflect a core Islamic value of shunning aggression. Muslims should not be involved in aggression at all. ". . . And let not the hatred of some people in (once) shutting you out of the sacred mosque lead you to transgression (and hostility on your part). Help one another in righteousness and piety. But help ye not one other in sin and rancor" (5:2). Lack of tolerance and hatred should not lead one to become an aggressor" or hostile to the other disputant, even if they shut you out of the house of God, which is an act of exclusion and violence. No doubt that Muslims have to settle their conflicts peacefully based on both the Qur'an and the Prophet's tradition: "The believers are but a single brotherhood: so make peace and reconciliation between your two (contending) brothers" (49:10).

From the Prophet's tradition, peacemaking was one of his central qualities while living in Mecca, even prior to his prophecy. Being known as al Amien (the faithful) allowed him to act as mediator and arbitrator in many disputes among the various tribes. During that period, his creative methods of peacemaking and advocating justice were highly praised by believers and nonbelievers; Islamic conflict resolution methods can easily rely on these classic cases of intervention.

Having established the primacy of peacemaking and peace at the core of Islamic tradition we would like to discuss, necessarily in briefer compass, some of the ancillary values that make such a goal and process possible; for any meaningful peace, as is well known today, depends on much more than the abstention from open conflict.

FORGIVENESS (*AFU*)

It is a higher virtue to forgive than bear hatred. While justice ought to be pursued and evil fought, forgiveness nevertheless, remains a higher virtue (see 42:40 and 24:43). In fact, believers are urged to forgive even when they are angry (42:37). The Prophet said: "God fills with peace and faith the heart of one who swallows his anger, even though he is in a position to give vent to it." When the Prophet entered Mecca with his Muslim followers, he set an example of a great forgiving attitude toward Meccans who fought him: "There is no censure from me today on you (for what has happened is done with), may God who is the greatest amongst forgivers forgive you."[27]

A saying in Islamic ethic: "The most gracious act of forgiving an enemy is his who has the power to take revenge."[28] Such a value is supported by a story about the Prophet when some of his followers came to him asking that he invoke the wrath of God on the Meccans because of their persecution of early Muslims. His reply was: "I have not been sent to curse anyone but to be a source of *Rahmah* (beneficence) to all."[29]

Successful conflict resolution process according to the above principles should result in forgiveness and reconciliation among disputants rather than temporary settlement. Despite the strict conditions of the use of violence or retributive justice, nevertheless, forgiveness is held in higher moral and ethical levels. The virtue of forgiveness is clearly favored.

TAKE INDIVIDUAL RESPONSIBILITY

Islam puts emphasis on doing; lip service is not enough, the real test of a virtue is in action: "If you do good, it will be for your own self; if you do evil, it will react on you" (17:7). An individual is responsible for his or her deeds. No one else can bear the responsibility of one's actions:

> Whoso bringeth a good deed will receive tenfold the like thereof, while whoso bringeth an ill deed will be awarded but the like thereof; and they will not be wronged (6:161). It is not that We wronged them but they wronged themselves. (11:101)

According to Islam, a person has three major levels of responsibilities on which he or she will be judged by God: (1) responsibility toward Allah to be fulfilled through the performance of religious duties faithfully; (2) responsibility to oneself by living in harmony with oneself; and (3) responsibility to live in harmony and peace with other fellow humans.

Persuasion of the other (as opposed to coercion) and allowing free choice are two important principles in Islam. Even the Prophet himself was not responsible for the others' decisions: "But if they turn away, Say: Allah sufficeth me: there is no god but He: on Him is my trust—He the Lord of the Throne (of Glory) Supreme!" (9:129). If others did not accept the message, it was their choice; therefore, you (as a person) are only responsible for your actions.[30] Allah is the sole arbitrator who judges the choices of the people.[31]

The sense of individual choice and call for involvement extends to the political governing system in which the ruler expects his followers to take full responsibility and stop injustice if it is committed. Abu Bakr told the people: "I am no better than you . . . I am just like any one of you. If you see that I am pursuing a proper course, then follow me; and if you see me err, then set me straight."[32] Thus, persuasion (being persuaded by evidence and faith) is a strong quality that puts humans in charge of their own fate; it is also a reason for individual actions. Persuasion as a main strategy in the Qur'an is reflected in the great number of verses that present the arguments and claims of opposition during the Prophet period, and the systematic nullification of these arguments through proof and evidence.[33]

PATIENCE (*SABR*)

Muslims are encouraged to be patient and to suspend their judgment of others, whether Muslims or non-Muslims. Patience is a virtue of the believers who can endure immense challenges and still maintain strong belief in God. Such a value is very appropriate to peace building and nonviolent resistance, because while it often produces few macro impacts or short-term changes, it is a long-term investment in the community. It may be noted that *sabr* often translates "nonviolence" in Arabic writing today.

COLLABORATIVE ACTIONS AND SOLIDARITY

There is a well-known traditional saying: "help your brother (Muslim) whether he is an aggressor or a victim of aggression." When the Prophet was asked, "How can we assist our brother when he is aggressor?" He replied, "By doing your best to stop him from aggression."[34] This is a clear message about solidarity among Muslims, in contrast to tribal solidarity (*Assabiyyah*); it also, of course, refutes the misconception that nonviolence is a kind of passivity.

UMMAH

The concept of *Ummah* or "community" has functioned as a base for collective action since the Prophet's period. During the early period of Islam in Mecca, where the Prophet lived for 13 years, he utilized such values as collaboration and collectivism to mobilize his followers and to respond nonviolently to those who did not follow his prophecy. Moreover, to this day, as Esack Farid argues, "The notion of Ummah . . . continues to give Muslims a deep sense of belonging . . . The universal community under God has always been a significant element in Muslim discourse against tribalism and racism."[35]

It has been even expanded to include God-believing non-Muslims. In supporting this argument scholars stress that the People of the Book, as recipients of the divine revelation were recognized as part of the Ummah, based on the Qur'anic verse: "Surely this, your community (Ummah), is a single community" (23:52). The charter of the Medina—the first constitution created by the Prophet—is also proof of such an inclusive and religiously diverse community.[36]

Islamic conflict resolution is based on the inclusion of communal and collective solidarity, which we often see in the public rituals for reconciliation (*Sulha*). In addition, most interventions (mediation or arbitration) are not restricted to the individual disputants and the semiprofessional third party, but involve additional people from the extended family and community at large.

INCLUSIVITY

Participatory forums and inclusive procedures are considered more productive and effective than authoritarian, hierarchical, and exclusionary decision-making approaches. Thus, peace-building strategies are based on either assisting parties in joint interest-based negotiation or bringing a third party to facilitate such processes, rather than using imposition and competition.

The Muslim tradition of mutual consultation (*Shura*) exhibits a number of key points:

1. It is not a mere consultation by the rulers, but an inclusive process in which all Ummah are asked to provide input. Consultation is not obligatory, but Shura is obligatory and a duty.
2. It involves all matters of concern to the Ummah.
3. The people of the Shura represent all the segments of the society (parties, religious groups, Muslim and non-Muslim, etc.). They are different from people of Ijtihad who are the Islamic faqihs or jurisprudents.

4. The freedom of expression is the core of Shura. If freedom of expression of all people is not guaranteed, then Shura is not practiced.[37]

The principle of inclusivity is seen dramatically in the way the religion encourages involvement and responsibility of the people rather than passivity or acceptance of oppression. In fact, it is the duty of the Muslim to resist the *Zulm* (oppression) and work against it. A saying of the prophet instructs: "Best of the jihad is a word of truth (Haq) to an oppressing sultan." "If people saw the oppressor and did not warn or consult him God is about to punish them."

PLURALISM AND DIVERSITY

The Qur'an supports diversity and tolerance of differences based on gender (49:13; 53:45); skin color, language (30:23); beliefs (64:2); ranks (6:165); social grouping and communities (2:213; 10:19; 7:38 13:30; 16:63; 29:18; 35:42; 41:42; 64:18). It asserts that differences are inherent in human life (11:118–119; 10:99; 16:93). Scholars cite a pertinent saying of the Prophet: "My Ummah's difference is mercy" (a highly disputed Hadith, however, very popular among Muslims).[38] The equality of the followers of different religions is reiterated in both the Qur'an and Hadith many times. Muslims are asked to remember that there is no difference in the treatment of people of different religions except in their faith and deed (3:113–114; 2:62; 5:68).

The Qur'an affirms the validity of the other religions and requires its followers to respect their scriptures (see 3:64; 5:68–69).

Among Muslims themselves, there was no single Islamic law or constitution and no standardization of the Islamic law. The Sunni tradition, when it standardized such laws, came up with four legitimate schools.[39] Moreover, the Qur'an is used to legitimize the validity of differences (Ikhtilaf). On the other hand, Islam is far less tolerant of the nonbelievers or infidels. Throughout history those who were cast as "Kufar" (Kafir is infidel) were persecuted and punished by rulers and followers.

The existence of differences is, as mentioned, a given in Islam; consequently, there is no justification in violating peoples' right to existence and movement due to their different religious affiliation (42:15). Islam thus spread and coexisted in many different cultures and ethnic groups in Asia, the Middle East, Africa, and South east Asia, where it typically created a new civilization that was multicultural and pluralist. Although not always perfectly observed in practice, these values have been integral parts of Islam since its inception.

ISLAMIC NONVIOLENT PROCESSES AND PROCEDURES

In North America and the West generally, conflict resolution has developed and been professionalized, including various processes and frameworks for resolving conflicts according to their nature, level, and scope: interest-based negotiation, arbitration, mediation, facilitation, joint problem solving, dialogue, etc. On the peace studies side, advocacy and nonviolent resistance have also been developed and conceptualized based on rich field experiences and solid empirical research. Such research has not been carried out in the same systematic manner in the developing field of Islamic peace and conflict resolution; however, since the early 1990s there have been serious efforts in this direction.[40]

Today there are a few academic courses, offered mostly in Western universities and institutes, that focus on Islamic sources of peace and conflict resolution[41] and practices such as arbitration (*tahkim*), mediation (*wasatah*), and reconciliation (*sulh*)—all of which often rely on Quranic foundations, such as:

> If you fear a breach between them (man and wife), then appoint an arbitrator from his people and an arbitrator from her people. If they desire reconciliation, God will make them of one mind. God is all knowing, all aware. (4:35)

The Prophet's numerous interventions and Seerah (Awus Khazraj; Black stone; negotiating the Hodaibyah agreement, Charter of Medinah, etc.), which have been well documented and verified by many Muslim scholars, constituted a path or a guide for Islamic third-party interventions.

Naturally, these mediation and arbitration processes rely on a particular set of cultural and religious principles that differs from the North American models; they are mostly collective in their nature, involving the entire community in settling a family, interpersonal, or tribal dispute, especially in rural or nonurban areas.

In short, there is no shortage of stories recounting practices of Islamic conflict resolution carried out by the Prophets and other Muslim leaders such as the first four Khaliphates. All Islamic educational curricula incorporate these stories of the Prophet's mediation, arbitration, and conciliation efforts.

CONCLUSION

The ideals of Islamic peace described in this brief survey have not been applied or adopted on a wide scale by most Muslims, due to both external and internal factors. Internally, Islamic communities often face a socialization that instills obedience to authoritarianism, supported and maintained by a set of cultural values, rewards, and punishment codes, for one example. It is true that these factors are maintained by educational systems that are corrupt and function as a force of oppression, by socializing young generations into conformity, obedience, and discouragement of self-critique or self-reflections. The outcome of such patterns is reflected in a cultural code of "shame and honor" that stifles creativity in dealing with conflict.

Needless to say, external factors such as colonial and post-colonial policies have greatly taken advantage of these internal drawbacks, often using them to reinforce control and continue extracting natural and human resources from Muslim societies. British, French, Spanish in North Africa and the Middle East, and Americans in the early 1950s, 1960s, and 1970s heavily relied on these policies of legitimizing authoritarian regimes, on patriarchal and hierarchical governance systems, and co-opted religious leaders.

Nevertheless, in our discussion we have identified important Islamic principles and values that constitute the basic elements of an Islamic peace building and conflict resolution approach to all types and levels of conflicts (interpersonal, organizational, family, community, and national, too). This framework if applied in a community context with an emphasis on peace building, could go far toward creating more just and peaceable societies within and among Muslim communities themselves and between them and this pluralistic but still violent world. Finally, it is the duty of Muslims who are living in Western societies to reach out to others without apologies or defensiveness, but with creative initiatives and constructive programs.

NOTES

1. Ahmad, 1993.

2. "He who does not show compassion to his fellow men is undeserving of God's compassion." Cited in Saiyidain, 1976.

3. A Muslim leader who created a nonviolent social and political movement to fight the British colonial forces in Pakistan, before independence.

4. Hwadi, 1993. Cites A. Zamakshari: "and in this-pursuing justice with enemies—there is a great warning that if justice is a duty to be applied when dealing with the infidels (Kufar) who are the enemy of God, if it had such a powerful characteristic then what is its duty among the believers who are God's supportive and favorites?"

5. Kelsay, 1993.

6. United Nations Development Program and Arab Fund for Economic and Social Development, 2002; Reza, 1984, see Nahjul Balagha, Letter No 53 "An Order to Malik-ul-Ashtar.

7. The notion that peace can not be achieved without justice is echoed by many peace-building researchers and activists. See Lederach, 1997 and Burgess and Burgess, 1994.

8. Based on this Hadith and others, Saiyidain, 1976, argues that refusal to support wrongdoing by one's country is either proof of patriotism or an act of virtue.

9. Saiyidain, 1976.

10. Ibid.

11. Zakah is also encouraged and described in detail with its rewards in the Koran.

12. Saiyidain, 1976.

13. Ibid.

14. Hwadi, 1993.

15. Kishtainy, 1990.

16. Saiyidain, 1976.

17. Siddiqi, 1976–1979: 838; as cited in Satha-Anand, 1993:11.

18. Saiyidain, 1976.

19. Kelsay, 1993.

20. A Syrian religious scholar who is known for his reformist writing.

21. Abu-Nimer, 2003.

22. Hashimi, 1996.

23. Esposito, 1988.

24. Unfortunately, the association of Muslims with jihad and violence has become very strong particularly in Western media. Such mischaracterization is reflected in the popular term "A people of the Sword." Some argue that the self-fulfilling prophecy of jihad has become a phenomenon of our times. Not only are Muslim activists (violent and nonviolent alike) suffering the imagery of age-old misperceptions and misrepresentation, but the religion and its followers also sustain the labeling and stereotyping as a result. There is much emphasis and domination of such stereotypes and generalization among writers when studying Islam in general and political Islam in particular. Esposito has captured such misperception when he stated: "A combination of ignorance, stereotyping, history, and experience, as well as religio-cultural chauvinism, too often blind even best-intentioned when dealing with the Arab and Muslim World." (Esposito, 1993).

25. There are several Hadith that support such interpretations. Also there are Muslim groups that emphasize the spiritual rather than the physical jihad (such as Sufism and Ahmaddiyya); others suggested that Da'awa or (Calling—the spreading of Islam through preaching and persuasion) to be the major form of Jihad for Muslim.

26. Sachedina, 1996.

27. Based on Ibn Sad Al-Tabaqa Al Kubra, vol. II., p. 142 Beirut 1957. Cited in Saiyidain, 1976.

28. Saiyidain, 1976.

29. Based on Ibn Sad Al-Tabaqa Al Kubra, vol. II., Beirut 1957. Cited in Saiyidain, 1976.

30. See other verses in the Koran emphasizing the same principle of individual choice and responsibility, 5:8; 9:6; 16: 125; and 42: 48.

31. Individual responsibility, choice, and God's arbitration in the Judgment Day are reflected in the verses 18:29; 109:6; 88: 21,22; and 34:28.

32. At the same time there is the Al-Ash'ari and Din ibn Jama'a (1333) who forbade uprising against tyrants. The duty of Muslims is obedience no matter how unjust the ruler. See Saiyidain cited in Thompson, 1988.

33. Hwadi, 1993.

34. Saiyidain, 1976.

35. See Esack, 1997. He has completed a pioneer study on the Islamic theology of liberation based on the experience of Muslims in South Africa in fighting against the apartheid. Esack describes an astonishing account of the utilization of Islamic beliefs and values in mobilizing Muslims to resist and fight the South African system, particularly by building community coalitions with non-Muslims. Such experience affirms the great potential to construct coalitions across religious boundaries and identities in resisting war, violence, and injustice.

36. Also Akbar Ahmad supports such a notion about the Ummah being a diverse religious and individual community particularly in the Medinan period in which the Qur'an mentions it 47 times, and only 9 times in Meccan period. See Ahmad, 1979: 38–39.

37. Tawfiq Al-Shadi Fiqh Al-Shura Walestisharah (the jurisprudence of Consultation and Shura), p. 293). Cited in Hwadi, 1993.

38. Hwadi, 1993: 23.

39. Esack, 1998.

40. See Abu Nimer, 1996; Crow, 1997; Jalabi, 1998; Sachedina, 1996; Sai'd, 1997; Said, 1994; and Kishtainy, 1990.

41. See American University International Peace and Conflict Resolution.

PART V

GENDER IN WAR AND PEACE

The history of women in the world of violence has unique aspects. Their work is consistently exploited and their bodies routinely violated in war and in economic mistreatment. Yet, there is a special role for women in the pursuit of peace. Women are associated with life-affirming tasks of caring for others. Their voices are needed to reclaim this life-affirming outlook for present and future needs.

Throughout the ages, patriarchal arrangements of society have co-opted human energy and knowledge to control and dominate other human beings and the natural world. Under industrial capitalism that model of domination has worsened. The great problems of our time—poverty, inequality, war, terrorism, and environmental degradation—are due largely to flawed economic systems that set the wrong priorities and misallocate resources to the ends of competition and acquisition. If we define ourselves by a patriarchal economic model, then success is measured by who and what we are able to dominate.[1] Conventional economic models fail to value and support the most essential human work of caring and caregiving. Hence basic human needs are neglected, and life becomes a struggle in which we fight over what we see as a scarcity of resources.

In the 21st-century reality, a different worldview is gaining momentum. Matriarchy, recognizing all forms of life as being interconnected, provides an alternative. Women's organized efforts most often reflect aspects of culture and environment particular to their immediate circumstances—lack of rights to own property or to gain education, sexual assault, or hunger for themselves and their children. But an underlying theme is opposition to a system of patriarchy and a demand that women have a prominent part in decisions affecting their lives.

One theme of Riane Eisler's book *The Power of Partnership*,[2] is that we are always in relationship not just with our immediate circle but with a wider web of relationships impacting every aspect of our lives. This echoes a theme showing that human health, well-being, and indeed survival are dependent primarily on our connections.[3] We are defined by our relations—by intimate relations, by relations in the workplace and local community, and by relationships with the nation, the international community, and Mother Earth. Spiritually we are related to life itself. All elements are interrelated.

Feminist theory, vision, and practice draw strength from humanity's common matriarchal history—uncovered in the stories of women from Africa, Asia, the Pacific, Europe, and the Americas. Heide Goettner-Abendroth's edited anthology on matriarchal societies demonstrates well that there is an alternative to patriarchy that has been widely practiced. Indigenous cultures and archaeological accounts of lost cultures show examples of common principles of matriarchy occurring in societies across time and geography. Societies as different as the Bear Clan of the Ohio Seneca, Iroquois, and the Yunnan of southwest China illustrate the link between roles assigned to women as peacemakers and the absence of violence in the greater community.[4]

War almost always has a most devastating impact on women and children, leaving them homeless, vulnerable to disease and sexual assault, and lacking in economic security. Women have also been leaders in challenging the destruction. In Argentina they have appeared as the *Mothers of the Disappeared* (The Mothers of the Plaza de Mayo) who have fought for the right to re-unite with their abducted children; in Liberia united Christian and Moslem women forced the resignation of a brutal ruler, Charles Taylor, and the withdrawal from violence of the rebel gangs.

In Colombia where a U.S.-supported government with an atrocious human rights record and an unaccountable paramilitary group, both fighting an often violent guerilla opposition, women have been in the leadership of peace communities that have declared their separation from this man-made nightmare (see Lozano, Chapter 7, Volume 3). The case of Malalai Joya,[5] the first woman elected to parliament in Afghanistan, is particularly instructive. Her country is among the world's poorest. The tribal society is ruled by warlords who came to power and increased their weapons through their liaisons with the invading Soviet Union and later though liaisons with NATO invaders. The invaders always worked with one group of warlords and promised to improve the well-being of women subjected to extreme fundamentalist groups. At great risk, Joya told her fellow parliamentarians that they were warlords unsuited to rule the country. But she has been equally clear that the U.S.-led NATO military incursion widens a war that is devastating to Afghan women and should end immediately.

The sacrifices of male warriors are sometimes honored. Women casualties of war go relatively unnoticed. In this section Gianina Pellegrini compiles the painful facts of the effects of both military violence and ongoing domestic violence against women. She goes on to describe the leadership taken by women's groups to eliminate such violence and to restore peaceful and sustainable communities. The variety of such activities and the impact they are having on peace and development is described by Kavita Nandini Ramdas of the Global Fund for Women. The change is profound, not only for its impact on ending inequality between men and women but also between the affluent and the landless, between masters and slaves, between militias and peasants. Women's groups have stepped beyond the divisions of class and caste, the pillars of a dominator society. Taken as a whole they describe a revolutionary change in the assumptions that have perpetuated inequality and violence.

Finally in this section Carol Cohn and Sara Ruddick describe "anti-war feminism" a concept that should make us all look critically at how we buy unwittingly into a language of abstractions that permit and encourage violence. The distancing language and male stereotypes, so common in the abstractions used to discuss war, serve to shelter us from the human capacities for caring and compassion. Not all feminists and certainly not all women view war in the same way. However one major thread has been labeled "anti-war feminism." Carol Cohn and Sara Ruddick[6] have drawn attention to the fundamental contribution of the concept. The values and language of domination are so deeply planted in Western imperial culture that they often go unnoticed. The typical public discussion of war has images of macho bravado neatly concealed by an abstract language of strategies and weapon systems. Emotional expressions of abhorrence for the killing, or compassion for the children being traumatized, and the despair over a bombed out-home; these are associated with feminine weakness. The claim to rationality is afforded those who can leave such human emotions out of their deliberations. We buy unwittingly into a language of abstractions that permits and encourages violence. The distancing language and male stereotypes, so common in the abstractions used to discuss war, serve to shelter us from the human capacities for caring and compassion. Anti-war feminism reclaims for all of us the right, indeed the necessity, to honor and to express our love of life.

The feminist traditions of the Western World were built on social movements involving the rights to vote, hold title to property, and to obtain an education. Another wave of feminism is aimed at the rights of women to choose in matters of sexuality, marriage, childbearing, and jobs. Despite historically important associations between women's movements and opposition to war, some aspects of feminism called for equal opportunity only for inclusion in a patriarchal society. Others have argued that such equality is not enough and that it continues to permit the institutions of war and poverty to victimize members of both genders and all ages. Women who take on the tough, sexist, and dehumanizing language of the military do not tap the special talents of women to be nurturers of families, communities, and the living environment and models for nonviolent power. Most women have less power than men in their families and poor women less power than either men or women in middle and upper classes. Having fewer options for inflicting serious harm, women, particularly through the experience of mothering, have become experts in the exercise of nonviolent methods. It is for most women the means by which they raise children and by which they talk with other women about how to confront challenges without turning to violence. Many women replicate the basic applications of Gandhian theory of nonviolence in the practice of their daily lives. This is a special wisdom and a special form for the exercise of power that must be honored lest the technology available to practitioners of the dominator model lead to unspeakable violence and war.

Markets do not always rule. Neither do strategists with advanced weapons. When caring is valued psychologically, the economy moves from competition over scarcity to sustainable, shared abundance, and the culture of war becomes a culture of peace. Women are leading a worldwide struggle to recover the humanity and harmony lost to patriarchy not so many years ago. They give us hope that this new world is possible.

—Marc Pilisuk and Michael N. Nagler

NOTES

1. Eisler, 2007.
2. Eisler, 2003.
3. Pilisuk and Parks, 1986.
4. Goettner-Abendroth, 2008.
5. Joya and O'Keefe, 2009.
6. Cohn and Ruddick, 2004.

CHAPTER 13

WOMEN: BATTLEGROUND FOR WAR, RESOURCE FOR PEACE

Gianina Pellegrini

It is now more dangerous to be a woman than to be a soldier in modern conflict.

—Maj. Gen. Patrick Cammaert, 2008[1]

There is one global resource located on every continent and in every corner of the world. This resource is more valuable and instrumental to human survival and development than oil, water, minerals, or land. This resource is often overlooked, its strength not fully realized, and its worth depreciated. This resource is women. Like many other valuable global resources, women are often neglected, abused, and exploited. For centuries, women in all parts of the world, from all ethnic, religious, and cultural backgrounds, have been victims of oppressive, patriarchal social systems that leave them vulnerable to numerous forms of abuse.

This chapter illustrates the abuse perpetrated against women in times of relative peace and specifically in times of war. Women experience extreme levels of abuse, exploitation, and discrimination in warring and nonwarring societies; and yet they also demonstrate a remarkable ability to transform their experiences into powerful forces for peace. After identifying some of the abuses perpetrated against women, the chapter closes with a brief description of the international efforts to include women in all levels of the peace process and highlights a few women's groups that have contributed to the worldwide movement toward peace.

Until recently, the world viewed violence against women as domestic, private affairs and failed to recognize the global impact such abuse would have on human development. Violence against women has a serious and potentially irreversible impact not only on the women who have been hurt but also on human development more generally. For the attainment of sustainable peace to be possible, the protection of women must be recognized as an essential concern and fundamental priority in the global peace movement. The assault on women is an assault on all of humanity.

Violence perpetrated against women, whether in times of violent conflict or relative peace, has reached epidemic proportions and must be acknowledged as a serious international human rights emergency that threatens global security. In stable, nonwarring societies, women are subjected to extreme forms of abuse including rape, sexual exploitation, mutilation, physical abuse, and honor killings.[2] Globally, at least one in three women and girls is beaten or sexually abused in her lifetime. Domestic violence causes more deaths and disability to women aged 15 to 44, than cancer, malaria, traffic accidents, and war. At least 60 million girls who would otherwise be expected to be alive are missing from various populations, mostly in Asia, as a result of sex selective abortions, infanticide, and neglect. Annually, 4 million women and girls are trafficked into forced labor and sexual exploitation, including prostitution and sexual slavery. Each year, an estimated 5,000 women are victims of honor killings[3] and an estimated 3 million girls are at risk of undergoing female circumcision and other forms of genital mutilation.[4]

Permitting violence against women during times of peace is directly reflected in the methods of warfare used in contemporary violent conflicts. The last two decades have seen a dramatic increase in the frequency and severity of gender-based violence deployed as a weapon of war in conflicts throughout the world. Contemporary warfare includes deliberate and strategic attacks on civilians, many of which are women and children. Intentionally targeting civilians is a military tactic used to intimidate, instill fear, and control entire groups of people, communities, and populations. An estimated 75 percent of casualties of war are civilians, many of who are women and children.[5] Eruption of violent conflict results in the breakdown of the social and political structures that once provided some level of civilian protection. During violent conflicts families and communities are dispersed, adequate health and human service resources diminish, and economic opportunities become limited. Women who are often subjected to some level of marginalization before the conflict become more vulnerable to violence, abuse, and discrimination within their communities. Although women are typically the minority of combatants and perpetrators of war, they are increasingly the most impacted by the violence.

There is an undeniable link between sexual, gender-based violence and armed conflict. Wars and violent conflicts that were once fought between combatants on battlegrounds removed from civilians are now being waged within communities and directly on women's bodies. Women's bodies have irrefutably become the battleground for many contemporary wars.

SEXUAL VIOLENCE AS A WEAPON OF WAR

> I was in the fields with five other women. My baby girl was on my back. Four interahamwe [FDLR] soldiers approached, wearing military fatigues and carrying grenades. They chose me and another woman and forced us with them into the forest. We walked for hours through the bush to reach their camp, which was like a village they'd organized in the middle of the forest. There were around 50 women there, like us, taken by force. The commander chose me as his woman and raped me every day. My baby was beside me when this took place. After, I was left bleeding and weak.
>
> —Testimony from Constance, a 27-year-old single
> mother from Rutshuru territory in the Democratic
> Republic of the Congo, 2007[6]

Constance is one of many women subjected to sexual violence during violent conflict. Sexual, gender-based violence, including rape, sexual slavery, gang rape, mutilation, physical abuse, forced pregnancy, and sexual exploitation, is being systematically deployed against women as a weapon of war in contemporary violent conflicts. Sexual violence attacks the most basic fabric of society, bringing pain, fear, and shame to the victim and also to her family and community. There are countless examples throughout the world and throughout history of sexual, gender-based violence being utilized as a military tactic in violent conflicts.[7]

Sexual-based violence occurs within all countries and communities throughout the world. What follows is a description of those countries where sexual, gender-based violence has been most documented. This does not imply these are the only countries where such violence occurs. Without a doubt, much of the sexual, gender-based violence that women experience goes underreported or undocumented. However, the accounts that follow present a clear description of the atrocities women encounter during violent conflicts.

In Europe, sexual, gender-based violence has been reported in conflicts in Azerbaijan, Croatia, Georgia, Russia, Serbia, and the former Yugoslavia. Most notably, the three-year, inter-ethnic war that followed Bosnia and

Herzegovina's declaration of independence from Yugoslavia in 1992 involved multiple reports of sexual violence perpetrated against women. During the war, thousands of women were raped, sexually tortured, abducted, and forced into sexual servitude. Muslim women were systematically targeted as a form of ethnic cleansing. Detention sites known as "rape camps" were developed where women, primarily Muslim women, were repeatedly raped, forcibly impregnated, and detained so that the pregnancy could not be terminated. Up to 162 detention camps were formed and estimates of 20,000 to 50,000 women and girls were raped.[8]

In the Americas, armed conflicts in Guatemala, Haiti, Nicaragua, Peru, and Colombia utilized sexual, gender-based violence as a military and often political tactic to terrorize women and their communities. Throughout the ongoing conflict in Colombia, government and paramilitary forces utilized sexual violence against women as a counter-insurgency tactic to punish those suspected of supporting rebels or on those merely residing in rebel-controlled territories. As a result, hundreds of women have been subjected to sexual violence, including rape, sexual slavery, forced prostitution, and sexual mutilation.[9] The United States has been accused of utilizing sexual violence against suspected terrorists and prisoners of war in military prisons operated on foreign land. Even among their own people, the United States is guilty of sexual violence against women: one in three women in the U.S. military is raped or sexually abused.[10]

Sexual violence has been reported in conflicts throughout the vast Asian continent, including Sri Lanka, Afghanistan, Tajikistan, India, Burma/Myanmar, Cambodia, Nepal, Philippines, Indonesia, Papua-New Guinea, and East Timor. In East Timor, Indonesian troops and Indonesian-backed militia have been accused of widespread sexual violence, including sexual torture, sex slavery, forced sterilization, and forced prostitution.[11] Sexual violence, including rape, abductions, sexual exploitation, and forced marriages has been widely reported in Afghanistan since post-Soviet rule and sexual violence continues to be a considerable problem in the region. In 2006, the Afghanistan Independent Commission on Human Rights registered 1,651 cases of sexual and gender-based violence, including 213 cases of forced marriage, 106 cases of self-burning, 50 cases of murder, 41 cases of girls being traded off for various reasons, and 34 cases of rape.[12]

Sexual, gender-based violence is less documented in the Middle East primarily due to the stigma associated with such assaults and the widespread repercussions, such as honor killings, that a woman could suffer when reporting sexual violence. Sexual violence has been most reported in Iraq and reports of gender-based violence have significantly increased since the United States occupation began in 2003. Soldiers from the American, British, Italian,

Polish, and Spanish military have been accused of raping thousands of women since the beginning of the occupation, and there has been a distinct rise in the number of abductions of women as well as women being tortured, raped, and killed in this region. Honor killings have also been reported in Lebanon, the Palestinian Territories, and Yemen.[13]

The use of sexual violence as a military and political tactic has ravaged the African continent during past and current armed conflicts in countries such as Burundi, Chad, Rwanda, Sierra Leone, Liberia, Uganda, Sudan, and the Democratic Republic of the Congo (DRC). In Sudan, rape, sexual mutilation, and torture of non-Arab women have been employed as acts of genocide and ethnic cleansing during the civil war between Northern and Southern Sudan and more recently in the Darfur region. Countless women have been victims of sexual violence perpetrated by Sudanese security forces, militias, rebel groups, and former rebel groups.[14] For over 15 years, the civil unrest and violent conflict in the DRC has subjected tens of thousands of women to sexual violence, including rape, gang rapes, rapes leading to serious injury or death, and the abduction of girls and women to be used as sexual slaves. A peace treaty was signed in 2003, yet the violence against women and girls has not subsided. In 2008, Human Rights Watch documented 15,966 new cases of sexual violence reported throughout the country. In the first five months of 2009, 143 cases of rape by army soldiers were reported in North Kivu, and an estimated 40 women and girls are raped each day in the South Kivu region.[15] The violent conflicts throughout the African continent have been especially brutal to women and girls. Extremely atrocious forms of sexual violence, such as mutilation, rape with inanimate objects, physically violent gang rape, forced pregnancy, and the rape of extremely young children and babies have been documented in numerous countries including Sudan, the DRC, Ethiopia, Rwanda, and Sierra Leone. The brutality of sexual violence has resulted in many women suffering traumatic gynecologic fistula.[16]

As the above examples illustrate, the magnitude of violence and injustices experienced by women during and following violent conflicts is overwhelming. Utilizing sexual, gender-based violence as a weapon of war during armed conflicts has detrimental, long-term consequences on human development. Violence against women, whether perpetrated during violent conflicts or times of peace, is a global epidemic that must be abolished.

EFFORTS TO ABOLISH SEXUAL ABUSE IN CONFLICTS

In a direct response to the increase of violence perpetrated against women in conflict zones, there has been an increase in international attention and global awareness of women's experience of armed conflict. International efforts such as the Beijing Declaration and Platform for Action brought forth at the UN Fourth World Conference on Women (1995), UN Security Council Resolution 1325 (Women, Peace, and Security, 2000), and the Convention on the Elimination of All Forms of Discrimination Against Women (CEDAW) are a few international mandates that have introduced strategies and tools to enhance women's empowerment and obtain gender equality in all spheres of private and public life.

The Beijing Declaration and Platform for Action was developed in an effort to accelerate the implementation of the Nairobi Forward-Looking Strategies for the Advancement of Women (1985).[17] The Platform for Action introduced methods to enhance women's social, political, and economic empowerment. advancement, and equality. The UN reconvened in 2000 and 2005 to discuss the implementation of the Beijing Platform for Action, reevaluate the challenges women continue to experience, and identify new initiatives to obtain full and accelerated implementation of the commitments made in 1995. In 2010, the UN will reconvene for a 15-year review of the Beijing Platform for Action.

In 2000, the UN Security Council passed Resolution 1325 (Women, Peace, and Security), the first UN resolution to specifically address issues pertaining to women's role in the formal peace process. Resolution 1325 calls for greater participation of women in conflict prevention, peace building, and peacekeeping processes. The resolution contains 18 provisions that call to all parties of conflict to acknowledge the impact of conflict on women's lives and to protect women and girls from gender-based violence, to institute policies that respond to women's needs during and after conflict, and to end impunity for crimes against humanity affecting women.[18]

The Convention on the Elimination of All Forms of Discrimination Against Women (CEDAW), often referred to as the international bill of rights for women, is the human rights treaty devoted exclusively to gender equality. CEDAW establishes legal standards that if incorporated into national law would enhance gender equality through the elimination of political, social, economic, and cultural discrimination against women. This global human rights treaty identifies steps to achieving gender equality in a wide range of areas relating to trafficking and prostitution, political participation, nationality, education, employment, health care, economic, social, and cultural life, and family relations. CEDAW has been ratified or acceded to in 183 countries, meaning that these countries are legally bound by international law to implement its provisions, including eliminating discrimination against women in all spheres of life and establishing institutional measures to advance gender equality.[19]

The Beijing Platform of Action, Resolution 1325, and CEDAW are a few examples of international efforts to obtain gender equality and enhance women's empowerment in both the private and public sectors. Sustainable peace relies on these international efforts that emphasize the inclusion of women in all aspects of society, and specifically a role in the reconstruction of their communities following violence. Women rightfully deserve a more inclusive role in all aspects of the peace process and failure to obtain equal representation has detrimental consequences to society and the aspirations of sustainable peace. The formal peace process provides the opportunity to reconstruct the social and political policies that have for centuries marginalized women in society. There is a vital link between women's experiences during violent conflict and their full participation in conflict resolution and post-conflict reconstruction. Their experiences as victims of violence make them key contributors in determining the terms surrounding any peace negotiations.

Unfortunately, international efforts to eliminate gender-based violence and enforce equal gender representation in the peace process are difficult to implement due to the existing social structures that marginalize women in society. In principle, these initiatives are promising, yet in practice they continue to leave much to be desired. It is often women that organize on the local, grassroots level that initiate effective change within their communities. Despite the lack of equal gender representation in most formal peace processes, women have mobilized within their communities to demand an end to violence and promote sustainable peace. Women on every continent have shown a remarkable ability to transcend their experience as victims and organize as leaders of peace movements. Often without the support of international or governmental entities, women have transformed the peace process through activism, leadership, and unprecedented action to obtain peace.

In 1955, Jean Sinclair founded the Black Sash organization to resist the apartheid government in South Africa and aid oppressed black women and men. Wearing black sashes to symbolize the mourning of those oppressed by the apartheid system, this nonviolent organization held street demonstrations, spoke at political meetings, held vigils outside Parliament and government offices, campaigned against apartheid legislation, and brought forth issues of injustice to members of Parliament. They assisted black women and men with legal issues and provided secure locations for them to reside when faced with racial and gender persecution.[20]

During the "Dirty War" in Argentina from 1976 to 1983, those opposed or thought to be opposed to the violent military dictatorship were abducted, tortured, and killed, though often referred to as "disappeared." Many of those captured and disappeared were youth who had spoken publicly about their opposition to the regime. In response to the thousands of disappeared youth, a group of mothers, known as Madres of the Plaza de Mayo formed nonviolent demonstrations at the Plaza de Mayo in Buenos Aires, the site of Argentina's government. The mothers wore white head scarves embroidered with their children's names in an attempt to draw attention to their missing children and to pressure the government to acknowledge the assaults that were taking place. The number of mothers that gathered each week grew significantly and gained international attention, forcing the government to recognize their demands for political, social, and legal reparations. The women first began their demonstrations as an effort to protect and save their children, and through this process they were educated on their children's views and reasons for opposing the dictatorship. The Madres of the Plaza de Mayo organization grew from mothers protecting their children to a large group of women, now human rights activists mobilizing for justice and to bring change to the oppressive government through political reform. Mothers from other South American countries, such as Bolivia, Brazil, Chile, Paraguay, and Uruguay, formed similar groups protesting against their "disappeared" sons and daughters.[21]

In 1988, in response to the Palestinian *Intifada*, Israeli Jewish women began a nonviolent organization to protest Israeli occupation of the West Bank and Gaza. The organization, Women in Black, held weekly vigils in public places holding signs in Arabic, English, and Hebrew calling for an end to the occupation of Palestinian territories. The women, dressed in black to symbolize the tragedy suffered by Israelis and Palestinians, maintained silence during their weekly vigils and often stood in busy, highly populated areas to raise public awareness of the severity of the occupation and to show support for the Palestinians. Women in Black groups sprung up throughout Israel, gaining support from Israeli Jewish women and Palestinian women living in Israel and the occupied territories. In some cases, vigils would be held at border crossings with demonstrations occurring on both sides of the border. Women in Black organizations began as a direct response to the Israeli occupation of the West Bank and Gaza, and have since grown into an international women's anti-war movement with an estimated 10,000 activists around the world. Although the international organizations began in solidarity with the Israeli group, many have also embraced other social and political issues. Women in Black organizations are located: in Europe, the United States, South America, India, the Philippines, Nepal, and China.[22]

In 2000, a group of West African women came together to promote full participation in the process of preventing and managing conflicts and restoring peace in Africa. The meeting was organized by the nongovernmental organization Femmes Africa Solidarité and the African Women's Committee for Peace and Development with the sole purpose of establishing a subregional project for and by the women of the Mano River countries that would complement national efforts to build and sustain peace and resolve and prevent conflicts in the region. From this initial meeting, women of Guinea, Sierra Leone, and Liberia started the Mano River Women's Peace Network with the goal of achieving sustainable peace in the region. The primary objective of the Mano River Women's Peace Network is to educate and raise awareness on issues pertaining to sustainable peace, such as human rights, democracy, gender equality, development, and conflict prevention and resolution. In solidarity with other women's organizations, such as African Women's Committee for Peace, and the African Women's Federation of Peace Networks, their goal is to become an instrumental player in the peace and reconciliation process in the region.[23]

The Naga women of northeastern India have demonstrated astounding leadership in the mediation of violent conflicts. In 1963, the formal state of Nagaland was established following the 50-year political conflict between the 40 tribes of the Naga Hills and post-colonial India. A long and violent conflict prevailed between the armed subgroups of the Naga people, the government of India, the Indian state of Nagaland, and border states and tribes as the Naga people fought for independence. The Naga women have played an instrumental role in reducing the violence and promoting peace by acting as mediators between the fighting forces. Women would act as physical barriers between civilians and soldiers and appeal to underground fighting groups by walking into their camps and pleading with the leaders to stop the violence. The leaders of the fighting forces recognize women as key contributors to the stabilization of violence in the region. The first cease-fire agreement was signed in 1997 and has been signed subsequently each year. Although some violence still prevails, women continue to be active participants in the peacebuilding and peacekeeping process and are often requested by leaders to attend public activities and formal negotiations.[24]

The above examples are merely a few illustrations of peace movements initiated by women throughout the world. An entire anthology could be dedicated to representing the multiple movements women have created in a response to violence within their communities. These few examples illustrate how women continue to play an important role in the attainment of peace within their families, communities, and nations. Despite the pain women experience, both in the absence and presence of conflict, women show an unmatched strength to transform their suffering into creative and effective ways to advocate for the end to violence. The global peace movement cannot ignore the disparities women face in the modern world, nor can it ignore the vital contributions women provide in the attainment of peace. Just as the world must preserve and protect its natural resources, an essential priority for human development and security is the protection and preservation of women.

NOTES

1. United Nations (UNIFEM), 2009.

2. The following statistics on violence against women were obtained from the UN Secretary-General's database on violence against women. "General Assembly. In-Depth Study on All Forms of Violence against Women: Report of the Secretary General,". July 6, 2006. http://webapps01.un.org/vawdatabase/home.action. Specific information on the prevalence of specific types of abuse can also be obtained on the World Health Organization Web site. http://www.who.int/gender/violence/en/ and the United Nations Inter-Agency Network on Women and Gender http://www.un.org/womenwatch/.

3. Honor killings is when a girl or woman is murdered by a relative, typically her husband or father to cleanse the family of the perceived shame associated with rape or other forms of sexual violence.

4. For more information on Female Genital Mutilation, see United Nations Population Fund (UNFPA) & United Nations Children's Fund (UNICEF), 2010.

5. United Nations Security Council, 2009.

6. Amnesty International, 2008.

7. For more information see Ward and Marsh, 2006 and Ren and Sirleaf, 2002.

8. Ward, 2009 Bastick et al., 2007.

9. Bastick et al., 2007.

10. Sadler et al., 2003.

11. Bastick et al., 2007.

12. Afghanistan Independent Commission on Human Rights, 2005.

13. Human Rights Watch, 2003.

14. Human Rights Watch, 2008.

15. Human Rights Watch, 2009.

16. Fistula is when a woman's vagina and her bladder or rectum, or both, are torn apart, sometimes during birth but in this context as a result of violent force to her genitals. Fistula results in the inability to control the constant flow of urine and/or feces. For more information on sexual violence in Africa, see Stop Rape Now, UN Action against Sexual Violence in Conflict, http://www.stoprapenow.org/updates_field.html.

17. Nairobi Forward-Looking Strategies, 1985.

18. United Nations (Resolution 1325), 2009.

19. United Nations (CEDAW).

20. Spink, 1991.

21. Bouvard, 1994.

22. Sharoni, 1995.

23. Mano River Peace Network, 2009.

24. Manchanda, 2005.

CHAPTER 14

NOTHING SHORT OF A REVOLUTION: REFLECTIONS ON THE GLOBAL WOMEN'S MOVEMENT

Kavita Nandini Ramdas

In Togo, West Africa, a women's legal rights group mobilizes widows to claim inheritance rights and demand pension payments from the government. A few years ago, they were living in penury, denied their rights to inherit their husbands' land, unable to support their families and often vulnerable to sexual abuse by male neighbors. Today they are leaders in their community and working to educate young women about their rights and their vulnerability to sexually transmitted diseases, including HIV/AIDS.

In Yunan Province in China, the group Ecowomen leads a regional campaign to reduce the use of pesticides in agriculture, drawing connections to the impact on women's health and reproduction, the well-being of children, and the safety of agricultural workers, most of whom are women. The group educates children on environmental sustainability and works to influence policy.

In Serbia and Montenegro, the Anti-Trafficking Center seeks to protect and defend the rights of girls and young women at high risk of being trafficked into sex work or other forms of exploitative labor. Its work begins

---

This article was originally printed in *Conscience Magazine: The Newsjournal of Catholic Opinion*, XXVII, No. 2, Summer 2006.

with self-help groups of high school girls who are experiencing violence, abusive relationships, and incest. The group's male allies also launched an initiative to deconstruct patriarchal stereotypes and behaviors among men and boys who have grown up in a culture of violence in the aftermath of the recent Balkan wars.

In Bolivia, Mujeres Creando organizes indigenous women to ensure that women's voices are included in the new Constitutional Assembly that is to be launched under the leadership of President Evo Morales. Women hold very few positions of political power in the country and continue to live under situations of extreme poverty, lacking access to basic health care and education.

Palestinian refugee women in Lebanon find hope and economic inde-pendence in the programs of Association Najdeh, which trains and educates women in income generation skills and business management. At the same time, women and girls receive education about their own rights and support for their struggles against violence at home and in the community.

Five stories, five continents, five examples of women-led initiatives for change in their own communities. Each one of these examples is local, small-scale, surviving on volunteer efforts and small grants. In many ways these may seem far from the kind of massive social interventions we have come to associate with the word "global." However, viewed through the lens of the Global Fund for Women, it is clear that these five efforts are part of an extraordinary, irreversible, and growing movement to advance wom-en's rights and participation in every part of the world. In its 18-year his-tory, the Global Fund for Women has heard from more than 25,000 women's organizations from countries as tiny as El Salvador and as huge as China. Indeed, its creators, Frances Kissling, Anne Firth Murray, and Laura Lederer, were at least in part inspired by the burgeoning women's move-ment already apparent in 1985 at the UN sponsored Nairobi conference for women when independent nongovernmental organizations organized the first parallel meeting to a UN conference.

WHAT IS A GLOBAL WOMEN'S MOVEMENT?

The dictionary defines the women's movement, or feminism, as a move-ment to secure legal, economic, and social equality for women. It has its roots in the 19th-century women's movement, which sought, among other things, to secure property rights and suffrage for women. The modern fem-inist movement in the West was galvanized by the publication of Betty Friedan's book *The Feminine Mystique.* Increasingly visible mobilization by women activists for equality began in the 1960s and continued through the

1970s across the United States and Europe. Among other goals, its advocates sought equal access to employment, equal pay for equal work, improved day care arrangements, and the right to safe and legal abortions.

Although the modern feminist movement became best known in the West as a struggle by women to be allowed into previously exclusively male preserves, in much of the rest of the world, women's liberation efforts were closely linked with broader social justice movements. This was particularly true of women in the so-called Third World who had been active and equal partners to men in anti-colonial or anti-imperial liberation movements. Thus, women in the Arab world struggled both against British and French imperialism and the traditional restrictions on women's freedom and mobility in their own societies. In South Africa, women played a critical leadership role in the African National Congress' battle against apartheid, while they also challenged long-held patriarchal beliefs that justified domestic violence and early marriage. In the Indian subcontinent, women fought alongside male colleagues in the freedom struggle while demanding changes in practices that harmed women and girls, such as dowry and the terrible treatment of widows. In the indigenous cultures of South America, women also waged a dual struggle, working alongside their men to push back the forces of industrialization and capitalist exploitation of natural resources while demanding recognition and dignity as women within their homes and communities. In each of these instances, women defined their struggle for justice and equality within the larger context of their own cultures and political realities. They eagerly sought solidarity and support from women around the globe, including Western feminists. But their movements were not anemic copies of a Western feminism; because of their connection to larger mass movements for national liberation, they tended to have a stronger class analysis than their counterparts in the developed world.

OUR DISTINGUISHING MARKS

A Shared Analysis

Women's movements worldwide are too scattered and too diverse to claim a narrowly defined ideology, but there is a broad, shared analysis that sees discrimination in the prevailing social structure that privileges men over women as the main problem; in a word, patriarchy. Although the phrase was coined by early feminist theorists who emerged from the West, its analysis and fundamental quest for equality, dignity, and justice are shared by movements of women in many different parts of the world. In the deepest sense, this analysis goes beyond merely seeking to make women equal with men. It dares to ask the fundamental question: equal to what? It does not simply seek to give women the opportunity to participate in the existing world order as it is, but rather asks what is the most beneficial and effective way to organize society—not to simply maximize profit, but to enhance the quality of life for all human beings, women and men. It challenges the underlying premises of current social, economic, and political structures with their assumptions of hierarchy, use of force, and the privileging of the individual over society and the earth. In turn, feminism privileges a sense of shared possibility, equal opportunity, compassion, and community over narrow linear definitions of tribe, nation, and state.

Linkages

The global women's movement has from its earliest stages seen itself as being in a struggle to transcend traditional boundaries of class, religion, nation, and region. It has a strong emphasis on building and strengthening alliances and networks and an understanding that isolation is one of the worst barriers to women's emancipation. Thus the movement seeks to dismantle the barriers that are used to control and restrict the free mobility of individual women and is determined to challenge those barriers in its own structures.

Equality

The movement is fueled by its belief in the equality of all human beings. From the earliest suffragettes to current activists there has been support for efforts that extend beyond gender equality—a vision that does not stop at equality between men and women, but calls for equality between slave and slave owners, between minority communities and majority populations, and between other groups of oppressed or marginalized people. Among a certain subset of feminist activists, sometimes referred to as ecofeminists, it also calls for equal consideration and care for other living beings and the planet Earth.

Freedom/Liberty of Individuals

A common theme for women's movements across the globe is a challenge to restrictions on personal freedom and mobility. Women are often not free to move outside the home on their own, nor free to make decisions about their own bodies or their education and marriage. Even in countries where they have formally been accorded these rights, the environment of violence, insecurity, and traditional expectations continues to confine and restrict women from exercising them.

Dignity of the Human Person

The women's movement is deeply concerned with preserving bodily integrity and places a high value on liberating women's bodies from the physical control of others. It also encourages women to take comfort, delight, and pride in the well-being and health of their own bodies. Around the globe, women and girls are often little more than beasts of burden who carry backbreaking loads and perform incredibly hard labor, mostly in service of others and with little control over the outcome or income generated as a result of that labor. In addition, women's bodies are routinely subjected to incredible violence both within and outside the home through rape, battery, and assault. Women's bodies have, from the earliest times, been viewed as the property of male guardians—fathers, brothers, husbands. Women and girls have traditionally lacked the ability to control what is done to their bodies by others. In particular, women's sexuality has been seen as something to be controlled by practices that range from mutilation (foot binding in China and female circumcision in Africa) to death (honor killings in many parts of Latin America and the Middle East). Today discrimination against lesbians and transgendered individuals continues as a legacy of this fear of women's independent sexuality. In most societies women's ability to move freely outside the home and/or to take pleasure in their own bodies has been tightly controlled and restricted.

Diversity and Tolerance

Ours is a movement that believes in diversity—it understands that the conditions and circumstances within which women live are incredibly varied and complex, and that movements for justice emerge from a specific context within which women articulate a need for their own independence, freedom, and equality. This is both the movement's greatest strength and its greatest challenge since it does not have the cohesion and centralized decision-making structures that can ensure it achieves the clout and influence it needs to make a consistent impact at national and international policy-making levels.

Nonviolence and Peace

For the most part, the women's movement worldwide repudiates violence as inimical to the goals and objectives of true freedom and equality for all. Women and girls are so often the subjects of violence that women's movements have sought to make nonviolence and peaceful strategies a high priority in all aspects of their work. This does not mean that women's movements cannot be forceful and determined and engage in resistance, but it does mean that activists for women's rights tend to be deeply suspicious of the use of force as a method of resolving conflict. This is especially true since throughout history, wars have often been waged allegedly to protect the weak and defenseless, that is, women and children, yet war almost always has the most devastating impact on the same women and children, leaving them homeless, vulnerable to disease and sexual assault, and lacking in economic security.

Education and Economic Independence

Although women do more than two-thirds of the world's labor, they own less than 1 percent of the world's assets. They are paid less for the same work and remain vulnerable to poverty and abuse because they are dependent on others for their own security and that of their children. Women have fought for decades for what has only recently been confirmed by numerous studies—giving women equal access to education and work and the ability to control their own income and inherit and own property benefits society as a whole by improving the health of children, reducing fertility levels, and providing higher levels of education for both girls and boys.

OUR CHALLENGES

The women's movement has never had an easy time; its challenges to the fundamental ways in which most societies have been organized have ensured that it has struggled from its inception. Among current social movements, it is one of the youngest, barely a century old.

As well as playing itself out on the world stage, ours is the only social justice movement that locates its struggle in the most private and personal of venues—the family and the home. For other movements, whether national liberation struggles, worker's rights efforts, or peasant mobilizations, the venues have tended to be public spaces: the factory, the fields, the polis, the state. But women's struggle must be fought and has always been waged on two extremely different yet connected levels. It is a struggle for equality and justice in the public venues of workplace, government, and international institutions, but it is also waged in the most intimate spaces where the individual woman and girl also face the most significant threats to their safety, mental and physical well-being, and personal self-esteem. As Nobel Peace Prize–winner Shirin Ebadi said recently, "The women's movement does not have big offices across the country, but we have a branch in every home in Iran!"

The nature of this struggle is what makes the famous feminist saying "The Personal Is the Political" so true.

This dual nature of the women's struggle poses a special challenge for the movement. Contrary to the commonly held view that it is a movement that is "anti-men," it is not a movement against any particular group of people—capitalists, colonialists, factory owners, or landlords. It is a movement against a system called patriarchy in which men benefit by oppressing women, gaining greater power and wealth in the process. It is a system in which both women and men are trapped in roles that prevent them from achieving or aspiring to their fullest potential. It is a movement in which both women and men can participate. Indeed what is striking about women's movements, particularly in the developing world, is how closely they work with and rely on male allies in their struggle. As a Zapotec woman working to end domestic violence in her village said to me some years ago in Oaxaca, Mexico, "We explained to the men that if they beat us we cannot be strong and they need us to be strong so that we can stand next to them and support them as their partners. We do not try to be strong against them—we want to be strong for them and for us."

But this reality is a challenge for maintaining momentum. If there is no "enemy," then what do we go after? Where do we seek to make an impact and how can we achieve sweeping changes in the ways families, societies, and laws are structured so that women and girls have a real chance? How can the movement challenge long-held assumptions about male roles and female roles without alienating men? How do we measure progress and what kinds of indicators are needed to show that the movement is making a difference?

OUR WEAKNESSES ARE OUR STRENGTHS

The contradictions outlined above are reflected in the fact that our strength arises out of those challenges. This is an intensely global and profoundly local movement all at once. It is not restricted to one country or one region—it is fought in small villages and big cities, in highly developed economies like Japan and desperately poor ones like Zambia. It is fought inside the home and at the workplace—to quote Eleanor Roosevelt, "in small places, close to home." Indeed, it seems that from its inception, the women's movement has understood the power of the personal connection that transcends boundaries of region, state, and nation.

Women's organizations in the global South have long counted on their sisters in the industrialized world to be allies in the struggle and have greatly valued the exchange of ideas, strategies, and tactics that has marked the international women's movement. From Mexico in 1975 to Nairobi in 1985 to the groundbreaking work done by women's groups at the Cairo conference in 1994, women's groups from North and South have worked in concert (not always in agreement about everything, but together on the broad issues) to advance an agenda for women's human rights. This was most evident in the Beijing Platform for Action, approved in 1995 at the UN Conference for Women. Today, there is not a country in the world that does not at least claim to be doing something to improve the status and position of women and girls. In most democracies, women have won the right to vote and run for office; within families women have gained the right to control their own financial resources, own and inherit property, and the ability to fight for the custody of their children. These are not insignificant achievements and they have certainly contributed to a world in which women's rights are hailed as a global good from almost as many pulpits as the equally celebrated notion of "democracy."

WHERE ARE WE TODAY?

The dramatic world events of the past 10 to 15 years, including the fall of the Berlin Wall, the dissolution of the former Soviet Union, rapid globalization and its accompanying discontents, and the rise of the United States as the global hegemon, have had a significant impact on the women's movement. The challenges faced by women in the developing world and in countries of so-called "transition" have been dramatic and extreme. They are also deeply connected to the inequality underlying the current economic and political status quo. In particular, the women's movement sees clearly how many aspects of globalization reinforce the oppression of those in the global South, with women, as always, bearing the brunt of new economic policies, even as narrowly defined structures of electoral democracy and free markets claim to be a source of liberation for women.

Meanwhile, in the West and especially in the United States, a certain kind of complacency has set in—there is a flawed assumption that the issues raised by both the women's movement of the 1970s and the civil rights movement of the 1950s and 1960s (from which it learned so much) have adequately addressed the needs of both women and minorities. Indeed, the gains that were hard-won by the feminists of the 1960s and 1970s—in schools, in sports, in higher education, in access to professional development, and in the protection of their basic reproductive health and rights—are all but forgotten by many young women in the United States. I often hear from individuals who speak about women's rights being natural to Western culture—forgetting that barely 100 years ago, U.S. women, like slaves, were considered the private property of white men.

Thus in many parts of the United States today, the word *feminist* is either derided or dismissed as describing a dated and irrelevant movement. Young women who are strongly committed to equality and justice are somewhat ambivalent about being described as feminists. Among the general population, there are widely held misconceptions about feminists being anti-male or men-haters. This is puzzling for many activists in other countries who are well aware of the achievements of previous and current generations of U.S. feminists, who took the lead in raising awareness about a range of issues, including female circumcision or genital mutilation, fistulas, early marriage and pregnancy, inheritance rights, the position of women under regimes like the Taliban, honor killings, unsafe abortions, the increased vulnerability of women to HIV/AIDS, and the connections between violence and the spread of sexually transmitted diseases (STDs). It is important to note that the United States remains the only Western industrialized country to have failed to sign CEDAW (the UN convention against discrimination against women), apparently for fear that this would force a re-examination of the struggle over equal pay for equal work. Under the Bush administration, much of the energy and efforts of the current U.S. women's movement have been directed to preserving the gains of the past few decades, particularly in the areas of reproductive health and rights. Simultaneously, in the age of the war on terror, there have been conservative forces pushing the women's movement further to the center and challenging its traditionally strong ties to women's struggles in the rest of the world. Indeed, to many outside observers, the women's movement in the United States seems to have lost much of the popular support, momentum, and energy that defined it in previous eras.

AN EMERGING LEADERSHIP

Yet, even as women in the United States seek to cope with growing conservatism within their own communities, there has been an explosion in creative, innovative, and inclusive strategies for revolutionary change in gender relations and social justice from women in the South. Despite pessimism about the state of play in the North, we are, in fact, witnessing a period of exciting growth and the flourishing of an increasingly strong and articulate leadership in the global women's movement.

The leaders of the new women's rights movement are not well known in the West. In fact, they often work on issues that are not even considered "women's issues" and often are groups of women working collectively rather than charismatic individuals. They are environmental activists like Medha Patkar in Gujarat, Oral Ataniyazova in Uzbekistan, and Wangari Maathai in Kenya; they are parliamentarians like Mu Sochua in Cambodia, Pregs Govender in South Africa, President Ellen Johnson Sirleaf in Liberia, and former president Michelle Bachelet of Chile, they are judges like Navi Pillay in South Africa and human rights lawyers like Shirin Ebadi in Iran, Asma Khader in Jordan, and Asma Jahangir in Pakistan; they are teachers like Sakena Yacoobi in Afghanistan and Betty Makoni in Zimbabwe; they may be reinterpreting religion in ways that empower and celebrate women like Fatima Mernissi in Morocco and Zainah Anwar of Sisters in Islam in Malaysia; they are entrepreneurs with new ideas about how to organize and protect women's labor rights like Nari Uddug Kendra in Bangladesh and the South Korean Workers Union in Seoul. They are young girls, often not more than 14 or 16 years of age, in places like Juarez, Mexico, or Rwanda, Zimbabwe, and Uganda, who have shown amazing leadership in challenging traditional practices like Female Genital Mutilation (FGM), sexual abuse and early marriage—not by running away from their communities but by seeking to work with their elders, their mothers and aunts, their fathers and brothers; they are peacemakers brokering dialogue between rebels in Liberia and Guinea like the Mano River Women's Network, or between Arabs and Israelis like the Jerusalem Women's Center in Palestine and Bat Shalom, Israel.

And, because the West in general (and this includes Western journalists, policy makers, academics, politicians, and, even some Western women's groups as well) is not used to recognizing or accepting leadership that does not come with titles, degrees, or even Western education, it will take time to develop a new relationship based on respect, trust, and equality. In this 21st century, the rest of the world is questioning many of the givens in so-called Western civilization. Women's rights organizations are delighted by the promise of some aspects of science and technology, but are not sure that the model of excessive consumption and disregard for the environment is the best one. They are not sure that the atomization and isolation of individuals in a community is what they should aspire to as an indication of development. Many grassroots organizations across the developing world are questioning the Western model of development—its reliance on petroleum chemicals, large dams, nuclear power plants, and genetically engineered food crops. There is growing pressure among women's groups to look for more sustainable strategies to ensure sufficient energy and food for all. They would like more equality and democracy in their societies, but they do not think that elections in and of themselves are a substitute for grassroots participatory processes, representation of all population groups, and the rule of law. In other words, they are challenging some of the underlying assumptions of progress as defined by the West. They are doing this in a fiercely contested space, since religious extremists of every faith are also reacting to the pressures of globalization and modernization with a reaction that is regressive and seeks refuge in a simplistic interpretation of religion (whether that is Christianity, Islam, Hinduism, or Judaism) and is determined to re-impose control over women as a way to return to a mythical golden era when men were men and women knew their place.

Women's groups in the rest of the world are grateful for the support and solidarity of their like-minded sisters and brothers in the West. They need investments and financial resources that are given with respect, but they do not need charity or missionary zeal. They do not need to be empowered—rather they need their allies in the West, especially women's organizations, to stand by the human rights principles they uphold and apply them fairly to all societies, not just the ones that are the current favorites of the U.S. government. They want fair trade, not free trade that provides huge subsidies to Northern farmers, while demanding that Senegal and Sri Lanka open their economies to large multinational corporations. They need our respect and our support for their own powerful efforts to re-envision their societies. They want us to acknowledge that cultures are not static, but are continually evolving. They know that there is nothing inherently democratic about Western societies. The best thing we can do for them is to set a good example ourselves and not be hypocritical (for example, bringing liberation to Afghan women while Southern Baptists require women to "obey" their husbands or turning a blind eye to Mormon polygamy even as we gasp about the harmful traditions of the Middle East or South Asia).

Lastly, women's groups in other countries urge U.S. women's organizations to strengthen the women's movement here to be more inclusive of poor women, of migrant women, of native or indigenous women, of black and Latina women. They urge them to recognize that the policies of the United States have damaging impacts on women—not just women-specific policies such as the "global gag rule," but other policies such as North American Free Trade Agreement (NAFTA), subsidies on cotton and sugar, unfair trade practices, the export of tobacco and substandard drugs and the refusal of pharmaceutical companies to provide retroviral drugs at low cost to AIDS victims so that the companies can preserve their intellectual property rights. They welcome tough laws on trafficking but urge the United States to remember that patriarchy, poverty, and lack of economic choices fuel trafficking in women and that women are worthy of dignity and respect regardless of what forced them into the sex trade. Most importantly, they are concerned that women and the women's movement in the United States do not recognize the huge impact of the U.S. war on terror and the export of military might and weapons on women in the rest of the world. They are concerned that the women's movement in the United States appears to be relatively disconnected from the global peace movement and that the fear factor created after 9/11 has made it difficult for women in the United States to understand their country's policies and have actually made thousands, if not millions, of women and their families around the world less secure and safe. This is not just because in places such as Iraq, Israel, and Afghanistan, war and conflict have actually threatened women's lives and those of their families, but because the war on terrorism has enabled both the United States and other governments to divert desperately needed development resources in the fields of health, education, and social services into military and defense expenditures. Jeffrey Sachs, an economist at Columbia University, recently stated that the U.S. government gives "just $16 billion in development assistance, but our defense budget is nearly $450 billion each year. . . . We are flying a lopsided plane and it is bound to crash."

Women's rights groups around the world want to be given the chance to shift and change attitudes within their own communities from within—without the pressure of feeling that they are being "saved" from either their own cultures or their own backwardness by Western forces of modernization and progress. They cannot do this if they feel that their societies as a whole are under attack from the West. They cannot successfully challenge domestic violence while their fathers, brothers, and husbands are assumed to be terrorists and their faith is dismissed as tribal. This does not mean they have all the answers and it does not mean that they do not make mistakes. It does mean that all of us in the West—and not just the women's movement—need to re-examine our relationships with women in the rest of the world and to proceed with a degree of humility and openness as we listen to and learn from and with them, allowing them to be their own articulate advocates for an alternative vision of a future that is just, peaceful, and sustainable.

CHAPTER 15

A Feminist Ethical Perspective on Weapons of Mass Destruction

Carol Cohn and Sara Ruddick

The world will note that the first atomic bomb was dropped on Hiroshima, a military base. That was because we wished in this first attack to avoid, insofar as possible, the killing of civilians.

—President Harry Truman, August 9, 1945[1]

I heard her voice calling "Mother, Mother." I went towards the sound. She was completely burned. The skin had come off her head altogether, leaving a twisted knot at the top. My daughter said, "Mother, you're late, please take me back quickly." She said it was hurting a lot. But there were no doctors. There was nothing I could do. So I covered up her naked body and held her in my arms for nine hours. At about eleven o'clock that night she cried out again "Mother," and put her hand around my neck. It was already ice-cold. I said, "Please say Mother again." But that was the last time.

—A Hiroshima survivor[2]

This piece is excerpted from a significantly longer chapter that originally appeared in Steven Lee and Sohail Hashmi, eds., *Ethics and Weapons of Mass Destruction* (New York: Cambridge University Press, 2004). Copyright © 2004 Cambridge University Press. Reprinted with permission.

ANTI-WAR FEMINISM

There is no single feminist position on war, armament, and weapons of mass destruction (WMD). We report here on one feminist tradition we call "anti-war feminism," which opposes war-making as a practice and seeks to replace it with practices of non-violent contest and reconciliation.[3]

Anti-war feminists' opposition to the practice of war is simultaneously pragmatic and moral. We have an abiding suspicion of the use of violence, even in the best of causes. The ability of violence to achieve its stated aims is routinely over-estimated, the complexity of its costs overlooked. Our opposition also stems from the perception that the practice of war entails far more than the killing and destroying in armed combat. It requires the creation of a "war system" that entails arming, training, and organizing for possible wars; allocating the resources these preparations require; creating a culture in which wars are seen as morally legitimate, even alluring; and shaping and fostering the masculinities and femininities which undergird men's and women's acquiescence to war. Even when it appears to achieve its aims, war is a source of enormous individual suffering and loss. Modern warfare is also predictably destructive to societies, civil liberties and democratic processes, and the non-human world. State security may sometimes be served by war, but too often human security is not.

The tradition as a whole is not typically "pacifist" as that term is usually understood. While some anti-war feminists are indeed pacifists, the tradition as a whole neither rejects all wars as wrong, nor condemns others because they resort to violence. Indeed, some anti-war feminists have supported military campaigns against oppressive regimes. Although they do not reject violence in principle, they are, however, committed to "translating" or "transfiguring violence into creative militant nonviolence."[4]

To suggest the distinctive character of anti-war feminism, we identify four of its constitutive positions.

1. War Is a Gendered Practice

First, anti-war feminists insistently underline the gendered character of war, stressing its domination by men and masculinity, thus making visible what has been taken for granted. But they also stress that women's labor has always been central to war-making—although it has also consistently been either unacknowledged, or represented as tangential, in order to protect war's "masculinity."[5]

Secondly, they challenge the view that war is *inherently* gendered—in particular, the view that biology renders men "naturally" war-like and war therefore a "natural" male activity. The simple link of some innate male aggression to the conduct of war is belied both by what men actually do in war[6] and by many men's reluctance to fight.[7] Anti-war feminists identify the association of manliness with militarized violence as the product of specific social processes which they try to change.[8]

Finally, anti-war feminists analyze the ways that war-making is shaped by a gendered system of meanings. We understand gender not just as a characteristic of individuals, but as a symbolic system—a central organizing discourse in our culture, a set of ways of thinking, which not only shape how we experience and represent ourselves as men and women, but which also provide a familiar set of metaphors, dichotomies, and values which structure ways of thinking about other aspects of the world. In other words, we see the ways in which human characteristics and endeavors are culturally divided into those seen as "masculine" and those seen as "feminine" (for example, mind is opposed to body; culture to nature; thought to feeling; logic to intuition; objectivity to subjectivity; aggression to passivity; confrontation to accommodation; war to peace; abstraction to particularity; public to private; political to personal; realism to moral reflection), and the terms coded "male" are valued more highly than those coded "female."

We see the devaluation of what is seen as "feminine" as distorting basic national security paradigms and policies. Once the devaluation-by-association takes place, it becomes extremely difficult for anyone, female or male to express concerns or ideas marked as "feminine." What then gets left out is the emotional, the concrete, the particular, human bodies and their vulnerability, human lives and their subjectivity.[9]

2. Start from Women's Lives

Applying a central tenet of feminist methodology, we look at war and weapons from the perspective of women's lives, making women's experiences a central rather than marginal concern. In the context of war, "women's lives" has two primary referents: the work women do and the distinctive bodily assaults war inflicts on them.

Women's work traditionally includes life-shaping responsibilities of caring labor: giving birth to and caring for children, protecting and sustaining ill, frail, or other dependents, maintaining households, and fostering and protecting kin, village, and neighborhood relations. War threatens the well-being, and even existence, of the people, relations, and homes that women maintain.[10] Women are often in effect conscripted for dangerous or demeaning work whose effects may also survive the official end of war.

The practice of war implies a willingness to inflict pain and damage on bodies, to "out-injure" the other in pursuit of war's aim.[11] Women are no more or less embodied than men; but their bodies are differently at risk. There has been a quantitative shift in the ratio of women to men sufferers as civilian casualties come to outnumber those of the military. Rape is the conqueror's reward and taunt. It is a weapon against women and also against the men and community to whom they belong. The woman who becomes pregnant by rape may be seen by the rapist, or by herself, as forced to join the enemy, to create him. She may fear, and her rapist may hope, that she is contributing to the destruction of her own people.[12]

Given the multiple ways that war commits violence against women, it is suspect, at the least, to look for security from militaries. Conceptions of security based in the military defense of state borders and interests often mean greater insecurity for women.

3. War Is Not Spatially or Temporally Bounded

Anti-war feminism rejects the conception of war as a discrete event, with clear locations, and a beginning and an end. In our vision it is crucial not to separate war from either the preparations made for it or its long-term physical, psychological, socio-economic, environmental, and gendered effects.[13]

War's violence is not separate from other social practices. There is a continuum of violence running from bedroom, to boardroom, factory, stadium, classroom, and battlefield, "traversing our bodies and our sense of self."[14] Weapons of violence, and representations of those weapons, travel through interlocking institutions—economic, political, familial, technological, and ideological.

Before the first gunfire is the research, development, and deployment of weapons; the maintaining of standing armies; the cultural glorification of the power of armed force; and the social construction of masculinities and femininities that support a militarized state. When the war is over, what remains is a ripped social fabric: the devastation of the physical, economic, and social infrastructure through which people provision themselves and their families; the havoc wrought in the lives and psyches of combatants, noncombatants, and children who have grown up in war; the surfeit of arms on the streets, and of ex-soldiers trained to kill; citizens who have been schooled and practiced in the methods of violence, but not in nonviolent methods of dealing with conflict; "nature" poisoned, burned, made ugly and useless.[15] Typically peace includes official punishment—retribution, reparations, domination, and deprivation.

4. Alternative Epistemology

Both in philosophy and in Western thought more generally, "objective" knowledge is produced by socially autonomous reasoners who have transcended institutional constraints, gender identifications, and emotion. Many feminists propose an alternative epistemology, which stresses that all thinkers are "situated" within epistemic communities that ask some but not other questions, and legitimate some but not other ways of knowing. We are each of us also situated by social identities and personal histories.[16] Knowing is never wholly separated from feelings. We begin with and return to concrete open-ended questions about actual people in actual situations. Finally, we measure arguments, and ideals of objectivity, partly in the goods they yield, the pleasures they make possible and the suffering they prevent.

ANTI-WAR FEMINISM AND WEAPONS OF MASS DESTRUCTION

Grounded in this alternative epistemology, we are ambivalent about making ethical distinctions among weapons. We recognize that some weapons, and uses of weapons, are worse than others. Some weapons can be carefully aimed to cause minimal damage; others cannot. Some weapons may be deliberately cruel (dum dum bullets), outlast the occasion that apparently justified them (land mines), harm indiscriminately (cluster bombs, land mines again, or poison gas in a crowded subway), or injure massively and painfully (incendiary bombs). While respecting these distinctions, we nonetheless fear that stressing the horror of some weapons diminishes the horrors that more "acceptable" weapons wreak. For us the crucial question is not, "How do we chose among weapons?" but rather, "How can we identify and attend to the specific horrors of any weapon?"

In contrast to the attention given to WMD, for example, the horrors of small arms and light weapons (SALW) are too often ignored. SALW are weapons light enough to be packed over a mountain on a mule, including stinger missiles, machine guns, grenades, assault rifles, small explosives, and handguns. They are inexpensive, require little or no training to use, and are easily available, often unregulated by state, military, civic, or even parental authority. They have a long shelf life, travel easily, and therefore can, in the course of time, be traded, turned against various enemies, and brought home. They are a staple of the arms market, and the principal instrument of violence in armed conflicts throughout the world. When one looks at it from the perspectives of women's lives, SALW are seen as the cause of enormous, sustained, and pervasive suffering of very specific kinds. They are an instrument and enforcer of sexual violence, they wreak havoc among the relationships women have tended, and destroy women's capacity to obtain food, water, and other necessary staples, to farm and to keep their animals safe. In the lives of women around the world, small arms and light weapons are "weapons of mass destruction in slow motion."

Regarding what are more typically thought of as WMD, anti-war feminists have focused on nuclear weapons, and the discourse through which their use is theorized and legitimated—what we call "technostrategic discourse."[17] Critically, this discourse functions in myriad ways to divert attention from the specific horrors of the weapons' use. Anti-war feminists have written about both the sexual and domestic metaphors that turn the mind's eye toward the pleasant and familiar, rather than toward images of indescribable devastation. They have identified in nuclear discourse techniques of denial and conceptual fragmentation. They have emphasized the ways that the abstraction and euphemism of nuclear discourse protect nuclear defense intellectuals and politicians from the grisly realities behind their words. [18]

Abstract discussion of warfare is both the tool and the privilege of those who imagine themselves as the users of weapons. The victims, if they can speak at all, speak quite differently as seen in the following two statements.

While a U.S. defense intellectual says:

[You have to have ways to maintain communications in a] nuclear environment, a situation bound to include EMP blackout, brute force damage to systems, a heavy jamming environment, and so on.[19]

In an account by a Hiroshima survivor we read:

Everything was black, had vanished into the black dust, was destroyed. Only the flames that were beginning to lick their way up had any color. From the dust that was like a fog, figures began to loom up, black, hairless, faceless. They screamed with voices that were no longer human. Their screams drowned out the groans rising everywhere from the rubble, groans that seemed to rise from the very earth itself.[20]

Needless to say, it is easier to contemplate and "justify" the use of nuclear weapons in the abstract language of defense intellectuals than in the descriptive, emotionally resonant language of the victim. Detailed, focal attention to the human impact of weapons' use is not only considered out of bounds in security professionals' discourse; it is also de-legitimated by its association with the "feminine," as is evident in this excerpt of an interview with a physicist:

Several colleagues and I were working on modeling counterforce nuclear attacks, trying to get realistic estimates of the number of immediate fatalities that would result from different deployments. At one point, we re-modeled a particular attack, using slightly different assumptions, and found that instead of there being 36 million immediate fatalities, there would only be 30 million. And everybody was sitting around nodding, saying, "Oh yeh, that's great, only 30 million," when all of a sudden, I heard what we were saying. And I blurted out, "Wait, I've just heard how we're talking—Only 30 million! Only 30 million human beings killed instantly?" Silence fell upon the room. Nobody said a word. They didn't even look at me. It was awful. I felt like a woman.[21]

ANTI-WAR FEMINISM AND THE FULL COSTS OF HAVING WEAPONS OF MASS DESTRUCTION

If we must accord full weight to their daily effects on the lives of women, we find that the development and deployment of nuclear weapons, even when they are not used in warfare, exacts costs that particularly affect women. In the words of an Indian feminist:

> The social costs of nuclear weaponization in a country where the basic needs of shelter, food and water, electricity, health and education have not been met are obvious. . . . Less food for the family inevitably means an even smaller share for women and female children just as water shortages mean an increase in women's labor who have to spend more time and energy in fetching water from distant places at odd hours of the day.[22]

Although the United States is not as poor a nation as India, Pakistan, or Russia, it has remained, throughout the nuclear age, a country in which poverty and hunger are rife, health care still unaffordable to many, low-cost housing unavailable, with crumbling public schools and infrastructure, while the American nuclear weapons program has come at the cost of $4.5 trillion.[23]

In addition to being economically costly, nuclear weapons development has medical and political costs. In the U.S. program, many people have been exposed to high levels of radiation, including uranium miners; workers at reactors and processing facilities; the quarter of a million military personnel who took place in "atomic battlefield" exercises; "downwinders" from test sites; and Marshallese Islanders. Politically, nuclear regimes require a level of secrecy and security measures that exclude the majority of citizens, and in most countries, all women, from defense policy and decision making.[24]

From the perspective of women's lives, we see not only the costs of the *development* of nuclear weapons, but also the spiritual, social, and psychological costs of *deployment*. One cost, according to some feminists, is that "Nuclearization produces social consent for increasing levels of violence."[25] Another cost, for many, is that nuclear weapons create high levels of tension, insecurity, and fear. As Arundhati Roy puts it, nuclear weapons "[i]nform our dreams. They bury themselves like meat hooks deep in the base of our brains."[26]

Further, feminists are concerned about the effect of nuclear policy on moral thought, on ideas about gender, and how the two intersect. Nuclear development may legitimize male aggression, and breed the idea that nuclear explosions give "virility" to the nation that men as individuals can somehow share.

The strange character of nuclear policy making, which not only sidelines moral and ethical questions, but genders them, creates an elite that represents itself as rational, scientific, modern, and of course masculine, while ethical questions—questions about the social and environmental costs—are made to seem emotional, effeminate, regressive, and not modern. This rather dangerous way of thinking, which suggests that questions about human life and welfare are somehow neither modern nor properly masculine questions, or that men have no capacity and concern for peace and morality, can have disastrous consequences for both men and women.[27]

All in all, we find the daily costs of WMD development and deployment staggeringly high—in and of themselves enough to prevent deterrence from being an ethical moral option.

A so-called "realist" response to this judgment might well argue that the results of a nuclear attack would be so catastrophic that the rest of these considerations are really irrelevant. We make two rejoinders to this claim. First, we question the very assumptions that bestow the mantle of "realism" on such a constrained focus on weapons and state power. Rather than simply being an "objective" reflection of political reality, we understand this thought system as (1) a partial and distorted picture of reality, and (2) a major contributor to creating the very circumstances it purports to describe and protect against.

Second, just as feminists tend to be skeptical about the efficacy of violence, they might be equally skeptical about the efficacy of deterrence. Deterrence theory is an elaborate, abstract conceptual edifice, which posits a hypothetical relation between two different sets of weapons systems, presided over by "rational actors," for whom what counts as "rational" is the same, independent of culture, history, or individual difference. It depends on those "rational actors" perfectly understanding the meaning of "signals" communicated by military actions, despite dependence on technologies that sometimes malfunction; despite cultural difference and the difficulties of ensuring mutual understanding even when best friends make direct face-to-face statements to each other. The dream of perfect rationality and control that underwrites deterrence theory is highly dangerous, since it legitimates constructing a system that only could be (relatively) safe if that perfect rationality and control were actually possible. "Realists" are quick to point out the dangers of *not having* WMD for deterrence when other states have them. Feminist perspectives suggest that that danger only appears so self-evidently greater than the danger of *having* WMD if you discount as "soft," the serious attention to the costs of development and deployment.

THE ETHICS OF PROLIFERATION

We have been asked to address the question, "If some nations possess weapons of mass destruction (either licitly or illicitly) for defensive and deterrent purposes, is it proper to deny such possession to others for the same purposes?"

We believe that the rampant proliferation of weapons *of all kinds*, from handguns to nuclear weapons, is a massive tragedy, the direct and indirect source of great human suffering. Given this starting point, we, of course, oppose the proliferation of WMD. But our opposition does not allow us to give a simple "yes" answer to the question above, as it is posed. Before turning to proliferation as a *phenomenon*, we must first consider current proliferation *discourse*.

Proliferation as a Discourse

Proliferation is not a mere description or mirror of a phenomenon that is "out there," but rather a very specific way of identifying and constructing a problem. Proliferation, as used in Western political discourse, does not simply refer to the multiplication of WMD on the planet. Rather, it constructs some WMD as a problem, and others as unproblematic. It does so by assuming pre-existing, legitimate possessors of the weapons, implicitly not only entitled to those weapons, but to modernize and develop new generations of them as well. The problematic WMD are only those that "spread" into the arsenals of other, formerly nonpossessor states. This is presumably the basis for the "licit/illicit" distinction in the question; it does not refer to the nature of the weapons themselves, nor even to the purposes for which they are intended—only, in the case of nuclear weapons, to who the possessor is, where "licitness" is based on the treaty-enshrined "we got there first."

Thus, use of the term *proliferation* tends to locate the person who uses it within a possessor state, and aligns him or her with the political stance favoring the hierarchy of state power enshrined in the current distribution of WMD. The framing of the question ". . . is it proper to deny [WMD] possession to others for the same purposes?" seems similarly based in a possessor state perspective, as it is presumably the possessor states who must decide whether it is proper to deny possession to others.

As we have already stated, we find WMD themselves intrinsically morally indefensible, no matter who possesses them, and we are concerned about the wide array of costs *to any state* of development and deployment. We therefore reject the discourse's implicit division of "good" and "bad," "safe" and "unsafe" WMD (defined as good or bad depending on who possesses them). Our concern is to understand how some WMD are rendered invisible ("ours") and some visible ("theirs"); some rendered malignant and others benign.

Here, we join others in noting that the language in which the case against proliferation is made is ethno-racist and contemptuous. Generally, in Western proliferation discourse as a whole, a distinction is drawn between "the "Self" (seen as responsible) versus the non-Western "Unruly Other."[28] The United States represents itself as a rational actor, while representing the Unruly Other as emotional, unpredictable, irrational, immature, misbehaving. Not only does this draw on and reconstruct an Orientalist portrayal of Third World actors;[29] it does so through the medium of gendered terminology. By drawing the relations between possessors and nonpossessors in gendered terms—the prudential, rational, advanced, mature, restrained, technologically and bureaucratically competent (and thus "masculine") Self, versus the emotional, irrational, unpredictable, uncontrolled, immature, primitive, undisciplined, technologically incompetent (and thus "feminine") Unruly Other—the discourse naturalizes and legitimates the Self/possessor states having weapons that the Other does not. By drawing on and evoking gendered imagery and resonances, the discourse naturalizes the idea that "We"/the United States/ the responsible father must protect, must control and limit "her," the emotional, out-of-control state, for her own good, as well as for ours.

This Western proliferation discourse has had a function in the wider context of U.S. national security politics. With the end of the "Evil Empire" in the late 1980s, until the attacks of September 11, 2001, the United States appeared to be without an enemy of grand enough proportions to justify maintaining its sprawling military-industrial establishment. This difficulty was forestalled by the construction of the category of "rogue states"—states seen as uncontrollable, irresponsible, irrational, malevolent, and antagonistic to the West.[30] Their unruliness and antagonism was represented as intrinsic to their irrational nature; if it were not in their "nature," the United States would have needed to ask more seriously if actions on the part of the West had had any role in producing that hostility and disorder.

The discourse of WMD proliferation has been one of the principal means of producing these states as major threats. To say this is neither to back away from our position opposing WMD, nor to assess the degree to which WMD in the hands of "Other" states actually do threaten the United States, the "Other" states' regional opponents, or their own population. But it is an assessment of the role of WMD proliferation discourse in naturalizing and legitimating otherwise-difficult-to-make-appear-rational programs and expenditures such as National Missile Defense.[31]

Proliferation as a Phenomenon

Within the logic of deterrence theory and proliferation discourse, the phenomenon of WMD proliferation is understandable in two main ways. States either acquire WMD for purposes of aggression—that is, to use WMD or to threaten their use in acts of aggression, intimidation, and/or coercion against other states or populations within their own state. States also acquire WMD to enhance their own security by deterring an opponent from attack. Within a strategic calculus, either is understood as a "rational" motivation for WMD possession, even if not everyone would view these reasons as equally morally defensible.

Some in the security community have argued that this "realist consensus" about states' motivations for development of WMD "is dangerously inadequate." They argue that "nuclear weapons, like other weapons, are more than tools of national security; they are political objects of considerable importance in domestic debates and internal bureaucratic struggles and can also serve as international normative symbols of modernity and identity."[32] We agree, but would add that the understanding any of those motivations will be incomplete without gender analysis.

We argue that gendered terms and images are an integral part of the ways national security issues are thought about and represented—and that it matters. During the Gulf War, for example, the mass media speculated whether George Bush had finally "beat the wimp factor." When in the spring of 1998 India exploded five nuclear devices, Hindu nationalist leader Balasaheb Thackeray explained that "we had to prove that we are not eunuchs." An Indian newspaper cartoon "depicted Prime Minister Atal Behari Vajpayee propping up his coalition government with a nuclear bomb. 'Made with Viagra,' the caption read."[33]

Feminists argue that these images are not trivial, but instead deserve analysis. Metaphors that equate political and military power with sexual potency and masculinity serve to both shape and limit the ways in which national security is conceptualized.[34] Political actors incorporate sexual metaphors in their representations of nuclear weapons as a way to mobilize gendered associations and symbols in creating assent, excitement, support for, and identification with the weapons and their own political regime. Moreover, gendered metaphor is not only an integral part of accomplishing domestic power aims. The use of these metaphors also appropriates the test of a nuclear weapon into the occasion for reinforcing patriarchal gender relations.

That a nation wishing to stake a claim to being a world power (or a regional one) should choose nuclear weapons as its medium for doing so is often seen as "natural": the more advanced military destructive capacity you have, the more powerful you are. The "fact" that nuclear weapons would be the coin of the realm in establishing a hierarchy of state power is fundamentally unremarked, unanalyzed, taken for granted by most (nonfeminist) analysts. Some anti-war feminists, by contrast, have looked with a historical and post-colonial eye, and seen nuclear weapons' enshrinement as the emblem of power not as a natural fact, but as a social one, produced by the actions of states. They argue that when the United States, with the most powerful economy and conventional military in the world, acts as though its power and security are guaranteed only by a large nuclear arsenal, it creates a context in which nuclear weapons become the ultimate necessity for and symbol of state security. And when the United States or any other nuclear power works hard to ensure that other states don't obtain nuclear weapons, it is creating a context in which nuclear weapons become the ultimate arbiter of political power.[35]

An Ethical Nonproliferation Politics?

Finally, after our critique of both the framing and political uses of Western proliferation discourse, and our questioning of the adequacy of the models through which proliferation as a phenomenon is understood, there remains the question: "If some nations possess WMD (either licitly or illicitly) for defensive and deterrent purposes, is it proper to deny such possession to others for the same purposes?"

We have spoken of the multiple costs of developing and deploying nuclear weapons *to their possessors* and the immense suffering that WMD would bring. Given what we have said, we should not be indifferent to other states' developing nuclear weapons unless we were indifferent to them. Additionally, we believe that more WMD in more places would make their "accidental" or purposive use by states, as well as their availability to terrorists, more likely. So we are opposed to the development and deployment of any WMD, by any state or non-state actor.

Despite this clear opposition to the spread of WMD, we are uneasy simply answering "no" to the question *as it is posed*. The question assumes that some states already have WMD, and asks only whether it is proper to deny WMD to others. Denying WMD to others implies maintaining the current international balance of power, in which the West is privileged, politically and economically. As feminists, we oppose the extreme inequality inherent in the current world order, and are troubled by actions that will further enshrine it. But at the same time, we cannot endorse WMD proliferation as a mode of equalization; nor do we see it as an effective form of redress.

Second, we come to the question not only as feminists, but as citizens of the most highly armed possessor state. As such, we must ask: are citizens of possessor states entitled to judge, threaten, allow, or encourage the decisions of nonpossessor states to develop WMD? On what grounds? In what discursive territory? As we have outlined above, we find the existing proliferation discourse too ethno-racist, too focused on horizontal rather than vertical proliferation, and too sanguine about the justifiability of "our" having what "they" are not fit to have.

Our task then, as anti-war feminists, is to learn how to participate in a constructive conversation,[36] eschewing the vocabulary of "proliferation," learning to listen, perhaps publicizing the warnings that women—and men—are issuing about the multiple costs and risks of WMD in their particular states. As citizens of the most highly armed possessor state, our credibility as participants in this conversation will be contingent on our committed efforts to bring about nuclear disarmament in our own state, and our efforts to redress the worldwide inequalities that are underwritten by our military superiority.

NOTES

1. Truman, 1945.
2. Thompson, 1988.
3. Certain figures are taken as representatives of anti- war feminism. Images of Kathe Kollwitz' art work and phrases from Virginia Woolf's writing appear on postcards and T-shirts. On a deeper look each of these women expresses complexities of anti-war feminism. Kollwitz, who sent her son "off to war" with flowers and a blessing, slowly and with difficulty achieved an anti-war stance. Woolf, whose imagination was fundamentally shaped by her fear and rejection of war, found her anti-militarism tested by Nazi aggression. Woolf explicitly situated her anti-war feminism within a particular class: "daughters of educated men." Yet Cynthia Enloe, who studies the effects of masculinist militarization on women's lives across the globe, finds that Woolf's Three Guineas (New York: Harcourt Brace, 1938) sheds "new light on the subtle practices of militarization" with each new group of students from "the United States, Japan, Mali, Korea, Bulgaria." See Cynthia Enloe, Maneuvers: The International Politics of Militarizing Women's Lives (Berkeley: The University of California Press, 2000). The editors of Feminist Studies chose for its post-September 11th cover a photograph of Jane Addams at 70 "campaigning for peace" with her friend Mary McDowell, who, like Addams, was a pacifist, suffragist, and unionist. Jean Bethke Elshtain, herself an engaged reporter on and ambivalent participant in anti-war feminism, has just produced a biography of Addams and a "reader" that collects Addams's writings. Addams was ostracized for reporting that many soldiers were loath to kill, that they could use

a bayonet only after they were given "dope." Were Addams now to become representative, as Kollwitz and Woolf are, she would highlight the typical commitments of anti-war feminism to social justice and to the well-being of men made killers in war.

Our tradition is represented by groups as much as by individuals. Among the most venerable is the Women's International League for Peace and Freedom (WILPF), which was founded in 1915 to protest World War I, and which today is actively involved in disarmament and non-proliferation issues, as well as in advocacy for gender analysis in security affairs at the United Nations. During the Cold War, many women's movements protested nuclear weapons. Many other women's protest movements represent some but not all aspects of anti-war feminism. The courageous protest of the Madres of Argentina against a military dictatorship only gradually became anti-militarist and seems never to have been conventionally feminist. Women in Black began in Israel/Palestine and has moved to many conflict-ridden sites around the world; though it nearly everywhere engages in struggles for peace, its members differ about the extent and generality of its anti-militarism. In armed conflict zones around the world, there are many other women's peace initiatives and groups, although many would identify themselves as anti-war, fewer would adopt the label "feminist." An excellent place to start researching these groups is the Web site www.peacewomen.org, which was started to provide a clearinghouse of information and Web site links for women's peace groups.

4. A substantial literature exists regarding feminism and pacifism. See Deming, 1984 and Woolf, 1953.

5. Cynthia Enloe has been a pioneer in this field. See Enloe, 1983, 1989, 1993.

6. On the multiple masculinities required by war-making, see Ruddick, 1995.

7. For men's reluctance to fight, see Goldstein, 2001 especially Ch. 5. The relation between masculinity, aggression, and war remains highly controversial. Goldstein provides a lucid, balanced assessment of this debate.

8. See Enloe, 1993.

9. Cohn, 1987, 1993.

10. On war's destructive effects on women's work, see Tripp, 2000 and Cockburn, 1999.

11. Scarry, 1985.

12. See original text for an extensive list of further reading on this topic of rape as an instrument of war.

13. For the classic statement of this perspective, see Woolf, 2009; Cuomo, 1996; and Schott, 1996.

14. Cockburn, 1999.

15. This is primarily a description of after-effects on societies whose territories have been the site of warfare. But even those societies whose soldiers fight in distant lands suffer related effects. Surviving soldiers may bring home the effects of violence: injured bodies and minds; remorse, rage and despair; habits of aggression and abuse; syndromes of suffering.

16. The phrase "alternative epistemology" comes from Margaret Urban Walker, "Moral Understandings: Alternative 'Epistemology' for a Feminist Ethics," Hypatia 4, no. 4 (1989): 15–28. See original text for an extensive list of further readings.

17. Cohn, 1987.

18. See Cohn, 1993; Griffin, 1992; and Wolf, 1984.

19. General Robert Rosenberg, formerly on the National Security Council staff during the Carter Administration, speaking at the Harvard Seminar on C3I. "The Influence of Policy Making on C3I," in Incidental Paper: Seminar on Command, Control, Communications and Intelligence, Spring 1980. Center for Information Policy Research, Harvard University, 59.

20. Hisako Matsubara, Cranes at Dusk (Garden City, NY: Dial Press, 1985). The author was a child in Kyoto at the time the atomic bomb was dropped. Her description is based on the memories of survivors. See Matsubara, 1985.

21. Cohn, 1993.

22. Some defenders of nuclear weapons argue that nuclear weapons are actually economically beneficial, as a form of "defense on the cheap" (in contrast to the costs of conventional weapons and armies). Sangari et al. reject this argument, pointing out that "Nuclearization will not eliminate the necessity for conventional weapons. On the contrary, by provoking neighboring countries severely, it has made the prospect of conventional warfare far more imminent, and has stepped up military investment altogether." See Sangari et al., 1998.

23. In 1995, a study by the Nuclear Weapons Cost Study Project Committee was the first systematic attempt to catalog the comprehensive cost of the U.S. nuclear weapons program from inception in 1940 to 1995. The amount, $ 4 trillion, did not include the cost of disposing of hundreds of tons of uranium and plutonium. It did not include the money spent on National Missile Defense nor the costs of environmental clean up necessitated by the "unprecedented legacy of toxic and radioactive pollution at dozens of sites and thousands of facilities across the country," which they estimated would cost at least half a trillion more, where it can be cleaned up at all. See Schwartz, 1995.

24. This point is made by Sangari et al., 1998.

25. Ibid.

26. Roy, 1999.

27. Sangari et al., 1998.

28. Wright, 2001. Manuscript by courtesy of the author.

29. Said, 1978; Biswas, 2001.

30. For "rogue states," see Klare, 1995 and Wright, 2001.

31. Berry, 2000.

32. Scott Sagan, for example, has argued that "nuclear weapons programs also serve other, more parochial and less obvious objectives." See Sagan, 1996. In our view all three of the models Sagan outlines—the "security model," the "domestic politics model," and the "norms model"—are seriously weakened by their failure to incorporate gender analysis.

33. Basu and Basu, 1999.

34. Cohn, 1993.

35. Arundhati Roy put it this way: "But let us pause to give credit where it's due. Whom must we thank for all this? The Men who made it happen. The Masters of the Universe. Ladies and gentlemen, the United States of America! Come on up here, folks, stand up and take a bow. Thank you for doing this to the world. Thank

you for making a difference. Thank you for showing us the way. Thank you for altering the very meaning of life." See Roy, 1999. Some Indian feminists have combined this attention to weapons as symbols in world power relations with an analysis of the gendered meanings of power. Basu and Basu argue that the Bharativa Janata party decision to explode five nuclear bombs was in part an attempt "to shatter stereotypes about the 'effeminate' Indian that date back to the period of British colonialism." The British particularly disparaged 'feminized' Hindu masculinity, while seeing Muslims as "robust and brave." See Basu and Basu, 1999.

36. The term "constructive conversation" was introduced to us through a conversation Carol had with Laura Chasin, the director of the Public Conversations Project. Their Web site, http://www.publicconversations.org, would be a valuable resource for anyone who is trying to think about political conflict.

PART VI

THE CHALLENGE BEFORE US

Poverty and hunger are particularly grievous results of structural violence. They are not consequences of one particular violent activity but rather of the way that society at all levels is organized. Poverty has a demographic distribution internationally and within cities. It also reflects the distribution of resources and the system of laws and rules that regulate the ways they are allocated. Poverty reflects the system of information exchange telling who gets what communication and who governs the flow of information. Finally, poverty relies on a system of values that permit all of these and other dimensions of inequality to continue. We should, of course, feed hungry people, and we should enhance their capacities to obtain and provide food; but serious reduction of the violence of poverty requires a change in a larger system. Similarly, the direct violence of war is embedded in a larger pattern of the way we do things, the way we obtain and protect wealth, the position we afford states to define personal identity and security—and ultimately the value we place on human life. Every violent incident we can prevent is important, but building a world in which the active pursuit of peace replaces the embedded activities of war is a greater task.

In this part we examine some of the central supports of the system of global violence, particularly those having to do with the prevailing system of resource distribution and economic activity. The three chapters included consider the difficulties of moving that system, the costs of not doing so, and the possibility of making such a change.

Jan Egeland writes about organized efforts at a global level to distribute resources vital to sustain life. His years of working with the UN to combat poverty provide a keen vantage point on the areas that have improved, but also the billion lives that face dire poverty and are not being reached. He notes the dangers to peace and security that have resulted and the rather stingy assistance offered by industrialized countries. David Korten addresses the power of corporations and of large centralized systems and suggests a mobilization to regain control of decisions by groups more attuned to the reality of local needs. Pilisuk and Gaddy extend that argument to show how corporate power and military decisions are related and how needed changes require an understanding and redefinition of the taboo topic—the monetary system. Where does money come from, who determines what it is worth, and what might it look like in a peaceful world? In general the three articles suggest that the system of violence runs deep, but that we made it and we can change it.

—Marc Pilisuk and Michael N. Nagler

CHAPTER 16

WAR, PEACE, AND CLIMATE CHANGE: A BILLION LIVES IN THE BALANCE

Jan Egeland

We can for the first time in a very long time say confidently that for a majority of us in this world, the situation is improving. There is 50 percent more peace and less war now than when the Berlin Wall fell in 1989, the watershed of our generation. Researchers found when they made the Human Security Report that there were 10 genocides in 1989. There are many fewer today. There was, in the 1960s, 1970s, and 1980s, an average of 10 to 20 military coups per year; now there are between two and four per year. And for the first time ever the World Bank economists found in their surveys in 2007 that there are fewer than 1 billion fellow human beings who struggle to survive on less than $1 per day. Given the growing world population, this means that hundreds of millions of people have been lifted out of poverty in China, India, Southeast Asia, Latin America, the Middle East, Eastern Europe, and elsewhere. Palestinians still constitute the largest segment of the world's refugees facing unique geopolitical circumstances. However, there were more than 20 million other refugees in the beginning of the 1990s. Four to five million of those were in Europe, where we had several

This is an address by Jan Egeland delivered on March 4, 2008, at the Joan B. Kroc School of Peace Studies, University of San Diego, San Diego, California. Thanks to Rebecca Norlander and Patrick Landewe for help in editing this and preparing it as a chapter for publication.

wars in the Balkans at the time. Today there are around 10 million non-Palestinian refugees, half as many today as there were only 15 years ago.

However, we live in a world of increasingly stark contrasts. Nations will be dismantling big arms that are remnants of the Cold War, as a consequence of the disarmament agreements between the NATO West and the old Warsaw Pact countries. But there will be a spread of small arms, some also left over from the same Cold War, to be used in the endless cruel wars of Africa and elsewhere. Although there are fewer refugees, the number of displaced people remains the same, around 23 million. Even though there are many more people in school, including higher education, there are still an enormous number of people who are deprived of even a minute of education and who will remain illiterate for the duration of their lives.

So, we have a world of contrasts where the good news is that there are only 1 billion people who live on around $1 a day; but that is, of course, also the bad news and is why I call my book *A Billion Lives*. We've never been richer as an international community, and still nearly 1 billion people will go to bed hungry today. They will not have had access to safe drinking water today. They will not even have access to primary health care. And surviving on $1 per day is, in relative terms, even more difficult now than before; they know how well off we are. And I think this is one of the new things of our time and age. The 2 billion under $2 per day is perhaps an even better measure; they know exactly how we are living in San Diego, in Oslo, in Geneva, in Tokyo, in Seoul—places where we are shielded in a degree of peace, prosperity, welfare, like no other generation before us. And that makes them angry like nowhere before, no time before. That resentment is perhaps strongest among the 1.3 billion human beings in the age group between 12 and 24 years. Of them, the majority will get education and jobs, but a very sizable minority, hundreds of millions of those 1.3 billion, will get neither of the two. If you deprive tens if not hundreds of millions of youth of all hope, they will get angry and want to move. They want to go north toward this fence at the U.S. border, or they want to go to the fences of Europe, or of Korea or Australia or of Japan.

Now, what are the biggest clouds on this horizon in addition to the contrast between the rich and the poor? Well, there is one new cloud that we're focusing on in particular, which is by far the biggest existential threat against mankind now in a time when we see so much improvement—and that is climate change. There have always been climate variations. I was in Oslo with the secretary general of the World Meteorological Organization in the spring of 2008. He went into detail to explain the difference between climate variation, which has always happened, and climate change, which is not induced by the globe going in a new pattern around the sun and thereby creating an ice age or an ice meltdown—it is human induced for the first time ever. And for the first time ever, there is no doubt anymore. There is a consensus among scientists that we do have climate change which is human induced through the emission of greenhouse gases.

Now, the question becomes, would this lead to war, would it lead to catastrophe, or can we adapt? On that the jury is out because we can still have influence on the outcomes. I have of late been more involved in the discussion of the possible climate wars. Many declared, perhaps a bit too early when the Nobel Peace Prize was given to Al Gore and the UN's Intergovernmental Panel on Climate Change, that that was in a way evidence that climate change is leading to climate wars. And some said that Darfur is one of the first climate wars. That is not necessarily true. We've now gone through, in the last 15 years, a unique period of end to wars. That is the period when we've seen, for example, in the Sahel or in the hurricane belts of the world, a tripling of natural disasters because of climate change. More vulnerable people live more exposed to extreme weather. Where it's dry it's getting drier; where it's wet it's getting wetter; where it's windy it's getting windier. That is the whole thrust of climate change. Whether that will lead to more conflict or more cooperation remains to be seen.

Many have predicted it will lead to more conflict, but we're actually seeing more peace as of late. There are indications that the world, the UN, the regional organizations have had some success in inducing cooperation instead of conflict. Fifteen years ago we were predicting water wars in the Middle East and elsewhere. It was predicted that there would be fighting around and for the water of the river Jordan, around and for the water of the river Euphrates and the river Tigris. None of those wars happened for those scarce water resources. Cooperation regimes were successful. The same thing is true in Africa around the river Niger and the river Mano. A Mano River initiative was successful. We can influence more cooperation in meeting the resource scarcity, but we can also see more conflict. Certainly in Darfur, which was a man-made disaster, a cruel regime armed some old militias and said, "Do whatever you want against the civilian population," which support two guerilla movements. Then all hell broke loose and there was an ethnic cleansing campaign. Now, the 6 to 7 million people in Darfur today live on less green land than they did 10 years ago, and there is also population growth. This means that it is very hard now for those of us involved in the peace efforts to help people back out of refugee camps, even with the peace agreement, to a new and good life in this desert that is more inhospitable because of climate change. That again means that we need to have a big international investment not only on the political level to get more cooperation, but also on the development level: give people hope, give people a new future in these circumstances. The nomads have to get help for a new life. There will have to be more irrigation. There will have to be more ways of doing agriculture. And there has to be more employment in other areas.

I mentioned the growth of natural disasters. Unfortunately, I don't think that it's widely known that there are three times more natural disasters in this decade than there were in the 1960s and 1970s because of more extreme weather and because more vulnerable people live more exposed. There are seven times more livelihoods devastated from natural disasters now than from war in our time and age. It is estimated that the Millennium Development Goals will be impossible to reach if this growth of natural disasters continues and if more is not done to adapt and mitigate the results. We can also safely predict that in the future there will be gradually fewer refugee flows coming from war and conflict (as the current positive trend continues), and there will be more migration from environmental degradation. Totally inhospitable areas can become wastelands, like parts of the Sahel or Yemen in the southern tip of the Arab peninsula, where there is no groundwater left even now. People cannot live there except at a great cost; they cannot afford to live there unless they are heavily subsidized by their Saudi Arabian cousins in the north, who seem not very willing to help them. Sea level rise, which is pretty certain under any of the predictions of the UN climate panel, will lead to coastal communities having to move inland. There are many reasons there will be migratory trends.

I hope and believe we will have cooperation in the international community to meet these climate changes to help make poor people survive those great changes. But the investment will be enormous. It is probable that the total global bill of preventative measures, fewer emissions, technology transfer (from all those who have technology to all those who need technology), and clean energy (all those places where they are using coal and other things that should not be used anymore)—will cost trillions of dollars. Is that more than is possible for humankind to invest? No. It is probably between 1 to 2 percent of the gross national income of the industrialized countries. It will be a totally different kind of investment than we've seen so far to foreign assistance, but it is possible. It is a question of will. And I, for one, having seen all of these places and visited all of these countries on all these continents, remain an optimist. I feel it is amazing what we can do when we work together as humankind.

When I started in the UN, I saw peace break out gradually in Angola, Liberia, Sierra Leone, Ivory Coast, southern Sudan, most parts of the Congo, East Timor, Kosovo, and Nepal, to mention a few. This is very often not recognized—what we did and how we managed to do that. For the United States it was a triumph, working with and through the UN, making peace in

Liberia. The United States was the lead country on that, just as Britain was the lead country on Sierra Leone's peace process. Those were places where people specialized in killing and massacring each other in the most brutal ways. At the time of this writing, Liberia has a female president who is an example of good governance; that's been a total, total change. And the warlord Charles Taylor, who specialized in using child soldiers to kill other children, is in jail at The Hague waiting for his verdict.

Let me give the other example of relief operations, which was my area of responsibility. In the Southeast Asian tsunami, 90 countries gave assistance and 35 militaries participated. The aircraft carrier USS *Abraham Lincoln* helped the UN jump-start operations after the tsunami all over Aceh. Nobody died because of lack of food, lack of medical services, or lack of basic relief. It's the same in northern Pakistan; 3.3 million people were without a roof after the earthquake. It was four weeks until the Himalayan winter would descend on us, and I was there to help start the relief operations. It was a race against the clock. We got enough helicopters. We got enough Pakistani and international efforts on the ground. And no more died that winter than would have in a normal year. And when spring came, there were more girls in school than in a normal year.

The UN can be very cost-effective in these efforts as well as effective in meeting the humanitarian goals. All of these places have been made peaceful with UN, African Union, and local and national efforts with a budget for peacekeeping of $6 billion a year. That is one-sixth of the U.S. military bill in Afghanistan this year, and it is around 5 percent of the cost in Iraq this year—5 percent: for peace in all of these countries through a multilateral effective action, where the United States played a very effective and constructive role with and in the UN.

I would like to sum up the lessons of my 31 years of international work since I came through San Diego as a 19-year-old with my friends from Norway, driving a second-hand car from Canada to Panama on the way to work as a volunteer in a Catholic relief organization in Colombia. In those 31 years, the little bit of wisdom which has accumulated has led me to the following 10 conclusions.

The first conclusion is: Prevention is better than cure. It's a strange thing perhaps to say for somebody who's had his salary from emergency relief. But it's insane how much we spend on the fire brigade, trying to cure the wound that could have been healed beforehand. Climate change makes this more important than at any time before. We're talking about mitigation, adaptation, preparedness, early warning; we're talking about environment work; we're talking about development work. That is how we can get out of this vicious cycle of returning again and again and again to certain countries like Ethiopia, which could feed itself and thereby make its own population resilient. There are enough natural resources and enough talent in the population to do so, but we have never had a coherent national and international effort to make them resilient to the droughts and the natural disasters and the internal strife that have come back again and again and again. An African friend said the approach we've had is, "Save me today, kill me tomorrow." Why don't we have an approach that says let's invest in long-term protection for these populations?

Now, the second lesson is related to what I just said about the UN, because I think the multilateral institutions must be empowered to become more effective. The world is getting increasingly multi-polar, with not only the United States as a superpower, but soon also China, India, the European Union, and to some extent Russia, Brazil, Nigeria, Indonesia—there will be many powers. Just look at Africa: who is doing most of the investment and who is providing most of the international presence now? We must look also at China and India. In this world, the UN must be empowered to become effective. I've been working in the UN; I've seen how it can be effective, but also seen how it can be ineffective. The second thing that has to happen with the UN is that we have to make the structure more operational. It takes a year to fill a post. It is nearly impossible to re-allocate posts. The secretary-general and others need more executive power within the organization so that it can respond more flexibly to world problems as they arise. I have time and again been surprised that we did so much good in so many countries, from the tsunami to the earthquakes to all of this peacemaking, not because of, but in spite of the organizational structure.

The third lesson is that there must be not only prevention through development and environment action, but there also needs to be early, predictable political and security action to protect civilian communities, which in this time and age are as exposed or more exposed to violations than before. Again, it's one of the paradoxes of our time that yes, there are fewer wars, but they appear to be crueler against the civilian population. I sat at the table when Darfur was going from a small emergency to a full-blown ethnic cleansing catastrophe. We saw that there were one or two cease-fires mediated with our humanitarian envoys—not the political ones, but humanitarian envoys—yet no real effort by our member states to enforce these cease-fires and restrain the armed men and the government that was arming them. Predictable security and political action has to happen. Too often, I find that humanitarian efforts become the alibi for lack of political and security action. You send the humanitarians, they provide enough food, water, and blankets to keep people alive, but we don't protect them. A woman who led a delegation from camps in western Darfur approached me during my last visit there. Conditions were so bad in the camps that I couldn't go because there probably would have been riots between the various groups.

There was so much anger in the camps, and they were surrounded by the militias. So, the women came to me. I always speak to the women because then you get the truth as it is. This very articulate lady—illiterate, had never gone to school—said more or less the following: "Thank you for the food. [It came from America.] Thanks for the school in a box [which came from UNICEF]. Thanks for the health post—we have never had a health post before, ever. We've got all of this in this camp. But do you know that tonight they may come back? They may rape us. They may pillage everything again. Do you realize how it has been 1,200 days and 1,200 nights in fear?" And I had to admit, "No, I don't know that. And it is a shame really that you have had to live 1,200 days and nights in utter fear and suffer so much when it should have been an international responsibility to protect you." In 2005, world leaders—from my prime minister to your president to all of these other national leaders—solemnly swore in the General Assembly hall of the UN the following: "[W]e are prepared to take collective action in a timely and decisive manner through the Security Council in accordance with the Charter including Chapter VII" that is the one which mandates the use of force—". . . should peaceful means be inadequate and national authorities are manifestly failing to protect their populations from genocide, war crimes, ethnic cleansing and crimes against humanity." We are now trying to remind these leaders what they solemnly swore, because they seem to be retreating from this commitment, because still there is no protection in Darfur, still there is no protection for the women in eastern Congo, for the people who are in the camps in Chad or in Colombia.

My fourth lesson is that, given our resources, given the situation, given our potential, we must set ourselves ambitious goals. We cannot do less and the sky is the limit. We felt that very strongly when we were four Norwegian individuals who in deepest secret facilitated the first talks ever between the Palestine Liberation Organization and the state of Israel in Norway, which led to the famous Oslo accords. We felt the same when we did the tsunami relief. I went in 2003 to northern Uganda to see conditions for myself because my first day on the job I asked my most experienced relief colleagues, "What is the most neglected place on earth?" And they said immediately, "It must be northern Uganda. Nobody's aware of what's really happening at the hands of the Lord's Resistance Army [LRA] in northern Uganda, and we failed to wake up the world." So, I said, "Okay, let's go." So, we went. And I was shocked to my bone by seeing a place where 20,000 children had been kidnapped by a terror organization which had made them into child soldiers, attacking their own population. Very often, they, the LRA, brought them to their own village from where they had been kidnapped and terrorized into becoming soldiers, and made them burn their own village. Then the LRA told the children, "Now you have nothing to return to. We are your new

family. You have to live and fight with us forever." Terror worked in northern
Uganda. So, what did we do? We put it on the international news media. We
got much more money for emergency relief, so we lifted standards in the
camps. We got it on the Security Council agenda, and when south Sudan
started discrete mediations between the government and the Lord's Resistance Army, we gave money, facilitation. I went myself to the jungle to meet
Joseph Kony—this elusive leader of the Lord's Resistance Army—and told
him that if you continue holding the cease-fire agreement, we will give food
to your soldiers, we will organize the assembly points, we will be observers
there so you are not attacked by the Ugandan army, but you have to stop
looting, pillaging, massacring. And it did stop. Two weeks ago, the permanent cease-fire was declared after nearly two years of effective cease-fire.
Hundreds of thousands of people are returning home as we speak, and the
children are coming back.

The fifth lesson is that we need to be more generous to be able to reach all
of these good, ambitious goals that we have set for ourselves. Many years ago
it was agreed at several international conferences that the goal should be 0.7
percent of gross national income in the rich industrialized countries that goes
to foreign assistance. It's not one-tenth we're talking about. We're talking
about 0.7 percent. So, how did it go in these 20 years of trying to meet that
goal? Well, the average is now I think 0.22 percent or so for the rich industrialized world. Neither in the Bible nor in the Quran do we read: Keep 99.8
percent to yourself and give 0.2 percent to the neediest in the world. What
we have now is not good enough. Moreover, it was interesting that the G-8
countries in 2005, at the good initiative of Tony Blair, said, "We will build up
to this goal of 0.7 percent and we will definitely by 2010 have $50 billion more
for Africa." I was very happy. I welcomed that in the world media. Next year, I
checked: How did it go? Foreign assistance decreased from the G-8 countries,
except the United Kingdom. So, my word was "stingy." I could have found perhaps better words, but it's not very generous when you give 0.2 percent and it
goes down in a world of great, great needs. Now, it's not only the Western
countries that should step up to the plate. What about the Association of
Southeast Asian Nations (ASEAN) countries and the Arab countries, who have
rapidly growing economies? I have been many times to Singapore and South
Korea and the Gulf countries to say, "Look, when my country was half as rich
as you are now, we had 0.7 percent of gross national income in foreign assistance. Why is it not happening here?" I think in a way there has to be a campaign which says there are 50 rich countries now—not 5, 50—that could help
lift up the bottom billion people to the levels which should be there.

We need to control the arms flows, and these are on two levels. One is the
proliferation of small arms. The Kalashnikov is really the most lethal weapon

in our time and age. It has spread all over contemporary armed conflicts and it's creating havoc. With unemployed, angry youth in so many places, as I mentioned previously, and access to small arms, it is nearly impossible to create security for ordinary people, and the wars continue and continue. The other big goal has to do with weapons of mass destruction, which are closer to being used than probably at any point since Hiroshima and Nagasaki. Why? Because you can today on the Internet find the prescription to make a dirty bomb by nuclear material or bacteriological, biological or chemical weapons. You can buy it through the black market from Eastern Europe and elsewhere. It is not widely acknowledged that a terror organization or a rogue government can pretty easily get all of the materials and all the prescriptions needed.

I think we have to be more consistent in speaking the truth always as we see it, hear it, smell it, feel it when we go to the field, to the trenches, to where people suffer. It has indeed put me in trouble many times. There were five heads of state in government who were after my scalp when I was in the UN and wanted me to leave my position. I was defended always by Secretary-General Kofi Annan. Why is it so important to speak the truth? Because it's what shields the voiceless, and the voiceless are the ones we are there to help. It's a strategic choice who should speak out, how, where, and in what format, and very often it is not the NGO worker in the field or even the UN fieldworker who should do it. It is people like me, people like you here in shielded San Diego, who can and must speak the truth as it is and without censorship. Whether or not this may be about our friend—John Foster Dulles said famously about the brutal ruler, Anastasio Somoza Garcia, "He's a son of a bitch, but he's our son of a bitch," we have to speak the truth as it is.

And the eighth lesson is derived from that: We have to focus more on the forgotten, the neglected, and the voiceless, because I feel too often that we prove again and again that we're great as humankind when CNN and all the limelight is there, such as the tsunami. In Lebanon, we really did what was needed to get the senseless war to end. It had escalated so fast; 1.2 million people fled in a fortnight. It ended; there was a UN force on the ground in no time, there was a billion dollars pledged in no time, a lot of things happened. This does not happen in French-speaking Africa and elsewhere because it is neglected.

There are special needs of the civilian population, especially children and women, who have to be focused on. I mentioned that the wars are fewer but crueler. Perhaps the one thing, next to the kidnapped children who become child soldiers in northern Uganda, which was really unbearable was to meet the raped and abused women of eastern Congo. At the hospital called Panzi there was a group of 1,200 women who assembled in a big field. They and the doctor wanted to meet me and hear what I had to say, which was not easy. They were all physically and mentally destroyed by the rapes they had been subjected to. Slowly but surely they were helped together physically, medically, mentally to return to society, which often rejected them because they had been so broken and abused. It is a cancer in modern war which has to end. And we have to focus on this abuse of women, often children, in armed conflict. This can only be done by a very systematic effort to bring the accountable for all of this abuse to justice. An end to impunity is what it is really a question about.

The tenth and final point is that those of us who are involved in international work—we're all involved in international work directly or indirectly—need to ensure there is quality control, transparency, accountability. I often try to explain to colleagues and young people joining that this is work where the difference between excellence and mediocrity is measured in human lives. If you make soap, it is good to have good soap and it is bad to have bad soap, but it's not a question of life and death. In international work, it is a question of life and death if we do bad work. We cannot allow ourselves not to do the best in all of this, and we cannot lose a penny on the way. We cannot allow any corruption; we cannot allow any kind of cowardice as we are on this quest for very big things. Now, are we first and foremost accountable to the donors? No. We are *also* accountable to the donors and the budget has to be audited for every penny, but the biggest accountability you have is to the vulnerable themselves. I remember one epic evaluation which was on drought relief in the 1980s in Africa, and the first sentence was that the dispossessed, the vulnerable, the poor should at least have one human right remaining, and that is to be protected against mediocrity in international relief work. So, that's why it's so important with work like you are doing here with peace studies, humanitarian studies, human rights studies; it's a question of being better and doing what is important.

I would like to end with the following question, which is a follow-up to my first question: Is the world getting better or not? It's a question of what we can do to make it even much better. My answer is, I think, for the generation now coming and studying here, the sky is really the limit. If my generation is now 50-and-a-half years old; if we, sort of half-asleep and with half-hearted efforts, managed to make these strides ahead, what can one not do now with resources, private and public, which are infinitely bigger than at any time before in human history; with technology that is infinitely stronger and better than at any point in human history; and with organizations—nongovernmental, multilateral, bilateral, governmental—that are much better tools than ever before? We have everything that is needed to do very great things. It's a question of will.

CHAPTER 17

THE MOMENT FOR TURNING: LIVING AS IF PEACE AND SUSTAINABILITY REALLY MATTERED

David C. Korten

For peace to reign, people everywhere need secure access to the resources essential to their survival and well-being. For far too long, if nations, corporations, or peoples consumed or destroyed their own natural resource base, they sought to acquire the resources of their neighbor through one means or another, traditionally through military conquest and more recently through trade agreements that open resources everywhere to expropriation by global corporations. Through such means, the more powerful parties advance their private interests by depriving those less powerful of their livelihood and their dignity. Economic expansion, concentration of wealth, and war are all linked.

We see the consequences of the underlying dynamic by which the powerful expropriate the resources of the weak in the current credit meltdown, a shrinking middle class, stagnant wages, escalating food and energy prices, a dramatic decline in U.S. manufacturing and research capability, billion-dollar

Portions of this article were drawn from "After the Meltdown: Economic Redesign for the 21st Century," which appeared in *Tikkun Magazine* and from an address to Veterans for Peace Northwest Regional Conference at Kirkland Unitarian Church, Kirkland, WA, March 8, 2009, "Real Security, Community, and the New Economy." The author and editors express appreciation to Ellen Gaddy for editorial help.

pay packages for hedge-fund managers, skyrocketing consumer debt, an unstable U.S. dollar, a multi-trillion-dollar bailout for Wall Street, and the spreading collapse of earth's ecological systems. In the world's richest country over 20 million Americans suffer regularly from hunger.[1] India, bolstered by international loans to increase its energy production, is now the fastest growing economy, yet the rapid development does nothing to change the fact that India is still home to 40 percent of the world's malnourished children.[2] Even with gross budget deficits, the Pentagon maintains an expanding empire of over 6,000 domestic and 725 overseas military bases comprising only a portion of the half of all U.S. government discretionary expenditures dedicated to military preparedness and actions.[3] By any credible measure, our economic system has failed.

When economic failure is systemic, temporary fixes, even expensive ones like the Wall Street bailout, are like putting a Band-Aid on a cancer. They may create a temporary sense of confidence, but the effect is solely cosmetic. Politicians and most pundits are looking only at the tip of the economic iceberg. Pull away the curtain to look behind the headlines, and we find a potentially terminal economic crisis with four defining elements:

1. Excessive human consumption, which is accelerating the collapse of earth's ecosystem.
2. Unconscionable inequality and the related social alienation, which are advancing the social collapse manifest in terrorism, genocide, crime, and growing prison populations.
3. An economic system ruled by financial markets, global corporations, and economic theories devoted to increasing consumption while rolling back real wages and benefits for working people to make money for the richest among us.
4. A gigantic military establishment needed to protect those who profit in the short term from the passions of those who are displaced by an economy of waste.

This is a time for decisive action. Getting out of this economic crisis requires a total commitment from every person on the planet who has a moral conscience and a sound mind. For those who believe there is a better way, this is in fact a truly exciting time to be alive. The old system is destroying itself to make way for a new economic system.

THE OLD ECONOMY ECONOMIST VERSUS THE NEW ECONOMY ECOLOGIST

The task before us is to replace the culture and institutions of a 20th-century economy designed and managed to serve financial values with the culture and institutions of a new 21st-century economy designed to serve life values. The former undoubtedly leads to global violence and environmental, social, and economic collapse. The later holds promise of leading to the world most humans really want for themselves and their children—a world of happy, healthy children, families, and communities living together, in peace, in vibrant, healthy, natural environments. It is ours to choose.

The choice between the path of failure and the path of possibility is framed with dramatic clarity by two influential authors, one a 20th-century economist and the other a 21st-century ecologist. Jeffrey Sachs, in *Common Wealth: Economics for a Crowded Planet*, prescribes a Band-Aid.[4] James Gustave Speth, in *Bridge at the Edge of the World: Capitalism, the Environment, and Crossing from Crisis to Sustainability*, prescribes a holistic cure grounded in a cultural and institutional transformation.[5]

Sachs opens *Common Wealth* with a powerful and unequivocal problem statement that raises expectations of a bold break with the economic orthodoxy of what Sachs refers to as "free-market ideologues":

> The challenges of sustainable development—protecting the environment, stabilizing the world's population, narrowing the gaps between rich and poor, and ending extreme poverty—will take center stage. Global cooperation will have to come to the fore. The very idea of competing nation-states that scramble for markets, power, and resources will become passé. . . . The pressures of scarce energy resources, growing environmental stresses, a rising global population, legal and illegal mass migration, shifting economic power, and vast inequalities of income are too great to be left to naked market forces and untrammeled geopolitical competition among nations.[6]

This statement would have served equally well as an opening statement for Speth. Beyond the problem statement, Sachs and Speth both agree that there is an essential role for government and for greater cooperation among nations. From there, however, as I will elaborate later, we might wonder whether they live in the same world.

Sachs assures us that we can easily end environmental stress and poverty using existing technologies. By his estimation, with modest new investments we can sequester carbon, develop new energy sources, end population growth, make more efficient use of water and other natural resources, and jump-start economic growth in the world's remaining pockets of persistent poverty. Sachs made clear his belief that there is no need to redistribute wealth, cut back material consumption, or otherwise reorganize the economy as stated in his lecture to the Royal Society in London, which was broadcast by the BBC:

> I do not believe that the solution to this problem is a massive cutback of our consumption levels or our living standards. I think the solution is

smarter living. I do believe that technology is absolutely critical, and I do not believe . . . that the essence of the problem is that we face a zero sum that must be re-distributed. I'm going to argue that there's a way for us to use the knowledge that we have, the technology that we have, to make broad progress in material conditions, to not require or ask the rich to take sharp cuts of living standards, but rather to live with smarter technologies that are sustainable, and thereby to find a way for the rest of the world, which yearns for it, and deserves it as far as I'm concerned, to raise their own material conditions as well. The costs are much less than people think.[7]

Far from calling for a restraint on consumption, Sachs projects global economic expansion from $60 trillion in 2005 to $420 trillion in 2050. Relying on what he calls a "back-of-the-envelope calculation," he estimates that the world's wealthy nations can eliminate extreme poverty and develop and apply the necessary environmentally friendly technologies to address environmental needs with an expenditure of a mere 2.4 percent of projected mid-century economic output—problem painlessly solved, at least in Sachs's mind.

Sachs gives no indication of why, if we can stabilize the global population and meet the needs of the poor with modest expenditure, we should need or even want a global economy six times larger than its present size. With most economists, and indeed the general public, Sachs simply assumes that economic growth is both good and necessary. In a dissenting voice, economist Kenneth Boulding once observed that anyone who believes that an economy can grow infinitely on a planet with finite resources must be either insane or an economist. But it apparently does not occur to Sachs to question this assumption, which Speth demonstrates to be false, as I will elaborate later. Furthermore, Sachs maintains that there is no need for more than the very modest redistribution he estimates is required to put the poorest of the poor on the path to economic growth; hence he seems to assume that consumption will continue to increase across the board. He says nothing, however, about what forms of consumption he believes can continue to multiply without placing yet more pressure on already overstressed natural systems. Unless more people are driving cars, living in big houses, eating higher on the food chain, traveling farther with more frequency, and buying more electronic gear, what exactly will we be consuming more of? And from what materials will they be fabricated? Sachs neither raises nor answers such questions.

Nor does Sachs mention the realities of political power and resource control; for example, the reality that in most instances poor countries are poor not for want of foreign aid but because we of the rich nations have used our military and economic power to expropriate their resources to consume beyond our own means. It is troubling, although not surprising, that Sachs's reassuring words get an attentive hearing among establishment power holders. To his credit, Sachs has used his public platform to remind both governments and the general population of the extent of poverty and the destitution it entails. It is his conclusion, however—that we can change to a world of peace and sustainability without vast changes in the functioning of a corporate economy—that must be questioned.

In stark contrast to Sachs, Speth concludes, "The planet cannot sustain capitalism as we know it," calling for nothing less than a complete economic redesign. No simple back-of-the-envelope projections for Speth. He takes a hard look at the research on growth and environmental damage in relation to gross domestic product (GDP) and concludes that despite a slight decline in the amount of environmental damage per increment of growth, growth in GDP always increases environmental damage. The relationship is inherent in the simple fact, which apparently escaped Sachs, that GDP is mostly a measure of growth in consumption, which is the driving cause of environmental decline. Speth is clear that although choosing "green" products may be a positive step, not buying at all beats buying green most every time:

> To sum up, we live in a world where economic growth is generally seen as both beneficent and necessary—the more, the better; where past growth has brought us to a perilous state environmentally; where we are poised for unprecedented increments in growth; where this growth is proceeding with wildly wrong market signals, including prices that do not incorporate environmental costs or reflect the needs of future generations; where a failed politics has not meaningfully corrected the market's obliviousness to environmental needs; where economies are routinely deploying technology that was created in an environmentally unaware era; where there is no hidden hand or inherent mechanism adequate to correct the destructive tendencies. So, right now, one can only conclude that growth is the enemy of environment. Economy and environment remain in collision.[8]

Speth is clear that we are unlikely as a species to implement the measures required to bring ourselves into balance with the environment so long as economic growth remains an overriding policy priority, consumerism defines our cultural values, and the excesses of corporate behavior are unconstrained by fairly enforced rules. To correct our misplaced priorities, he recommends replacing financial indicators of economic performance, such as GDP, with wholly new measures based on nonfinancial indicators of social and environmental health—the things we should be optimizing.

Speth quotes psychologist David Myers, whose essay "What Is the Good Life?" claims that Americans have:

> Big houses and broken homes, high incomes and low morale, secured rights and diminished civility. We were excelling at making a living but too often failing at making a life. We celebrated our prosperity but yearned for purpose. We cherished our freedoms but longed for connection. In an age of plenty, we were feeling spiritual hunger. These facts of life lead us to a startling conclusion: Our becoming better off materially has not made us better off psychologically.[9]

This is consistent with studies finding that beyond a basic threshold level of about $10,000 per capita per year, equity and community are far more important determinants of health and happiness than income or possessions. Indeed, as Speth documents, economic growth tends to be associated with increases in individualism, social fragmentation, inequality, depression, and even impaired physical health.

Speth gives significant attention to social movements grounded in an awakening spiritual consciousness that are creating communities of the future from the bottom up, practicing participatory democracy, and demanding changes in the rules of the game:

> Many of our deepest thinkers and many of those most familiar with the scale of the challenges we face have concluded that the transitions required can be achieved only in the context of what I will call the rise of a new consciousness. For some, it is a spiritual awakening—a transformation of the human heart. For others it is a more intellectual process of coming to see the world anew and deeply embracing the emerging ethic of the environment and the old ethic of what it means to love thy neighbor as thyself.[10]

Finally, Speth examines the abuses of corporate power and endorses calls to revoke the charters of corporations that grossly violate the public interest, exclude or expel unwanted corporations, roll back limited liability, eliminate corporate personhood, bar corporations from making political contributions, and limit corporate lobbying. He recommends a redesign of "the operating system of capitalism" to support the development of local economies populated with firms that feature worker and community ownership and to charter corporations only to serve a public interest.

The differences between the worldviews of Sachs and Speth are instructive, because any effort to address the current potentially fatal threats to the human future necessarily begins with deciding whether to focus on adjustments at the margin as recommended by Sachs, the economist, or deep system redesign as recommended by Speth, the systems ecologist. By this point in time, given the strength of the evidence to the contrary, it is difficult to consider seriously an analysis that assumes, without question, that the global economy can expand six times between now and 2050 without collapsing earth's life support system. The perspective, widely shared in economics, reflects the myopic limitations of perspectives from a single discipline. When we seek guidance on dealing with the complex issues relating to interactions between human economies and the planetary ecosystems in which they are embedded, we are best advised to turn to those, like Speth, who view the world through a larger and less ideologically clouded lens.

RALLYING THE "TROOPS" FOR SUSTAINABILITY AND PEACE

We cannot resolve the issues of environmental destruction, extreme inequity, and global violence by treating the symptoms. Instead, we must turn our present economic system upside down and inside out. We must replace so-called "free-trade" agreements based on the misguided ideology of market fundamentalism, which has hollowed out our national industrial capacity, mortgaged our future to foreign creditors, and created global financial instability, with a system of trade that is fair and balanced between nations. Fair and balanced trade between nations means that we, in the global North, cannot consume more than our fair share. We should begin by taking stock of all of our available resources and ensure that each and every one is used responsibly and sustainably to meet the needs of all people and all living beings. To accomplish this task, we must rein in the economic power of transnational corporations.

An unprecedented concentration of power in transnational corporations that owe no allegiance to any nation, place, or purpose undermines democracy, distorts economic priorities, and contributes to a socially destructive concentration of wealth. The only legitimate reason for a government to issue a corporate charter, which gives a group of private investors a legally protected right to aggregate and concentrate economic power under unified management, should be to serve a well-defined public purpose under strict rules of public accountability. Because absentee ownership invites irresponsibility, we should urge our government to create incentives for publicly traded corporations to break themselves up into their component units and convert to responsible ownership by their workers, customers, or small investors in the communities in which they are located. We must create a true ownership society in which all people have the opportunity to own their own home and to have ownership stakes in the enterprises on which their livelihoods depend.

In summation, we must replace the Wall Street economy, whose main purpose is to make money for people who have money without the burden of producing anything of value in return, with the Main Street economy, comprised of local businesses and working people engaged in producing real goods and services to meet real needs. The Main Street economy requires new, nonfinancial performance indicators that evaluate economic performance against indicators of what we really want—healthy children, families, communities, and natural systems. This would place life values ahead of money values and dramatically reframe both our public and private economic priorities. The Main Street economy has been battered and tattered by the predatory intrusions of Wall Street corporations. We must help communities declare independence from Wall Street and, in so doing, revitalize Main Street and the middle class.

A strong, middle-class society is an American ideal. Our past embodiment of that ideal made us the envy of the world. We must act to restore that ideal by rebalancing the distribution of wealth. Necessary and appropriate steps should be taken to ensure access by every person to quality health care, education, and other essential services, and to restore progressive taxation, as well as progressive wage and benefit rules, to protect working people. We must take the necessary steps to eliminate automobile-dependence in favor of compact communities that bring home, work, recreation, shopping, and other aspects of our lives into close proximity; curtail advertising and redirect those creative and media resources to education; and end financial speculation and redirect investment to sustainable enterprises devoted to meeting community needs. Examples of sustainable enterprises include locally owned family businesses, cooperatives, community banks, and the many other forms of community- or worker-owned enterprises that promote a more equitable distribution of wealth. Main Street policies that favor local ownership of local enterprises by people who have a stake in the health of their communities and economies may seem familiar to older Americans; this is because they are the policies that created the middle class in the first place, the policies to which we must now turn to help create a peaceful and sustainable worldview.

In addition to converting from the Wall Street economy to a Main Street economy, we must convert from the war economy of our past to a green economy of the future. War is an outmoded institution that serves no beneficial purpose, other than to enrich the unscrupulous, and it has become an act of global scale collective suicide.

Marine Major General Smedley Butler warned of this in 1935:

There are only two things we should fight for. One is the defense of our homes and the other is the Bill of Rights. War for any other reason is a racket. There isn't a trick in the racketeering bag that the military gang is blind to. It has "finger men" to point out enemies, its "muscle men" to destroy enemies, its "brain men" to plan war preparations, and a "Big Boss" Super-Nationalistic-Capitalism.[11]

The greatest threats to U.S. security do not come from any foreign army, but rather from weather chaos, oil dependence, disruption of food supplies, water scarcity, environmental degradation and toxicity, domestic gun violence, and highly speculative financial institutions. The greatest *military* threat to our domestic security is from a handful of terrorists armed primarily with a willingness to die for their cause. Yet, U.S. military expenditures account for more than half of the U.S. federal discretionary budget and account for roughly *half of the world's military expenditures.* We must mobilize our human and material resources to address the real threats to our security and use our global influence and take the lead in renouncing war as an instrument of national policy and dismantling the means of conducting war.

Now is the time to create a world of peace—to turn our swords into ploughshares and our spears into sickles so that one nation shall no longer lift its sword against the life of another. It is time to convert our economies from war to peace and to devote every resource at our command to the vitalization, rather than the destruction, of life. Our need is to create societies that affirm and celebrate the love that is life. We must work to build cooperation among people and nations with the ultimate goal of eliminating terrorism and its underlying causes. To accomplish our goal of global peace, we will have to resolve conflicts through peaceful diplomacy, roll back military spending and demilitarize the national economies of all nations, restore environmental health, and increase economic stability. Additionally, we must work to replace a global system of economic competition with a global system of economic cooperation based on the sharing of beneficial technology and the right of the peoples of each nation to own and control their own economic resources to meet their needs for food, energy, shelter, education, health care, and other basic needs. This is our work, and it is a Great Work.

CONCLUSION

The time has come to make real the world of peace, justice, and ecological sustainability for all—the world of which most humans have dreamed for millennia. We must either work for the good of all or collapse into ecological and global violence. Our collective wisdom endows us with the knowledge that peace is more than the absence of war. True peace is community, sharing, and partnership—a world in which we each care for our neighbors as we care for ourselves. Forging a peaceful and sustainable worldview is the greatest creative challenge our species has ever faced. It requires that we replace the culture and institutions of an economy devoted to the service of money with the culture and institutions of an economy devoted to the service of life. It requires that we rebuild in ways that actualize the founding ideals of liberty and justice for all on which our nation was founded. It requires new leadership from all of us as we put aside outmoded assumptions and false values that have led our nation, species, and ecological environment to the brink of ruin. Above all else, it requires that we rediscover that which makes us truly human and reinvent our societies to nurture our human capacity to create, care, and cooperate rather than our capacity to dominate and destroy.

The time has come to break the silence and acknowledge the sins of our collective past even as we celebrate the possibilities of our future. We need to break the isolation that has separated us by race, class, ethnic origin, and religion so we may become a true national community within a larger planetary community of peoples and nations. We must enact our shared dream of a world in which people and nature live in dynamic, creative, cooperative, and balanced relationship. Despite all our differences, people need and want the same things. We want to breathe clean air and drink clean water. We want nutritious food uncontaminated with chemicals and pesticides. We want our children to be healthy and happy. We want meaningful work, a living wage, and security in our old age. We want a say in the decisions our government makes. We want a vibrant natural ecological *and social* environment. We want world peace.

Unfortunately, we have become so accustomed to cultures and institutions that reward and celebrate the pathologies of individualism, greed, hubris, deceit, ruthless competition, and material excess that some of us have come to doubt even the possibility that we humans might have, as a species, the capacity to cooperate in the interest of a common good. We fail to notice what science has recently been saying, and the world's wisdom traditions have never ceased saying, that service to the common good is our most important value. We may even fail to notice that most people daily demonstrate our human capacity for caring, sharing, honesty, cooperation, compassion, peacemaking, service, and material sufficiency. Now is the time to join together and redesign and reshape our culture and institutions to consign the promotion of global violence and ecological destruction to the dustbin of history. We have the power to turn this world around for the sake of ourselves, our children, and life's continuing creative journey. We are the ones we've been waiting for.

NOTES

1. Food Research and Action Center, Hunger and Food Insecurity in the United States. (2005) Available at: http://www.frac.org//html/hunger_in_the_us/hunger_index.html.

2. Watson, 2006.
3. Hagan and Bickerton, 2007.
4. Sachs, 2008.
5. Speth, 2007.
6. Sachs, 2008.
7. Sachs, 2007.
8. Speth, 2007.
9. Ibid.
10. Ibid.
11. Butler, 1935.

CHAPTER 18

AGAINST SO MUCH MONEY AND POWER, CAN THE PEACE MOVEMENT SUCCEED?

Marc Pilisuk and Ellen Gaddy

This set of books can scarcely acknowledge, in three volumes, the inspiring work for peace accomplished every day. To recognize and celebrate these efforts is a joy. To assess their potential for ending mass violence and war is more daunting. Here, we examine the forces that enable large-scale violence so that we may better answer the central question for the peace movement: *Can it bring peace?*

The endless struggles by peace advocates are sometimes effective, sometimes futile, over whether a particular war should be continued or ended, whether modest measures will be adopted toward saving our increasingly warm and toxic environment, and whether some private-sector exploitation of the global South and its resources will cease. We rejoice over our victories and see the potential of advances in global communication and social networking for the creation of a more aware and engaged citizenry. Then, a harsh reality sets in. Despite tireless efforts, we have little power to bring crucial items to the public agenda. Hence, our larger concerns and questions remain unheard.

Can we prevent rather than merely respond to the heart-wrenching suffering and ecological destruction that surrounds us? Must war, military preparedness, and the military-industrial-media complex continue unabated? Should not all people have the right to derive resources from their own communities, sufficient to sustain healthy lives, before transnational corporations are permitted to usurp those resources to appease the global North's insatiable appetite? Will electoral and legislative processes be made free of the influence of corporate money? And finally, could the vast resources currently being used to promote enmity be used instead to promote community? The absence of these items from the public agenda is not an accident, but rather a product of a social system created and maintained by humans. Even as we celebrate our victories, we know that the hidden wheels of the larger destructive and inequitable system continue to turn.

Audre Lorde once warned, ". . . the master's tools will never dismantle the master's house. They may allow us temporarily to beat him at his own game but they will never enable us to bring about genuine change."[1] Lorde believed that the efficacy of any approach to social change still embedded in the systems and institutions of the dominant worldview will be greatly diminished. Why? Because the master is the architect of the game, knows better than anyone how to win, how to lose, and when to change the rules. Our goal is to unmask the often-concealed master, the major beneficiary of the existing social, economic, and monetary system. We will also uncover the master's increasingly apparent game of imperial hegemony, characterized by the concentration of power within elite networks and the transfer of wealth and resources from the public to the private sector, from the global South to the global North, from Main Street to Wall Street.[2] Imperial hegemony consolidates wealth while spreading poverty and ecological destruction. The ensuing conflicts over resources result in direct military violence. Innocent people suffer and die from the unholy marriage of war and industry, as destitution follows from militarily protected procurement of local resources by remote corporations.

THE COSTS OF WAR

We live under an existential burden in which the exchange of nuclear weapons, by accident or intent, could put an end to humankind and the natural environment. Thus far, we have escaped this fate. However, we have yet to escape the hell of global violence and war. Although war is often glorified in history as the triumph over evil, revered in the memory of soldiers as a time of ultimate camaraderie and courage, and used as a rallying point by political leaders calling for patriotism, unity, and sacrifice, the actual human consequences of armed conflict are increasingly devastating. Since the end of World War II, upward of 250 major wars have claimed over 50 million lives and left tens of millions homeless.[3] Genocides and asymmetrical conflicts, in which civilians constitute the majority of casualties, have ushered in the 21st century in Darfur, Congo, Iraq, Afghanistan, Chechnya, Burma, Tibet, Gaza, Lebanon, Colombia, Somalia, and Sri Lanka.

The heartrending consequences of such violence include the suffering of displaced refugees, mostly children and women; civilian deaths and injuries; the creation of orphans; abused and tortured prisoners of war; and the soldiers who are killed, as well as those who are driven to suicide or who return disabled and psychologically scarred in ways that diminish the quality of their own lives and the lives of their families and communities. The costs of war include the money spent on weapons and the scientific talent to develop destructive capabilities, both of which might have been used to improve the quality of human life and the fragile ecology. Additional hidden costs of war include cancer and radiation sickness among those who worked in, or lived downwind of, nuclear weapons facilities and war zones; the continuing calls for retribution by the losers; the costs of rebuilding infrastructure; and the killing and maiming of unsuspecting children and farmers from hidden landmines long after hostilities have ended.

The gains of war are questionable. Historian Barbara Tuchman's *The March of Folly: From Troy to Vietnam* outlines a history of humankind's propensity to engage in violent wars.[4] This history of bloodshed includes numerous cases in which the potential gain for participants, on either side of the conflict, was small compared to the costs. Indeed, a detailed review of all U.S. wars and military intervention since World War II demonstrated that most conflicts have produced unintended consequences, detrimental to the United States and her people.[5] Unlike the costs of natural disasters, these consequences result from the decisions by humans who have historically demonstrated a propensity for inflicting suffering and death on their own kind. *So, why do we do it? And, why have our efforts, thus far, failed to stop us from advancing this tragic game?*

THE COSTS OF STRUCTURAL VIOLENCE

In the most widespread form of mass violence, giant transnational corporations, owing no allegiance to any one nation and maintaining the right of corporate personhood, usurp control over arable land, water, oil, gas, and other minerals. They control market places, workforces, media, and the regulatory functions of government, and leave in their wake the casualties of structural violence. These casualties include children who die of curable and preventable disease; impoverished villagers forced to travel long distances to work in dangerous factories for negligible wages; children and young women forced into hard labor, some enslaved, some trafficked for the global sex industry, and some forced into the only viable local economy—drugs. Dissenters to the game of imperial hegemony are often labeled as revolutionaries or terrorists. These labels justify the reigns of terror and torture against dissenters and often result in their untimely disappearances. Government leaders seeking to regain control of local resources from the corporate network have been isolated, coerced, bribed, and assassinated, which begs the question *"By whom?"*[6]

Militarism, patriarchy, capitalism, human aggression, and fundamentalism have each been named as the essential cause. Each of these identifies a genuine problem. However, the most compelling answer for why violence continues is that a small group of powerful people benefit greatly from the havoc. By looking at the primary beneficiaries of the destructive system, we may gain a clearer perspective on what social transformation is required to create a peaceful and sustainable world.

THE POWER ELITE

A common belief is that the United States is the economic, political, and military hub of the game of imperial hegemony.[7] Economist James Galbraith has a slightly different perspective. He sees the United States as the primary *vehicle* for the dealings of a supranational "Predator State," controlled by the elite group, with the sole purpose of diverting wealth from public to private interests.[8] According to Galbraith, the Predator State is the culmination of the neoliberal path toward deregulation, privatization, and free trade. It is characterized by an intricate network of corporate and financial elites working together to make money off the state and the global economy "so long as they control it."[9] Like the mandarins of imperial China, the strategists funded by this elite weave the rationale for imperial rule.

Power is typically a taboo subject. Rarely do we see identified the persons who, often from behind the scenes, dominate a policy process that favors calling for war and for the displacement and impoverishment of people. Telling this neglected story is not for the purpose of placing blame. Those with inordinate power may be kind or cruel and are often acting in ways they believe will help everyone. Whether cruel or kind, the roots of continuing violence are to be found among a network of powerful beneficiaries, a force, so far, sufficient to constrain the nurturing potential of humans and to conceal the destructive system and avert the mayhem of war and poverty. This elite group of individuals with enormous wealth, social capital, and influence use their resources and connections to ensure that the system in which they have succeeded does not change.[10]

Whose special interests are intrinsically protected by their network connections and who gets left out of the vital connections needed to thrive in today's global economy? To find out, one might start with an examination of the multiple positions held by the occupant of an important political office. Take, for example, former Secretary of the Navy Gordon England. Secretary England was appointed 72nd Secretary of the Navy in May 2001. While holding this position, Mr. England led America's Navy and Marine Corps and was responsible for more than 800,000 military and civilian personnel and an annual budget of more than $120 billion. He joined the Department of Homeland Security in January 2003. Prior to joining the administration of President G. W. Bush, Mr. England was executive vice president of General Dynamics Corporations where he was responsible for two major corporate sectors: Information Systems and Technology and International Contracting. Previously, he had served as executive vice president of the Combat Systems Group, president of General Dynamics Fort Worth aircraft company (now Lockheed Martin), president of General Dynamics Land Systems Company, and also as the principal of a mergers and acquisition consulting company.[11]

Such corporate-government connections are commonplace within the imperial game. But corporations are also connected with one another. One can track the board memberships of England's General Dynamics (GD) colleagues as well as the accounting and law firms that serve GD. Among the GD board are retired generals and admirals; directors of major financial firms (Morgan Chase and LLC investment banking), the food industry (Sara Lee), and pharmaceutical companies (Schering Plough). The web of interconnections extends further. With high-level government and corporate officials one finds multiple links to certain financial institutions, law firms, accounting firms, and trade organizations like Petroleum Institute or PhRMA. The networks include links to managers of major media corporations and to research centers and think tanks. People central in these powerful networks are sought after for boards of universities and major medical centers where they help to attract donors and play an integral role in ensuring the continuous supply of trained persons to help turn the wheels of an acquisitive society and the imperialist game.[12] England's situation is more the rule than the exception. A "revolving door" exists in which corporate and financial officials assume roles in government and then return to corporate and financial lobbying activities with greater influence resulting from their past government ties.[13] The future efficacy of the peace movement will be determined by its ability to demystify and address these networks and systems of power.

THE CENTRALIZED MONETARY SYSTEM

To understand how and why a well-positioned group has gained sufficient power to impede change, it is important to examine their dominant currency of power and interaction, namely, money. As David Korten observed: "Money is a system of power and . . . the more dependent we are on money as the mediator of human relationships, the more readily those who have the power to create money and to decide who gets it can abuse that power."[14] Centralized monetary systems, both national and international, on which the free-market system rides, are the foundation for the game of imperial hegemony. To create a peaceful, sustainable, and equitable world we must gain an understanding of how centralized monetary systems, governed by central banks, consolidate wealth and power by monopolizing and politicizing the money supply. So what is a centralized monetary system? How is money created? And for that matter, what *is* money?

In centralized monetary systems, central banks, such as the Federal Reserve, control the money supply.[15] They also serve as the state's bank, providing the state with the money necessary to carry out its operations. Thus, in centralized monetary systems money, banking, and finance have been politicized because, as Thomas H. Greco, Jr., a leading authority on free-market approaches to monetary and financial innovation, revealed, "national governments have arrogated to themselves virtually unlimited spending power, which enables them to channel wealth to favored clients, to conduct wars on a massive scale, and to subvert democratic institutions and the popular will."[16]

Essentially, central banks fund state operations directly, so that the state does not have to tax its citizenry to raise funds for its deficit spending. Indeed, the military-industrial complex could not maintain itself were it not for the U.S. government's arrangement with the Federal Reserve.[17] Convincing the public to fight a war is one matter. Convincing the public to both fund *and* fight a war is altogether different. Many have argued that the arrangement between the U.S. government and the Federal Reserve constitutes a threat to both civil liberty and democracy.[18]

MONEY AND ITS CREATION

On August 15, 1971, President Nixon took the U.S. dollar off the gold standard internationally, which shifted the entire global monetary system to a fiat standard. Fiat money is money that is no longer grounded to the natural world. It is backed by nothing, and created out of nothing, by a central authority.[19] The U.S. Federal Reserve is the central authority that controls the money supply by buying or selling primarily U.S. Treasury securities on the open market, which is referred to as the monetization of government debt.[20] The amount of securities bought or sold on the open market determines the amount of money available to the banking system as a whole. The amount of money a commercial bank is allowed to borrow at the federal funds rate, to be lent to its customers at a significantly higher interest rate than the federal funds rate, is determined by the commercial bank's reserves.[21]

Centralized monetary systems are based on the fractional reserve banking system.[22] The fractional reserve system allows banks to loan up to 10 times the amount of their actual reserves, which greatly increases the private banks' income derived from interest and overall investment potential.[23] For example, say the Federal Reserve writes a check to the U.S. government for $100,000. By the time this money works its way through the banking system as a succession of deposits and loans, $900,000 in credit money will be added to the monetary system as a whole, all of it bearing an interest charge to be paid to the bank.[24] So what is money?

At various junctures in its history, money was backed by tangible objects of value such as gold, silver, cattle, or grain.[25] At present, all money, except for coins and some special notes in circulation today, is created from debt and backed by nothing more than the government or debtor's promise to repay the loan plus interest.[26] For example, a bank may, with a few keystrokes on a computer, make a loan of up to $10,000 to a debtor, so long as that bank retains $1,000 in reserve on that loan, effectively creating $9,000 in money that does not exist. Concurrently, the debtor acquired a legal obligation to repay the principal amount of $10,000, plus interest.[27] Interest is the fee charged for use of the central bank's monopolized credit money and places an unnecessary burden on debtors. The classic argument used to justify interest is that banks take on a risk when they loan money. This argument holds weight if money were actually backed by something of intrinsic value, such as gold, and/or the lender had actually labored to earn the money being loaned. But this is simply not the case in a debt-based monetary system in which banks create money from nothing the moment a loan is approved. Furthermore, if the money supply were not monopolized, then competition among currencies (credit) would temper commercial banks' profits and reduce them to reasonable service fees.[28] Indeed, the charging of interest, although highly profitable for the super class, has serious consequences for the majority of the population as well as the natural environment.

THE PROBLEM WITH INTEREST

The charging of undue interest, known as usury, undermines social justice and threatens the sustainability of the ecological environment. We already noted that commercial banks create money the moment a debtor takes out a loan. However, commercial banks only increase the amount of money in the economy to match the *principal* amount of a loan. Commercial banks do not increase the amount of money in the economy to cover the *interest* on that loan. In this way, money is made intentionally scarce, which forces debtors to compete against each other for the interest. As there is never enough money in the system at any one time to cover both the collective's principal and the collective's interest, default is inevitable. Worse, the charging of interest on debt money results in a debt imperative in which debt is exponentially growing at all times.[29] This debt imperative leads to a growth imperative in which the economy must grow fast enough to maintain the demand for new loans, thus creating enough new money to cover the interest on old loans.[30] Hence an elite group of wealthy investors benefit from an endlessly expanding economy.

The real growth of goods and services in the economy rarely keeps up with the average interest rate and, even if it did, limits on the natural environment and its resources will eventually check economic growth. Thus, the centralized monetary system guarantees the consolidation of wealth and power in the hands of the super class by way of profits derived from the charging of interest, which is multiplied tenfold in a fractional reserve system; by accumulating assets when debtors default on loan payments; and by investing upward of 30 percent of money created in their own accounts.[31] Next, Wall Street takes over and, using a myriad of inventive and speculative investing, trading, and lending vehicles, helps the super class create and consolidate even more phantom wealth.[32] That this option is not readily available to victims of war or economic displacement, or simply to members of the poor and working classes, leads to the creation of a class structure that is strikingly similar to that of feudal, medieval Europe.[33]

The debt imperative and growth imperative, fueled by the competition for scarce money, prohibit the creation of a steady-state, sustainable economy based on growing real wealth, such as quality goods and services and healthy communities. Our monetary system demands that we appease the growth imperative by churning out as many cheap, environmentally ruinous, and unnecessary goods as possible in an attempt to outrun exponentially increasing debt. Furthermore, the growth imperative, based on competition for interest, pressures the financial system for short-term returns, usually derived by speculation, rather than long-tem sustainability. Within our centralized monetary system, the creation of a steady-state, sustainable economy is not profitable enough in the short-term to keep apace with the debt imperative.

Unfortunately, war has the effect of staying abreast of the debt imperative, at least in the short term. War results in the expansion of credit money, which whether intentional or not, has the effect of "priming the pump" of the economy.[34] Thus, history suggests that, in addition to a debt and growth imperative, the centralized monetary system lends itself to a war imperative as well. The problem of interest makes it unlikely that a peaceful, sustainable world can be created without addressing the centralized monetary system.

THE PROBLEM OF INFLATION

Inflation occurs in an economy with "too much money chasing too few goods."[35] It results from the improper issue of money whereby the money supply is expanded without the proportional expansion of goods and services in the market place. Greco likened inflation to a form of legal counterfeit, as both decrease the purchasing power of money.[36] As money becomes worthless, the prices of goods and services must rise to offset the watered-down money supply. Thus, inflation creates a growth imperative to offset the decreased value of money. Effectively, the Federal Reserve inflates the money supply any time it monetizes long-term government debt, particularly war debt.[37] The problem is that inflation must be reigned in, at which point the Federal Reserve restricts the amount of credit (money) available in the economy. At this time, the economic cycle "busts," massive defaults ensue, and wealth is further consolidated in the hands of those few who are able to buy up the assets now available at bargain prices.

A BAILOUT FOR THE FINANCIAL ELITE

The recent financial crisis presented an opportunity for the current administration to curtail Wall Street's speculative ventures and make radical changes to our inequitable monetary system. It might also have replaced expenditures on the war sector with investments in education and health that produce significantly more jobs. Instead, the politicized money power triumphed, and Wall Street was rewarded for its recklessness in the form of a multi-trillion-dollar bailout, a significant portion of which was used for bonuses, vacations, and golden parachute executive payouts. The bailout is testament to the power elite's commitment to maintaining the status quo and revealed the revolving door between the U.S. government and Wall Street. Take for example the case of Goldman Sachs, the world's most powerful investment bank.

According to Matt Taibbi, the history of the financial crisis and resulting bailout "reads like a Who's Who of Goldman Sachs graduates."[38] Henry Paulson, President George W. Bush's Treasury secretary and former CEO of Goldman Sachs was the architect of the bailout, which seemingly benefited the interests of Goldman Sachs and friends over other financial institutions and, more importantly, the American people. For example, Robert Rubin, President Clinton's former Treasury secretary and former Goldman Sachs employee of 26 years, received $300 billion in taxpayer dollars for Citigroup, of which he is chairman; former Goldman Sachs employee John Thain, now head of Merrill Lynch, received billions of taxpayer dollars, funneled through

Bank of America; and Robert Steel, former executive of Goldman Sachs, who was rewarded with a $250 million golden parachute executive payout for running his bank, Wachovia, into bankruptcy. Other notable Goldman Sachs alums include Joshua Bolten, President Bush's chief of staff during the bailout; Mark Patterson, the current Treasury chief of staff under President Obama; the heads of the Canadian and Italian national banks, the head of the New York Stock Exchange, and the last two heads of the Federal Reserve Bank of New York. The financial and political power and reach of Goldman Sachs is behemoth, and Taibbi's outline of Goldman Sach's involvement in, and profit derived from, every major market manipulation (bubble) since the Great Depression exposed the damage that results from the centralized and politicized monetary system.

The centralized monetary system is an important tool for the proliferation of the master's game because it consolidates private wealth and power in interlocked hierarchies between government, industry, and the financial elite, influences the direction of the economy by favoring short-term gains over long-term sustainability, contains a built-in war imperative, and burdens governments and people with debt. The global debt-based, centralized monetary system has also proved ruinous for the economies of underdeveloped and developing nations. As Jubilee South proclaimed, "Debt is essentially an ideological and political instrument for the exploitation and control of our peoples, resources, and countries by those corporations, countries, and institutions that concentrate wealth and power in the capitalist system."[39] Members of Jubilee South call for nothing less than debt cancellation, debt repudiation and reparation, and for the creation of community-oriented, socio-economic and political systems based on serving the needs of the people.

CONCENTRATING WEALTH

In addition to the centralized, debt-based monetary system, which was designed to consolidate wealth and power, the power elite have enriched themselves by buying out their competitors and by acquiring resources of the world for a pittance while leaving the environmental and health costs of their activities to be paid by others. Some of their wealth has come from loans made to governments of poor countries in the form of a structural adjustment package. The stipulations for the procurement of a loan from the IMF and World Bank, largely controlled by nations in the global North, almost always include economist Milton Friedman's "triumvirate of privatization, deregulation/free trade and drastic cuts to government spending."[40] The privatization of poor countries and their resources enables the siphoning of wealth from the global South to the global North.

Beyond privatization, the elite group has found other ways to concentrate wealth and promote inequity. For example, they have welcomed into the workplace immigrants and women, to whom they can pay shamefully low wages. They have overseen technological advances in industry and communications, which have replaced still more workers. They have sold the dream that every generation will have more than the previous generation. The dream of collective enrichment was true from the 1820s through times of boom and bust, including even the Great Depression. However, it ceased to be true in the 1970s when more workers and more members of a family began to invest longer hours at work to maintain the same income. Corporate globalization forced demands for higher productivity on workers without raising their wages or benefits. With limited labor costs and an increase in productivity, profits soared among the wealthiest. Incidentally, the 1970s also marked the time when President Nixon took the U.S. dollar off the gold standard internationally, thereby forcing international currencies to "float" against each other in a highly speculative, and exploitable, currency exchange market.[41] Currency speculation allowed for the further concentration of wealth at the expense of poorer nations and their people. Herve Kempf effectively demonstrated the excessive concentration of wealth among a small minority: 793 billionaires possess $2.6 trillion dollars, which, according to the Committee for the Cancellation of Third World Debt (CADTM) is the sum equal to "the entirety of developing countries' foreign debt."[42]

The corporate elite marketed excessive consumption by selling the myth that "the good life" was to be had by buying more stuff that could be paid off on installments. Instead of providing higher wages to match increases in productivity, the financiers extended credit, once again turning ordinary people into supporters of the most wealthy through interest payments on their loans and credit cards.[43] The elite limited safety nets by selling the idea that people were individually responsible for their own well-being, even though their own enterprises relied heavily on government subsidies, sweetheart contracts, and tax loopholes. In the wake of their growth, corporations left a population deeply stressed and heavily in debt, wanting change, but still hoping that it might come without undue sacrifice.

CONSENT OF THE PEOPLE

From the inception of the nation state, there have always been dominating elites, distrustful of the capacity of ordinary people to make the decisions of the state, and therefore needing to be controlled, whether by persuasion or by police force. This system is inordinately influenced, as we have demonstrated, by a small interconnected group of corporate, financial, military, and government leaders. They have the power to instill fear, to protect and to increase their excessive fortunes, and to restrict information, particularly information that concerns their own clandestine dealings or information that threatens the imperialist game.

Over the past century leaders of this elite became more skilled in the art and science of propaganda by tapping into emotional needs, both conscious and unconscious. The media are used with even greater sophistication to manage perceptions and to manufacture consent.[44] They were carefully used to bring a reluctant U.S. public into World War I. They were central to the demonization of the Soviet Union following World War II and crucial for the development of a permanent war economy.[45] Additionally, media were used to turn ordinary citizens into passive consumers who measure their identities against what they purchase, thereby leaving poor people deficient not only in goods but in self-esteem as well.

THE MYTH OF PROGRESS

Some excessive spending of the elite class on ridiculously expensive clothing, multiple homes, vacations, art collections, and "yacht wars," has the effect of establishing prestige. The super-rich live in secluded mansions, gated communities, and restricted penthouses, apart from the common space shared by others.[46] The image of their lifestyle is an object for both envy and mimicry. The illusion that ordinary people can realistically aspire to the lifestyle of the elite fuels the idolization of successful superstars, the purchase of lottery tickets, and the gullibility of electorates for the message, repeated each electoral season, that corporate-selected candidates are just like the rest of us. Although they may be like us in their personal human qualities, they differ from the rest of us in the roles they play in the master's game. Though many recognize the absurdity of the vast inequity, they have lived so long with a plantation mentality that they cannot imagine an equitable and peaceful life beyond the master's game.

Indeed, the hopes of people have been cast in the mold of progress and growth. When failures occurred, there was always a new frontier, or a new technology, that would sustain the myth of exponential growth.[47] Now, there is no new frontier waiting to be discovered and exploited, which has led many to view the future green economy as the savior of a fledgling global economy and financial system.[48] But alas, in a world of finite resources, even a green economy will be insufficient for the task of saving a system run by, and for, an elite addicted to their own game, who have demonstrated a willingness to use violence to protect their own interests. We must work to change the myth of progress from a faith in new frontiers and exponential economic growth to a hope that life can be fuller and healthier with better stewarding and sharing of resources and power. Only then will we be able to dismantle the master's house and bring about genuine social change.

WHAT NEXT?

The failures of globalization have resulted in a collective scrutiny of the master's game. The stage may now be set for social transformation in the inseparable directions of ecological sustainability, economic justice, and non-violent resolution of differences. Paul Hawken, author of *Blessed Unrest*, optimistically describes a revolution presently occurring, without any discernable leader, subscribed doctrine, headlines, or coordination, in which people the world over are actively engaged in transforming society.[49] We hope Hawken is right, but fear that this ignores the taboo topic of power and the privatization and consolidation of power and wealth.

Many of the wonderful projects we see are affirmations of the values and practices that were necessary for the viability of the bands, tribes, and villages in which most of humanity lived for centuries prior to the industrial revolution. The groups that survived and flourished were the ones that worked out ways to live peacefully among themselves, to preserve their ecological nests, and to use the wisdom of their elders for the betterment of the community. The current flood of grassroots actions for peace and sustainability undoubtedly taps into the human capacity for caring and empathy, and they are critical for the success of the movement.

However, change must be both local and global. Some issues, like control and elimination of nuclear weapons, accountability for war crimes, the prevention of epidemics, the clean-up of toxic wastes, the conversion to a peacetime economy, and the forgiveness of Third World debt, require governments and international regulatory agencies to play a major role. The creation of community-oriented, socio-economic, and political systems based on serving the needs of all people, rather than the needs of the wealthy elite, is not possible, we believe, without a concerted, global effort on the part of governments, their people, and international regulatory agencies.

The plantation we now occupy is heading for potential economic and ecological disaster and collapse. Replacing it will require that we dismantle the master's house. Those now heading recovery efforts strive mainly to return to a point where we are able to resume consumption of things we do not need with credit and thereby restore a system requiring growth and military action to protect it. On the most personal level, the changes must encompass the values we live by and the way we create self-esteem. As a global society, we face changes in the control over money and over the means to kill. We come close to the heart of what must change by raising the issue of complementing the centralized monetary system with a decentralized, abundant, and inexpensive monetary system that is not embedded in the power network.[50] Given the interlocking of the U.S. government and the money power, it is doubtful that any significant transformation will come about from within the existing monetary system, whether nationalized or privatized. Former senior Central Bank executive Bernard Lietaer recognized the perils of challenging the money power. He suggested that monetary transformation must arise from private initiative in the form of a complementary monetary system, which will operate alongside the centralized monetary system.[51]

The goal is to create democratic, locally controlled, depoliticized, interest-free monetary systems designed to strengthen local economies and communities, while simultaneously providing a buffer against the inflationary and monopolized national currency with its inevitable cycles of boom and bust. The result is a mutual credit system in which money is created at the moment of exchange between parties. At present, one of the most comprehensive mutual credit systems is ROCS—Robust Complementary Community Currency.[52] The system was designed to provide the best buffer against the centralized monetary system and the fairest means of exchange between parties.[53] Though no complete ROCS systems are presently in use, elements of the system are seen in existing mutual credit systems such as LETSystems, Ithaca Hours, and Time Dollars.

ROCS is a robust currency designed to withstand external shocks such as economic bust cycles, inflation, or even economic collapse. ROCS are issued by participants, rather than a central authority, which means that the amount of credit in the system is always balanced. Unlike some mutual credit systems, which are tied to the national currency, ROCS are measured in hours of service. However, mutual credit systems are not limited to the hour for their unit of account. Any unit of account that is beyond the grasp of state and financial hierarchies, such as a basket of commodities, could be used in place of hours. Unlike other mutual credit systems, the ROCS system allows participants to negotiate the rate of exchange. In this manner, participants whose hour of service required more training, skills, hard and/or undesirable labor, or the use of expensive equipment is worth more than those whose hour of service required less demanding work. Finally, the ROCS system contains a demurrage fee that is applied to both positive and negative balances. Demurrage can be thought of as a negative interest rate, the purpose of which is to help keep the mutual credit circulating, rather than hoarded. The collective demurrage fee can then be used for operational costs, community projects, or to help the most impoverished in the community gain the skills and training necessary to participate in the local mutual credit system.

Despite the potential of the ROCS system to provide a buffer against external shocks and empower the people with an abundant, inexpensive, and fair means of exchange, the problem of the centralized money power remains. Articulating a comprehensive strategy for the transformation of the current global monetary system into one that promotes sustainability, justice, and equity is beyond the scope of this article. However, the wisdom of Bernard Lietaer points in the right direction. Lietaer called for the private sector to create a global reference currency (GRC), which he called the Terra, whose unit of account is grounded in the natural world in the form of a basket of commodities.[54] The purpose of the Terra is to provide a reliable and stable reference currency for international trade and to reinstate the international standard of value, which was removed by President Nixon in 1971, thereby hampering the speculative global currency casino. Additionally, the Terra would contain a demurrage fee, which can also be thought of as a sustainability fee. The purpose of the sustainability fee is to both counter the global growth imperative and prevent hoarding during periods of external economic shock. Thus, the Terra would serve a similar purpose for the global economy as a local mutual credit system serves for the local economy. The hope is that local and global democratic, sustainable, and equitable monetary systems might, one day, build sufficient support to peacefully supplant the money power's centralized monetary system. A second big change in the master's game must be the removal of war. The United World Federalists express hope for an international federation of separate governments that would have great accountability to its member states, but which would have predominant control over the military force which would be used only for the restoration of peace after all other efforts have failed.[55] The question is again one of accountability. With governments now accountable to the corporate sectors with whom they are also closely connected, it is remarkable that the UN continues to address some of the issues of the inclusion of all people in the world community. In addition to the UN, new institutions like a nonviolent police force and a World Social Forum will need to grow in power and influence on the world stage. Indeed, projects reflecting our humanity on a local level may have to be melded into programs and agencies with global impact. Additionally, local communities and the people who work in corporate structures will have to find ways to share in the responsibility for these structures, to keep them accountable to local needs. We will have to welcome conflicts as well as creative resolutions among local projects that promote life with global regulatory institutions that prevent violence.

With a newfound respect for the responsibilities of preserving a sustainable world at peace, we confront the elephant in our living room. We will enter the plantation, bring light to its dark corners, and gradually replace the needs of the master with the needs of all stakeholders on the global plantation. To create a peaceful worldview, the power elite, now central to a system requiring violence, must be faced. We must remind ourselves that revolutionary transformations do occur. However, the magnitude of the revolutionary transformation needed for peace and sustainability to reign requires many shifts. We may need to find meanings in our self-concept that unite us more closely to the web of life and to our local communities. This can guide us to eat differently, to invest in the health of our communities, to use the gifts of our planet wisely, to be more accepting of differences and more knowing of nonviolent ways to resolve disputes, and to care more deeply for those most deserving of that care. It is the special task of this generation to liberate both the oppressed and the oppressors from the monetary, economic, and political systems that perpetuate injustice and engender violence. We can and must demystify and confront the master's game, in which we are all entangled, and write a peaceful and sustainable story for our species.

NOTES

1. Lorde, 1984.
2. Korten, 2006, 2009.
3. Peace Pledge Union, 2005.
4. Tuchman, 1984.
5. Hagan and Bickerton, 2007.
6. Perkins, 2004.
7. Korten, 2006.
8. Galbraith, 2008.
9. Ibid.
10. Perruci and Wysong, 1999.
11. Pilisuk, 2008.
12. Ibid.
13. Public Citizen Report, 2009.
14. Korten, 2009.
15. Greco, 1990.
16. Greco, 2009.
17. Rockwell, 2008.
18. Ibid.
19. Lietaer, 2001.
20. Brown, 2007.
21. The Federal Reserve System Board of Govenors, 2005.
22. Zarlenga, 2002.
23. Brown, 2007.
24. Lietaer, 2001.
25. Zarlenga, 2002.
26. Wolff, 2009.

27. Korten, 2009.
28. Greco, 2009.
29. Ibid.
30. Brown, 2007.
31. Ibid.
32. Korten, 2009.
33. Kelly, 2001.
34. Rockwell, 2008.
35. Greco, 2009.
36. Ibid.
37. Ibid.
38. Taibbi, 2009.
39. South, 2002.
40. Klein, 2007.
41. Brown, 2007.
42. Kempf, 2008.
43. Wolff, 2009.
44. Pilisuk, 2008.
45. Ibid.
46. Kempf, 2008.
47. Ibid.
48. Sachs, 2008.
49. Hawken, 2007.
50. Greco, 2009.
51. Lietaer, 2001.
52. Ibid.
53. Ibid.
54. Ibid.
55. Tetalman and Belitsos, 2005.

A FINAL WORD

Marc Pilisuk and Michael N. Nagler

Like the surface of the earth itself, the prevailing war system is a relatively thin and unstable layer that effectively conceals intense energies of greater fluidity beneath its surface—energies that occasionally burst forth. Our journey through the manifold energies and projects that are represented in the chapters of these three volumes did not reveal a single, unified world peace movement, but it certainly did reveal wellsprings of activity, more intense, more creative and more widespread than one would imagine. The bubbling energies appear as contributions to a gigantic wave surging against the barriers that societies have entrenched into laws and ideologies that make inequality, exploitation, and violence appear inevitable. Slowly but with increasing likelihood, individuals and groups of individuals, facing incredibly diverse manifestations of that age-old inhumanity, are finding courage, as people have done through history, to rise up against it. But in this generation many more of us are also identifying the existing exploitative system underlying diverse violence and recognizing that this system is failing. And some are daring to view the movements toward peace, justice, and sustainability as a yet-unrealized but potentially unstoppable movement. This emergence is all the more amazing as it comes on the heels of a century in which control over human identity has become all-pervasive and quite often malicious; when the war propaganda is based, ironically enough, on adaptations of Sigmund Freud's theories about the power of appealing to basic needs and fears; when such propaganda hurled masses of humanity into paroxysms of anti-Semitic hatred, among other examples of targeted dehumanization; and when the self-image of human beings as "happiness machines that have become the key to economic progress" (to paraphrase President Hoover) came to predominate.[1] The power of such manipulation and control is breaking apart and yielding to a culture in which the better natures of people can assert themselves.

One cannot review the efforts described in these volumes, and the many more that we could not include, without realizing that the wave is powerful and has not yet reached its crest. The power and impact of these healthier alternatives are evident and they are springing up everywhere. They remain seriously under-reported by the mainstream media that instead deliver a constant stream of tragedies, local and national, as though they were singular occurrences rather than looking deeply into the failures of unfettered corporate expansion and the war system. It is an ironically hopeful sign that the failures of that system are becoming apparent to people the world over, despite the impressive capacity of a powerful elite to "spin" the coverage. Some former powerful players of that system, some of whom appear in these pages, have recognized the failure of an unbridled quest for development and unending search for enemies.

A more heartening sign is that the activists described in the final chapter of Volume 3 do not wait for powerful officials to lead them. In ways small and large, people are devoting their creativity, their energy, their dreams, and their quest for a meaningful life to make peace a reality. One cannot come away from the story of these efforts without being heartened by the fact that so many others have stepped forward. We are resourceful and caring custodians of the force of life. The peace movement worldwide is an inchoate but amazing force. It grows because it must prevail. And if we nurture it, it will.

NOTE

1. BBC documentary, 2002.

BIBLIOGRAPHY

Abu-Nimer, Mohammed. "Conflict Resolution in an Islamic Context." *Peace and Change* 21, no. 1 (1996): 22–40.

Abu-Nimer, Mohammed. *Nonviolence and Peace Building in Islam: Theory and Practice.* Gainesville: University of Florida Press, 2003.

Ackerman, Peter, and Jack DuVall. *A Force More Powerful: A Century of Non-Violent Conflict.* New York: Palgrave, 2000.

Adams, David. "Internal Military Interventions in the United States." *Journal of Peace Research* 32 (1995): 197–211.

Adams, David. *The History of the Culture of War.* 2008. Available for reading online or mail order at http://culture-of-peace.info/books/history.html.

Adams, David. "The Seville Statement on Violence: A Progress Report." *Journal of Peace Research* 26 (1989): 113–21.

Adams, David. *World Peace through the Town Hall.* 2009. Available for reading online or for mail-order at http://culture-of-peace.info/books/worldpeace.html.

Adams, David, ed. "The Seville Statement on Violence." General Conference of UNESCO, 25th session. Paris, November 16, 1989.

Adams, David, ed. *UNESCO and a Culture of Peace: Promoting a global movement.* Paris: UNESCO, 1995.

Adams, David. "Why There Are So Few Women Warriors." *Behavior Science Research* 18, no. 3 (1983): 207.

Adkins, Christopher P. "Is Empathy the Missing Link in Teaching Business Ethics? A Course-Based Educational Intervention with Undergraduate Business Students." PhD diss, The College of William and Mary, 2009.

Afghanistan Independent Commission on Human Rights. *A Call for Justice: A National Consultation on Past Human Rights Violations in Afghanistan*, 2005, http://www.aihrc.org.af/Rep_29_Eng/rep29_1_05call4justice.pdf.

Ahmad, Razi. "Islam, Nonviolence and Global transformation." In Islam and Nonviolence. Edited by Glenn D. Paige, Chaiwat Satha-Anand, and Sarah Gilliant. 27–33. Center for Global Nonviolence Planning Project, Matsunaga Institute for Peace, University of Hawaii, 1993.

Ahmed, Akbar. *Discovering Islam: Making Sense of Muslim History and Society.* London: Routledge & Keagan Paul, Ltd., 1988.

American University International Peace and Conflict Resolution Master Program (IPCR) http://www1.sis.american.edu/academics/fieldofstudy/ipcr.htm.

Amnesty International, "Killer facts: The impact of the irresponsible arms trade on lives, rights and livelihoods." New York: Amnesty International, May 6, 2010, http://www.amnesty.org/en/library/info/ACT30/005/2010/en (accessed November 29, 2009).

Amnesty International. "North Kivu: No End to War on Women and Children," http://www.amnesty.org/en/librry/asset/AFR62/005/2008/en/f23caedf-8e4a-11dd-8e5e-43ea85d15a69/afr620052008en.html (accessed November 29, 2009).

Angier, Natalie. "Why We're So Nice: We're Wired to Cooperate." *The New York Times*, July 23, 2002.

Anthony, David W. *The Horse, the Wheel, and Language.* Princeton, NJ: Princeton University, 2007.

Appiah, Kwame Anthony. *Cosmopolitanism: Ethics in a World of Strangers.* New York: W. W. Norton, 2006.

Appiah, Kwame Anthony. *The Ethics of Identity.* Princeton, NJ: Princeton University Press, 2005.

Appleby, Scott. *The Ambivalence of the Sacred: Religion, Violence, and Reconciliation.* Lanham, MD: Rowman & Littlefield, 2000.

Arendt, Hannah. *Eichmann in Jerusalem: A Report on the Banality of Evil*, rev. ed. New York: Viking, 1968.

Arnould, Dominique. *Guerre et paix dans la poesie grecque. De Callinos a Pindare.* New York: Arno Press, 1981.

Ashghar, Ali Engineer. "Sources of Nonviolence in Islam." In *Nonviolence: Contemporary Issues and Challenges*, edited by M. Kumar. New Delhi: Gandhi Peace Foundation, New Delhi, 1994.

Augros, R., and George Stanciu. *The New Biology.* New York and London: Shambala, 1988.

"Autism." *Science Daily*, April 18, 2005, http://www.sciencedaily.com/releases/2005/04/050411204511.htm.

Bandura, Albert. "Mechanisms of Moral Disengagement." In *Origins of Terrorism: Psychologies, Ideologies, Theologies, States of Mind*, edited by W. Reich, 161–91. New York: Cambridge University Press, 1988.

Bandura, Albert, Bill Underwood, and Michael E. Fromson. "Disinhibition of Aggression through Diffusion of Responsibility and Dehumanization of Victims." *Journal of Research in Personality* 9 (1975): 253–69.

Bastick, Megan, Karin Grimm, and Rahel Kunz. *Sexual Violence in Armed Conflict: Global Overview and Implications for the Security Sector.* Geneva Center for the Democratic Control of Armed Forces, 2007.

Basu, Amrita, and Rekha Basu. "India: Of Men, Women, and Bombs," *Dissent*, Winter 1999, 39–43.

Bates, Stephen. "Slaps on the Wrist." *The Guardian* (London), June 23, 1997.

BBC documentary, *Happiness Machines*, available at http://www.bbc.uk//bbcFour/docimentraries/features/century_of_the_self_episode_1.shtml (accessed April, 29, 2002).

Beales, A. C. F. *The History of Peace; A Short Account of the Organized Movements for International Peace*. New York: Garland Publishers, 1971 (1931).

Beck, Peggy V., and Anna Lee Walters. *The Sacred: Ways of Knowledge: Sources of Life*. Tsaile, AZ: Navajo Community College, 1977.

Bennett, Milton J. "A Developmental Approach to Training for Intercultural Sensitivity." *International Journal of Intercultural Relations* 10, no. 2 (1986): 179–96.

Bensahel, Nora, Olga Oliker, and Heather Peterson, "Improving Capacity for Stabilization and Reconstruction Operations," RAND Corporation, 2009, http://www.rand.org/pubs/monographs/2009/RAND_MG852.pdf.

Bernstein, Elizabeth, and Institute for Defense and Disarmament Studies, eds. *Peace Resource Book of 1986*. Cambridge, MA: Institute for Defense and Disarmament Studies.

Berry, Nicholas. "Too Much Hysteria Exists over the Increasing Proliferation of Weapons of Mass Destructions and Ballistic Missile Technology: A More Modest Hysteria Would Be Wiser." *Asia Forum*, January 21, 2000.

Berryman, Phillip. *Liberation Theology*. New York: Meyer Stone Books, 1987.

Biswas, Shampa. "'Nuclear Apartheid': Race as a Postcolonial Resource?" *Alternatives* 26, no. 4 (Oct.–Dec. 2001).

Bitsas, Constantine. "Food for Thought: The Role of Nutrients in Reducing Aggression, Violence and Criminal Behavior." *Corrections Today* 66, Part 2 (2004): 110–115, http://www.biobalance.org.au/articles/16 (accessed October 13, 2009).

Black, Peter W., and Kenneth Avruch. "Some Issues in Thinking about Culture and the Resolution of Conflict." *Humanity and Society* 13, no. 2 (1989): 187–94.

Blumberg, Herbert A., Paul Hare, and Anna Costim. *Peace Psychology: A Comprehensive Introduction*. New York: Cambridge University Press, 2007.

Blumenthal, Max. *Republican Gomorrah: Inside the Movement that Shattered the Party*. New York: Nation Books, 2009.

Boff, Leonardo. "Spirituality and Politics." In *Liberation Theology: An Introductory Reader*, edited by Curt Cadorette, Marie Giblin, Marilyn J. Legge, and Mary Snyder, 236–43. Maryknoll, NY: Orbis Books, 1992.

Boulding, Kenneth. "Evolutionary Movement toward Peace." In *World Encyclopedia of Peace*, edited by Ervin Laszlo and J. L. Yoo. Oxford: Pergamon, 1986.

Bouvard, Marguerite Guzman. *Revolutionizing Motherhood: The Mothers of the Plaza de Mayo*. Oxford: SR Books, 1994.

Bredemeier, Harry C., and Jackson Toby. *Social Problems in America*. New York: Wiley, 1972.

Bronfenbrenner, Urie. "The Mirror Image in Soviet-American Relations." *Journal of Social Issues* 16, no. 3 (1986): 45–56.

Brown, Ellen. *The Web of Debt*. Baton Rouge, LA: Third Millennium Press, 2007.

Buber, Martin. *I and Thou*, 2nd ed. New York: Charles Scribner's Sons, 1958.

Burgess, Heidi, and Guy Burgess. "Justice without Violence: A Theoretical Framework." In *Justice without Violence*, edited by Paul Wehr, Heidi Burgess, and Guy Burgess. Boulder, CO: Lynne Rienner Publishers, 1994.

Burton, John W. *Resolving Deep Rooted Conflict: A Handbook*. Lanham, MD: University Press of America, 1987.

Bush, Robert A. B., and Joseph P. Folger. *The Promise of Mediation: Responding to Conflict through Empowerment and Recognition*. San Francisco: Jossey-Bass, 1994.

Butler, Smedley. *War Is a Racket*. New York: Round Table Press, 1935.

Cahill, Lisa. *Love Your Enemies: Discipleship, Pacifism, and Just War Theory*. Minneapolis, MN: Augsburg Press, 1994.

Cantril, Hadley. *Human Nature and Political Systems*. New Brunswick, NJ: Rutgers University Press, 1961.

Chatfield Charles. *Peace Movements in America*. New York: Schocken Books, 1973.

Chatfield, Charles, and Robert Kleidman. *The American Peace Movement: Ideals and Activism*. New York: Maxwell Macmillan International, 1992.

Christianson, Drew. "Catholic Peacemaking, 1991–2005: The Legacy of Pope John Paul II." *The Review of Faith and International Affairs* (Fall 2006): 23.

Christianson, Drew. "Peacebuilding in Catholic Social Teaching," response given at Catholic Peace Building Conference, Notre Dame, IN, April 15, 2008, session V, panel 1. Audio at http://cpn.nd.edu/2008CPNConference%20-%20Post-Program.shtml.

CNN.com Transcripts, "America Strikes Back: Secretary of Defense Rumsfeld and Secretary of the Army Thomas White Hold a Press Conference," CNN.com, http://transcripts.cnn.com/TRANSCRIPTS/0110/11/se.18.html.

Christie, Dan, Barbara S. Tint, Richard V. Wagner, and Deborah DuNann Winter, eds. *Peace Psychology for a Peaceful World*. Washington, DC: American Psychological Association, 2008.

Cock, Jacklyn. *Women and War in South Africa*. Cleveland: Pilgrim Press, 1993.

Cockburn, Cynthia. *The Space between Us*. London: Zed Books, 1999.

Cohn, Carol. "Sex and Death in the Rational World of Defense Intellectuals." *Signs* 12, no. 4 (1987): 687–728.

Cohn, Carol. "War, Wimps and Women." In *Gendering War Talk*, edited by Miriam Cooke, 227–246. Princeton, NJ: Princeton University Press, 1993.

Cohn, Carol, and Sara Ruddick. "A Feminist Ethical Perspective on Weapons of Mass Destruction. In *Ethics and Weapons of Mass Destruction*, edited by Steven Lee and Sohail Hashmi. New York: Cambridge University Press, 2004.

Congolese Women's Campaign Against Sexual Violence in the DRC, "Sexual Violence in the East of DRC." http://www.rdcviolencesexuelle.org/site/en/node/44.

Congress Watch is the author for this piece. "Congressional Revolving Doors: The Journey from Congress to K Street." *Public Citizen Reports*, July 2009.

Coomaraswamy, Radhika. "Reinventing International Law: Women's Rights as Human Rights in the International Community." *Bulletin of Concerned Asian Scholars* 28, no. 2 (April–June 1996).

Creswell, J. David, Baldwin M. Way, Naomi I. Eisenberger, and Matthew D. Lieberman. "Neural Correlates of Dispositional Mindfulness during Affect Labeling." *Psychosomatic Medicine* 69, no. 6 (2007): 560–65.

Crow, Douglas Karim. *Nurturing an Islamic Peace Discourse.* Washington, D.C.: Center For Global Peace, American University (unpublished paper), 1997.

Cuomo, Chris J. "War Is Not Just an Event: Reflections on the Significance of Everyday Violence." *Hypatia* 11, no. 4 (1996): 30–45.

Day, Dorothy. *The Long Loneliness: The Autobiography of the Legendary Catholic Social Activist.* New York: Harper & Row, 1952.

deMause, Lloyd. "The Childhood Origins of the Holocaust." *The Journal of Psychohistory* 33, no. 3 (2006): 204–22.

DeMello, Cajetan. "Acting the Culture Contrast." In *Intercultural Sourcebook: Cross-Cultural Training Methods,* edited by S. M. Fowler and M. G. Mumford, 69–79. Yarmouth, ME: Intercultural Press, Inc., 1995.

Deming, Barbara. "Revolution and Equilibrium." In *We Are All Part of One Another.* Philadelphia: New Society Publishers, 1984.

Devall, Bill, and George Sessions. *Deep Ecology: Living as if Nature Mattered.* Layton, UT: Gibbs Smith Publisher, 1985.

de Waal, Frans. *Good Natured: The Origins of Right and Wrong in Humans and Other Animals.* Cambridge, MA: Harvard University Press, 1996.

de Waal, Frans. *Peacemaking among Primates.* Cambridge, MA: Harvard University Press, 1989.

Diamond, Irene, and Gloria Orenstein, eds. *Reweaving the World: The Emergence of Ecofeminism.* San Francisco: Sierra Club Books, 1990.

Doidge, Norman. *The Brain That Changes Itself.* New York: Vintage, 2007.

Donais, Timothy. "Empowerment or Imposition? Dilemmas of Local Ownership in Post-Conflict Peacebuilding Processes." *Peace & Change* 34, no. 1 (2009): 3–26.

Eisler, Riane. *The Chalice and the Blade.* San Francisco: Harper & Row, 1987.

Eisler, Riane. *The Power of Partnership: Seven Relationships That Will Change Your Life.* Novato, CA: New World Library, 2003.

Eisler, Riane. *The Real Wealth of Nations: Creating a Caring Economics.* San Francisco: Berrett-Koehler Publishers, 2007.

Ember, Mel, and Carol R. Ember. "Making the World More Peaceful: Policy Implications of Cross-Cultural Research." In *Prevention and Control of Aggression and the Impact on Its Victims,* edited by Manuela Martinez, 331–38. New York: Kluwer/Plenum, 2001.

Embry, Dennis D. "The Neuroscience of Peace." The Praxis Institute, http://74.125.155.132/search?q=cache:DNZC48InUp8J:www.creducation.org/resources/Christa_Tinari_CRE_Summit_Packet.doc+neuroscience+and+peace&cd=26&hl=en&ct=clnk&gl=us

Emminghaus, Wolf B., Paul Kimmel, and Edward Stewart. "Primal Violence: Illuminating Culture's Dark Side." *Journal of Peace and Conflict* 3 (1997): 167–91.

"Emotion." In *Encyclopædia Britannica.* http://search.eb.com/eb/article-283143

Enloe, Cynthia. *Bananas, Beaches, and Bases: Making Feminist Sense of International Politics.* Berkeley: University of California Press, 1989.

Enloe, Cynthia. *Does Khaki Become You? The Militarization of Women's Lives.* Boston: South End Press, 1983.

Enloe, Cynthia. *Maneuvers: The International Politics of Militarizing Women's Lives.* Berkeley: The University of California Press, 2000.

Enloe, Cynthia. *The Morning After: Sexual Politics at the End of the Cold War.* Berkeley: University of California Press, 1993.

Esack, Farid. *Liberation and Pluralism: An Islamic Perspective of Interreligious Solidarity Against Oppression.* Oxford: One World Publications, 1997.

Esack, Farid. "Religion and Cultural Diversity: For What and With Whom?" Islam and Cultural Diversity, A Conference at American University (unpublished paper, 1998).

Esposito, John. *Islam: The Straight Path.* New York: Oxford University Press, 1988.

Esposito, John. *The Islamic Threat.* New York: Oxford University Press, 1993.

Esposito, John, and James Piscatori. "Democratization and Islam." *Middle East Journal* (Summer 1991).

Etheridge, Lloyd. *Can Governments Learn?* New York: Pergamon Press, 1987.

Federal Reserve System Board of Governors. "The Federal Reserve System Purpose and Function," June 2005. Available at: http://www.federalreserve.gov/pf/pf.htm.

Feldman, Lily G. *Reconciliation and Structural Peace: The Case of the Federal Republic's Relations with France, Israel and the United States.* Washington, DC: The U. S. Institute of Peace, 1991.

Ferrer, Jorge N. *Revisioning Transpersonal Theory.* Albany: State University of New York Press, 2002.

Fiore, Quentin, and Marshall McLuhan. *War and Peace in the Global Village.* New York: McGraw-Hill, 1968.

Fisher, Luke, and Anthony Wilson-Smith. "Somalia's Ghosts Haunt Canada." *Macleans.* July 14, 1997.

Fisher, Roger, and William L. Ury. *Getting to Yes: Negotiating Agreement without Giving In.* New York: Penguin Books, 1983.

Food Research and Action Center, Hunger and Food Insecurity in the United States. (2005) Available at: http://www.frac.org//html/hunger_in_the_us/hunger_index.html.

Frady, Marshall. "The Outsider, II." *New Yorker,* March 10, 1992, 70.

Fr. Cantalamessa. Third Lenten Sermon, 2005. http://centerforchristiannonviolence.org/downloads/Eucharist_Gods_No2Violence_03.pdf.

Fromm, Erich. *The Anatomy of Human Destructiveness.* New York: Holt, Rinehart and Winston, 1973.

Fromm, Erich. *Escape From Freedom.* Austin: Holt, Rinehart and Winston, 1941.

Fromm, Erich. *Sane Society.* New York: Holt Rinehart, 1955.

Fry, Douglas P. *Beyond War: The Human Potential for Peace.* New York: Oxford University Press, 2007.

Fukuyama, Francis. *Trust: The Social Virtues and the Creation of Prosperity.* New York: The Free Press, 1995.

Galbraith, James K. *The Predator State.* New York: Free Press, 2008.

Galtung, Johan. "Three Approaches to Peace: Peacekeeping, Peacemaking, and Peace Building." In *Peace, War and Defense: Essays on Peace Research,* vol. 2, edited by Johan Galtung. Copenhagen: Christian Ejlers, 1976.

Galtung, Johan. *Peace by Peaceful Means. Peace and Conflict, Development and Civilization.* Oslo, Peace Research Institute of Oslo; London: Sage, 1996.

Galtung, Johan. "Violence, Peace and Peace Research." *Journal of Peace Research* 3 (1969): 176–91.

Gandhi, Mahatma. *Collected Works of Mahatma Gandhi*, Vol. 34:11 (February 1926–April 1, 1926).

Gandhi, Mohandas. *Hind Swaraj.* Ahmedabad: Navajivan Press, 1944http://www.gandhiserve.org/cwmg/cwmg.html (accessed November 13, 2009).

Gandhi, Mohandas. "Panchayats in Independent India," *Harijan*, July 28, 1946.

Geertz, Clifford. *The Interpretation of Cultures.* New York: Basic Books, 1973.

Gilligan, James. *Violence: Reflections on a National Epidemic.* New York: Random House, 1996.

Gladwell, Marlcolm. *The Tipping Point: How Little Things Can Make a Big Difference.* Boston: Little, Brown, 2000.

Glazer, Steven. *The Heart of Learning.* New York: Jeremy P. Tarcher/Putnam, 1999.

Glenn, Edmond S. *Man and Mankind: Conflict and Communication between Cultures.* Norwood, NJ: Ablex Publishing, 1981.

Goettner-Abendroth, Heide. *Societies of Peace: Matriarchies Past, Present and Future.* Toronto: Inanna Publications, 2008.

Goldman, Alvin. "Mirror Systems, Social Understanding, and Social Cognition." *Interdisciplines*, 2009. http://www.interdisciplines.org/mirror/papers/3.

Goldstein, Joshua S. *War and Gender: How Gender Shapes the War System and Vice Versa.* Berkeley: University of California Press, 2001.

Gottleib, Gidon. *Nation against State.* New York: Council on Foreign Relations Press, 1993.

Gottlieb, Roger, ed. *This Sacred Earth: Religion, Nature, Environment*, 2nd ed. New York: Routledge, 2003.

Grant, Kevin. "Mayor's Street Outreach Program," Part of Measure Y. Oakland, CA, 2004, http://measurey.org/index.php?page=mayor-s-street-outreach.

Greco, Thomas H., Jr. *Money and Debt: A Solution to the Global Crisis.* Tucson, AZ: Thomas H. Greco, Jr., Publisher, 1990.

Greco, Thomas H., Jr. *The End of Money and the Future of Civilization.* White River Junction, VT: Chelsea Green Publishing, 2009.

Greenough, Paul R. "Indian Famines and Peasant Victims: the Case of Bengal in 1943–44." *Modern Asian Studies*, 1980, 14(2), 205–235.

Griffin, Susan A. *Chorus of Stones.* New York: Doubleday, 1992.

Grille, Robin. *Parenting for a Peaceful World.* Sydney: Longueville Media, 2009.

Gross, Rita M. *Buddhism after Patriarchy: A Feminist History, Analysis, and Reconstruction of Buddhism.* Albany: State University of New York Press, 1993.

Grossman, Lt. Col. Dave. *Let's Stop Teaching Our Kids to Kill.* New York: Crown Publishers, 1999.

Grossman, Lt. Col. Dave. *On Killing. The Psychological Cost of Learning to Kill in War and Society.* Boston: Little, Brown, 1995.

Gusterson, Hugh. "Orientalism and the Arms Race: An Analysis of the Neo-colonial Discourse on Nuclear Nonproliferation," Working Paper #47, The Center for Transcultural Studies, 1991.

Hagan, Kenneth J., and Ian J. Bickerton. *Unintended Consequences of War: The United States at War.* Chicago: University of Chicago Press, 2007.

Halifax, Joan. Foreword to *Buddhist Peacework: Creating Cultures of Peace*, by David W. Chappell, 11–14. Somerville, MA: Wisdom Publications, 1999.

Hanh, Thich Nhat. *Love in Action: Writings on Nonviolent Social Change.* Berkeley, CA: Parallax Press, 1993.

Haring, Bernard. *Virtues of an Authentic Life.* Liguori, MO: Liguori Publications, 1997.

Hashimi Sohail. "Interpreting the Islamic Ethics of War and Peace." In *The Ethics of War and Peace: Religious and Secular Perspectives,* edited by Terry Nardin. Princeton, NJ: Princeton University Press, 1996.

Hawken, Paul. *Blessed Unrest: How the Largest Social Movement in History Is Restoring Grace, Justice, and Beauty to the World.* New York: Penguin Group, 2007.

Hedges, Chris. *War Is a Force That Gives Us Meaning.* New York: Anchor, 2003.

Heschel, Abraham Joshua. *The Prophets,* Vols.1-2. New York: Harper & Row, 1962.

Heschel, Susannah, ed. *On Being a Jewish Feminist: A Reader.* New York: Schocken Books, 1983.

Himes, Kenneth. "Peacebuilding as a Developing Norm in Catholic Social Teaching," presented at Catholic Peacebuilding Conference. Notre Dame, IN, Apr. 15, 2008, session V, panel 1. Audio at http://cpn.nd.eu/2008CPNConference%20-%20Post-Program.shtml.

Holden, C., ed. "Attachment Chemistry." *Science* 310 (2005): 1421.

Holmes, Robert L. *Basic Moral Philosophy,* 4th ed. Belmont, CA: Thomson Wadsworth, 2007.

Holmes, Robert L. *On War and Morality.* Princeton, NJ: Princeton University Press, 1989.

Holmes, Robert L., and Barry L. Gan, eds. *Nonviolence in Theory and Practice,* 2nd edition, Long Grove, IL: Waveland Press, 2005.

Holsti, Ole R. "The Belief System and National Images: John Foster Dulles." *Conflict Resolution* 6, no. 3 (1982): 244–52.

Human Rights Watch. *Climate of Fear: Sexual Violence and Abduction of Women and Girls in Baghdad,* July 16, 2003, E1508, http://www.unhcr.org/refworld/docid/3f4f595615.html.

Human Rights Watch. "Five Years On: No Justice for Sexual Violence in Darfur," http://www .hrw.org/en/reports/2008/04/06/five-years-0.

Human Rights Watch. "Soldiers Who Rape, Commanders who Condone: Sexual Violence and Military Reform in the Democratic Republic of Congo," http://www.hrw.org/en/reports/2009/07/16/soldiers-who-rape-commanders-who-condone;.

Hwadi, Fahmi. *Islam and Democracy.* Cairo Center for Translation and Publication, 1993.

Iacoboni, Marco. "Mental Mirrors," Adapted from *Mirroring People: The New Science of How We Connect with Others.* New York: Farrar, Straus and Giroux, 2008.

Iacoboni, Marco, Istvan Molnar-Szakacs, Vittorio Gallese, Giovanni Buccino, John C. Mazziotta, and Giacomo Rizzolatti. "Grasping the Intentions of Others with One's Own Mirror Neuron System." *PLoS Biol* 3, no. 3 (2005): e79.

Imam Muslim, *Sahih Muslim,* translated by Abdul Hamid Siddiqi. Baltimore, MD: International Islamic Publishing House, 2009.

Ingles, Paul. "The Neuroscience of Compassion." *Peace Talks Radio*, May 20, 2008. http://www.prx.org/pieces/26259-peace-talks-radio-the-neuroscience-of-compassion.

Isenberg, David. "Contractors vs. Genocide," Middle East Times, August 8, 2008. http://www.cato.org/pub_display.php?pub_id=9586.

Jacob, Pierre, and Marc Jeannerod. "The Motor Theory of Social Cognition: A Critique." *TRENDS in Cognitive Science* 9, no. 1 (2005): 21–25.

Jacoby, Russell. *The Repression of Psychoanalysis: Otto Fenichel and the Political Freudians.* Chicago: University of Chicago Press, 1986.

Jalabi, Khalis M. *The Psychology of Violence and the Strategy of 'Peaceful Action'.* Damascus: Dar al-Fikr, 1998.

James, William E. "The Moral Equivalent of War." *Peace and Conflict: Journal of Peace Psychology* 1 (1995): 27–36.

Johnston, Douglas, and Cynthia Sampson, eds. *Religion, The Missing Dimension of Statecraft.* New York: Oxford University Press, 1994.

Joya, Malalai, and Derrick O'Keefe. *A Woman among Warlords: The Extraordinary Story of an Afghan Who Dared to Raise Her Voice.* New York: Scribner, 2009.

Kandel, Eric R., James H. Schwartz, and Thomas M. Jessell. *The Principles of Neuroscience,* 4th ed. New York: McGraw-Hill, 2000.

Kant, Immanuel. *Groundwork of the Metaphysics of Morals,* translated by Lewis White Beck. New York: Liberal Arts Press, 1959.

Kaplan, Robert D. "The Coming Anarchy." *The Atlantic Monthly* 273, no. 2 (1994): 44–76.

Kelly, Marjorie. *The Divine Right of Capital: Dethroning the Corporate Aristocracy.* San Francisco, CA: Berrett-Koehler Publishers, 2001.

Kelman, Herbert C. "Informal Mediation by the Scholar/Practitioner." In *Mediation in International Relations: Multiple Approaches to Conflict Management,* edited by J. Bercovitch and J. Rubin, 64–96. London: Macmillan, 1992.

Kelsay, John. *Islam and War: A Study in Comparative Ethics.* Louisville, KY: Westminster/John Knox Press, 1993.

Kempf, Herve. *How the Rich Are Destroying the Earth.* White River Junction, VT: Chelsea Green Publishing 2008.

Kimmel, Paul R. "Assessing the Impact of Peace Building Processes." *Modern Science and the Vedic Science* 5, no. 1–2 (1992): 125–33.

Kimmel, Paul R. "Culture and Conflict." In *The Handbook of Constructive Conflict Resolution: Theory and Practice,* rev. ed., edited by Morton Deutsch and Peter T. Coleman. San Francisco: Jossey-Bass, 2006.

Kimmel, Paul R. "Cultural and Ethnic Issues of Conflict and Peacekeeping." In *The Psychology of Peacekeeping,* edited by Harvey Langholtz, 101–29. Westport, CT: Greenwood Publishing Group, 1998.

Kimmel, Paul R. "Cultural Perspectives on International Negotiation." *Journal of Social Issues* 50, no. 1, (1994): 179–96.

Kimmel, Paul R. "Facilitating the Contrast-Culture Method." In *Intercultural Sourcebook: Cross-Cultural Training Methods,* edited by Sandra M. Fowler and Monica G. Mumford, 69–79. Yarmouth, ME: Intercultural Press, Inc., 1995.

Kimmel, Paul R. *International Negotiation and Intercultural Explorations: Toward Cultural Understanding.* Washington, DC: U.S. Institute of Peace report, 1989.

Kimmel, Paul R. "Learning about Peace: Choices and the U.S. Institute of Peace As Seen from Two Different Perspectives." *American Psychologist* 40 (1985): 525–41.

Kimmel, Paul R. *Peace and Culture Shock: Can Intercultural Communication Specialists Help Save the World?* Abstracts, Tenth Annual SIETAR Conference, 1–4, 1984.

Kimmel, Paul R. "Sustainability and Cultural Understanding: Peace Psychology as Public Interest Science." *Peace and Conflict: Journal of Peace Psychology* 1, no. 2 (1995): 101–16.

King, Martin Luther, Jr. "Where Do We Go from Here." In *A Testament of Hope: The Essential Writings and Speeches of Martin Luther King, Jr.*, edited by James M. Washington. San Francisco: HarperCollins, 1986.

Kishtainy, Khalid. "A Violent and Nonviolent Struggle in Arab History." In *Arab Non Violent Political Struggle in the Middle East*, edited by R. E. Crow, P. Grant, and S. E. Ibrahim. Boulder, CO: Lynne Rienner Publishers, 1990.

Klare, Michael. *Rogue States and Nuclear Outlaws: America's Search for a New Foreign Policy.* New York: Hill and Wang, 1995.

Klein, Naomi *The Shock Doctrine: The Rise of Disaster Capitalism.* New York: Metropolitan Books, 2007, 163.

Koestler, Arthur. *The Ghost in the Machine.* New York: Macmillan, 1968.

Kohls, L. Robert. *Models for Comparing and Contrasting Cultures.* Paper presented at the National Association for Foreign Student Affairs Meetings, Washington, DC, 1987.

Kohls, L. Robert. *Models for Contrasting and Comparing Cultures.* Paper presented as part of the USIA's Tenth Annual Intercultural Communication Course, Washington, DC, 1977.

Kok, Bethany. "The Process of Other-Focus: A Synthetic Social Psychophysiological Model." M.A. thesis, University of North Carolina at Chapel Hill, 2008.

Kool, V. K. *The Psychology of Nonviolence and Aggression.* London: Macmillan, 2009.

Korten, David. *Agenda for a New Economy: From Phantom Wealth to Real Wealth.* San Francisco: Berrett-Koehler Publishers, 2009.

Korten, David. *The Great Turning: From Empire to Earth Community.* San Francisco: Berrett-Koehler Publishers, 2006.

Kotva, Joseph J. *The Christian Case for Virtue Ethics.* Washington, DC: Georgetown University Press, 1996.

Kremer, Jürgen W. "Ethnoautobiography as Practice of Radical Presence: Storying the Self in Participatory Visions." *ReVision* 26, no. 3 (2004): 5–13.

Kremer, Jürgen W. "Shamanic Initiations and Their Loss: Decolonization as Initiation and Healing," *Ethnopsychologische Mitteilungen* 9, no. 1/2 (2000): 109–48.

Kumar, Ravindra. "India, Its Concept of Peace and Gandhi." *Los Angeles Chronicle,* May 7, 2009, http://www.losangeleschronicle.com/articles/view/93665.

Kurtz, Lester, and Jennifer Turpin, eds. *Encyclopedia of Violence, Peace, and Conflict.* San Diego: Academic Press, 1999.

Lakey, George. "How to Develop Peace Teams: The Light Bulb Theory," 2010. http://www.trainingforchange.org/light_bulb_theory.

Lakoff, George P. *Moral Politics: What Conservatives Know That Liberals Don't.* Chicago: University of Chicago Press, 1996.

Landau, Elizabeth. "Charting the Psychology of Evil: Decades After the 'Shock' Experiment." *CNN*, December 19, 2008.

Langer, Suzanne. *Philosophy in a New Key: A Study of the Symbolism of Reason, Rite, and Art.* Cambridge, MA: Harvard University Press, 1942.

Langholtz, Harvey, ed. *The Psychology of Peacekeeping.* Westport, CT: Greenwood Publishing Group, 1998.

Lazlo, Ervin, and John Yoo, eds. *World Encyclopedia of Peace.* Oxford: Pergamon Press, 1986.

Lederach, John Paul. *The Little Book of Conflict Transformation.* Intercourse, PA: Good Books, 2003.

Lederach, John Paul. *Moral Imagination: The Art and Soul of Building Peace.* New York: Oxford University Press, 2005.

Lederach, John Paul. *Peace Building in Divided Societies.* Syracuse, NY: Syracuse University Press, 1997.

Lederach, John Paul. Reina Neufeldt, and Hal Culbertson. *Reflective Peacebuilding: A Planning, Monitoring, and Learning Tool Kit.* South Bend, IN: Kroc Institute University of Notre Dame, 2007.

Leighton, Taigen D. *Faces of Compassion: Classic Bodhisattva Archetypes and Their Modern Expression,* rev. ed. Boston: Wisdom Publications, 2003.

Lerner, Michael. *The Left Hand of God: Taking Back Our Country from the Religious Right.* San Francisco: HarperOne, 2006.

Leighton, Taigen D. *Spirit Matters.* Charlottesville, VA: Hampton Roads, 2000.

Lietaer, Bernard A. *The Future of Money: A New Way to Create Wealth, Work and a Wiser World.* London: Century, 2001.

Lifton, Robert Jay. *The Protean Self: Human Resilience in an Age of Fragmentation.* New York: Basic Books, 1993.

Linton, Ralph. *The Study of Man.* New York: Prentice Hall, 1936.

Lorde, Audre. *Sister Outsider.* Berkeley, CA: Crossing Press, 1984.

Loy, David R. *Money Sex War Karma: Notes for a Buddhist Revolution.* Boston: Wisdom Publications, 2008.

Lumsden, Malvern, and Rebecca Wolfe. "Evolution of the Problem-Solving Workshop: An Introduction to Social-Psychological Approaches to Conflict Resolution." *Peace and Conflict: Journal of Peace Psychology* 2, no. 1 (1996): 37–67.

Macy, Joanna, and Molly Y. Brown. *Coming Back to Life: Practices to Reconnect Our Lives, Our World.* Gabriola Island, British Columbia: New Society Publishers, 1998.

Maharshi, Ramana. *Talks with Ramana Maharshi.* Carlsbad, CA: Inner Directions, 2000.

Manchanda, Rita. *Naga Women Making a Difference: Peace Building in Northeastern India.* Women Waging Peace Policy Commission. Hunt Alternatives Fund, 2005.

Mano River Peace Network, http://www.marwopnet.org/history.htm (accessed August 23, 2009).

Marsella, Anthony J. "Diversity in a Global Era: The Context and Consequences of Differences." *Counseling Psychology Quarterly* 22, no. 1 (2009): 119–136.

Mason, Christine. "Women, Violence and Nonviolent Resistance in East Timor." *Journal of Peace Research* 42, no. 6 (2005): 737–49.

Matsubara, Hisako. *Cranes at Dusk*. Garden City, NY: Dial Press, 1985.

Mauk, Ben. "Neuroscience at War" Mind Wars. Trans-Atlantic Discussion at The Dana Foundation, New York, September 26, 2007.

Mayer, Jane. "The Secret History: Can Panetta Move the CIA Forward without Confronting Its Past?" *The New Yorker*, June 27, 2009.

McCarthy, Rev. Emmanual. *The Nonviolent Eucharistic Jesus: A Pastoral Approach*, Wilmington, DE: Center for Christian Nonviolenve, 1992. http://centerforchristian nonviolence.org/downloads/NV_Eucharist_PastoralApproach_01d.pdf.

McCarthy, E. "A Virtue Ethic Assessment of Nonviolent Peacemaking: Toward Public Discourse and Policy." PhD Diss., Graduate Theological Union, 2009.

McLuhan, Marshall. *The Global Village: Transformation in World Life and Media in the 21st century*. New York: Oxford Press, 1989.

Meisler, Stanley. "Baby-Sitters in Blue Berets, Peacekeepers Ease Tensions." *Los Angeles Times*, November 16, 1992, A1, A14–15.

Meisler, Stanley. "Mission Impossible for the U.N.?" *Los Angeles Times*, November 15, 1992, A1, A14–15.

Meisler, Stanley. "U.N. Peacekeepers Face a Crisis of High Expectations." *Los Angeles Times*, November 17, 1992, A1, A22.

Melko, Matthew. *52 Peaceful Societies*. Oakville, ONT: Canadian Peace Research Society, 1973.

"Mental Illness Common among Returning US Soldiers." *Reuters News*, March 12, 2007, http://www.reuters.com/article/healthNews/idUSTON27935120070312.

Merchant, Carolyn. *The Death of Nature: Women, Ecology, and the Scientific Revolution*. San Francisco: Harper & Row, 1980.

Merton, Thomas, ed. *Gandhi on Non-violence: A Selection from the Writings of Mahatma Gandhi*. New York: New Directions, 1965.

Milburn, Michael A., and Sherrie D. Conrad. *The Politics of Denial*. Cambridge, MA: The MIT Press, 1996.

Milgram, Stanley. *Obedience to Authority: An Experimental View*. New York: Harper & Row, 1974.

Miller, Alice. *For Your Own Good: Hidden Cruelty in Child-Rearing and the Roots of Violence*. New York: Farrar, Straus, Giroux, 1983, 204–222.

Montville, Joseph V., ed. *Conflict and Peacemaking in Multiethnic Societies*. Washington, DC: Lexington Books, 1990.

Muslim, Imam. *Sahih Muslim*. Translated by Abdul Hamid Siddiqi, n.d.

Muste, A. J. A. J. Muste Memorial Institute, http://www.ajmuste.org/ (accessed November 11, 2009).

"Mutual Aid: A Factor in Evolution." In *Encyclopædia Britannica*. http://www.britannica.com/EBchecked/topic/399850/Mutual-Aid-A-Factor-in-Evolution

Nagler, Michael. *The Search for a Nonviolent Future: A Promise of Peace for Ourselves Our Families, and Our World*. Maui, HI: Inner Ocean Publishing, 2004.

Nairobi Forward-Looking Strategies for the Advancement of Women, 1985. http://www.un.org/womenwatch/confer/nfls.

National Peace Academy. http://www.nationalpeaceacademy.us/.

Nietzsche, Friedrich. *Untimely Meditations*, translated by R. J. Hollingdale, edited by Daniel Breazeale. New York: Cambridge University Press, 1997.

Njeri, Itabari. "The Conquest of Hate." *Los Angeles Times Magazine* 46 (1993): 20–26.

Nordhaus, Ted, and Michael Schellenberger. *Break Through: From the Death of Environmentalism to the Politics of Possibility.* Boston: Houghton Mifflin, 2007.

Nussbaum, Martha. *Women and Human Development: The Capabilities Approach.* New York: Cambridge University Press, 2001.

Nuttall, Geoffrey. *Christian Pacifism in History.* Oxford: Blackwell, 1958.

Office of the Coordinator for Reconstruction and Stabilization. "Introduction to the Civilian Response Corps," http://www.crs.state.gov/index.cfm?fuseaction=public .display&shortcut=4QRB.

O'Neill, William. "What We Owe to Refugees and IDP's: An Inquiry into the Rights of the Forcibly Displaced." In *Refugee Rights*, edited by David Hollenbach. Washington, DC: Georgetown University Press, 2008.

O'Neill, William "The Violent Bear It Away: Just War and U.S. Military Policy in the Eyes of Catholic Teaching." *Journal of Religion and Society* 4, 2008, http://moses.creighton.edu/JRS/2008/2008-31.html.

Orwell, George. "A Hanging." In *Shooting an Elephant, and Other Essays.* New York, Harcourt Brace, 1968.

Osgood, Charles E. *An Alternative to War or Surrender.* Urbana: University of Illinois Press, 1962.

Paris, Roland. "Peacebuilding and the Limits of Liberal Internationalism." *International Security* 22, no. 2 (1997): 56.

Peaceful Societies: Alternatives to Violence and War. "http://peacefulsocieties.org/" http://peacefulsocieties.org

Peace Pledge Union. *War and Peace.* (2005). Available at: http://www.ppu.org.uk/war/facts/.

Pease, H. "The Peace Triad: Peacekeeping, Peacemaking, and Peace Building." *Peace Institute Reporter* (April edition). Washington, DC: National Peace Institute Foundation, 1987.

Perkins, John. *Confessions of an Economic Hitman.* San Francisco: Berrett-Koehler Publishers, 2004.

Perrucci, Robert, and Earl Wysong. *The New Class Society.* Lanham, MD: Rowman & Littlefield, 1999.

Perry, Bruce D. " Child Maltreatment: A Neurodevelopmental Perspective on the Role of Trauma and Neglect in Psychophathology." In *Child and Adolescent Psychopathology,* edited by Theodore P. Beauchaine and Stephen P. Hinshaw, 93–129. Hoboken, NJ: John Wiley & Sons, 2008.

Philpott, Dan. "Lessons in Mercy: Justice and Reconciliation in the Aftermath of Atrocities." *America*, May 4, 2009.

Pilisuk, Marc. "Experimenting with the Arms Race." *Journal of Conflict Resolution* 28, no. 2 (June 1984): 296–315.

Pilisuk, Marc. *Who Benefits from Global Violence and War: Uncovering a Destructive System* (with Jennifer A. Rountree). Westport, CT: Greenwood/Praeger, 2008.

Pilisuk, Marc, and Joanne Zazzi. "Toward a Psychosocial Theory of Military and Economic Violence in the Era of Globalization." *Journal of Social Issues* 62, no. 1 (2006): 41–62.

Pilisuk, Marc, and Susan Hillier Parks. *The Healing Web: Social Networks and Human Survival.* Hanover, NH: University of New England Press, 1986.

Plato. *Crito.* 48d–49e.

Pontifical Council for Justice and Peace. *Compendium of the Social Doctrine of the Church.* Libreria Editrice Vaticana, 2004.

Pope Benedict. *Deus Caritas Est,* (2005), para. 14, http://www.vatican.va/holy _father/benedict_xvi/encyclicals/documents/hf_ben-xvi_enc_20051225_deus -caritas-est_en.html.

Pope Benedict. "Midday Angelus," 2007, http://www.catholicpeacefellowship.org/ nextpage.asp?m=2308.

Pope Benedict. Vatican City, February 18, 2007, Zenit.org.

Pope John XXIII. *"Pacem in Terris: Peace on Earth."* In *Catholic Social Thought: The Documentary Heritage,* edited by David O'Brien and T. Shannon. Maryknoll: Orbis, 1992.

Pope John Paul II. "Homily at Drogheda, Ireland, Sept. 29, 1979." In *The Pope in Ireland: Speeches and Homilies.* Dublin: Veritas Publications, 2004.

Pope John Paul II. "No Peace without Justice, No Justice without Forgiveness," in celebration of the *World Day of Peace,* Jan. 1, 2002.

Pope John Paul II. *"Sollicitudo Rei Socialis: On Social Concern."* In *Catholic Social Thought: The Documentary Heritage,* edited by D. O'Brien and T. Shannon. Maryknoll, NY: Orbis, 1992.

Pope John Paul II. "War, a Decline for Humanity." *Origins* 20, no. 33 (January 24, 1991): 527, 530.

Postman, Neil. *Technopoly: The Surrender of Culture to Technology.* New York: Alfred A. Knopf, 1992.

Powers, Roger, and William Vogele, eds. *Protest, Power, and Change: An Encyclopedia of Nonviolence from ACT-UP to Women's Suffrage.* New York: Garland, 1997.

Prigogine, Ilya, and Isabelle Stengers. *Order Out of Chaos.* New York: Bantam, 1984.

Public Citizen. "Congressional Revolving Doors: The Journey from Congress to K Street." *Public Citizen Reports,* July 2009.

Public Conversations Project. http://www.publicconversations.org.

Pyszczynski, Tom, Sheldon Solomon, and Jeff Greenberg, *In the Wake of 9/11: The Psychology of Terror.* Washington, DC: American Psychological Association, 2003.

Queen, Christopher S., ed. *Engaged Buddhism in the West.* Boston: Wisdom Publications, 2000.

Queen, Christopher S, and Sallie B. King, ed., *Engaged Buddhism: Buddhist Liberation Movements in Asia.* Albany: State University of New York Press, 1996.

Rapoport, Anatol. *Fights, Games and Debates.* Ann Arbor: University of Michigan Press, 1960.

Raymond, Nathaniel. "New Yorker: Former APA president worked with CIA and on board of mitchell and jessen." Blog Entry. Physicians for Human Rights, http://phrblog.org/blog/2009/06/14/new-yorker-former-apa-president-worked-with-cia-and-on-board-of-mitchell-and-jessen/ (accessed September 5, 2009).

Rehn, Elisabeth, and Ellen Johnson Sirleaf. *Women, War, and Peace: The Independent Experts' Assessment on the Impact of Armed Conflict on Women and Women's Role in Peace-Building*, Vol. 1. New York: United Nations Development Fund for Women (UNIFEM), 2002.

Reza, Sayed 'Ali (trans.). *Nahj al-balaghah: Peak of Eloquence*. (3rd ed.) Elmhurst: Tahrike Tarsile, 1984.

Rilling, James K., David A. Gutman, Thorsten R. Zeh, Giuseppe Pagnoni, Gregory S. Berns, and Clinton D. Kilts. "A Neural Basis for Social Cooperation." *Neuron* 35 (July 18, 2002): 395–405.

Roberts, Adam. "Transarmament to Civilian Defence." In *The Strategy of Civilian Defence*, edited by A. Roberts. London: Faber and Faber, 1967, 292–293.

Robichaud, Carl. "Buying Time in Afghanistan." *World Policy Journal*, 2007.

Rockwell, Llewellyn H., Jr. "War and Inflation." Delivered at the *Future of Freedom Foundation's conference on "Restoring the Republic: Foreign Policy and Civil Liberties,"* on June 6, 2008, Reston, Virginia, http://mises.org/daily/3010.

Roman, Leslie G. "This Earthly World: Edward Said, the Praxis of Secular Humanism and Situated Cosmopolitanisms." *Discourse: Studies in the Cultural Politics of Education* 27, no. 3 (September 2006): 357–68.

Rosenberg, Marshall. *Nonviolent Communication: A Language of Life*. Encinitas, CA: Puddle Dancer Press, 2003.

Rosenberg, Robert. Harvard Seminar on C3I. "The Influence of Policy Making on C3I," in Incidental Paper: Seminar on Command, Control, Communications and Intelligence, Spring 1980. Center for Information Policy Research, Harvard University, 59.

Roth-Douquet, Kathy, and Frank Schaefer. *AWOL: The Unexcused Absence of America's Upper Classes from the Military and How It Hurts Our Country*. New York: Collins, 2006.

Rothberg, Donald. "The Crisis of Modernity and the Emergence of Socially Engaged Spirituality." *ReVision* 15, no. 3 (1993): 105–14.

Rothberg, Donald. *The Engaged Spiritual Life: A Buddhist Approach to Transforming Ourselves and the World*. Boston: Beacon Press, 2006.

Rothberg, Donald, with Anisah Bagasra and Jürgen Kremer. *Approaches to Socially Engaged Spirituality*. San Francisco: Saybrook Graduate School Course Guide, 2007.

Roy, Arundhati. "The End of Imagination." In *The Cost of Living*. New York: The Modern Library, 1999, pp. 91–126.

Rubin, Jeffrey Z., Dean Pruitt, and Sung Hee Kim. *Social Conflict: Escalation, Stalemate, and Settlement*, 2nd ed. New York: McGraw-Hill, 1994.

Ruddick, Sara. *Maternal Thinking: Toward a Politics of Peace*. Boston: Beacon Press, 1989.

Ruether, Rosemary. *Sexism and God-talk: Toward a Feminist Theology*. Boston: Beacon Press, 1983.

Sachedina, Abdulaziz A. "Justification for Violence in Islam." In *War and Its Discontents: Pacifism and Quietism in the Abrahamic Traditions*, edited by J. P. Burn. Washington, DC: Georgetown University Press, 1996.

Sachs, Jeffrey. "Bursting at the Seams." BBC Radio, April 11, 2007, Podcast and transcript, http://www.bbc.co.uk/radio4/ reith2007/lecture1.shtml.

Sachs, Jeffrey. *Common Wealth: Economics for A Crowded Planet.* New York: The Penguin Press, 2008.

Sadler, Anne G., Brenda M. Booth, Brian L. Cook, and Bradley N. Doebbeling. "Factors Associated with Women's Risk of Rape in the Military Environment." *American Journal of Industrial Medicine* 43 (2003): 262–73.

Sai'd, Jawdat. "Peace - Or Nonviolence - in History and with the Prophets." (Unpublished Paper) Forum on Islam and Peace in the 21st Century. American University, 1997.

Said, Abdul Aziz. "Cultural Context of Conflict Resolution: And Reference to An Arab-Islamic Perspective." Unpublished Paper. American University, 1994.

Said, Edward. *Covering Islam.* New York: Pantheon Book, 1981.

Said, Edward. *Culture and Imperialism.* New York: Knopf/ Random House, 1993.

Said, Edward. *Orientalism.* New York: Pantheon, 1978.

Said, Jawdat. "Peace—Or Nonviolence—in History and with the Prophets." A Paper presented at a conference on Islam and Peace in the 21st Century. Washington, DC: American University, 1998.

Sagan, Scott D. "Why Do States Build Nuclear Weapons?" *International Security,* 21, no. 3 (1996/1997): 54–86.

Saint Augustine. *St. Augustine, City of God.* Translated by Gerald G. Walsh, Demetrius B. Zema, Grace Monohan, Daniel J. Honan, and Vernon J. Bourke. New York: Doubleday Image, 1950.

Saiyidain, K. G. *Islam, the Religion of Peace: Islam and Modern Age Society.* New Delhi: Leaders Press, 1976.

Sandel, Michael. "The Source of Discontent: America's Search for a New Public Philosophy." *Atlantic Monthly* 277 (1996): 57–74.

Sangari, Kumkum, Neeraj Malik, Sheba Chhachhi and Tanika Sarkar. "Why Women Must Reject the Bomb." In *Out of Nuclear Darkness: The Indian Case for Disarmament,* edited by Movement in India for Nuclear Disarmament (MIND), 45–56. New Delhi: MIND. 1998, pp. 47–56.

Satha-Anand, Chaiwat. "The Nonviolent Crescent: Eight Theses on Muslim Nonviolent Actions." In *Islam and Nonviolence,* edited by Glenn Paige, Chaiwat Satha-Anand, and Sara Gilliat, 7–26. Honolulu: Center for Global Nonviolence Planning Project, Matsunaga Institute for Peace, University of Hawaii, 1993.

Scarry, Elaine. *The Body in Pain.* Oxford: Oxford University Press, 1985.

Schechter, Danny. In Debt We Trust: America Before the Bubble Bursts, DVD. New York: Globalvision, Inc., Disinformation Company, 2007.

Schiffer, Frederic. *Of Two Minds: The Revolutionary Science of Dual Brain Psychology.* New York: The Free Press, 2002.

Schirch, Lisa. "Building Bridges and Preventing Conflict: A Memo to the New Administration," supported by 3D Security-Initiative, Alliance for Peacebuilding, and Global Partnership for the Prevention of Armed Conflict, December 28, 2008. http://3dsec.sockhead.com/sites/3dsecurity.org/files/3D%20AfP%20and%20 GPPAC%20Memo%20to%20Obama%20Admin%20December%2028%202008.pdf.

Schore, Allan N. "Early Relational Trauma, Disorganized Attachment, and the Development of a Predisposition to Violence." In *Healing Trauma: Attachment, Mind, Body, and Brain*, edited by Marian F. Solomon and Daniel J. Siegel, 107–67. New York/London: W. W Norton, 2003.

Schott, Robin May. "Gender and Post Modern War." *Hypatia* 11, no. 4 (1996): 19–29.

Schwartz, Stephen I. "Four Trillion Dollars and Counting." *Bulletin of the Atomic Scientists*, November/December, 1995.

Schweitzer, Albert. *Civilization and Ethics*. London: Adam and Charles Black, 1946.

Schweitzer, Albert. *The Philosophy of Civilization*. Buffalo: Prometheus Books, 1987.

Seager, Joni. *Earth Follies: Coming to Feminist Terms with the Global Environmental Crisis*. New York: Routledge, 1993.

Segal, David R., and Katharine S. Gravino. "Peacekeeping as a Military Mission." In *The Hundred Percent Challenge*, edited by Charles D. Smith, 38–69. Cabin John, MD: Seven Locks Press, 1985.

Sen, Amartya. *Identity and Violence: The Illusions of Destiny.* New York: W. W. Norton, 2006.

Shalaby, Ibrahim. "Islam and Peace." *Journal of Religious Thought* 34, Fall/Winter (1978): 42–49.

Sharoni, Simona. *Gender and the Israeli-Palestinian Conflict: The Politics of Women's Resistance*. Syracuse, NY: Syracuse University Press, 1995.

Sharp, Gene. *The Politics of Nonviolent Action*. Boston: Porter Sargent, 1973.

Sharp, Gene. *Waging Nonviolent Struggle: 20th Century Practice and 21st Century Potential*. Boston: Porter Sargent Publishers, 2005.

Shephard, Mark. *The Community of the Ark*. Arcata, CA: Simple Productions, 1990.

Shils, Edward A. "Primordial, Personal, Sacred and Civil Ties." *The British Journal of Sociology* 8 (1957): 130–45.

Siddiqi, Abdul Hamid (trans.). *Sahib Muslim Vol. 3*. Lahore: Sh. Muhammad Ashraf, 1976–1979.

Smith, Martin. "Learning To Be A Lean, Mean Killing Machine." CounterPunch, October 20, 2007. http://www.counterpunch.org/smith02202007.html

Snell, Bruno. *The Discovery of the Mind*. Oxford: Blackwell, 1953.

South, Jubilee. "South-South Summit Declaration." In *Global Backlash: Citizen Initiatives for a Just World Economy*, edited by R. Broad. New York: Rowman & Littlefield, 2002.

Speth, James. *The Bridge at the Edge of the World: Capitalism, the Environment, and Crossing from Crisis to Sustainability.* New Haven, CT: Yale University Press, 2007.

Spink, Kathryn. *The Black Sash: Beginning of a Bridge in South Africa*. London: Methuen Publishing, 1991.

Spohn, William. *Go and Do Likewise: Jesus and Ethics*. New York: Continuum, 2003.

Stahl, Leslie. "The Unreported Consequences of Sanctions and War on the People of Iraq: Leslie Stahl interviews Madeline Albright." *CBS, 60 Minutes*, May 12, 1996. Uncover Iraq.com http://home.comcast.net/~dhamre/docAlb.htm.

Stapp, Henry. "Quantum Physics and Human Values." Paper presented at the Symposium on Science and Culture for the 21st Century, 1–14. British Columbia, Canada, September 1989.

Starhawk. *Truth or Dare: Encounters with Power, Authority, and Mystery.* San Francisco: Harper & Row, 1987.

Stassen, Glen, ed. *Just Peacemaking: The New Paradigm for the Ethics of Peace and War.* Cleveland, OH: Pilgrim Press, 2008.

Stassen, Glen, and David Gushee. *Kingdom Ethics: Following Jesus in Contemporary Context.* Downers Grove: Intervarsity Press, 2003.

Staub, Ervin. "The Psychological and Cultural Roots of Group Violence and the Creation of Caring Societies and Peaceful Group Relations." In *A Natural History of Peace,* edited by T. Gregor, 129–55. Nashville, TN: Vanderbilt University Press, 1996.

Staub, Ervin. *Roots of Evil. The Psychological and Cultural Origins of Genocide.* New York: Cambridge University Press, 1990.

Stephenson, June. *Poisonous Power: Childhood Roots of Tyranny.* Palm Desert, California: Diemer Smith Publishing, 1998.

Stewart, Edward C. "Contrast-Culture Training." In *Intercultural Sourcebook: Cross-Cultural Training Methods,* edited by S. M. Fowler and M. G. Mumford, 47–58. Yarmouth, ME: Intercultural Press, 1995.

Stewart, Edward C. "The Primordial Roots of Being." *Zygon* 22 (1987): 87–107.

Stewart, Edward C., Jack Danielian, and Robert J. Foster. "Simulating Intercultural Communication through Role-Playing." *Technical Report* 69–7 (May 1969). Alexandria, VA: Human Resources Research Organization.

Storm, Hyemeyohsts. *Lightningbolt.* New York: Ballantine, 1994.

Suedfeld, Peter, ed. *Psychology and Torture.* Washington, DC: Hemisphere Publishing, 1989.

Summers, Frank. "Making Sense of the APA: A History of the Relationship between Psychology and the Military." *Psychoanalytic Dialogues* 18, no. 5 (2008): 614–37.

Sumner, William G. *Folkways.* Boston: Ginn & Co., 1906.

"Talks with Sri Ramana Maharshi," http://en.wikipedia.org/wiki/Ramana_Maharshi (accessed October 28, 2010).

Taibbi, Matt. "The Great American Bubble Machine." *Rolling Stone,* July 13 2009, http://www.rollingstone.com/politics/story/29127316/the_great_american_bubble_machine.

Tetalman, Jerry, and Byron Belitsos. *One World Democracy: A Progressive Vision for Enforceable Global Law.* San Rafael, CA: Origin Press, 2005.

Thompson, Henry. *World Religion in War and Peace.* Jefferson, NC: McFarland, 1988.

Tolstoy, Leo. "Letter to Ernest Howard Crosby." In *Writings on Civil Disobedience and Nonviolence.* Philadelphia: New Society Publishers, 1987. Reprinted in *Nonviolence in Theory and Practice,* edited by Robert L. Holmes and Barry L. Gan, 73–74. Long Grove, IL: Waveland Press, 2005.

Transaction Net. "ROCS—a Robust Complementary Community Currency," http://www.transaction.net/money/rocs/ (accessed August 10, 2009).

Tripp, Aili Mari. "Rethinking Difference: Comparative Perspectives from Africa." *Signs* 25, no. 3 (2000): 649–75.

Truman, Harry S. "Radio Report to the American People on the Potsdam Conference." *New York Times,* August 10, 1945, p 12. http://www.trumanlibrary.org/publicpapers/index.php?pid=104&st=&st1.

Tuchman, Barbara. *The March of Folly: From Troy to Vietnam.* New York: Random House, 1984.

Tyson, Peter. "Daniel Glaser's Latest Study With Ballet and Capoeira Dancers." *NOVA Science Now,* 2005, http://www.pbs.org/wgbh/nova/sciencenow/3204/01-resup.html (accessed November 15, 2009).

Tzu, Sun. *On the Art of War.* Translated from the Chinese by Lionel Giles, 1910. Available at http://www.chinapage.com/sunzi-e.html.

UN Department of Peacekeeping Operations. "UN Peacekeeping." http://www.un.org/Depts/dpko/dpko/.

UN, Millennium Development Goals: 2008 Progress Chart, http://www.un.org/millenniumgoals/2008highlevel/pdf/newsroom/MDG_Report_2008_Progress_Chart_en_r8.pdf.

UNESCO. "Guidelines Preparation of National Plans of Action." 2000. http://unesdoc.unesco.org/images/0012/001219/121911e.pdf.

United Nations. See Homepage at http://www.un.org.

United Nations. Millennium Development Goals: 2008 Progress Chart, http://www.un.org/millenniumgoals/2008highlevel/pdf/newsroom/MDG_Report_2008_Progress_Chart_en_r8.pdf.

United Nations. Consolidated Report. Document A/53/370 (1998). Available at http://www.culture-of-peace.info/annexes/resA-53-370/coverpage.html.

United Nations. Convention on the Elimination of All Forms of Discrimination Against Women (CEDAW), http://www.un.org/womenwatch/daw/cedaw/.

United Nations. Declaration and Programme of Action on a Culture of Peace. Document A/53/243 (1999). Available at: http://www3.unesco.org/iycp/uk/uk_sum_refdoc.htm.

United Nations Action against Sexual Violence in Conflict, "Stop Rape Now," http://www.stoprapenow.org/updates_field.html.

United Nations Development Fund for Women (UNIFEM). "Facts and Figures on Peace and Security," http://www.unifem.org/gender_issues/peace_security/facts_figures.php (accessed December 1, 2009).

United Nations Development Program (UNDP). 2009. Human Development Reports, http://hdr.undp.org/en/.

United Nations Development Program & Arab Fund For Economic and Social Development. "Arab Human Development Report 2002: Creating Opportunities for Future Generations." 2002. http://hdr.undp.org/en/reports/regionalreports/arabstates/name,3140,en.html.

United Nations Population Fund (UNFPA) & United Nations Children's Fund (UNICEF). "Annual Report 2009 for the UNFPA/UNICEF Joint Programme on Female Genital Mutilation/Cutting." 2010. http://www.unfpa.org/public/publications/pid/2944.

United Nations Population. Fund—UNICEF (UNFPA_UNICEF 2009), "UNFPA-UNICEF Joint Programme on Female Genital Mutilation/Cutting," http://www.unfpa.org/public/publications/pid/2944.

United Nations Resolution 1325, http://www.peacewomen.org/un/sc/1325.html.

United Nations Security Council. "Report of the Secretary-General to the Security Council on the protection of civilians in armed conflict." March 2001, http://www.securitycouncilreport.org/site/c.glKWLeMTIsG/b.1203269/k.4C3E/

December_2005brProtection_of_Civilians_in_Armed_Conflict.htm (accessed November 25, 2009).

U.S. Catholic Bishops. "Challenge of Peace: God's Promise and Our Response." In O'Brien, David J. and Thomas A. Shannon, eds. *Catholic Social Thought: The Documentary Heritage.* Maryknoll, NY: Orbis Books, 1992.

U.S. Catholic Bishops. "The Harvest of Justice Is Sown in Peace." *Origins* 23, no. 26 (Dec. 9, 1993).

Useem, Michael. *Investor Capitalism: How Money Managers Are Changing the Face of Corporate America.* New York: Basic Books, 1996.

Vision of Humanity. Global Peace Index, http://www.visionofhumanity.org/gpi/results/rankings.php.

Volkan, Vamik D. "Psychological Processes in Unofficial Diplomacy Meetings." In *The Psychodynamics of International Relationships*, Vol. II: *Unofficial Diplomacy at Work*, edited by V. D. Volkan, J. V. Mont Maryknoll, NY: Orbis Books, 1992. ville, and D. A. Julius, 207–22. Lexington, MA: Lexington Books, 1991.

Volkan, Vamik D. "Ethno Nationalistic Rituals: An Introduction." *Mind and Human Interaction* 4, no. 1, (1992): 3–19.

Voll, John, and John Esposito. "Islam's Democratic Essence." *Middle East Quarterly* http://www.meforum.org/151/islams-democratic-essence (accessed September 1994).

Wadud, Amina. *Qur'an and Woman: Rereading the Sacred Text from a Women's Perspective.* New York: Oxford University Press, 1999.

Wagner, Richard, and Dan J. Christie. "Psychology and Peace." In *Peace and World Security Studies: A Curriculum Guide*, edited by M. T. Klare, 230–42. Boulder, CO: Lynne Rienner Publishers, 1994.

Wahiduddin, Khan. "Nonviolence and Islam." A paper presented at a conference on Islam and Peace in the 21st Century. Washington, DC: American University, 1998.

Walker, Margaret Urban. "Moral Understandings: Alternative 'Epistemology' for a Feminist Ethics." *Hypatia* 4, no. 4 (1989): 15–28.

Wallis, Jim. *The Soul of Politics: A Practical and Prophetic Vision for Change.* New York and Maryknoll, NY: The New Press and Orbis Books, 1994.

War Resister's League. "Where Your Income Tax Money Really Goes," http://www.warresisters.org/pages/piechart.htm (accessed December 2009).

Ward, Jeanne. *If Not Now, When? Addressing Gender Based Violence in Refugee, Internally Displaced and Post-Conflict Settings: A Global Overview*, on behalf of the Reproductive Health Response in Conflict Consortium (RHRC). http://www.rhrc.org/resources/gbv/gbvintro.pdf (accessed October 2009).

Ward, Jeanne, and Mendy Marsh. *Sexual Violence against Women and Girls in War and Its Aftermath: Realities, Responses, and Required Resources.* A Briefing Paper Prepared for the Symposium on Sexual Violence in Conflict and Beyond, June 21–23, 2006.

Washington, James M., ed. *A Testament of Hope: The Essential Writings and Speeches of Martin Luther King, Jr.* San Francisco: HarperOne, 1986.

Watson, J. R. I. "Investigation into De-individuation Using a Cross-Cultural Survey Technique." *Journal of Personality and Social Psychology* 25 (1973): 342–45.

Watson, Paul. "Some Say India Deal Ignores Another Energy Need: Food." *Los Angeles Times*, March 7, 2006, A3.

Welch, Bryant. *State of Confusion: Political Manipulation and the Assault on the American Mind.* New York: St. Martin's Press, 2008.

West, Cornel. *The Cornel West Reader.* New York: Basic Civitas Books, 1999.

Wheeler, Mary E., and Susan T. Fiske. "Controlling Racial Prejudice." *Psychological Science* 16, no. 1 (2005): 56–63.

White, Leslie A. *The Evolution of Culture.* New York: McGraw-Hill, 1959.

Wikipedia, "Bengal Famine of 1943." http://en.wikipedia.org/wiki/Bengal_Famine_of_1943 (accessed October 28, 2010).

Wikipedia, "Sniper Alley." http://en.wikipedia.org/wiki/Sniper_Alley (accessed October 28, 2010).

Williamson, Richard S. *The United Nations as Peacekeeper.* Center paper, 1. Washington, DC: Center for the Study of Foreign Affairs, Foreign Service Institute, U.S. Department of State, March 1989.

Wolf, Christa. *Accident: A Day's News.* New York: Farrar, Straus & Giroux, 1989.

Wolf, Christa. *Cassandra.* New York: Farrar, Straus & Giroux, 1984.

Wolff, Richard. *Capitalism Hits the Fan: Richard Wolff on the Economic Meltdown.* Northampton, Mass.: Olive Branch Press, 2010. http://www.capitalismhitsthefan.com/.

Woolf, Virginia. "Thoughts on Peace in an Air-raid." In *Collected Essays*, vol. 4. New York: Harcourt Brace, 1953.

Woolf, Virginia. *Three Guineas*, New York: Harcourt Brace, 1938.

World Civil Society. *Report on the Culture of Peace*, 2005. Available at http://decade-culture-of-peace.org.

World Health Organization. *Violence Prevention: The Evidence.*, http://www.who.int/violence prevention/publications/en/index.html (accessed September 20, 2009).

Wurmser, David, and Nancy B. Dyke, *The Professionalization of Peacekeeping. A Study Group Report.* Washington, DC: United States Institute of Peace, 1993.

Zahn, Franklin. *Alternative to the Pentagon: Nonviolent Methods of Defending a Nation.* Nyack, NY: Fellowship Publications, 1996.

Zarlenga, Stephen. *The Lost Science of Money: The Mythology of Money and the Story of Power.* Valatie, NY: American Monetary Institute, 2002.

Zimbardo, Philip. *The Lucifer Effect: Understanding How Good People Turn Evil.* New York: Random House, 2007.

Zimmerman, Jack, and Virginia Coyle. *The Way of Council.* Las Vegas, NV: Bramble Books, 1996.

INDEX

About the Editors and Contributors

Co-editor **Marc Pilisuk** got his PhD in clinical and social psychology from the University of Michigan in 1961 and went on to teach, research, and write at several colleges ending up at the University of California and Saybrook University. His various departmental affiliations—psychology, nursing, administrative sciences, social welfare, public health, community mental health, human and community development, city and regional planning, peace and conflict studies, and human sciences—convinced him that academic disciplines could be blinders and should be crossed. He was a founder of the first Teach-in on a University Campus (Michigan) and the Psychologists for Social Responsibility, helped start SANE (now Peace Action), and is a past president of the Society for the Study of Peace Conflict and Violence. He has received several lifetime contribution awards for work for peace. Marc's books cover topics of underlying social issues, poverty, international conflict, and the nature of human interdependence. His most recent (*Who Benefits from Global Violence and War*) uncovered information that was sufficiently shocking to motivate this new undertaking on *Peace Movements Worldwide*.

Co-editor **Michael N. Nagler** was sensitized to issues of peace and justice (the usual term is "radicalized") through folk music and various influences by the time he left his New York City birthplace. After attending Cornell University and finishing his BA at New York University, he arrived in Berkeley, CA, in 1960, in time to finish a PhD in Comparative Literature before the advent of the Free Speech Movement. The successes and failures of that movement broadened his outlook so that he joined the group forming around meditation teacher, Eknath Easwaran, late in 1966 and soon launched a parallel career—inward. Nonviolence, and Gandhi in particular, became a way to carve out a meaningful niche for himself within academia. At Berkeley, he went on to found the Peace and Conflict Studies Program (PACS; now probably the largest in terms of student majors in the United States) and off campus co-founded the Metta Center for Nonviolence (www.mettacenter.org). He also became chair of Peaceworkers (www.peaceworkers.org) and eventually co-chair of the Peace and Justice Studies Association (www.peacejusticestudies.org). He stopped teaching at the university in 2007 to devote his time to Metta and the Blue Mountain Center of Meditation. A frequent speaker on nonviolence and related themes around the world, his most recent recognition is the Jamnalal Bajaj International Award for Promoting Gandhian Values Outside India. His books include *The Upanishads* (with Eknath Easwaran, 1987), *Our Spiritual Crisis* (2004), and *The Search for a Nonviolent Future*, which won a 2002 American Book Award and has been translated into six languages, most recently Arabic.

Mohammed Abu-Nimer is a professor in the International Peace and Conflict Resolution program at the School of International Service. In addition to his teaching position, he is also director of the Peacebuilding and Development Institute at American University and founder of the Salam Institute for Peace and Justice. An expert on conflict resolution and dialogue for peace, Abu-Nimer has conducted research on conflict resolution and dialogue for peace among Palestinians and Jews in Israel. His work has focused on the Israeli-Palestinian conflict and on application of conflict resolution models in Muslim communities. Abu-Nimer has also conducted interreligious conflict resolution training, and interfaith dialogue. In the last decade, he has completed many evaluation projects and reports of peace building and development programs. As a scholar/practitioner, he has been intervening and conducting conflict resolution training workshops in many conflict areas around the world, including Palestine, Israel, Egypt, Northern Ireland, Philippines (Mindanao), Sri Lanka, and other areas. In addition to his numerous articles and publications, he is also the co-founder and co-editor of the *Journal of Peacebuilding and Development*.

David Adams, since his retirement from UNESCO in 2001, has continued to devote his energies to the Global Movement for a Culture of Peace. In addition to the books listed in the references to his article, Adams has established a number of Web sites: the Culture of Peace info Web site (http://www.culture-of-peace.info); the Culture of Peace News Network (http://cpnn-world.org); the Web site of the Civil Society Report to the UN on the Culture of Peace (http://decade-culture-of-peace.org); and the culture of peace game (http://culture-of-peace-game.org). At UNESCO, he was the director of the Unit for the International Year for the Culture of Peace, proclaimed for the year 2000 by the UN General Assembly. He came to UNESCO in 1992 to develop the national culture of peace programs as a supplement and alternative to military peacekeeping operations. On behalf of UNESCO he drafted UN documents, including the Declaration and Programme of Action on a Culture of Peace (1999). Previously, at Yale and Wesleyan, he published many studies on the brain mechanisms of aggressive behavior, the evolution of war, and the psychology of peace activists, and he helped to develop and publicize the Seville Statement on Violence.

Jamal A. Badawi completed his undergraduate studies in Cairo, Egypt, and his MA and PhD degrees at Indiana University, Bloomington. He is professor emeritus at St. Mary's University in Halifax, Nova Scotia, where he served as a professor of both management and religious studies. During its May 2008 Convocation, Saint Mary's University granted him an Honorary Doctorate of Civil Law in recognition of his promotion of "a better understanding of Islam" and contribution "to civil society around the world." Badawi is the author of several works on Islam, including books, chapters, articles, and a 352-segment television series on Islam. Some of his works such as "Muslim and Non-Muslim Relations," "Gender Equity in Islam," "Muslim Contribution to Civilization and Apostasy" are available on various sites especially islamonline.net under "Reading Islam," "Contemporary issues," and other headings. In addition to his participation in lectures, seminars, and interfaith dialogues in North America, Badawi has been invited to speak on Islam in 38 other countries. He is a member of the Islamic Juridical [Fiqh] Council of North America, The European Council of Ifta and Research, and the International Union of Muslim Scholars.

Carol Cohn, is the director of the Boston Consortium on Gender, Security and Human Rights. Carol is a leader in the scholarly community addressing issues of gender in global politics generally, armed conflict, and security. Cohn's research and writing has focused on gender and security issues ranging from work on the discourse of civilian defense intellectuals to gender integration issues in the U.S. military, weapons of mass destruction, and the gender dimensions of contemporary armed conflicts. She conducts training and workshops on 1325 and consults on gender mainstreaming and gender and organizational change. She has worked actively with the NGO Working Group on Women, Peace and Security since 2001 and is now working with the Social Science Research Council to design a Global Centre for Research on Gender, Crisis Prevention and Recovery for the UN Development Programme. In addition to her research and policy consulting, Cohn is deeply committed to teaching in the area of gender and global security. She came to the position as director of the Consortium after 20 years of teaching at the college and university level.

Jan Egeland is the director at NUPI and is currently professor II at the University of Stavanger. He has substantial experience in the field of humanitarian relief and conflict resolution within the UN system. From 2006 to 2008 he was special advisor to the UN secretary-general for Conflict Prevention and Resolution. From 2003 to 2006 he was under-secretary-general for Humanitarian Affairs and Emergency Relief Coordinator at the UN Headquarters. From 1999 to 2001, he was under-secretary-general and special advisor to the secretary-general for International Assistance to Colombia. He has long-time experience in conflict resolution from Colombia, the Middle East, Sudan, Guatemala, and the Balkans. From 1990 to 1991, he was state secretary in the Ministry of Foreign Affairs. Egeland holds a magister in political science from the University of Oslo. He has received a number of awards for his work on humanitarian and conflict resolution issues. In 2008 he published *A Billion Lives—An Eyewitness Report from the Frontlines of Humanity.*

Ellen Gaddy is a graduate student in psychology and social transformation at Saybrook University, where she studies the psychology of sustainability and sustainable monetary systems. Ellen also co-directs Smokey Mountain Hollers Cooperative, which operates a local currency and trade exchange located in Asheville, North Carolina, as well as NewDay Africa, a not-for-profit organization that supports community-based programs for the orphaned, the ill, and the impoverished in East Africa.

Johan Galtung, widely considered the founder of peace research, gained the equivalents of MA and PhD degrees in respectively mathematics and sociology at the University of Oslo in 1955 and 1956. Seeing his beloved father arrested by the Nazis when he was 12 years old was a defining event that turned him to a lifelong career in peace. After teaching briefly at Columbia University, he returned to Norway and founded the Peace Research Institute of Oslo (PRIO). It was the first of many groundbreaking institution foundings that culminated most recently in 1993 when, leaving behind a distinguished academic career that spanned the world, he co-founded TRANSCEND to employ a new method of conflict reduction and train others to continue it. Galtung has published more than 1,000 articles and over 100 books, most of which contain extremely cogent if not groundbreaking contributions to the understanding of nonviolence and peace, leading economist and fellow peace researcher Kenneth Boulding to comment that Galtung's "output is so large and so varied that it is hard to believe that it comes from a human."

Barry L. Gan is professor of philosophy and director of the Center for Nonviolence at St. Bonaventure University. He is co-editor with Robert L. Holmes of a leading anthology on nonviolence, *Nonviolence in Theory and Practice* (2nd edition) and editor of *The Acorn: Journal of the Gandhi-King Society.* He has served as co-editor of *Peace and Change: A Journal of Peace Research, Journal of the Peace History Society* and the *Peace and Justice Studies Association*; and for two years he served as program committee chair of the oldest and largest interfaith peace group in the United States, the Fellowship of Reconciliation. He has taught at St. Bonaventure University for the past 25 years after receiving his MA and PhD degrees in philosophy from the University of Rochester. Prior to that, he taught high school and junior high school English for six years.

Hildegard Goss-Mayr is an Austrian Catholic pioneer in teaching the philosophy and practice of nonviolence amid great historical events of the past half century. During childhood and as a young person she experienced Nazism, the persecution of her family, and World War II. After graduation with a doctorate in philosophy from the University of Vienna she worked, together with her husband, Jean Goss, as a staff person of the International Fellowship of Reconciliation for East-West-Dialogue during the Cold War. She supported nonviolent struggles to overcome colonialism and racism (Angola, Mozambique, South Africa) and helped to build up "People Power" in the Philippines to overthrow the dictatorship of President Marcos. During the Second Vatican Council the Goss-Mayrs set up a peace lobby in Rome to promote the out-ruling of the just war concepts and the development of a theology of peacemaking built on the nonviolence of Jesus. During recent years she helped to build up nonviolent movements in francophone

African countries. She published several books and numerous articles and interviews. She has been awarded several peace prizes.

Mitch Hall is a peace activist, children's rights advocate, scholar, writer, and speaker. He currently works with a nonprofit mental health clinic as a counselor for underprivileged children and youth who live in a high-violence urban area and have suffered significant trauma. His interests include peace psychology, attachment research, interpersonal neurobiology, human rights, social justice, psychohistory, meditation, yoga, and natural healing. Mitch serves on the Board of Parents and Teachers against Violence in Education, which promotes nonviolent childrearing and education. He is a certified yoga teacher with the Niroga Institute, a nonprofit organization dedicated to bringing the transformative life skills and benefits of meditation, breathing practices, and yoga poses to underserved populations, including children who have been traumatized, at-risk youth, seniors, and medical patients recovering from serious disorders. He is also on the board of AHIMSA Berkeley, a nonprofit organization that explores how spirituality, science, and social action can contribute to peace building. Mitch is a member of Psychologists for Social Responsibility and has posted on their Web site blogs about children's issues in relation to structural violence and cognitive dissonance. He has many publications and has spoken at numerous conferences, primarily about peace building and the personal and societal importance of providing for children's attachment security in nurturing, nonviolent homes, schools, and communities.

Paul R. Kimmel received a doctorate in social psychology from the University of Michigan in 1963. He is currently teaching at the Saybrook University. He has also taught at Iowa State University, American University, UCLA, and Pepperdine University. He was the first public policy fellow at the American Psychological Association and in the first group of peace fellows at the U.S. Institute of Peace. He has published articles and book chapters about intercultural communication, peace building, and the culture of peace. His research includes major evaluations for the State Department, the U.S. Agency for International Development, the National Academy of Sciences, and the Washington International Center. For over 40 years he has been designing and conducting programs in intercultural understanding for diplomats, UN personnel, the police, Americans going abroad, and international business persons. He has been an officer and is currently active in the Society for the Psychological Study of Social Issues, Psychologists for Social Responsibility, and the Division of Peace Psychology of the American Psychological Association. He recently edited a book on the psychological consequences of America's war on terrorism.

David C. Korten is the author of *Agenda for a New Economy: From Phantom Wealth to Real Wealth* and *The Great Turning: From Empire to Earth Community.* His previous books include the international best-seller *When Corporations Rule the World* and *The Post-Corporate World: Life after Capitalism.* Korten is co-founder and board chair of the Positive Futures Network, which publishes *YES! Magazine,* and is founder and president of the People-Centered Development Forum, a board member of the Business Alliance for Local Living Economies (BALLE), and co-chair of the New Economy Working Group. He is also a founding associate of the International Forum on Globalization (IFG) and a major contributor to its report on Alternatives to Economic Globalization. Korten holds MBA and PhD degrees from the Stanford Business School, has 30 years' experience as a development professional living and working in Asia, Africa, and Latin America, and has served as a Harvard Business School professor, a captain in the U.S. Air Force, a Ford foundation project specialist, and a regional advisor to the U.S. Agency for International Development.

Anthony J. Marsella is professor emeritus, Department of Psychology, University of Hawaii, Honolulu, where he was a member of the faculty for 33 years. He earned his PhD from Pennsylvania State University in clinical psychology. During his tenure at the University of Hawaii, Marsella served as vice president for Academic Affairs, director of Clinical Psychology Training, director of the WHO Psychiatric Research Center, and director of the Disaster Management and Humanitarian Assistance Training Program. Marsella has published 14 books and more than 200 book chapters, journal articles, technical reports, and popular articles. He also served as co-editor for two encyclopedias of psychology and currently serves as editor for a book series on cultural and international psychology for Springer SBM Publications. He is the recipient of numerous research and training grants for studies of (1) culture, psychology, and psychopathology; (2) serious mental disorders; and (3) global challenges. He has received several American Psychological Association awards for contributions to the advancement of international psychology, the Asian-American Psychological Association Presidential Award for lifetime contributions to Asian American and Pacific Island psychology, and numerous other professional and scientific awards. The University of Copenhagen awarded him an honorary doctorate degree for his contributions to international peace and understanding.

Eli Sasaran McCarthy is a PhD candidate at the Graduate Theological Union in the area of ethics and social theory with a particular focus in peace and justice studies, such as nonviolent peacemaking and Truth and

Reconciliation Commissions. His dissertation project is a "Virtue Ethic Assessment of Nonviolent Peacemaking." This project examines how to more adequately assess nonviolent peacemaking practices, and more effectively draw them into public discourse and policy. His article titled "The Virtue Ethic Difference in the Just War Discourse of James Turner Johnson and Catholic Social Teaching" is coming out in the *Journal of Political Theology*, and he has an article is under review called "Truth and Reconciliation Commissions: Toward a More Just U.S. Society." He has taught courses at St. Mary's College and Holy Names University, as well as being a teaching assistant at the University of California, Berkeley, and the Graduate Theological Union. He is a member of the Community of Sant' Egidio, created a conflict transformation program for undergraduates at the Berkeley, did peace building in Israel and Palestine with the Nonviolent Peaceforce and UN, and spent five months in Haiti doing grassroots peace building and learning about structures of injustice.

Rebecca Joy Norlander has a master's degree in French cultural studies from Columbia University and is currently pursuing a doctoral degree in human science at Saybrook University, with a concentration in social transformation. Her primary areas of interest are post-conflict education curriculum development and peace building. Rebecca has spent much of her life living, working, traveling, studying, and volunteering abroad; cultivating an interest in intercultural communication and conflict resolution that she hopes will further the interests of grassroots change initiatives that aim to improve the quality of life for all of earth's inhabitants.

Gianina Pellegrini is a doctoral student at Saybrook University, pursuing a degree in psychology with a concentration in social transformation and certification in international peace and conflict resolution. While obtaining a master's degree in psychology, Gianina researched how spiritual, religious, and traditional customs in sub-Saharan Africa influenced the care and treatment of HIV-positive children. Her primary areas of interest include issues pertaining to human rights, public health, and social justice.

Kavita Nandini Ramdas has served as president and CEO of the Global Fund for Women since 1996. She has dedicated herself to empowering women worldwide with the financial resources to increase girls' access to education, defend women's right to health and reproductive rights, prevent violence against women, and advance women's political participation, as well as other vital issues. Kavita has served on the boards of the Women's Funding Network, the Women's Rights Prize of the Gruber Foundation, and the Ethical Globalization Initiative. She is the recipient of numerous philanthropic and leadership awards, including most recently, the Haridas and Bina Chaudhuri Award for Distinguished Service presented by the California Institute of Integrated Studies (CIIS). Kavita recently joined the Global Development Advisory Panel of the Bill and Melinda Gates Foundation, the Advisory Panel of the Asian University for Women, and the board of trustees of Princeton University.

Donald Rothberg is a member of the Spirit Rock Meditation Center's Teachers Council in Northern California, writes and teaches on Buddhist meditation, spiritual practice in daily life, transpersonal studies, epistemology and spirituality, and socially engaged Buddhism. He has helped to guide training programs in socially engaged spirituality for the Buddhist Peace Fellowship (a number of six-month "BASE" programs), Saybrook University (several 18-month interfaith programs), and Spirit Rock (the "Path of Engagement" 24-month program). An editor of *ReVision: A Journal of Consciousness and Transformation* for 10 years, he is the co-editor (with Sean Kelly) of *Ken Wilber in Dialogue: Conversations with Leading Transpersonal Thinkers* (Quest Books, 1998) and the author of *The Engaged Spiritual Life: A Buddhist Approach to Transforming Ourselves and the World* (2006).

Sara Ruddick received her PhD in philosophy from Harvard University. She then taught for many years at Eugene Lang College, New School University where she is now Faculty Emerita. She co-edited three feminist anthologies: *Working It Out, Between Women,* and *Mother Troubles.* She is the author of *Maternal Thinking: Toward a Politics of Peace* (Beacon Press, 1989, 1995). For the 20th anniversary of this book Andrea O'Reilly prepared a collection of essays entitled *Maternal Thinking: Philosophy, Politics, Practice.*

Angel Ryono is a master's degree student in the human sciences at Saybrook University. She was inspired to pursue graduate studies after working as a researcher and associate editor for Toda Institute for Global Peace and Policy Research in Honolulu, Hawaii. Currently, Angel is affiliated with the War Crimes Studies Center at University of California, Berkeley, particularly in working to support transitional justice projects in Southeast Asia. Her research focuses on the historical and structural challenges to peace building in Cambodia.

ABOUT THE SERIES EDITOR AND ADVISORY BOARD

SERIES EDITOR

Chris E. Stout, PsyD, MBA, is a licensed clinical psychologist and is a Clinical Full Professor at the University of Illinois College of Medicine's Department of Psychiatry. He served as an NGO Special Representative to the United Nations. He was appointed to the World Economic Forum's Global Leaders of Tomorrow and he has served as an Invited Faculty at the Annual Meeting in Davos. He is the Founding Director of the Center for Global Initiatives. Stout is a Fellow of the American Psychological Association, former President of the Illinois Psychological Association, and a Distinguished Practitioner in the National Academies of Practice. Stout has published or presented over 300 papers and 30 books and manuals on various topics in psychology. His works have been translated into six languages. He has lectured across the nation and internationally in 19 countries and has, visited 6 continents and almost 70 countries. He was noted as being "one of the most frequently cited psychologists in the scientific literature" in a study by Hartwick College. He is the recipient of the American Psychological Association's International Humanitarian Award.

ADVISORY BOARD

Bruce Bonecutter, PhD, is Director of Behavioral Services at the Elgin Community Mental Health Center, the Illinois Department of Human Services state hospital serving adults in greater Chicago. He is also a Clinical Assistant Professor of Psychology at the University of Illinois at Chicago. A clinical psychologist specializing in health, consulting, and forensic psychology, Bonecutter is also a longtime member of the American Psychological Association Taskforce on Children and the Family. He is a member of organizations including the Association for the Treatment of Sexual Abusers, International, the Alliance for the Mentally Ill, and the Mental Health Association of Illinois.

Joseph Flaherty, MD, is Chief of Psychiatry at the University of Illinois Hospital, Professor of Psychiatry at the University of Illinois College (UIC) of Medicine and a Professor of Community Health Science at the UIC College of Public Health. He is a Founding Member of the Society for the Study of Culture and Psychiatry. Dr. Flaherty has been a consultant to the World Health Organization, the National Institute of Mental Health, and also the Falk Institute in Jerusalem. He is the former Director of Undergraduate Education and Graduate Education in the Department of Psychiatry at the University of Illinois. Dr. Flaherty has also been Staff Psychiatrist and Chief of Psychiatry at Veterans Administration West Side Hospital in Chicago.

Michael Horowitz, PhD, is President and Professor of Clinical Psychology at the Chicago School of Professional Psychology, one of the nation's leading not-for-profit graduate schools of psychology. Earlier, he served as Dean and Professor of the Arizona School of Professional Psychology. A clinical psychologist practicing independently since 1987, his work has focused on psychoanalysis, intensive individual therapy, and couples therapy. He has provided Disaster Mental Health Services to the American Red Cross. Horowitz's special interests include the study of fatherhood.

Sheldon I. Miller, MD, is a Professor of Psychiatry at Northwestern University, and Director of the Stone Institute of Psychiatry at Northwestern Memorial Hospital. He is also Director of the American Board of Psychiatry and Neurology, Director of the American Board of Emergency Medicine, and Director of the Accreditation Council for Graduate Medical Education. Dr. Miller is also an Examiner for the American Board of Psychiatry and

Neurology. He is Founding Editor of the *American Journal of Addictions*, and Founding Chairman of the American Psychiatric Association's Committee on Alcoholism. Dr. Miller has also been a Lieutenant Commander in the U.S. Public Health Service, serving as psychiatric consultant to the Navajo Area Indian Health Service at Window Rock, Arizona. He is a member and Past President of the Executive Committee for the American Academy of Psychiatrists in Alcoholism and Addictions.

Dennis P. Morrison, PhD, is Chief Executive Officer at the Center for Behavioral Health in Indiana, the first behavioral health company ever to win the Joint Commission on Accreditation of Healthcare Organizations (JCAHO) Codman Award for excellence in the use of outcomes management to achieve health care quality improvement. He is President of the Board of Directors for the Community Healthcare Foundation in Bloomington, and has been a member of the Board of Directors for the American College of Sports Psychology. He has served as a consultant to agencies including the Ohio Department of Mental Health, Tennessee Association of Mental Health Organizations, Oklahoma Psychological Association, the North Carolina Council of Community Mental Health Centers, and the National Center for Heath Promotion in Michigan. Morrison served across 10 years as a Medical Service Corp Officer in the U.S. Navy.

William H. Reid, MD, is a clinical and forensic psychiatrist, and consultant to attorneys and courts throughout the United States. He is Clinical Professor of Psychiatry at the University of Texas Health Science Center. Dr. Miller is also an Adjunct Professor of Psychiatry at Texas A&M College of Medicine and Texas Tech University School of Medicine, as well as a Clinical Faculty member at the Austin Psychiatry Residency Program. He is Chairman of the Scientific Advisory Board and Medical Advisor to the Texas Depressive and Manic-Depressive Association, as well as an Examiner for the American Board of Psychiatry and Neurology. He has served as President of the American Academy of Psychiatry and the Law, as Chairman of the Research Section for an International Conference on the Psychiatric Aspects of Terrorism, and as Medical Director for the Texas Department of Mental Health and Mental Retardation. Dr. Reid earned an Exemplary Psychiatrist Award from the National Alliance for the Mentally Ill. He has been cited on the Best Doctors in America listing since 1998.

ABOUT THE SERIES

THE PRAEGER SERIES IN CONTEMPORARY PSYCHOLOGY

In this series, experts from various disciplines peer through the lens of psychology, telling us answers they see for questions of human behavior. Their topics may range from humanity's psychological ills—addictions, abuse, suicide, murder, and terrorism among them—to works focused on positive subjects, including intelligence, creativity, athleticism, and resilience. Regardless of the topic, the goal of this series remains constant—to offer innovative ideas, provocative considerations, and useful beginnings to better understand human behavior.

Series Editor
Chris E. Stout, Psy.D., MBA
Northwestern University Medical School
Illinois Chief of Psychological Services

Advisory Board
Bruce E. Bonecutter, Ph.D.
University of Illinois at Chicago
Director, Behavioral Services, Elgin Community Mental Health Center